The Polish Wa

Chopin: A Biography
Paderewski
The Battle for the Marchlands

The Polish Way

A THOUSAND-YEAR HISTORY
OF THE POLES AND THEIR CULTURE

Adam Zamoyski

HIPPOCRENE BOOKS
New York

Contents

Figures

Maps

Illustration Acknowledgments

I should like to thank the following institutions for supplying illustrations and for their permission to reproduce them:

The Archaeological Museum, Warsaw, 1,2,3,4; the Trustees of the British Museum, London, 66; the deBrzezie Lanckoro ski Foundation, London, 36, 43; the Czartoryski Collection, Kraków, 64, 67, 68, 71, 99, 113; the Institute of Art of the Polish Academy of Leaning, 9, 10, 13, 14, 16, 17, 23, 32, 33, 34, 35, 39, 40, 53, 58, 76, 77, 79, 80, 81, 82, 87, 92, 94, 101, 102; the Museum of the Jagiellon University, Kraków, 56, 57; the Museum of Weaving, ód , 132; the National Archives, Warsaw, 44; the National Museum, Kraków, 7, 24, 25, 26, 27, 28, 89, 117, 138; the National Museum, Warsaw, 12, 60, 70, 72, 75, 84, 85, 86, 90, 96, 97, 98, 104, 106, 107, 109, 110, 111, 116, 121, 124, 126, 128; the Polish Army Museum, Warsaw, 69, 122; the Polish Library, Paris, 63; the Pomeranian Museum, Gda sk, 140; Puls Publications, London, 141, 142, 143, 144; the State Art collection at the Wawel, Kraków, 11, 59, 73, 78.

The photographs were taken by the following: T. Biniewski, 2; Miros aw Ciunowicz, 69, 122; W adys aw Gumu a, 56, 57; M. Kopyd owski, 40; Adam Kossakowski, 103; J. Ksi ek, 71; Edmund Kupiecki, 15, 21, 22, 38, 45, 46, 47, 48, 49, 50, 51, 52, 61, 74, 91, 118; Zbigniew Malinowski, 138; Stanis aw Michta, 6, 64, 67, 68; G. Nawrocki, 143; Lech Oko ski, 18; Popperfoto, 137; E. Rachwa , 73; ukasz Schuster, 59, 78; B. Serdy ska, 107; Teresa Szymonowicz, 132; Witalis Wolny, 77; Teresa Zó towska, 12, 60, 70, 72, 75, 84, 85, 86, 90, 97, 98, 104, 106, 110, 111, 116, 121, 126, 128, 140; The remaining photographs were taken by the author. All the maps were drawn by Trevor Allen.

Preface

No satisfactory synthesis of Poland's history has so far been achieved, principally because attempts at producing one have tended to reflect nationalist and even political viewpoints. Foreign historians have patronised, while Poles have fought back with all the handicaps of the besieged. More recently, fashion has guided historians away from synthesis towards analysis and insight, and while this has resulted in some interesting literature, it has not filled the paramount need, which is for a brief general history. The present contribution is made with all these factors in mind.

The principal aim of this book is to chart the course of Polish history within its European context, highlighting those political and diplomatic events which had repercussions beyond the boundaries of the country itself. From this angle, the most striking features of Polish history are: the evolution of a parliamentary state in Central Europe; its spectacular expansion in the early modern period; its equally spectacular decay and disintegration in the eighteenth century; and finally, the transformation of the multi-ethnic 'nation without a state' into one of the most homogenous and vigorous nations of contemporary Europe.

I have therefore concentrated on tracing the evolution of Polish society, its mentality, outlook, behaviour and taste, and this has led me to devoting a larger proportion of the book than is usual to the period 1400–1800. It was during this period that the Poles were in a position to shape their own destiny and created an original world personal to themselves. It was also then that they ascended to greatness and declined into inadequacy, leaving a legacy with which they, and the rest of the world, have had to live ever since.

To be consistent in the matter of spelling and nomenclature is impossible, and every historian makes his own rules. I have preferred the more euphonius and traditional rendering of *wojewoda* as 'palatine' to the currently fashionable 'voivod', but have used the original *starosta* instead of the possible equivalents such as 'sheriff'. For the sake of simplicity I have used the original spelling of *Seym* rather than the later and current form *Sejm*. In the text I have only given the titles of those families of Jagiellon, Rurik or Ruthene princely blood entitled to bear them under the provisions of the Union of Lublin. Virtually all other titles were bestowed by the Holy Roman Empire, Russia, Prussia, Austria or the Holy See. Although many of these were confirmed by the Senate of the Kingdom of Poland in 1824, and others were obtained in the states to which the partitions had assigned territory and people, I have ignored them, since they contribute little to an understanding of Polish history or social conditions. Finally, I have included no source-notes, since all the dates and statistics given here are standard and uncontroversial figures, to be found in any reliable literature on the subject. The same goes for the quotations I have used, which are all easily traceable in printed sources.

This has not been an easy book to write, and I should never have attempted it or persevered without the encouragement, advice and support of Professor Aleksander Gieysztor of Warsaw, whom I must also thank for devoting so much time to reading Chapters 1–19 of the manuscript. Many others have helped me in specific areas and I beg their indulgence in not mentioning them all individually. I owe a great deal to my patient and inspired editor Antony Wood, and I am deeply indebted to Shervie Price for her unstinting and intelligent help in editing the manuscript.

Polish words may look complicated, but pronunciation is at least consistent. All vowels are simple and of even length, as in Italian, and their sound is best rendered by the English words 'sum' (*a*), 'ten' (*e*), 'ease' (*i*), 'lot' (*o*), 'book' (*u*), 'sit' (*y*).

Most of the consonants behave in the same way as English, except for *c*, which is pronounced 'ts'; *j*, which is soft, as in 'yes'; and *w*, which is equivalent to English *v*. As in German, some consonants are softened when they fall at the end of a word, and *b*, *d*, *g*, *w*, *z* become *p*, *t*, *k*, *f*, *s* respectively.

There are also a number of accented letters and combinations peculiar to Polish, of which the following is a rough list:

ó = *u*, hence *Kraków* is pronounced 'krakooff'.
ą = nasal *a*, hence *sąd* is pronounced 'sont'.
ę = nasal *e*, hence *Łęczyca* is pronounced 'wenchytsa'.
ć = *ch* as in 'cheese'.
cz = *ch* as in 'catch'.
ch = guttural *h* as in 'loch'.
ł = English *w*, hence *Bolesław* becomes 'Boleswaf', *Łódź* 'Wootj'.
ń = soft *n* as in Spanish '*mañana*'.
rz = French *j* as in '*je*'.
ś = *sh* as in 'sheer'.
sz = *sh* as in 'bush'.
ż = as *rz* (Ż is the accented capital).
ź = A similar sound, but sharper as in French '*gigot*'.

The stress in Polish is consistent, and always falls on the penultimate syllable.

1

'A Country in the Moon'

They reached the heights of the Kahlenberg just before nightfall. From this vantage-point the king and his generals surveyed the great plain stretching into the distance, cut across by the winding course of the Danube. At their feet lay the city of Vienna. Only the occasional flash of a cannon from its battered ramparts and the distress-rockets rising periodically into the evening sky from the tower of St Stephen's Cathedral confirmed that after sixty days of siege the garrison was still holding out.

The proud Habsburg capital was dwarfed by a larger city, a sprawling encampment of many thousand tents which pullulated with a quarter of a million soldiers, slaves, camp-followers and houris; with horses, camels and buffalo. Every province the Sultan of Sultans could command had offered its exotic warriors to the Almighty for the *Jihad*, the Holy War. Janissaries from Turkey, Spahis and Mamluks from North Africa, mountain tribesmen from Georgia and Tatars from the Crimea had pitched their homes of leather, canvas or silk. The last rays of the setting sun played on the multicoloured domes and peaks, and lingered on a silken palace rising up in the centre of the camp. A pleasure-ground of embroidered tents which surrounded improvised gardens, menageries and seraglios led up to the quarters of the Grand Vizir, Kara Mustafa.

'He's badly camped – we shall beat him!' said the king, turning to his generals. Few of them shared his confidence, but they trusted his experience, his reputation, and the renown of the strange-looking regiments he had brought with him. A beacon was lit on the heights to inform the defenders of the dying city that help was at hand. This signal did not unduly worry Kara Mustafa. He had over a hundred thousand fighting men securely entrenched with plenty of artillery, and he was convinced that no serious threat could come from the Kahlenberg: a large army would have chosen a longer route through the plain. His own victorious army did not fear the solid but slow-moving Austrian and German troops, their unadventurous generals or their pusillanimous emperor, who had abandoned his capital. The only Christian general they held in awe was Jan

Sobieski, the King of Poland. But he, Kara Mustafa believed, was still hundreds of miles away in Kraków.

Just before dawn on the following day, 12 September 1683, the King of Poland attended Mass in the ruins of an old convent on the Kahlenberg and then dictated the *ordre de bataille*. The left wing was given to the Duke of Lorraine. It consisted of three corps of Imperial and Saxon infantry under Count Caprara, the Duke of Baden, and the Elector of Saxony, supported by a large force of Polish cavalry under Stanisław Lubomirski. It was to advance along the Danube to relieve Vienna itself. The centre, under the Prince of Waldeck, was made up of troops from Franconia and Bavaria – with the young Elector going into his first battle as a mere soldier. The right wing, lost from sight throughout most of the day as it swept round through the Vienna Woods, consisted of Polish infantry and cavalry under Stanisław Jabłonowski. Only the Polish artillery had been nimble enough to haul their ordnance over the mountain roads, so their twenty-eight guns would have to race about from one corner of the battlefield to another – at one stage they were to run out of wadding and had to commandeer the fine wigs of some indignant French gentleman-volunteers. Only about one third of the 68,000 troops were Polish – the rest were Germans, Italians, Frenchmen, Spaniards, Scots and Irishmen. It was a crusading army, come together from all corners of the Christian world to face the Infidel, and in its ranks fought no fewer than nine sovereign princes.

As they began their descent from the Kahlenberg, a Turkish force came out of the camp to face them. The janissaries took up defensive positions on hillocks, along gullies and in vineyards, and the Christian troops had to pick their way through difficult terrain to dislodge them. It was a sweltering day, and by early afternoon when the Christian army had pushed the Turks off the last foothills, the men were thoroughly exhausted. Around three o'clock there was a lull in the fighting, as they consolidated their new positions and the Turks fell back to regroup.

The king felt tempted to put off the decisive battle to the following day, even though this would give the Turks time to turn the heavy guns bombarding Vienna to face his army. Through his telescope he saw fresh Turkish regiments being drawn up and a red tent being put up behind them. Beside it stood a pole bearing the horse-tails which were the sign of the Grand Vizir's rank. At about four o'clock Kara Mustafa unfurled the banner of the Prophet, emblem of Ottoman victory, to loud cries from the ranks of Janissaries. Instinct made the king change his mind, and he sent a galloper to Jabłonowski on the right wing. Then he rode forward himself.

As Sobieski's mounted figure appeared on a prominent hillock in the front line, over to the right the leafy gloom of the Vienna Woods burst into blossom, as a few, then a few hundred, then a few thousand brightly-coloured lance-pennants thrust out between the branches. One by one, the glittering squadrons of the Polish heavy cavalry, the *Husaria*, detached themselves from the mass of the woods and trotted forward. Led by senators and senior dignitaries of the Most Serene Commonwealth of Poland, its ranks made up exclusively of the highest-born, this great war-machine shimmered with the wealth of vast acreages. Each rider was helmeted and plumed; his breastplate encrusted with gold and gems; cloaked with leopard-skins; winged with great arcs of eagle-feathers rising over his head; mounted on a magnificent charger caparisoned in silk and velvet embroidered with gold. Each *husarz* carried sabres and pistols with jewelled handles, and a twenty-foot lance with streaming pennant. As they broke into a lumbering canter and lowered their lances, the pennants and the wings on their backs set up an evil hiss while the ground shook with the pounding of fifteen thousand hooves.

Selim Girey, Khan of the Crimean Horde, had been waiting to pounce on the right wing of the Christian attack. When he recognised the Polish king and the winged riders who had defeated his Tatars before, he turned about and led his riders away. Everything now hinged on whether the janissaries could stand firm against the Husaria, which lumbered on purposefully, sparing its horses, diagonally across the whole battlefield, making for the landmark of the Vizir's tent. Idle soldiers on both sides stared in disbelief at the slow, mesmeric charge. Then the Husaria broke into a wild gallop and the heavy mass of men and horses cascaded over the Turkish ranks, bowling over the first, slicing through the second, surging on towards the exquisite red tent, before which the Grand Vizir sat and watched. He saw the Pasha of Aleppo fall and the horse-tail banner of Kara Mehmet of Mesopotamia go down in the fray. Next came the turn of the Pashas of Silistria and Buda. Their janissaries hesitated for a moment, then turned and fled, followed by the rest of the army. The Grand Vizir leapt on to a horse and made his own escape moments before the winged riders thundered up to the tent and the banner was struck.

The entire Christian army moved forward and the king rode into the Turkish camp to take possession. One of the Vizir's servants handed him a jewelled stirrup which had broken off as Kara Mustafa heaved himself into the saddle to flee. A true *galant*, the king gave it to one of his young gentlemen, bidding him ride hard all the way to Kraków to lay it at the feet of his French queen. Another messenger was sent to Rome, to the Pope, bearing the standard of the Prophet; the *Jihad* had been defeated by the last Crusade.

This battle, which was crucial to the future of the whole of Europe, had not been hard-fought, and the casualties on both sides were light. It had been won principally by the prestige of Jan Sobieski and his army. In 1683 Poland was the largest state in Europe, its territory exceeded only by the vast expanses of Muscovy, and a powerful arbiter of war in that part of the world. Yet when the fighting was over, the Poles went home, hung the captured Turkish trophies in their castle halls, and returned to their own pursuits. There was no Polish participation in negotiations between the Sultan and the Emperor, no claims, no compensation, no diplomatic victory.

The size and power of Poland repeatedly thrust it into a vital international role, but it was one for which its people felt no calling. The ruling classes and their institutions were inward-looking, preferring to remain in a state of diplomatic hibernation, oblivious to and aloof from what was being planned at Versailles, Schönbrunn or Whitehall. In her moment of crisis, Poland could count on the sympathy of every state in Europe, and on the support of none.

Only a century after the Battle of Vienna a declining Poland was neatly removed from the map of Europe by a coalition of Russia, Prussia and Austria. The civilised world was horrified. Here was surreptitious power-politics at its shameful worst. Three crowned heads aspiring to the name of enlightened monarchs had haggled greedily over the spoils before committing an act of cannibalism which cut across every concept of legality, morality and honour held at the time. In the House of Commons, the action of the coalition was branded as 'the most flagrant instance of profligate perfidy that has ever disgraced the annals of mankind'. No less indignant sentiments were voiced in other countries. When the rhetoric evaporated, however, it had to be admitted that the disappearance of one of the half-dozen great states in Europe did not in this case seem to make any difference in practical terms. Even Edmund Burke, the staunchest ally of Poland at Westminster, had to concede that as far as England was concerned, 'Poland might be, in fact, considered as a country in the moon.' By the end of the nineteenth century, Poland had been relegated to an even remoter planet as far as western European consciousness was concerned, and even if recent events have brought it back to a central position on the globe, its past remains shrouded in all the mystery of a lunar prospect. To the average inhabitant of Western Europe, the history of Poland is a yawning chasm whose edges are obscured by an overhang of accepted commonplaces – that the Poles are a romantic people, good at fighting, riding, dancing and drinking, pathologically incapable of organisation or stable self-government, condemned by geography and their own ineptitude to be the victims of history.

This is of course nonsense. The Poles are neither romantic nor passionate; they are one of the least military nations in Europe; they established one of the largest and most ambitious political structures of early modern times; and for much of history they dominated their neighbours. There is less sorrow and suffering in their history than in that of many nations –

they were not traumatised for decades by the devastation of the Black Death; they did not, like the Germans, see over half of their population slaughtered by religious wars; they have experienced no horrors akin to those of the Russian Revolution or the Spanish Civil War. When disaster did strike, however, it coincided with the birth of the Romantic Movement, which exalted the tragedy into something monumental. Again, in 1945, a martyred nation was abandoned and condemned to moral and physical misery, the spectre of which haunts the world's view of Poland's past.

Polish history was an early casualty of political propaganda. Russia and Prussia built their imperial structures with materials taken from the Polish edifice which they had dismantled. They realised that any attempt at rebuilding Poland would strike at the very foundations of their new power. They therefore found it imperative to make people forget there had ever been a Polish state which they had so indecorously pillaged. Two years after Russia, Prussia and Austria had taken apart the Polish Commonwealth, on 26 January 1797, they signed a convention which was 'to secure the three Powers in a real, actual and unchangeable possession of the provinces which they had annexed.' They added a secret article which stressed 'the recognised necessity of abolishing everything which might recall the existence of a Polish kingdom in face of the performed annihilation of this political body.'

In this spirit, the Prussians melted down the Polish crown jewels, the Austrians turned royal palaces into barracks, and the Russians grabbed everything they could lay their hands on and shipped it out. They destroyed books and documents on an industrial scale and rewrote history, seeking to justify their action by explaining to the world that the Poles were so hopeless as to be unable to govern themselves, and that the country had never really been a sovereign state. The Poles refused to be subjugated, and hardly a generation passed without a rebellion. A Polish state re-emerged in 1918, and although it was re-enslaved in 1945, it remains obvious to all that nothing will stop the Poles from aspiring to independence. On the other hand the plan to occlude and rewrite Poland's history has been so successful that many outside central Europe are unaware of Poland ever having been independent, let alone a major power.

The reasons for this success are fascinating in themselves. The nineteenth century saw the eclipse of Poland's friends and cultural allies – France, Italy, Spain, Hungary and Turkey. The running was made in Central Europe by Russia and Germany, and in the West by Great Britain. It was the age of triumph for the industrial nations of the north and for the Protestant bourgeoisie, which learnt to associate Catholicism with poverty, dirt and indolence, as well as with *ancien-régime* priestcraft and obscurantism. With their German royal family and their own 'burden' in Ireland and the Empire, the British were not prepared to look too closely at

German or Russian doings in Poland. The German view of the swashbuck-ling, adventurous, disorganised Polish past was picturesque but not designed to appeal to middle-class cultures based on thrift and hard work. German historians demonstrated eloquently that Poland had been a chaotic backwater which needed stabilising and civilising. Their obsession with racial theories ensured that the achievements of any Pole were denigrated, and that any Pole whose achievements were beyond dispute was saddled with German origins.

British historians swallowed most of this. A typical work written at the turn of the century by the Oxford historian C.R.L. Fletcher informs the reader that 'as the Slav has never shown any capacity for civilisation, the proper method to apply to him was that of Otto the Great, to push him steadily back eastwards and to colonise his territory with sturdy Teutons, to leave him, if at all, only in a completely inferior position with no separate political existence.' Such an attitude is principally the result of ignor-ance but there has also been an element of prejudice involved. In the nineteenth century the Poles were forced to become the enemies of the status quo. They were therefore generally viewed as trouble-makers impeding the march of orderly progress. In the present century they have been seen as reactionary and unprogressive, since they alone of all European nations vigorously rejected the new idols. Consumed with reverence for Russian communism, many Western intellectuals and histor-ians have shown an unprofessional exasperation with the Poles not only for the lack of enthusiasm with which they greeted Russian ideological exports, but also for the way in which they have turned theory on its head. The fact that radical workers have been staging a revolution against the dictatorship of the proletariat wearing a picture of the Madonna on their lapels has derailed many a marxist argument.

The dramatic events of the summer of 1980 started a flurry of interest in Poland, but many of the new books on the subject still take for granted that Poland is somehow 'different'. 'Poland is a terribly dangerous project for the assumptions and categories of a conventional historian,' writes the reviewer of a recent history; 'Is Poland a state? . . . Is Poland even a place? . . . Is there a Polish people?' While the author reviewed sees Poland as 'an immensely complex phenomenon – both land, and state, and nation, and culture; a community in constant flux, forever transmuting its composi-tion, its view of itself, its *raison d'être*: in short, a puzzle with no clear solution.'

All of this applies equally well to Britain, France, Germany, and any other major nation. Britain is more racially mixed than Poland has ever been. France, originally a hybrid construction of several kingdoms, races and languages, is also forever transmuting its view of itself and its *raison d'être*. German frontiers have fluctuated more than those of Poland over the last thousand years, and Germany has been little more than a concept for much of that time. A hundred and fifty years ago, 'Italy' was, as Metternich put it, no more than a geographical expression. Italy is now a thriving sovereign state: Poland is still, for many, 'a country in the moon'.

It is neither helpful nor conducive to good history to regard Poland as a special case. Like any other nation, it has its idiosyncrasies and nurtures its paradoxes, which are neither more nor less baffling than those of others. There is, however, one respect in which the case of Poland is unique. Of the six major nations of Europe, the Germans, the French, the English, the Italians, the Spanish and the Poles, the first five have between them created everything that Europe stands for, while the Poles would seem to have contributed virtually nothing. A closer inspection will reveal that their influence has been much greater than is commonly thought, but still, there are few fields of human activity in which the Poles can rival the other great nations. Both the cause and the effect are a certain distance between the Poles and their sister peoples. The other European nations have sailed through the ages as a fleet, encountering storms and becoming becalmed more or less together. The Polish barque has sailed in the same direction, but at a distance, usually avoiding those storms, occasionally hitting others which it has had to weather on its own. This would not be surprising if it were just one of the small boats of the fleet, peripheral to its operations – a Finland, Albania or Ireland – but Poland was one of the half-dozen ships of the line, even if the helmsman sometimes failed to realise it.

The origins of this discordant relationship with Europe must lie somewhere in the fact that Poland was the product of an entirely different set of dynamics from other states. It was the only major medieval political unit not to have been built on the spiritual foundations laid by the Roman Empire. It was not just that the Romans never reached Poland – no part of Russian soil was ever trodden by a legionary, yet the whole of Russian civilisation is deeply marked by Rome in its Byzantine form. It is simply that by the time medieval Christianity brought the influence of Rome to what is now Poland, there was already a nation-state in existence.

Throughout the last three centuries, the Poles have been at pains to stress that they belong to the West, to Christendom and to Rome. There are strong ideological reasons for this claim, since they have absorbed so much of the moral and cultural heritage of Rome, and this constitutes the greatest distinction between them and their Slav brothers to the East. Their zeal, however, is the zeal of the convert, for they were not conceived by Rome or born in Christianity.

2

The Polish Crown

When Charlemagne was crowned Roman Emperor in the year AD 800 he knew less about the area which is now Poland than about any other part of the European mainland. His Frankish and Saxon dominions ended on a line roughly equivalent to that of the Iron Curtain today, beyond which stretched a limitless Slav sea. The occasional expedition undertaken against the westernmost Slavs living along the river Elbe revealed them to be primitive and disorganised, which was assumed to be symptomatic of the whole murky hinterland with its thick forests, swamps and treacherous moving sands.

While most of Europe evolved from the Dark Ages in mutual interaction, while Celtic monks from Ireland carried the religion of Rome to Germany, and Vikings from Scandinavia linked England and France with Sicily and the Arab world or sailed down the rivers of Russia to Kiev and Constantinople, Poland existed in a vacuum. The whole of what is now Poland, East Germany and Czechoslovakia had been settled by a number of Slav peoples. Roman merchants who had come from the south in the first century in search of amber, the 'gold of the north', had recorded that they were unwarlike and agricultural, living in a state of 'rural democracy'. The largest of these peoples even took their name from their trade, being known as 'the people of the fields', *Polanie* in their language. Their profound attachment to the land kept them introverted, and they were cushioned from the outside world. In the north, the Pomeranians (*Pomorzanie*, or people of the seaboard) were linked by Viking trade with the whole of Europe. In the south, the *Vislanie* of the upper Vistula were alternately attacked and evangelised by Christian Moravians. In the west, a whole series of smaller Slav peoples warred and traded with the Germans and Saxons. Neither invasion nor ideas penetrated this buffer-zone, and the Polanie could therefore develop their way of life and their institutions undisturbed throughout the eighth and ninth centuries.

Their methods may have been primitive, but the defensive earthworks and places of worship they left behind testify to large forces of organised

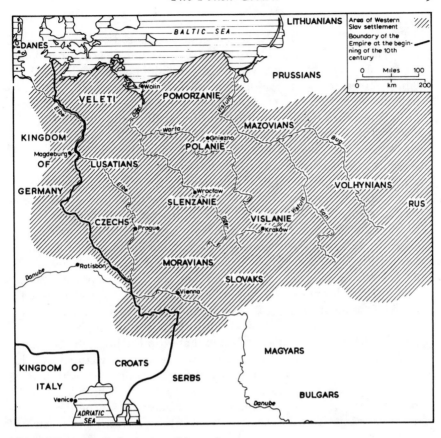

Central Europe at the beginning of the tenth century

manpower, while excavations have shown that open-cast mining and iron-smelting were carried on in the south of the country on an industrial scale. This is the more surprising as the pattern of settlement was not one of large tribal centres, but of clusters of homesteads and small villages separated from each other by expanses of virgin land, each a self-sufficient unit within a larger community. This pattern provides a clue to the exceptionally strong regionalist tendencies manifest throughout Polish history – a regionalism which cannot be explained, as in Britain, France or Italy, by ethnic differences. The Polanie shared a common way of life, and a uniform language which differed slightly from that spoken by the Bohemians or

Czechs to the south-west and that of the eastern Slavs of Rus.

The western Slavs also shared a common religion. It was based on the same pantheon as other Indo-European cults but lacked a developed pattern of ritual. The gods were mostly worshipped through objects in nature – trees, rivers, stones – in which they were held to dwell, and less so in the shape of idols, or in circles and temples. As practised by the Polanie, this religion was neither organised nor hierarchical, and was not a politically unifying force. What did provide the cohesion whose signs are everywhere were the rulers of the Polanie, the Piast dynasty established in Gniezno at some time during the ninth century.

Throughout the second half of the ninth century and the beginning of the tenth, these princes gradually extended their sway outwards to embrace the neighbouring peoples. Most of these were under some kind of pressure from the outside world, so making it easier for the Piast princes to act as protectors and overlords, and by the middle of the tenth century they controlled a considerable area. This dominion was described, in the first written source of any worth, by Ibrahim Ibn Yaqub, a Jewish traveller from Spain, who noted that the ruler, Prince Mieszko, had imposed a relatively sophisticated fiscal system, and exercised control through a network of castles and a standing army of three thousand horsemen.

It was these troops and these castles that Otto I, King of the Germans, encountered in the year 955. Otto had won a series of victories over his troublesome eastern neighbours and fortified his boundaries with a string of bastion-provinces or Marches. He then crossed the Elbe in force. As he advanced eastward, routing small bands of Slav warriors on the way, he eventually came up against something resembling an army and a system of defences. For the Polanie, the period of isolation had come to an end, and Prince Mieszko could no longer ignore the outside world, in the shape of the powerful Germans.

He could even less afford to ignore them after 962, when Otto was crowned Roman Emperor by the Pope. The Empire was more of a theoretical than a material institution, but it drew considerable strength from its association with the centre of Christianity. Mieszko was aware of the political and cultural benefits Christianity had brought the Bohemians. Only by adopting Christianity himself would he be able to avoid war with the Emperor, and at the same time provide himself with a useful political instrument. In 965 he sought the approval of Otto and married the Bohemian Princess Dobrava. The following year, 966, Mieszko and his court were baptised. The Duchy of Polonia formally became a part of Christendom.

Mieszko had no intention of playing the obedient godchild, and continued to pursue his own aims, even if they conflicted with those of the Empire. One of these was to gain control of as much of the Baltic coastline

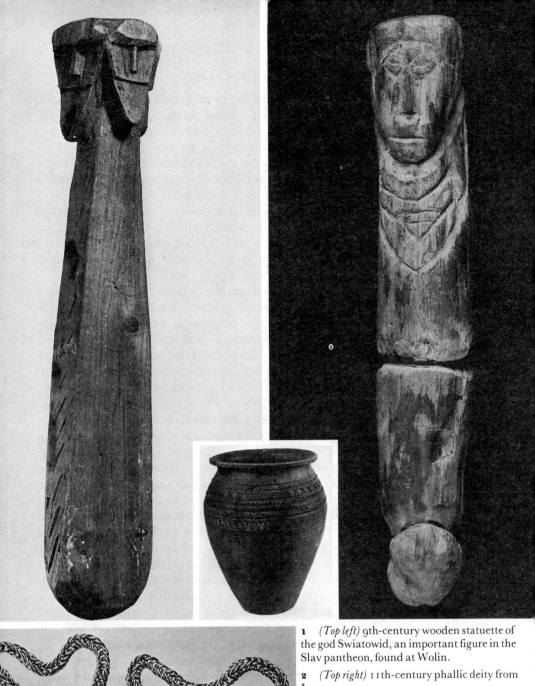

1 *(Top left)* 9th-century wooden statuette of the god Swiatowid, an important figure in the Slav pantheon, found at Wolin.

2 *(Top right)* 11th-century phallic deity from Łęczyca.

3 *(Left)* Silver chain and pectoral casket from Borucin in Kujavia, dating from the first half of the 11th century.

4 *(Centre)* Earthenware vase from Bródno, near Warsaw, 10th century.

as possible. He invaded Pomerania, but soon encountered the Margrave of the Norther March, who was attempting to conquer the area for the Empire. Mieszko defeated him at Cedynia in 972 and reached the mouth of the Oder in 976. The Margrave called on his new master Otto II for assistance, and the latter mounted a major expedition against the Poles. Mieszko defeated him too in 979, and became undisputed lord of the whole of Pomerania. He marked this triumph in the following year by planting a new city at the mouth of the Vistula to balance the existing ports of Szczecin and Wolin on the Oder. This city, which was to play a unique and important role throughout Polish history, and which was to mark its millennium in a way that drew to itself the eyes of the world, was called Gdańsk.

Mieszko continued to advance along the coast until he joined up with the Danes, who had been extending their dominion eastward. He ensured good relations with his new neighbours by giving his daughter Świętosława in marriage to King Eric of Sweden and Denmark. After Eric's death, she married Swein Forkbeard, King of Denmark, and bore him a son who visited Poland in 1014 to collect a force of three hundred horsemen who would help him reconquer his kingdom of England. His name was Canute.

The first ruler of Christian Poland was a remarkable man. Consistently successful in war, he did not neglect diplomacy, seeking contacts with powers as distant as the Moorish Caliphate of Cordoba in Spain to reinforce his policy of expansion and independence from the Empire. His last enterprise was to invade and absorb the lands of the *Slenzanie* (which came to be known as Silesia). There in 992 he drew up a document, the *Dagome Iudex*, laying down the boundaries of his realm, which he dedicated to St Peter and placed under the protection of the Pope.

The Pope was to prove immensely useful to Mieszko's son and successor, Bolesław the Brave, who carried his work through to a glorious conclusion, using the institutions and paraphernalia of the Church with flair. In 996 a distinguished monk called Adalbertus (actually Vojteh, a Bohemian prince) appeared at the court of Bolesław, who received him with all due honours. He had been sent by Pope Sylvester I with the mission of evangelising the Prussians, a non-Slavic people inhabiting the Baltic seaboard to the east of the mouth of the Vistula. The Prussians made short work of putting the missionary to death. On hearing the news, Bolesław sent to Prussia and bought the remains of the monk for their weight in gold. He then laid them to rest in the Cathedral of Gniezno.

When Pope Sylvester heard of this, in 999, he canonised Adalbertus. He also took the momentous step of elevating Gniezno to the level of an Archbishopric, and creating new bishoprics at Wrocław, Kołobrzeg and Kraków. This underlined the independence of the Polish Church hierarchy from the influence of the older diocese of Magdeburg, which had hoped to control it in the German interest. It also strengthened the Polish state, for in the conditions prevailing all over Europe, ecclesiastical networks were instruments of stability and control. In Poland, parishes were originally established beside the castles which were centres of royal administration, a connection between religious and temporal power which is enshrined in the etymology of the Polish word for 'church' – *kościół*, which derives from the Latin *castellum*.

These events had even more far-reaching repercussions. The new Emperor Otto III had been a friend of Adalbertus, as well as of Pope Sylvester, and in the year 1000 he came on a pilgrimage to the saint's shrine at Gniezno. His visit is best described by the chronicler Gallus, who wrote:

> Bolesław received him with such honour and magnificence as befitted a King, a Roman Emperor and a distinguished guest. For the arrival of the Emperor he prepared a wonderful sight; he placed many companies of knights of every sort, and then his dignitaries, in ranks, every different company set apart by the colours of its clothes. And this was no cheap spangle of any old stuff, but the most costly things that can be found anywhere on earth. For in Bolesław's day every knight and every lady of the court wore not linen or woollen cloth, but coats of costly weave, while furs, even if they were very expensive and quite new, were not worn at his court unless doubled with fine stuff and trimmed with gold tassels. For gold in his time was as common as silver is now, silver was as cheap as straw. Seeing his glory, his power and his riches, the Roman Emperor cried out in admiration: 'By the crown of my Empire! What I see far exceeds what I have heard!' And taking counsel with his magnates, he added, before all those present: 'It is not fit that such a man should be titled a prince or count, as though he were just a great lord, but he should be elevated with all pomp to a throne and crowned with a crown.' Taking the Imperial diadem from his own brow, he placed it on the head of Bolesław as a sign of union and friendship, and for an ensign of state he gave him a nail from the Holy Cross and the lance of Saint Maurice, in return for which Bolesław gave him the arm of Saint Adalbertus. And they felt such love on that day that the Emperor named him brother and associate in the Empire, and called him the friend and ally of the Roman nation . . .

According to one source, Bolesław then accompanied Otto back to Aix-la-Chapelle, where the latter had the tomb of Charlemagne opened. From the trappings of imperial power it contained, Otto is reputed to have taken the throne itself and presented it to Bolesław, who responded with the gift of a bodyguard of Polish knights.

Otto had come not only to pray at the tomb of his saintly friend. He needed to assess Poland's strength and establish its status within the Holy Roman Empire. He was impressed by what he saw, and decided the country must be treated not as a tributary duchy, but as a fully-fledged kingdom, alongside Germany and Italy. From the moment the embryonic Polish state had come into contact with the Empire, two possibilities arose: it would either be sucked into the position of a vassal, like Bohemia, to be slowly digested by Germany, or it could enter the club of Europe as a sovereign state. The events of the year 1000 had decided the issue, in principle at least.

As soon as Otto was succeeded by the less idealistic Henry II the principle had to be defended. Neither German nor Bohemian *raison d'état* could tolerate the idea of a strong Polish state, and a new German offensive was launched, supported by Bohemia on the southern flank, and the pagan Slavs in the north. Bolesław defeated Henry in battle. He then brought diplomatic pressure to bear on Bohemia by a timely alliance with the Hungarians, and on Henry himself by arranging a dynastic alliance with the Palatine of Lorraine. Pressed from all sides, Henry was obliged, at the treaty of Bautzen (1018), to cede to Poland not only the disputed territory along the Elbe, but the whole of Moravia as well.

Like his father, Bolesław was not a man to rest on his laurels, and when an opportunity for action arose, he took it. He had married his daughter to Prince Svatopolk, ruler of the Principality of Rus, whose capital of Kiev was a great centre of Slav culture. Svatopolk was ousted by a rebellion, whereupon Bolesław invaded on his son-in-law's behalf. He took the opportunity of annexing a slice of land separating his own dominions from those of Kiev, the area between the rivers Bug and San, which neatly rounded off his state in the east.

The Polish realm was now large by any standards, and its sovereign status seemed beyond doubt. To stress this, in the last year of his life, 1025, Bolesław had himself crowned King of Poland in Gniezno Cathedral. It was a great moment, but it was hollow of real significance. As the chronicler laments, with the hindsight of almost a century:

> With the passing from this world of King Bolesław, the golden age turned into a leaden one. Poland, hitherto a queen crowned with shining gold and precious stones, now sits on ashes, dressed in widow's weeds, while the sound of the zither has turned to wailing, joy to sorrow, and the voice of the organ to a bitter sigh.

The reality behind the chronicler's poetic image was that the empire-building policies of Mieszko and Bolesław had outstripped the means of

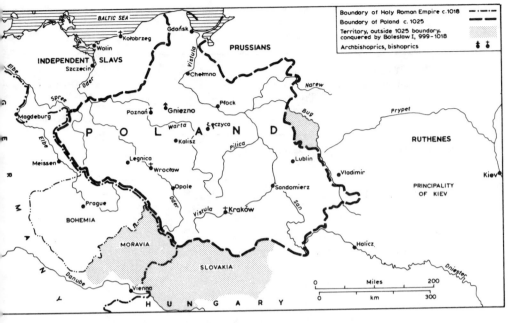

The Kingdom of Bolesław the Brave in 1025

the nascent state, which could not digest all their conquests at such a rate. At the same time, the regionalist tendencies inherent in the patterns of settlement of the Poles made themselves felt with the accession of Bolesław's son Mieszko II, who was not a strong ruler.

While he attempted to hold together his dominions, jealous brothers obtained the support of Kiev by promising to cede the lands between the Bug and San rivers, and that of the Empire by promising to give back areas annexed by Bolesław. They had no difficulty in toppling Mieszko, and he had to flee the country in 1031. The unfortunate man was then set upon by some Bohemian knights who, according to the Polish chronicler, 'used leather thongs to crush his genitalia in such a way that he would never sire again.' Although he managed to return and regain his throne, he died in 1034 leaving the country divided. His son, Kazimierz I, was hardly more successful, and he too had to flee when civil war broke out.

The Duke of Bohemia took advantage of this to invade and seize Gniezno, which he looted thoroughly, taking not only the attributes of the Polish crown, but also the body of St Adalbertus, or Wojciech as he is called in Poland. This act was to become one of many landmarks punctuating an eternity of mistrust and hostility between the Poles and the Czechs. This mutual dislike was based on practical as well

THE PIAST PRINCES OF THE POLANIE

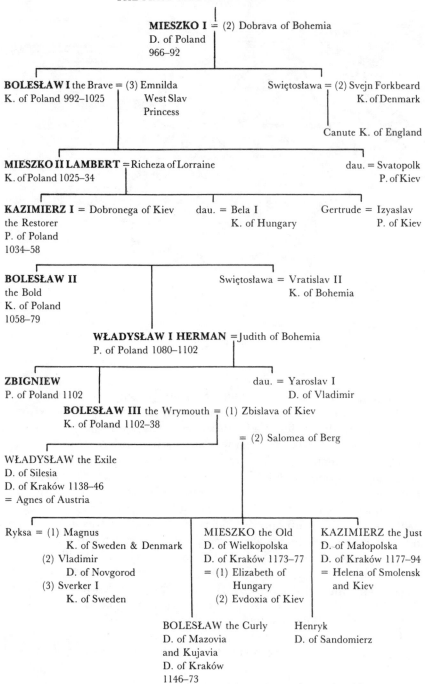

Fig. 1 *The early Piast kings. (Only the more important members of the dynasty are shown. Dates given are those of reigns. The family tree continues on p.32)*

as emotional factors. Bohemia had been Christian at least a century before the conversion of Poland and had benefited from contact with the Celts. It was culturally more developed than Poland and enjoyed a special relationship with the Empire. The Poles mistrusted Bohemia's links with the Empire, seeing in it an instrument of German influence and aggression. The two states were also in continuous conflict over a number of border areas, particularly Silesia. The position was in many ways analogous to that between France and Britain, whose special relationship with the United States offers tempting parallels. The tendency of the French to admire the British yet to view them as perfidious shopkeepers with a sinful talent for success is at times reminiscent of the Polish view of the Czechs. The Czech vision of the Poles as a nation of arrogant adventurers surfaces as often in history as the similar British attitude to the French. These irrational love-hate relationships outlast every possible justification. They are often inexplicable. Yet they provide much of the stuff of which history is made. At a moment when concepts of nationhood were in their infancy, and when distinctions were so blurred as to be almost imperceptible, the first Czech chronicler, Cosmas of Prague, and his contemporary Polish one, the monk Gallus, each saw the other nation as the worst enemy of his own.

This may come as a surprise to those fed on the German-Slav conflict theories of the great nineteenth-century historians like von Ranke, who divided Europe neatly into Germanic, Latin and Slav spheres and chose to ignore the fact that there was neither a dogma of conflict nor a hermetic ethnic frontier. In fact, Germans fought amongst themselves more often than they fought Slavs, and the Slavs were constantly at war with each other. When the Germans occupied the lands up to the Oder, they absorbed so much Slav blood that the later master-race of Brandenburg was heavily mixed. In what became Mecklenburg, the Slav ruling classes became the German aristocracy. On the other hand, the rulers of Poland repeatedly intermarried with Germans.

After about 1050, when the Germans began to feel a strong urge to expand, they backed it up with the theory that they were bringing civilisation to heathens and savages. They struck a crusading note which sounded down the ages, echoed by Frederick the Great, Bismarck and the leaders of the Third Reich. But the underlying conflict was over the question of Poland's position in the Christian world. For a century and a half after Otto III had sanctioned Bolesław the Brave's royal ambitions, Poland's status remained uncertain, with the Empire continually trying to place it in the position of a vassal state, and Poland continually trying to establish its sovereignty. The ebb and flow of this struggle is reflected in the way Polish monarchs are variously referred to as *dux, princeps* and *rex* in Western sources of the time. In spite of its own internal dissensions and civil wars, the Empire was the theoretical arbiter on such questions. The Polish monarch could strengthen his position by building up his own power, by seeking the support of other countries and by alliance with the Pope against the Emperor. The problems involved are clearly illustrated by the hundred years after the death of Kazimierz I in 1058.

After regaining his throne in 1040, Kazimierz had made Kraków his capital. Gniezno, the centre of Wielkopolska (Greater Poland), the land of the Polanie, demanded a strong boundary along the Oder and the Polish domination of Pomerania in the north and Silesia in the south. Kraków, the capital of Małopolska (Lesser Poland), was likely to be more affected by what happened in Kiev than what was going on in Pomerania. Both Kazimierz, who was married to the sister of the Prince of Kiev, and his son Bolesław II, the Bold, who also married a member of that royal house, had turned their eyes to the east and Bolesław occupied Kiev twice on his uncle's behalf. At the same time, Hungary was emerging as an important factor in Polish affairs. A rich, attractive land with a population sympathetic to Polish attitudes, it was an obvious ally against Bohemia and the Empire. Wars in the west against the Germans were costly and destructive, and Polish kings learned to eschew them in favour of diplomatic manoeuvres based on the Poland-Hungary-Rome axis, which at this moment extended all the way to Spain in a great web of anti-Empire papal policy. One of the fringe benefits of this alliance was that the Pope granted Bolesław a royal crown, with which the latter crowned himself in great ceremony in 1076.

The fiery king's friendship with the Papacy came to grief only three years after this event. Less than a century after his namesake had made such mileage out of a saint, Bolesław lost his throne over one. A number of magnates, including Stanisław, Bishop of Kraków, had started to plot against him. When Bolesław uncovered the conspiracy he reacted with his usual violence, putting to death a number of the conspirators, including the bishop. It was a move that aroused widespread indignation, and the unfortunate king was obliged to abandon his throne to his brother Władysław Herman. The killing of the bishop, who was later canonised, brought about a sharp decline in Poland's position, and in 1085 the Emperor Henry IV allowed the Duke of Bohemia to crown himself King of Bohemia and Poland. This was a slap in the face to Władysław, although it did not actually entail Bohemian domination in Poland.

At home, Władysław was unable to curb the rising power of local lords, who stipulated that Poland should be divided between his two sons at his death. When this came, however, in 1102, the younger son, Bolesław the Wrymouth, drove his brother out of the country. As his name suggests, he was an ugly, cunning, sardonic man, but he was also extremely capable, and quickly earned the respect and even the love of his subjects, in spite of his determination to rule with a strong arm. He was aided in this by his ability as a general. In 1109 he won a victory over the Emperor and the Duke of Bohemia at the Battle of Psie Pole near Wrocław, forcing them

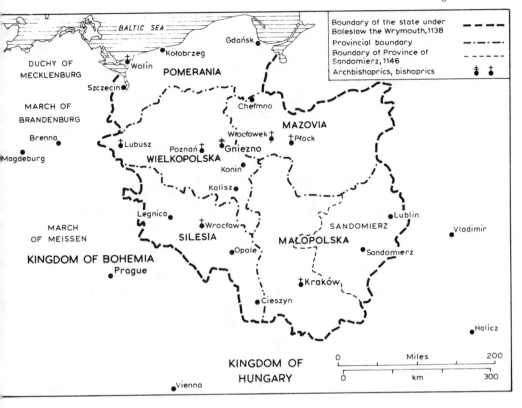

The Division of Poland, 1138

to renounce all their claims to Polish territory. He also invaded Pomerania, where a gradual German incursion had over the years weakened the Polish position. He recaptured the whole area up to and well beyond the Oder, as far as the Island of Rügen.

The last years of his reign brought defeat during expeditions in support of his Hungarian allies, provoking renewed Bohemian invasions. A group of nobles took advantage of the situation, forcing Bolesław to make a political testament which carved Poland up into duchies. Each of his five sons was to rule over one of these. Pomerania, whose Dukes were closely related but not of the main Piast line, was given equal status. The eldest son was to reign in the small but symbolic duchy of Kraków as well as his own and exert suzerainty over the others. Thus when Bolesław the Wrymouth died in 1138, the country embarked on a political experiment designed to compromise between the strong regionalist tendencies, and the feeling of kinship and political unity which already existed throughout Poland.

To be specific about Poland at this time is not easy. Frontiers fluctuated, and great expanses of land, particularly in Pomerania, were considered to be Polish by the ruler of Poland and to be German by the Emperor. Every so often one monarch or the other would appear at the head of an army to restate his claim, but no such thing as a permanent boundary existed, and the fact that the population was Slav did not count either way. There were also a great many foreigners settled in the cities, mainly Germans and Jews from Western Europe. Nevertheless, by the year 1100 there was a fairly well-defined area inhabited by about two million racially and linguistically homogeneous people which can be defined as Poland, even though it did not necessarily correspond to political frontiers. Provinces such as Silesia, which were lost to Poland for several hundred years, retained into the twentieth century their consciousness of being a limb of the Polish body.

This sense of nationhood, more marked in Poland at this stage than in France, England and most of the other future states of Europe, was not the result of the mere century-and-a-half since Christianization. A sense of unity was in evidence much earlier, and one can trace its origins to the moment the Piast dynasty had begun to hold sway in Gniezno, in the middle of the ninth century and perhaps even before. It was Mieszko I who translated this into political terms by effectively creating the Polish state.

He and his successors applied themselves with energy to the task of developing this state economically. They had established over eighty castle-towns by the end of the eleventh century and endowed market-towns with royal charters granting rights and protection. They encouraged the replacement of barter with their own coinage, and did what they could to ensure the security necessary for the development of international trade-routes through the country.

Cities like Kraków, which became the capital in 1040, Sandomierz, Kalisz, Wrocław, Poznań and Płock flourished and began to give an impression of opulence. The shortage of good building stone in Poland meant that they were almost entirely wooden, but stone buildings were not unknown, and the palace in which Bolesław I entertained Otto in 1000, for instance, was built of stone. It was the Church, however, which played the most significant role here, and stone architecture in the Romanesque style appeared in the wake of its progress through the country.

Originally, the stone-masons and craftsmen came from Burgundy or Germany and the earliest churches in Poland proclaim these origins by their stylistic purity. Local craftsmen, some of whom were probably of foreign origin, began to produce works of remarkable quality, as a number of surviving artefacts from the last quarter of the twelfth century reveal. The Kalisz patten (c.1195) and the original Trzemeszno chalice (c.1180) bear comparison with objects produced anywhere else in the Christian world, while the magnificent bronze doors of Gniezno Cathedral (1170–

5 The Church of St Andrew in Kraków, built in 1086, but altered in later centuries. It was originally much taller, since the floor is now more than three metres below street level. The church was the only building in the city to withstand the Tatar sack of 1241, and those who took refuge inside survived.

6 The Lance of St Maurice presented to Bolesław the Brave by the Emperor Otto III in the year 1000.

7 11th century silver bowl from Włocławek, decorated with biblical scenes. The bowl, which is a fine example of the Romanesque style imported from the West, shows strong Sassanian stylistic influences, which testify to continued contact with other cultural centres.

8 The Collegiate Church of St Alexis, Tum, near
Łęczyca, built between 1141 and 1161 on the site of an
earlier Benedictine foundation.

9 The bronze doors of Gniezno Cathedral, made by
local craftsmen in the 1170s, which depict the life and
martyrdom of St Adalbertus (Wojciech), and the
purchase of his remains from the pagan Prussians by
Bolesław the Brave in 998.

10 Gold paten presented by Duke Konrad of Mazovia
to the Cathedral of Płock. Made locally c. 1238, the paten
is Romanesque in style and conception, but shows the first
traces of Gothic. Duke Konrad is depicted on the right,
presenting the chalice, with his wife Agafia opposite, and
his sons Ziemowit and Kazimierz below.

80) are unique in style and quality, and remain one of the masterpieces of Romanesque art.

The Church was central to the spread of culture and education, and to the whole process of modernisation, providing as it did technical expertise, administration, and schooling for would-be priests and young noblemen. The arrival of the Benedictines, whose great monastery at Tyniec on the Vistula dates from the second half of the eleventh century, and later of the Premonstratensians and Cistercians, added impetus to this process. Most of the cathedrals had schools attached to them, and through the institution of the Church it was possible for Polish students to travel to other countries in search of learning. A local Latin *chanson de geste* made its appearance, and between 1112 and 1116 the first Polish chronicle, a Latin text of some literary quality, was written down in Kraków by Gallus, probably a Benedictine monk from Provence.

A distinction must be drawn between the great impact of the Church's educational and even political activities, and the considerably lesser impact it produced at the purely religious level. Pagan cults survived the official conversion of the country in 966, and the next two centuries witnessed several major revivals, during which churches.were burnt and priests put to death. The pagan survivals were particularly strong in areas such as Pomerania, which were attempting to maintain a measure of autonomy in the face of pressure to submit to either Polish or Imperial overlordship. Until the 1120s there was a much-visited shrine of the god Trzygława in Szczecin, a grandiose temple covered in frescoes housing a live black horse which was consulted as an oracle.

The Church could do little about this in the face of a general lack of zeal, which is well illustrated by the Polish response to Rome's summons to the Crusades. Apart from Prince Henryk of Sandomierz, few heeded it. Duke Leszek the White explained in a long letter to the Pope that neither he nor any self-respecting Polish knight could be induced to go to the Holy Land, where, they had been informed, there was no wine, mead, or even beer to be had. While it is probably true that then as now the Poles did not like drinking water, there were in fact less frivolous reasons for staying at home.

There were enough aggressive and troublesome pagans on Poland's own frontiers – the Prussians and Lithuanians – but little was being done to evangelise them. This stemmed from a mixture of toleration and indifference, both of which were reflected elsewhere. The Synod of the Polish Church at Wrocław in 1266 was berated by the Papal Legate for allowing Jews to dress like everyone else and to live without restriction in Poland, a complaint which would be voiced again and again. Polish lack of crusading zeal and the easygoing attitude towards those of other religious persuasions had deeper causes.

A major motor in propelling great numbers of European knights across the seas to fight crusades in Palestine and the Baltic (and settlers to follow them) was the great population explosion of the Middle Ages which produced serious overcrowding. The still underpopulated Poland felt no such need for expansion, and tolerated the large-scale immigration of Jews, Bohemians and Germans who provided useful services. The feelings towards Jews and 'infidels' in general were less violent in a country which was still a newcomer to Christianity, and which viewed the Empire and the Papacy with considerable mistrust.

It could almost be said that the Poles had come to view all higher authority with mistrust. The realm continued to fragment after the death of Bolesław the Wrymouth in 1138 had transformed it into five duchies. The eldest of his sons, Władysław, made an attempt at reuniting it from his position as ruler of Kraków, but he came up against the resistance not only of his brothers but of most of the local lords as well. Over the next hundred years successive dukes reigning in Kraków proved less and less successful in enacting the formal suzerainty which went with the position, and eventually abandoned the attempt altogether. The various branches of the royal family established local dynasties, in some cases subdividing the original five duchies of Wielkopolska, Mazovia-Kujavia, Małopolska, Sandomierz and Silesia into smaller units in order to accommodate their offspring.

There was more to such fragmentation than the claims of rival siblings. Regional lords and the larger towns contributed a strong yearning for autonomy, and the trend towards devolution went hand-in-hand with a demand for wider power-sharing. Władysław of Wielkopolska, also known as Spindleshanks on account of his bony legs, made a valiant attempt to reassert his authority as Duke of Kraków, but a number of powerful barons forced him to grant them substantial prerogatives by the Privilege of Cienia in 1228, just twelve years after a similar document, the Magna Carta, had been extorted from a king of England.

There was nevertheless a profound difference between the barons of England and the magnates of Poland. The power of an English or French lord at this time was held from the crown and fitted into a whole system of vassalage. Polish society had evolved from clannish structures, and the introduction of Christianity and all that went with it did not alter these significantly. The feudal system which regulated society all over Europe was never introduced into Poland, and this fact cannot be stressed too heavily.

The highest estate were the gentry, the *szlachta*, who inherited both status and land. They were obliged to perform military service for the king and to submit to his tribunals, but they were the independent magistrates over their own lands. They upheld the customary laws of the country, the *Ius Polonicum*, based entirely on precedent, and resisted attempts at the imposition of foreign legal practices by the crown. Beneath the szlachta there were a number of estates, including the *włodyki*, who were knights without noble status, and the *panosze*, who formed a sort of yeoman class. The peasants were mostly free and able to rise to a different status. A small proportion belonged to their masters, but these gained greater personal freedom during the first half of the thirteenth century, and were not generally tied to the land as in Western Europe.

The adoption of the three-field system at the beginning of the thirteenth century and the agrarian boom it brought about differentiated between those who owned land and those who did not. Those who did grew richer, those who did not were revealed to have nothing to offer except their labour. Thus while they gained greater personal freedom and legal protection, the poorer peasants began to be caught up in the mesh of economic bondage, resulting in a form of economic feudalism that had nothing to do with the feudal system as such.

The cities were, literally, a law unto themselves. Most of them had been either founded by or endowed with special charters which gave them a large measure of autonomy. As they grew, they attracted foreigners – Germans, Italians, Walloons, Flemings and Jews – whose presence served to increase this independence. The Germans imported with them the *Ius Teutonicum* or Magdeburg Law, which was first adopted for Silesian towns in 1211, and quickly spread, in modified form, to others all over Poland. These laws, which regulated criminal and civic offences and all trade practices, meant that the area within a city's walls was both administratively and legislatively in another country from that lying without. The city-dwellers evolved as a separate class having nothing in common with the others. The same was true of the growing Jewish community, which was granted a royal charter in 1264, the first of a number of such privileges which were to turn it into a nation within a nation.

Since there was no framework of vassalage there were no natural channels for the exercise of central authority. Royal control therefore depended not on a local vassal as elsewhere in Europe, but on a functionary appointed by the king. He was known by his function, and his title of Castellan (*Kasztelan*) derived from the royal castle from which he exercised judicial, administrative and military authority on the king's behalf. There were over a hundred of these castellans administering the Polish lands by 1250, but their importance had waned along with central authority when the country was divided. In terms of power, they began to be superseded by the ministers of the individual dukes, the Palatines (*Wojewoda*).

These divergences from European norms are characteristic. Poland had joined Christendom in 966 as a relatively mature if unsophisticated political unit. It had not been absorbed in the manner of a frontier province or colony, and it continued to reject those religious and cultural elements which it could not accommodate. Politically, it fought hard to keep both the Empire and the Papacy at arm's length throughout the crucial period. By the 1250s, when the power of the Empire had gone into decline as a result of internal struggle in Germany, the sense of political unity was gaining ground throughout the Polish lands in spite of their divided condition and it was thanks to this that the kingdom survived, to flourish in the next two centuries. To the historian, thirteenth-century Poland provides the unusual spectacle of an unsophisticated, even primitive society refusing to obey the cultural and economic laws which would have it absorbed into the powerful European mainstream, apparently determined to find its own course.

3

Tatars and Teutons

In 1241 the hordes of Genghis Khan broke over Europe in a great wave. These short powerful men with their flat, yellow, beardless faces, sunken noses and slit eyes issued from the heart of Central Asia, the fiercest of all Mongol peoples. They drank horse's milk mixed with blood, ate raw meat, and on this rancid diet they could travel fast and endure surprising extremes of climate. They were fine warriors, manoeuvring with all the instinctive cunning and discipline of a pack of wolves. European armies of knights and men-at-arms were no match for them.

With terrible ease they overran and put to fire and sword the principalities of Rus, and then divided into two bodies. The larger swept into Hungary, the other ravaged Poland. The knighthood of Małopolska gathered to face them at Chmielnik, but were swamped and massacred. The Duke of Kraków, Bolesław the Chaste, fled south to Moravia. (His nickname designates not so much a virtue as a predicament; he was married to St Kunegunda who, chroniclers maintain, exclaimed 'Ave Regina Coeli' as she issued from her mother's womb, suckled less on Fridays, not at all on fast-days, and, of course, refused to consummate her marriage.)

The Tatars kept going. They sacked Kraków and burnt it to the ground on Easter Day, then rode on westwards into Silesia. Here Duke Henryk the Pious had massed all his own forces, as well as those of Wielkopolska, a contingent of foreign knights, and even the regimented miners from his goldmines of Złotoryja. On 9 April 1241 he led them out of the city of Legnica to face the oncoming Tatars. His forces were decimated and Duke Henryk himself was surrounded and hacked to pieces. 'After this disaster, unleashed on a Christian people by the just sentence of God', the chronicler records, 'every man trembled in his soul, terror and doubt took hold of every mind.'

Happily for Western Europe, the Tatars veered south to rejoin their brothers in Hungary and there news reached them of the death of their Khan. They abandoned their westward advance and rode back whence

Tatars and Teutons

they had come. Christendom was saved. Although they never again attempted a conquest of Europe, they did not leave Poland or Hungary alone. In 1259 they swept through Poland, sacking Lublin, Sandomierz, Bytom and Kraków. They returned in 1287, again putting everything to fire and sword, with only the fortresses of Sandomierz and Kraków holding out.

These raids left an indelible mark on the country. In the space of a few decades, the whole of eastern and southern Poland had been seriously depopulated and its cities burnt to the ground. The horror was vividly captured in chronicle, legend and song, and kept alive to this day in the hourly trumpet-call from the tower of St Mary's Church in Kraków, which breaks off in the middle to commemorate the Tatar arrow that cut short the medieval trumpeter's call. In his various religious and political guises the eastern barbarian is to this day a bogeyman in the Polish political mind.

The Tatar invasions showed up the vulnerability of a country divided. Although there was a community of interest, there had been no coordination of action, and regional militias were defeated one by one. Just as the Tatar threat died away, this vulnerability was beginning to be demonstrated on the other side of the country, where the other great bogeyman of modern Polish history was born, swaddled in polished steel marked with the black cross.

At a time when Poland had already been a Christian state for two hundred years, much of the Baltic coastline was still inhabited by heathens, and the Polish Dukes of Gdańsk-Pomerania and of Mazovia carried on endless wars against the Prussian tribes. Further east and north, where the Baltic coast curves upwards, the Danes were making inroads into Livonia. The motives for this fighting were self-defence, the desire for land, or the need to open up trade routes. The missionary urge lagged far behind, until St Bernard of Clairvaux started preaching the crusade all over Europe.

It was he who persuaded the Pope to use North European crusaders in Northern Europe rather than the Middle East, and to grant the same dispensations and indulgences to those who fought against the heathen Slavs or Prussians as to those fighting the Saracens. Although the first northern crusade was a failure, the heathen Slavs in western Pomerania were gradually subjugated by the Saxons and the Danes over the next fifty years. The advantage of a crusade was that a local duke who launched what was in effect a private war against his enemies could, by making an arrangement with his bishop, recruit foreign knights who would come and fight for him as unpaid soldiers. And the fruits of this crusade whetted the appetites of Danes, Poles and Germans alike.

Throughout the early 1200s the Dukes of Mazovia tried to make inroads into Prussia, but this only provoked counter-raids from the heathen

11 The *Szczerbiec*, which became the coronation sword of the kings of Poland. Originally made for Bolesław of Mazovia in the first half of the 13th century, probably in Płock, it was first used by his nephew Władysław the Short at his coronation as King of Poland in 1320.

12 The Battle of Legnica (1241) in which the Tatar army of Genghis Khan routed the forces of Henryk the Pious of Silesia Panel of a tryptych by the Master of Wielowieś, c. 1430, depicting the Legend of St Jadwiga.

13 Tympanum representing David playing the harp before Bathsheba, in the Cistercian Church at Trzebnica, dating from the first half of the 13th century.

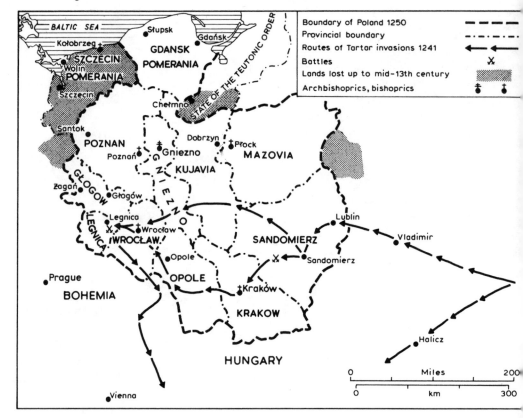

The Polish Duchies, 1250

Prussians. A methodical military takeover of the area was needed, and the only armies which could take up such a challenge were the Military Orders, the most famous of which, the Templars and Hospitallers, had proved their efficiency in Palestine. The Germans formed a military brotherhood known as the Knights of the Sword to conquer Livonia. Duke Konrad of Mazovia imitated them by founding Christ's Knights of Dobrzyn as the regular army of the Polish 'mission' to Prussia, but this body was too small to cope with the task.

An altogether more radical solution was called for, and so, in 1226, Konrad of Mazovia took a step whose consequences for Poland and for Europe were to be incalculable. He invited the Teutonic Order of the Hospital of St Mary in Jerusalem, known as the Teutonic Knights, to establish a commandery at Chełmno and help him conquer Prussia. The Teutonic Knights had been set up at Acre in Palestine on the model of the Templars, but were keen to find a niche of their own. They seemed to have found it in Hungary, where they were given the task of holding the Tatars at bay, but the King of Hungary grew wary of their political and territorial ambitions and shortly expelled them.

They could see the advantages of the Polish offer, but this time they were determined to guarantee their future. They made a number of diplomatic moves, obtaining a bull from the Pope to conquer Prussia and thereafter to hold it in perpetuity as a papal fief. They also forged a document whereby the lease Konrad of Mazovia gave them on the territory of Chełmno became a freehold.

The Teutonic Knights were a form of life which post-renaissance man finds it impossible to comprehend. They applied the principles of the Templars with truly Teutonic thoroughness. Vowed to chastity and poverty, reading their breviary on the march and keeping monastic silence in camp, they gave up all amenities and led a dour military life in order to expiate their sins. From the moment he took his vows, a knight-brother did not own his horse or his armour and gave up his own coat of arms, sinking his identity within that of the Order. This monastic discipline and uniformity equipped them superbly for the job in hand.

They started their operations in the Baltic by taking over the Knights of the Sword with their province around Riga in Livonia. The two brotherhoods winkled out the Danish missionary colony at Reval in Estonia, and then proceeded to launch a two-fronted offensive against the Prussian tribes. Progress was slow. Great forays would be organised, using Polish, German and visiting Burgundian and English knights to supplement the crusaders, but while the Prussians could be defeated in battle, they carried on a guerilla campaign which prevented the setting up of Christian outposts. There were squabbles too, involving Polish Dukes of Pomerania or Mazovia, the Order, Prussian tribes, and even the Lithuanians to the north-east.

Nevertheless, by 1283 the whole area of Prussia had been conquered. Although it was settled by a considerable number of landless Polish and German knights who were not members of the Order, it was the Order that ruled the province. The Knights built a stronghold at Marienburg and garrisoned a number of castles throughout the territory. Where it had not been slaughtered the local Prussian population was subjugated, and colonisers of every estate were brought in from Germany and Poland. Agriculture began to flourish, and the Knights established a port at Elbing (Elbląg) to carry trade from the province.

In the space of fifty years, the Prussian nuisance on the Mazovian border had been replaced by a Germanic state. Politically, this was independent of any dominant influence, since it was virtually the private estate of a religious order – a sort of monastic version of the East India Company. It was therefore not in itself a threat to the Polish Duchies. Yet as part of a

32

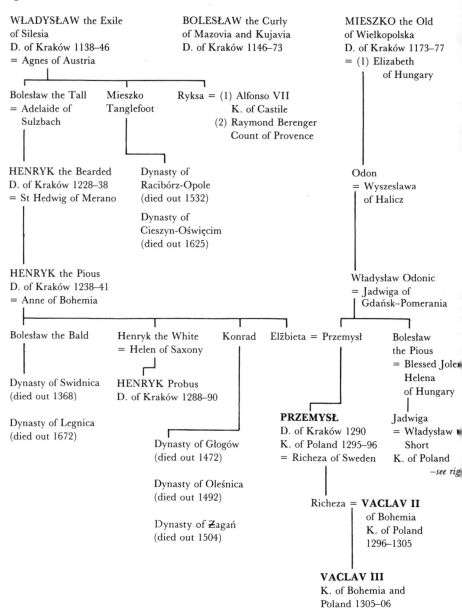

WŁADYSŁAW the Exile
of Silesia
D. of Kraków 1138–46
= Agnes of Austria

Bolesław the Tall
= Adelaide of
Sulzbach

Mieszko
Tanglefoot

Ryksa = (1) Alfonso VII
K. of Castile
(2) Raymond Berenger
Count of Provence

HENRYK the Bearded
D. of Kraków 1228–38
= St Hedwig of Merano

Dynasty of
Racibórz-Opole
(died out 1532)

Dynasty of
Cieszyn-Oświęcim
(died out 1625)

HENRYK the Pious
D. of Kraków 1238–41
= Anne of Bohemia

Bolesław the Bald

Henryk the White
= Helen of Saxony

Konrad

Elżbieta = Przemysł

Bolesław
the Pious
= Blessed Jolen
Helena
of Hungary

Dynasty of Swidnica
(died out 1368)

Dynasty of Legnica
(died out 1672)

HENRYK Probus
D. of Kraków 1288–90

Dynasty of Głogów
(died out 1472)

Dynasty of Oleśnica
(died out 1492)

Dynasty of Żagań
(died out 1504)

PRZEMYSŁ
D. of Kraków 1290
K. of Poland 1295–96
= Richeza of Sweden

Jadwiga
= Władysław
Short
K. of Poland
—see rig

BOLESŁAW the Curly
of Mazovia and Kujavia
D. of Kraków 1146–73

MIESZKO the Old
of Wielkopolska
D. of Kraków 1173–77
= (1) Elizabeth
of Hungary

Odon
= Wyszeslawa
of Halicz

Władysław Odonic
= Jadwiga of
Gdańsk–Pomerania

Richeza = VACLAV II
of Bohemia
K. of Poland
1296–1305

VACLAV III
K. of Bohemia and
Poland 1305–06

Fig. 2 The division and reunification of Poland under the later Piasts

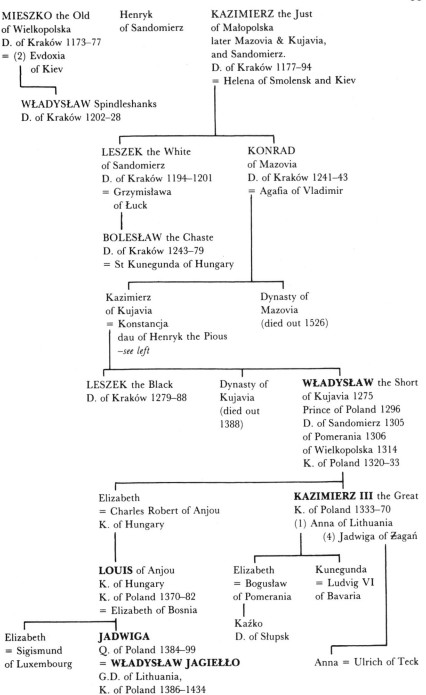

MIESZKO the Old
of Wielkopolska
D. of Kraków 1173–77
= (2) Evdoxia
of Kiev

Henryk
of Sandomierz

KAZIMIERZ the Just
of Małopolska
later Mazovia & Kujavia,
and Sandomierz.
D. of Kraków 1177–94
= Helena of Smolensk and Kiev

WŁADYSŁAW Spindleshanks
D. of Kraków 1202–28

LESZEK the White
of Sandomierz
D. of Kraków 1194–1201
= Grzymisława
of Łuck

KONRAD
of Mazovia
D. of Kraków 1241–43
= Agafia of Vladimir

BOLESŁAW the Chaste
D. of Kraków 1243–79
= St Kunegunda of Hungary

Kazimierz
of Kujavia
= Konstancja
dau of Henryk the Pious
—see left

Dynasty of
Mazovia
(died out 1526)

LESZEK the Black
D. of Kraków 1279–88

Dynasty of
Kujavia
(died out
1388)

WŁADYSŁAW the Short
of Kujavia 1275
Prince of Poland 1296
D. of Sandomierz 1305
of Pomerania 1306
of Wielkopolska 1314
K. of Poland 1320–33

Elizabeth
= Charles Robert of Anjou
K. of Hungary

KAZIMIERZ III the Great
K. of Poland 1333–70
(1) Anna of Lithuania
(4) Jadwiga of Żagań

LOUIS of Anjou
K. of Hungary
K. of Poland 1370–82
= Elizabeth of Bosnia

Elizabeth
= Bogusław
of Pomerania

Kaźko
D. of Słupsk

Kunegunda
= Ludvig VI
of Bavaria

Elizabeth
= Sigismund
of Luxembourg

JADWIGA
Q. of Poland 1384–99
= WŁADYSŁAW JAGIEŁŁO
G.D. of Lithuania,
K. of Poland 1386–1434

Anna = Ulrich of Teck

series of developments in the north and east of the Polish world, it was ominous.

A century earlier, in the 1150s, the last Slav prince of Brenna died, to be succeeded by a German. The March of Brandenburg, as it then became, embarked on a policy of aggrandisement in the east, driving a wedge between Slav states on the Baltic, where the outflanked Prince Bogusław of Szczecin was forced to accept German overlordship, and those to the south, like the small principality of Lubusz, which was annexed to Brandenburg outright. In 1266 Brandenburg took Santok, and in 1271 Gdańsk, thus joining its own territory to that of the Order. The Poles retook both Gdańsk and Santok in the following year, but a precedent had been set. The Polish western frontier along the river Oder had been breached for good. From the stronghold they had set up at Berlin on the river Spree in 1231, the Margraves of Brandenburg would watch and dream for centuries of extending their dominion eastwards.

The *Drang nach Osten* had begun. German settlers poured in, often encouraged by Polish rulers seeking to repopulate areas devastated by the Tatars. By the end of the thirteenth century not only Silesian and Pomeranian cities like Wrocław and Szczecin, but even the capital, Kraków, had become virtually German. In Silesia and Pomerania, the influx of landless knights and farmers from Germany also increased the German element in rural areas, radically affecting the will as well as the ability of local Piast rulers to stand by a disunited Poland unable to help them. Like so many small shopkeepers, these minor rulers had to pay tribute to whoever was strong enough to impose protection. One by one the princes of Pomerania, outflanked by German states and undermined by German control of the cities, particularly Hanseatic centres like Szczecin and Stargard, had to accept the German Emperor instead of the Duke of Kraków as their overlord. Poland had begun to disintegrate. In 1300 King Vaclav II of Bohemia was able to invade Wielkoposka, and with the blessing of the Emperor have himself crowned King of Poland.

The idea of reunification had remained alive within certain branches of the Polish royal family and among the szlachta. The experience of the Tatar invasions gave stimulus to the movement, and a real phobia of the encroaching Germans was beginning to manifest itself at all levels. After yet another attempt by Bohemia to take Kraków with the connivance of some of the townspeople, the Polish troops which retook it in 1312 proceeded to round up all the citizens and to behead those who could not pronounce the Polish tongue-twisters they were made to repeat. This mounting resistance to things German also helped to prepare the climate for reunification.

The crucial part in the process was played by the Church. Until now, it had not played a political role, merely an administrative one. Under the early Piast kings, the bishops had been royal functionaries without a power-base of their own. The period of devolution of the country into separate duchies changed this. The local rulers were not as strong as the kings had been, and they needed the support of local bishops. These had grown in influence, and they were quick to perceive that if the Polish duchies were swallowed up by Bohemia and Germany, the Polish Church would lose its autonomous status. The clergy of Silesia were the first to realise this, and took steps to counter the creeping Germanisation. At the Synod of Łęczyca in 1285 the Polish bishops adopted a resolution that only Poles could be appointed as teachers in church schools.

The earliest written examples of Polish prose and verse, from the first half of the thirteenth century, emanated not from ducal courts, but from the Church, which in most countries preferred to set down hymns and prayers in Latin. Not long after the canonisation of Stanisław, the Bishop of Kraków put to death by Bolesław II and recognised as patron of Poland in 1253, the monk Wincenty of Kielce wrote his *Vita Maior Sancti Stanislai*. In this the alleged miraculous growing together of the saint's quartered body is described as prophetic of the way in which the divided Poland would become one again. Another Bishop of Kraków, Wincenty Kadłubek, wrote a Polish chronicle in the first years of the thirteenth century in which he showed off not only his Parisian education but also his nationalism, producing a work of literary rather than historical merit in which the Poles are shown as a superior nation. The more reliable *Kronika Wielkopolska*, written by a churchman in Poznań in the 1280s, also reveals a deep-rooted and rather modern sense of nationalism.

The message was taken up by various dukes, who decided to abandon the hereditary principle and to elect from their number the overlord who would rule effectively in Kraków. Henryk Probus of Silesia was the first to be chosen in this way, and on his death in 1290 the Kraków throne was given to Przemysł II of Gniezno, a strong partisan of reunification. He was actually crowned King of Poland in 1295, but was assassinated two years later by agents of Brandenburg. He was succeeded by a prince of the Mazovian line, Władysław the Short, who was to become one of the greatest of Polish kings.

The Bohemian invasion of 1300 forced him to flee the country for a time, and Władysław went straight to Rome in search of allies. As his sobriquet suggests, he was a very small man, but he knew what he wanted and how to get it, laying his plans with consummate skill. The Papacy was locked in one of its perennial conflicts with the Empire, and therefore looked kindly on the anti-Imperial Polish duke. Władysław was impressed by the figure of Charles Robert of Anjou, the erstwhile King of Naples and Sicily who had just succeeded to the Hungarian throne. With the Pope's support he sealed an alliance by marrying his daughter to the Angevin. Having also secured the cooperation of the Ruthenian princes of Halicz and Vladimir he set off on the reconquest of his realm.

In 1306 he took Kraków and in 1314 Gniezno, thus gaining control of the two principal provinces, while a third, Mazovia, recognised his over-lordship. In 1320 he was crowned King of Poland. By making an alliance with Sweden, Denmark and the Pomeranian Principalities, Władysław forced Brandenburg onto the defensive while he dealt with the Teutonic Knights, who were in a difficult position. The fall of Acre to the Saracens in 1291 had deprived them of their headquarters. The indictment in 1307 of the Templars, on whom the Teutonic Knights were closely modelled, their subsequent dissolution and savage persecution, were a chilling warning to any order which grew too powerful. Władysław lost little time in taking the Teutonic Order to a Papal court not only on charges of invasion and rapine, but on more fundamental questions of whether the Order was fulfilling its duty. The Papal judgement went against the Order, but the very fact that the Knights had been cornered brought about a subtle change in their attitude.

Their headquarters, located in Venice after the fall of Acre so as to be ready for future crusades in the Holy Land, was quickly moved to Marienburg in Prussia in 1309. Prussia now became not a crusading outpost, but a state, and it would settle its disputes with neighbours not through Papal courts but on the battlefield. In concert with its ally John of Luxemburg, King of Bohemia, the Order invaded Poland. The Silesian Duke Bolko of Swidnica held off the Bohemians while Władysław marched against the Teutonic Knights and defeated them in a costly battle at Płowce in 1331. Too weak to pursue his advantage, he did not manage to reassert a Polish ascendancy in Pomerania or Silesia, where the German hegemony persisted. Nevertheless, by the time of his death in 1333, Władysław the Short had managed to reunite the central provinces and to establish at least nominal control over a number of other areas. His son Kazimierz III (1333–70), known as the Great, was able to carry through this process and to place the sovereignty of Poland beyond question.

While Western Europe pitched in the waves of calamity succeeding each other throughout the century, Poland enjoyed an unprecedented respite. As a minor ice-age reduced yields and ruined harvests throughout the continent, Poland basked in a more than usually warm and temperate spell, which produced not only bumper crops but also conditions in which all kinds of Mediterranean fruit could be grown and good wine produced in abundance. While the Hundred Years' War devastated the richest lands in Western Europe and wrought financial havoc as far afield as Italy, Poland was spared lengthy conflicts. Finally, as the entire continent was engulfed by one of the greatest catastrophes it has ever experienced – the Great Plague of 1348 – most of Poland remained unaffected, mainly as a result of

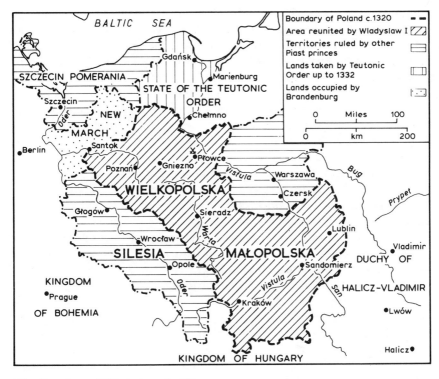

The Kingdom of Władysław the Short, c.1320

the scarcity of great concentrations of population. The populations of England and France, of Italy and Scandinavia, of Hungary, Switzerland, Germany and Spain were more than halved. Poland's grew. It grew from internal causes and as a result of conditions elsewhere. The depredations of the plague were accompanied by widespread famine which began a great exodus from towns and villages. Refugees roamed Europe in search of a haven. The need for a scapegoat had provoked the greatest wave of anti-Jewish atrocities in medieval history, and terrified survivors fled eastwards. They were welcomed in Poland, which insisted only on a period of quarantine.

Kazimierz was a fitting ruler for these halcyon days. Physically handsome, with a broad forehead and a remarkable head of hair, he was a regal figure, combining courage and determination with the tastes of a voluptuary. Above all, he was a man of generous understanding and wisdom, traces of which are everywhere visible to this day.

The introduction of brick in the first half of the thirteenth century had a great impact on a country poor in building stone. The gothic style, whose

first traces can be seen in the portal of the chapel at Trzebnica dating from
1270, stimulated building. The king himself was directly responsible for
much of this, as he put into effect a building programme which included
the creation of sixty-five new fortified towns, the fortification of twenty-
seven old towns, and the erection of fifty-three new castles. He also
rerouted the Vistula at Kraków, and constructed a canal linking the
salt-mines of Wieliczka with the capital. Some of his castles and city walls
survive, but the real monuments to his reign are the Cathedrals of Gniezno
and Kraków, with its beautiful Lady Chapel, the Collegiate Church of
Sandomierz, and a host of other new churches.

The monuments he left behind were not only of brick and stone. In 1347
he codified the entire corpus of existing laws in two books, one for
Wielkopolska, one for Małopolska. He reformed the fiscal system, created
a new centralised chancellery, and regulated the monetary situation with
the introduction of the Kraków grosz in 1338. In the towns he established
guilds, amended and extended the Magdeburg Laws, and granted a
separate law for the Armenians living within them, while he gave the Jews
their own fiscal, legal, and even political organisation.

These measures laid the foundations of a new boom, based on the
favourable climatic conditions, the agrarian crisis outside the country, and
the influx of refugees from Western Europe. Polish cities gained considerable numbers of merchants and skilled artisans, while the influx of Jews
provided them with banking and other facilities. This had a stimulating
effect on the growth of industry. Newly-discovered deposits of iron, lead,
copper, silver, zinc, sulphur and rock salt were exploited and mining
techniques improved, with the use of remarkable technology which can
still be seen in the great salt-mine of Wieliczka. The old exports of grain,
cattle, hides, lumber and other forest produce were supplemented by
manufactured goods such as finished cloth, which was carried all over
Central Europe, as far west as Switzerland.

Contact with the outside world was increasing, largely thanks to the
Church which, having played such a significant role in the process of
reunification, was enjoying considerable power and prestige. At one level,
this was translated into a cultural mission carried on throughout the
country by the expanding religious orders and collegiate chapters, particularly the Cistercians and the Premonstratensians, and the mendicant
orders of Dominicans and Franciscans. A large proportion of these clerics
were foreign, but they trained Polish priests who in turn travelled abroad.
Some went to spread the faith, like the friar Benedictus Polonus who
reached the capital of the Mongol Khan in the Gobi desert in 1245. Others
went to study, particularly at the universities of Bologna and Paris. As a
result, the Poles began to play a part, albeit a humble one, on the European
academic stage. The Dominican Martin the Pole became famous for his

The reign of Kazimierz the Great (1333–70) was a period of intense artistic activity.
14(*Left*) The east end of Gniezno Cathedral, rebuilt c. 1350 on the foundations of
Mieszko I's original rotunda. **15** (*Right*) The Church of St Catherine, consecrated in
1373, was one of several built in Kraków by the King. The stone-faced porch on the left
dates from the 15th century (the small wooden building in the foreground is the belfry).

16 Enamelled gold chalice presented to the Collegiate Church in Kalisz by the king in
1363. **17** Reliquary of St Sigismund presented to the Cathedral of Płock by the King in
1370. The diadem worn by the Saint is made from 13th-century royal coronets.

history of the Popes; Nicolaus Polonus, erstwhile physician to Duke Leszek the White, was noted for the medical works he wrote at Montpellier at the end of the thirteenth century; Franco de Polonia became a name in the world of astronomy; and Vitelo, a native of Silesia, wrote a revolutionary treatise on optics.

Another consequence of education was the beginning of a Polish literature. Henryk Probus, Duke of Silesia, wrote his lyrics in German, and Czech was much favoured at court, but the vernacular was gaining ground as a literary vehicle. Extant texts, mainly religious verse or epigrams, are fragmentary and little more than touching or amusing, yet the *Bogurodzica*, a hymn to the Mother of God written sometime before 1300, is a sophisticated poem of great force and beauty.

Kazimierz the Great exerted a strong personal influence on the development of learning and culture, and laid the foundations of the flowering of the next century. In 1364 he founded a university in Kraków. Coming just after the foundation of the Charles University of Prague and before those of Vienna and Heidelberg, this was the second such academy in central Europe. Unlike most English, French and German universities, which evolved from religious institutions, Kraków was based on the Italian models of Padua and Bologna, which were secular establishments. Kraków had chairs in civil law, canon law, medicine and the liberal arts, but none in theology, and the invigilator was the Chancellor of Poland, who was not necessarily a cleric.

That same year, 1364, Kazimierz put his capital on the map in another respect, by offering it as the venue for a congress of monarchs convened to discuss a possible Crusade. He was the first Polish monarch since Bolesław I to appreciate the value of prestige in asserting the country's international status. His family ties with the Hungarian Angevins had helped to make his court more cosmopolitan, while the period of prosperity enabled him to enhance its splendour. He lavished pomp and luxury on his guests, who included the Emperor Charles IV and the kings of Hungary, Denmark, Sicily, Cyprus and Austria. Kazimierz had little interest in the subject of the conference, seeing it principally as a means for establishing his power in the eyes of the world and pursuing his own international aims. The success with which he met in these can be gauged from the fact that he inherited a kingdom of 106,000 square kilometres, and left one of 260,000. This was the result of a mixture of war and diplomacy, in both of which he excelled. He warred with John of Luxemburg, King of Bohemia, over rival claims to Silesia, finally defeating him in 1345, just one year before the unfortunate blind king lost his plumes to the Prince of Wales at Crécy. Having thus secured his position in the west, Kazimierz could turn his attention elsewhere.

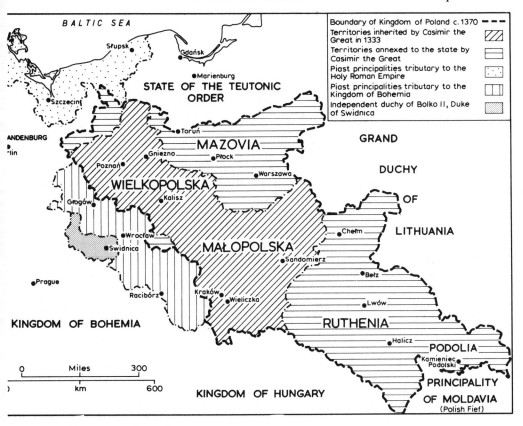

Poland under Kazimierz the Great, 1370

The Tatar invasions of the previous century had annihilated the Principality of Kiev, and the smaller Russian principalities were only allowed to survive at the cost of yearly tribute to the Tatars, who had settled in southern Russia. Two such principalities, those of Halicz and Vladimir, were adjacent to Poland's south-eastern border. Both were dynastically connected with Poland, and after the princes of Halicz died out, in 1349, Kazimierz incorporated their lands into his own dominion.

This elongation of Poland to the south-east was inevitable and permanent. The move of the Polish capital from Gniezno to Kraków three hundred years before was now beginning to affect Polish policy significantly. The king viewed his dominions from a different vantage-point, and the most pervasive influence at court was that of the magnates of Małopolska, the 'Kraków Lords'. There was more at stake in this eastern theatre than territorial gain. The disintegration of Kiev had left an enormous power-vacuum into which Poland was inevitably drawn, all the more so since another power was taking more than a passing interest in the area – the Duchy of Lithuania.

The Lithuanians were a Baltic people like the Prussians and the Letts, between whom they were settled. Theirs was a forest culture which included the worship of fire and of snakes, a complicated, ill-defined, yet cohesive religion which gave the savage and robust Lithuanians remarkable dynamism. Long after their kindred Letts and Prussians had been subjugated by the Knights of the Sword and the Teutonic Knights respectively, the Lithuanians continued to defy all attempts at conquest. The Knights could mount huge military expeditions into their very heartland, crusades with mass participation of European chivalry. They could invest and bombard the Lithuanian capital of Vilnius, and foreign crusaders like the Duke of Lancaster, the future Henry IV, could plant their banners on the captured ramparts, but within weeks the small men clad in skins would have beaten them back and retaken possession of their sacred forests and marshes.

The Lithuanians were ruled by a turbulent, cunning and ruthless dynasty well suited to the people and its needs. They were prepared to make peace and accept token Christianity from the Knights in order to gain support against the Russians of Novgorod, and from Novgorod in order to defeat the Knights. Their policy was so wily and volatile that nobody could keep up with it, and none of their neighbours could ever rest easy. After the debacle of Kiev, there was no stopping the Lithuanians, who poured into the devastated area and annexed vast tracts of masterless land. In 1362 the Lithuanian Duke Algirdas defeated the Tatars at the battle of the Blue Waters, and in the following year he occupied Kiev itself. In less than a hundred years, the Lithuanian state had quadrupled in size, but while this made it more formidable to its enemies, it endeared it to none and enmeshed it in problems which, for once, were too great even for the ravenous appetite of its rulers. They could not hope to administer the huge area populated with Christian Slavs by whose multitude they were to be eventually swamped. Their takeover of these lands had brought them into vicious confrontation with the Tatars on one front, while the Teutonic Knights were straining all their resources to crush them on the other. The Russian principalities were hostile, while Poland, which now shared a very long frontier with Lithuania, was growing tired of sporadic Lithuanian raids into Mazovia. Lithuania needed an ally in this sea of enemies. The problem of which to choose was the most pressing issue facing Grand Duke Iogaila when he came to the Lithuanian throne in 1382. And that same year had placed Poland in a dilemma, for different reasons.

Kazimierz the Great had died in 1370. Although married four times, he left no legitimate heir. This would have been a matter of little consequence, since there were plenty of Piast princes of other branches to pick from, had it not been for the fact that he left the throne to his nephew, Louis of Anjou, King of Hungary. King Louis attended the funeral and then went back to Hungary leaving his mother, the late king's sister, to rule in his name. She would have been unable to rule the country without the support of the more powerful nobles of Małopolska, the 'Kraków Lords'. They seized the chance to assume a greater share in the running of the country, and indeed in its status. The fourteenth century saw the establishment of a new concept of the state, according to which sovereignty was no longer seen as being vested in the person of the monarch, but in a specific geographical area, the *Corona Regni Poloniae*, embracing all the Polish lands, even those which had fallen under foreign domination. In 1374 the Polish nobles wrested from King Louis the Privilege of Kosice, which stressed the indivisibility of his patrimony, and stipulated that no part of it was his to give away. They were looking to a future which remained uncertain, since Louis, too, had no male heir. He did, however, have two daughters. He had married the elder, Maria, to Sigismund of Luxemburg, and intended him to take the Polish throne. The younger, Hedwig, was betrothed to Wilhelm of Habsburg, who was to have Hungary. But when Louis died in 1382, the Kraków Lords refused to bow to these wishes and made their own plans.

They rejected the already married Maria and brought the ten-year-old sister Hedwig, Jadwiga in Polish, to Kraków, where in 1384 she was crowned very emphatically *King (rex)*. The chronicler Długosz noted: 'The Polish lords and prelates were so taken with her, so greatly and sincerely loved her that, almost forgetting their masculine dignity, they did not feel any shame or degradation in being the subjects of such a gracious and virtuous lady.' In fact, they saw her principally as an instrument, and they disregarded her feelings entirely. When young Wilhelm of Habsburg turned up to claim his betrothed, he was kept away from her and she was locked in the castle on Wawel hill. She is even reputed to have seized an axe and tried breaking down the door of her chamber to get to him, all to no avail. He was sent off, and she was prepared by the Polish lords for the bed of another.

They had found a husband for her in Iogaila, Grand Duke of Lithuania. She was so frightened by the prospect of succumbing to this hairy heathen much older than herself that she pleaded with the lords, and was only placated after a favourite young knight of hers, Zawisza of Oleśnica, had been sent to inspect Iogaila in his bath-house and reported back favourably on the details of the barbarian's body.

The idea of a union between Poland and Lithuania had germinated simultaneously in both countries. On 14 August 1385 a basic agreement was signed at Krewo. This was followed by more specific agreements at

The Combined Kingdom of Poland and Lithuania in 1466

Wołkowysk in January 1386, and at Lublin a few weeks later. On 12 February, Jagiełło, as his name had crystallised in Polish, entered Kraków, and three days later he was baptised as Władysław. On 18 February he married Jadwiga, and on 4 March was crowned King of Poland.

Poland had linked its destiny to a backward pagan state three times its size, which it never quite managed to control. The benefits to Poland of the arrangement were not always clear. Most of the power and riches added by Lithuania were spent on Lithuanian ambitions and it was the problems generated by the alliance which were largely responsible for bringing the whole Polish world crashing down four centuries later. Yet the benefits were immense, and there is no doubt that the Kraków Lords had foreseen some of them when making their choice. They did not find Jadwiga a husband amongst the Silesian or Mazovian branches of the Piast royal house, because his hereditary right to rule would have placed him in a strong position. They did not want the Habsburg, because he was an agent of German hegemony. By choosing Jagiełło, they took someone whose position would never be entirely secure, someone who would rule only by their consent. They opted for a constitutional monarchy, and this was to permit Poland to flourish in a way uniquely her own.

4

The Jagiellon Adventure

The marriage of the thirty-five-year-old warrior to the twelve-year-old girl was not bound to be fruitful. Queen Jadwiga did not enjoy her marital duties, and took solace in a saintly life of charity and care for the poor. She died young, having borne her husband no heir. Yet the fruits of this marriage were prodigious. From this bed sprang a new Polish world, as different from the Poland of the twelfth or twentieth centuries as the Habsburg world was from the Austria of today.

The union of the two countries and the conversion of Lithuania sounded the knell for the Teutonic Order; the need for crusading vanished, and with it the whole *raison d'être* of the Knights in Prussia. Worse still, the two enemies whom the Order had often played off against each other had become firm allies. The Knights responded by trying to break up the alliance. This was made simpler for them when Władyslaw Jagiełło installed his cousin Vytautas (Witold) as regent in Lithuania. Vytautas was, like most of the Lithuanian ducal family, fiercely ambitious. 'No prince of his day could rival him in haughty spirit or the competence with which he conducted his affairs', in the words of a contemporary historian. He immediately began to champion the pagan separatist opposition to the union with Poland, at the same time accepting baptism and the alliance of the Teutonic Knights. Instead of concentrating on his anti-Polish policy, Vytautas was tempted to lead an expedition against the Tatars first. The crushing defeat he received at the hands of Tamerlane in 1399 brought him back to Władysław's heel. While the Order continued to intrigue with Vytautas and negotiate with Władysław, it could not hope to avoid confrontation with the Polish-Lithuanian alliance indefinitely. When this came in the great war of 1409–10, it resulted in the devastating defeat of the Order on the battlefield of Grunwald (Tannenberg) by a combined force under the command of Władysław and Vytautas.

The battle was one of the largest and longest of the middle ages. It was also one of the bloodiest. The Grand Master Ulrich von Jungingen and all the Order's officers but one were killed in the field, and the whole of Prussia was there for the taking. Much to the exasperation of the Polish commanders Władysław reined in the pursuit and in the treaty signed later he demanded only a thin strip of land to be ceded to Lithuania, and nothing for Poland. A decade later the Order made war again, was again defeated, and again got away with insignificant concessions to Poland. In 1453 a revolt against the Order by local knights and cities, aided by Poland, started a war which dragged on for thirteen years. This was notable for the fact that it saw the first Polish victory at sea, in 1493, when twenty-five privateers defeated and captured the Order's fleet of forty-four ships off Elbing. The Knights were defeated, and once again spared by the Treaty of Toruń in 1466. Poland took the coastline around Gdańsk and Elbing, the area of Warmia, and even the stronghold of Marienburg, but did not suppress the Order, which moved its capital to Königsberg and retained the rest of its dominions as vassal of the King of Poland.

This forbearance is surprising in view of the ruthless methods applied by the Teutonic Knights. In Prussia they had a job to do, and they did it efficiently, applying protonationalist policies of extermination and resettlement which bring to mind more recent events in those areas. When the war was taken on to Polish territory, the same brutalities were applied and extended to the raping of Christian women, and even the burning of priests in their churches. There were, however, factors involved in the relations between Poland and the Order which transported the border squabbles of Prussia into an infinitely greater context, that of a religious debate of European proportions.

The Teutonic Knights had representatives and friends at every court, and they were masters of propaganda. Their first line of attack had been that the bethrothal of Jadwiga to Wilhelm of Habsburg had been consummated (chamber-maids and page-boys were produced to give intimate details) and that her marriage to Władysław Jagiełło was therefore bigamous. They also argued, with some justification, that the alleged conversion of Lithuania was a sham. Therefore, they maintained, the Order was more than ever carrying on a real and vital crusade. At Grunwald, they pointed out, the Catholic Polish knights had been the minority in an army made up of Lithuanian pagans, Christians of the Eastern rite, and even Muslims (the Tatars who had settled in Lithuania some time before). They suggested that Władysław Jagiełło's army was hardly more Christian than Saladin's.

They had a point, and that point assumed importance in the context of a minor reformation which was sweeping Europe, a nationalist, reformist, anti-clerical, anti-Imperial movement, whose greatest exponent was the Bohemian Jan Hus. The Hussite movement was itself connected with Wycliffe's Lollards in England, and both causes enjoyed considerable sympathy in Poland. It was no coincidence that many prominent Hussites

48

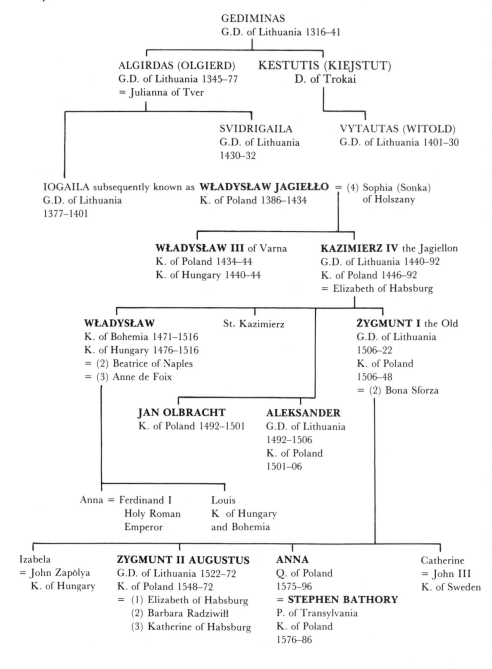

Fig. 3   The Jagiellon dynasty of Poland-Lithuania

fought in the Polish ranks at Grunwald, or that the victory earned Władysław a panegyric from Hus.

The Teutonic Knights ranged themselves on the side of the Empire, the established Church, and traditional dogma on such subjects as crusading. The Polish-Lithuanian alliance was cast in the role of champion of nationalism and of the view that infidels were also children of Christ, to be converted not slaughtered. The matter came to a head at the Council of Constance which met in 1415. Arcane canonical arguments were spun out in endless debates to prove that an infidel was not a human being in the full sense of the word, and that by allying themselves with infidels against other Christians, the Poles had made an alliance with the Devil against Christ.

The Polish delegation to the Council, led by Paweł Włodkowic (Paulus Vladimiri) of Kraków University, included a number of Lithuanians and schismatics, and caused uproar. Włodkowic ran rings around the defenders of the Order and managed to discredit it in the public mind – a change of opinion reflected in the fact that after 1415 foreign knights eager for glory no longer came to Prussia. But there was no clear-cut victory. The Teutonic Knights continued to wield diplomatic weapons and they still had an ally in the Empire, which had political objections to the Polish-Lithuanian stand. The issues involved continued to haunt all Polish-Order and Polish-Empire conflicts, and the spectre of a German crusade against Poland-Lithuania shadowed them, dictating caution to the Poles. At the same time it must be remembered that not everything which was good for Poland was good for Lithuania. It may be that Władysław Jagiełło consciously saved the Order after Grunwald on the grounds that it might prove useful if the union were to be dissolved and he were to lose the Polish throne.

The arrangement itself was under frequent review. In 1413, after Grunwald, a new treaty of union was signed at Horodło. This attempted to bind the two states together more firmly, and was epitomised by the Polish szlachta adopting the Lithuanians as brothers in chivalry, bestowing on them their own coats of arms. In 1430, Vytautas' successor as Grand Duke of Lithuania undid all this by allying himself with the Teutonic Knights and adopting an anti-Polish policy. Ten years later, the union was formally dissolved, but this made little difference, since the ruler of Lithuania was the son of the King of Poland, whom he succeeded in 1446, once again uniting the two states under one crown.

The unstable nature of the union was largely the result of incompatibility. Poland was a nation-state with developed institutions and strong constitutional instincts. Lithuania was a mixture of pagan Balts and Orthodox Christian Slavs. The Lithuanian dynasty were autocratic, and showed little desire for settled progress. The two states were pulling each other in different directions, and in the field of foreign policy it was Lithuania, or rather the Jagiellon dynasty, which pulled the hardest, dragging the combined kingdom into an imperial adventure.

It is no coincidence that the oldest extant letter from a king of England to a king of Poland dates from 1415, when Henry V begged Władysław Jagiełło 'to assist him' in the war against the French 'with his strong arm'. The union with Lithuania and the victory over the Teutonic Order had firmly placed Poland among the Great Powers of Europe, a status she was to hold for three hundred years. It is hardly surprising that with such a power behind them, the ambitious and dynastically-minded Jagiellons should have taken advantage of the boundless possibilities on offer in the first half of the fifteenth century.

The extinction of the two dynasties of Luxemburg and Anjou in Bohemia and Hungary respectively marked the beginning of a new contest for hegemony in the area between two new dynasties – the Habsburgs of Austria and the Jagiellons of Poland-Lithuania. Hungary, which had been ruled successively by Anjou, Luxemburg and Habsburg, fell to the Jagiellons in 1440 when the Magyars offered the throne to the stripling Władysław III of Poland, Władysław Jagiełło's eldest son. Władysław did not rule long as King of Poland and Hungary, for his new dominion lured him into its own foreign problems. Three years after he was crowned at Buda, the chivalrous young king was drawn into the anti-Turkish league, and slain while charging the Sultan at the Battle of Varna on the Black Sea in 1444. The throne of Poland passed to his younger brother, Kazimierz IV. That of Hungary went to Mattias Corvinius, but after his death in 1490 it reverted to Kazimierz's eldest son, Władysław. This Władysław was King not of Poland, but of Bohemia, the Czech Diet having elected him in 1471.

The Jagiellon dreams of conquest had come true; by the end of the century they ruled over about one third of the entire European mainland. Their gigantic domain stretched from the Baltic to the shores of the Black Sea and the Adriatic. But the Jagiellons did not use the power accumulated in their hands to further the vital interests of Poland and Lithuania. In the next generation they lost all the thrones outside Poland to the Habsburgs, and Poland found itself none the richer for the experience of having been the heart of a great empire.

There were compensations. The most tiresome and belligerent neighbour, Lithuania, had become an ally. The Teutonic Order had been curbed. The Jagiellon policies had shifted the struggle with the Empire from the Polish doorstep out into the plains of Hungary and the shores of the Black Sea. As a result, Poland itself enjoyed a period of hitherto unknown freedom from invasion, and foreign affairs occupied the minds of the monarchs more than those of the population. It is true that in 1442 the assembly of the szlachta at Sieradz begged Władysław III to abandon Hungary and to concentrate on ruling Poland, but on the whole they appreciated the advantages of having wayward and often absentee kings. It permitted them to assume a greater share in the running of the country, and the crown's frequent demands for funds and armies supplied them with the levers for extorting the concessions which shaped the forms of parliamentary government.

The principle of government by consensus was already enshrined in practice under the early Piast kings. By the beginnings of the thirteenth century this practice was established firmly enough to play a major role in the government of the various provinces when the kingdom was divided. Provinces such as Wielkopolska or Mazovia would hold an assembly called *seym*. This was made up of delegates elected at a smaller meeting, which was called a *seymik*, at which the entire szlachta of the district could join in discussion and vote.

The consent of the seym of every province was of vital importance in the process of reunification of the Polish lands, and by the time this was achieved the seyms had become part of the process of government. Władysław the Short convoked seyms four times during his reign (1320–33), and his successor Kazimierz the Great (1330–70) almost as often, acknowledging them as the basis of his right to govern.

The heirless death of Kazimierz and the ensuing regency of Queen Elizabeth furnished the opportunity for one group of the szlachta to steal a march on their fellows. These were the dignitaries of the realm, the castellans, who had been the mainstay of royal authority in the regions, and the palatines, who had grown into the virtual governors of their provinces – the provinces themselves came to be known as 'palatinates' as a result. Representing as they did the forces of regional autonomy, the palatines were poor instruments of royal control, and Władysław the Short when reuniting the country had been obliged to bring in yet another tier of royal administration. He instituted the *starosta*, a kind of royal sheriff, often described as the king's arm (*brachium regale*), who henceforth represented the king in his area, while the palatines turned into a political force. With the exception of the Castellan of Kraków, who remained the premier temporal dignitary, it was the palatines, particularly those of Małopolska, who now made a bid for oligarchy, in unison with the bishops. Over the years, this clique had assumed the function of royal council, and in the critical moments following the death of Kazimierz the Great they took the fate of Poland into their own hands. It was they who decided on Jadwiga against Maria and chose her a husband, Władysław Jagiełło. And they made it clear that it was they who would select his successor. His failure to produce an heir with Jadwiga only strengthened their hand on this point.

In the course of the fifteenth century all the palatines and castellans were allowed a seat in the Grand Council (*consilium maius*), but policy-making was jealously guarded by the caucus of palatines and bishops who sat in the Privy Council (*consilium secretum*). This body was dominated by the bishops, for the Church was at the zenith of its temporal power. A typical figure is Zbigniew Oleśnicki, Bishop of Kraków, secretary to Władysław Jagiełło, regent during the minority of Władysław III and mentor of his successor Kazimierz IV. Educated, tough, and absolutist in his convictions, a cardinal who was a born statesman, guided by a vision which combined his own advancement with that of Poland and the Church, he had no room in his scheme of things for a vociferous seym.

The szlachta were not fond of him or the oligarchy he stood for. They were imbued with an aversion to central government, with a belief that they should be consulted, and with the suspicion that any decision taken behind closed doors was a threat to their position. They made it clear that Władysław Jagiełło needed their support as well as that of the magnates in order to secure the succession of his son. This enabled them to extort a number of privileges and rights from the king during the 1420s, the most important of which, granted in 1425, was the edict *Neminem captivabimus nisi iure victum*. An equivalent to the later English *Habeas corpus* act, it meant that nobody could be held or imprisoned without trial. This law, the basis of all civilised life, freed the szlachta from all fears of 'persuasion' or reprisal on the part of the magnates and officers of the crown. Once it had become clear that royal power and prerogatives were being ceded, the magnates and the szlachta leapfrogged each other to claim them. This race had the twofold effect of accelerating the development of the parliamentary system, and of defining the two groups which were eventually to crystallise into the upper and lower chambers.

Feeling hemmed in by the magnates, Kazimierz IV sought the support of the szlachta, which was eager to give it, at a price. The price was the Privilege of Nieszawa, granted in 1454, which stipulated that the king could only raise troops and taxes with the approval of the district assemblies, the seymiks of the eighteen palatinates of Poland. It enshrined the principle of no taxation without representation for the rank-and-file szlachta, who all had a vote at these assemblies, and the measure also made the seyms of Wielkopolska and Małopolska more directly answerable to their electorate. In 1468, these decided to meet together, at Piotrków, and henceforth constituted the national Seym, bringing together dignitaries of the kingdom, and the representatives of all the provinces and the major towns (Lithuania was still ruled despotically by the grand duke, and Mazovia, ruled by a vassal Piast, kept its own separate seym for another century). The next step came in 1493, when it divided into two chambers: the Senate, consisting of 81 bishops and dignitaries, and the Seym proper, which consisted of 54 deputies of the szlachta and the largest cities.

The death of Kazimierz IV in the previous year afforded the new parliament an ideal opportunity to flex its muscles and lay down further precedents in its determination to show that the existence of a natural heir to the throne did not impinge on its right to choose the successor. For two weeks the Seym discussed the merits of a number of candidates, including the king's sons and a Piast prince from the Mazovian line, and finally chose Kazimierz's son, Jan Olbracht. The actual election took one hour and was unanimous.

From now on not even the only son of the deceased king would sit on the Polish throne before being vetted by the Seym. After the death of Jan Olbracht in 1501 his brother Aleksander was elected, and forced to sign over yet more royal power to the Seym before he could take his throne. Four years later, the Seym sitting at Radom passed the act *Nihil novi*, which formally bound the king to take no action whatsoever until it had been debated and endorsed by the two chambers.

The constitutional developments of the fifteenth century are mirrored in the development of the legal system. The regional castellans' courts (*sąd grodowy*) had declined steadily in influence. Their jurisdiction was encroached upon by the manorial courts, in which landowners dispensed justice to their tenantry, seymik courts, whose judges were appointed by the regional assemblies, and most of all by ecclesiastical courts. The latter, which originally governed those living on Church-owned lands, gradually extended their competence to cover all cases involving a cleric or church property, as well as all those with a religious dimension (marriages, divorces, sacrilege). The division of the country allowed the ecclesiastical courts to extend their activity into other areas, by providing what was in effect an independent inter-provincial legal system which proved very convenient in cases where the litigants were residents of different provinces. They complemented the rising power of the Church hierarchy, and directly challenged the influence of the central legal system. This was reinforced through the new county courts (*sąd ziemski*), whose judges were appointed by the crown, and whose executive officers were the starostas or sheriffs. The crown also re-established its jurisdiction, through the Supreme Crown Court, over all the gravest criminal and civil offences, and retained the role of supreme court of appeal. But these functions were ultimately to be taken over by the Seym.

Jagiellon rule had provided greenhouse conditions for the growth of parliamentary institutions. At the death of Kazimierz the Great in 1370, Poland had been in advance of most European countries in this respect, but only a hundred and fifty years later it had surpassed even England. The power of the crown was so hamstrung by a series of checks and balances that it could never be used arbitrarily. The Seym had taken over

Fig. 4   A selection of Polish coats-of-arms. These were never personal to the bearers; each was borne by all members of the family, and often of dozens of families of different names which may or may not have shared their origins. Many are clearly hieroglyphic emblems of some kind (the origin of which still evades historians), others are constructs of real objects which make up similar emblems, while others represent everyday objects which were probably chosen for their resemblance to such emblems.

all legislative functions. The degree of representation, with some ten per cent of the population having a vote, would not be bettered until England extended the franchise by the Reform Act of 1832. Yet the basis of Polish democracy was flawed at the outset, as the running had been made exclusively by the noble estate, the szlachta. This was as restricted in its interests as it was varied in its makeup. One cannot substitute the terms 'nobility' or 'gentry' for szlachta because it had little in common with those classes in other European countries either in origin, composition or outlook.

The origins of the szlachta remain obscure. Polish coats of arms are utterly unlike those of European chivalry, and were held in common by whole clans which fought as regiments. It is not known whether these originated as family or tribal groupings, but their existence has suggested an analogy with the clans of Scotland. A more apt analogy might perhaps be made with the Rajputs of northern India. Like both of these, and unlike any other gentry in Europe, the szlachta was not limited by nor did it depend for its status on either wealth, or land, or royal writ. It was defined by its function, that of a warrior caste. Clannish and arrogant as it was, the szlachta did not underpin its position with the feudal pillars of gentle kinship on the one hand and contempt for the villein on the other. Its bases were subtly but markedly different; mutual solidarity, and fierce rivalry with other classes. Its attitude was often indistinguishable from that of a modern trade union.

As the contemporary historian Długosz summed up, 'the Polish gentry are eager for glory, keen on the spoils of war, contemptuous of danger and death, inconstant in their promises, hard on their subjects and people of the lower orders, careless in speech, used to living beyond their means, faithful to their monarch, devoted to farming and cattle-breeding, courteous to foreigners and guests, lavish in hospitality, in which they exceed other nations.' Gradually, the outlook of the szlachta was changing, and from being a warrior caste, they were turning into a class of entrepreneurs.

The Teutonic Order had used its position straddling the lower Vistula to promote its own exports by imposing heavy duties on Polish grain. After the defeat of the Order and the Treaty of Toruń in 1466 this changed and exports shot up. The Vistula and its many tributaries provided a natural system of waterways which assisted cheap and rapid concentration of agricultural produce at Gdańsk. The city's trade with England quadrupled in volume in the years following 1466. By the end of the century, the number of ships calling at Gdańsk had risen to eight hundred a year, most of them bound for Bruges.

Meadows were drained, scrub woods cut back, and acreages under cultivation increased in order to produce more as the szlachta began to feed a hungry European market. Poland had become the granary of Europe, and this was to determine the direction taken by Polish society over the next centuries. The question of how to increase yields and minimise expenses began to obsess the szlachta, dictating attitudes which

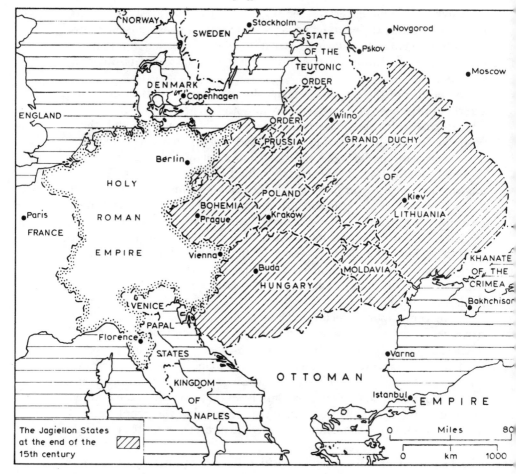

The Jagiellon Dominions at the end of the fifteenth century

were to congeal their mentality. Landowners could best exploit their
estates by forcing peasants to work free for them, rather than by accepting
money-rents and then employing casual labour. The dramatic fall in the
value of the coinage in the early 1400s had halved the real value of
money-rents received from tenants, further convincing the landlords of the
desirability of transferring to labour-rents – the productivity of a day's
work did not fluctuate. Hence the onslaught on the freedom of the peasant.
Just as the rest of Europe was beginning to doubt the value of serfdom,
Poland found excellent reasons to adopt it.

In 1496 the Seym passed measures restricting the freedom of movement
of peasants. Tenants who wished to move to a different area were obliged

to put their tenancies in order, pay off all dues, and to sow the land before they left. The economic effort involved in moving was therefore prohibitive, and peasants who were determined to go often simply absconded; the terminology 'peasants in flight' did not refer to fugitive slaves, but to defaulting contractors. The comparatively high proportion who owned their land outright were not affected by this legislation. Nor were the inhabitants of the 'free settlements', sometimes referred to as 'Dutch settlements'. These had arisen in areas where the landlord, eager to found new villages on unexploited land, enticed peasants (often of foreign origin) to settle by offering them an advantageous set of terms and obligations set down in special charters. It was the normal tenant on szlachta estates who was the most vulnerable. In 1400 he had a minimum unit of seventeen hectares, about three times as much as his descendant in People's Poland today. The annual rent for this was fifteen *grosze* (the price of a pig or a calf) and a few bushels of grain. In addition, he had to perform up to twelve days' work a year in the landlord's fields, using his own implements and horses, usually at the busiest times. There were plenty of tenants rich enough to employ casual labour to perform the labour-rent on their behalf, but even their resources were strained when, in 1520, the Seym increased the labour-rent from twelve days to fifty-two days per annum for all tenants. Their legal position was dramatically weakened at about the same time, when they lost their right of appeal to other courts and could only seek justice in the manorial courts, in which their landlord sat as magistrate.

The ease with which the szlachta could promote its economic interests through the legislative and political institutions had a detrimental effect on its whole outlook. Gentle birth provided the land, God provided the rain and the sun, and the excellent order of things in the kingdom provided the necessary services. At no point in this divinely ordained process of gathering in the good things due to them did the szlachta need to make an investment or calculate with market forces: notions of thrift, risk, investment and the value of money were ignored by the average landowning gentleman, and this average landowning gentleman represented virtually the only articulate and enfranchised section of the population. Taking root as it did on the eve of a general European shift into commerce, banking and industry, this state of mind was bound in time to affect Poland's relationship with the rest of the continent.

The evolution of such attitudes is the more unexpected as fifteenth-century Poland was essentially an urban culture. While land provided the majority with a livelihood, it was not the only or even the predominant source of wealth for the magnates, whose estates were not large by the standards of the barons of England or the great lords of France. So far, only the Church had managed to build up extensive *latifundia* through the monastic orders and the dioceses, which made the great prelates such as the Bishop of Kraków the richest people in the land.

The magnates only started accumulating property on a large scale at the beginning of the fifteenth century. Jan of Tarnów (1367–1432), Palatine of Kraków, built up an estate of one town, twenty villages and one castle. His son, Jan Amor Tarnowski, Castellan of Kraków, increased this estate to two towns and forty-five villages – more than doubling it in the space of fifty years. Jan of Oleśnica, father of Cardinal Zbigniew Oleśnicki, only had one village in 1400, yet by 1450 his other son owned fifty-nine, along with a town and a castle.

Taken alone, the revenues from such estates were not great enough to support rampant ambition. The magnates were therefore obliged to supplement them by lucrative or at least influential public office, and by various business ventures. A favourite was mining, in which fortunes could be made with a little influence at court and some capital. It was necessary to obtain a concession from the crown, which owned all underground deposits. Personal capital or that of specially set up joint-stock companies was then used to employ engineers and build machines to work the mines, which were among the deepest in Europe, and to keep them drained and aerated. These were ambitious operations, but the fruits were abundant – salt, sulphur, tin, lead, zinc, and even gold. It was only by being on the spot that noblemen could make fortunes, and the Tenczyński, Szafraniec, Szydłowiecki, Tarnowski and other great families of the fifteenth century based themselves in or near the cities. In this, as in other things, they are more akin to the civic magnates of Italy than to the regional nobility of France or England.

The cities were not large. Only Gdańsk, with 30,000 inhabitants, and Wrocław with 20,000, could rival important centres in western or southern Europe. Kraków had a paltry 15,000; Lwów, Toruń and Elbing 8,000; and Poznań and Lublin only some 6,000. What they lacked in numbers they made up in diversity. Kraków was an extraordinary Babel in which German predominated in the streets over other languages, while patrician circles rang with Polish, Italian and Ruthene. A similar cosmopolitanism can be detected in the diet of city-dwellers, which had come to include such unlikely items for northern Europe as rice, figs, raisins and citrus fruits. It was also to be seen in manners and fashions. There were no less than twelve public baths in Kraków, a legacy of the Scandinavian north. At the same time Burgundian and Italian styles influenced dress, and the contemporary historian Długosz noted with considerable disapproval in 1466 that 'men comb their hair and twist it into curls in the manner of women. They dress up in long robes, both indoors and abroad, morning and night, mincing and vying with women, whom they imitate with their ringlets and ribbons.'

Poland's principal links with the outside world until the end of the fourteenth century had been Germany and Bohemia. As Poland was often in a state of conflict with both, the links were often severed, and western European culture tended to be associated with the enemy. One consequence of the Jagiellon forays into Hungary and southern Europe was that a new vista was opened towards Italy. For the best part of a century Jagiellon dominions bordered with the Republic of Venice. The new Humanism awakening in Italy was quickly transmitted to Poland, both by travelling Poles and by growing numbers of immigrants.

The previous century, the calamitous fourteenth, had radically altered the balance between Poland and the more developed countries of Europe. Poland had escaped the ravages of the Black Death and the concomitant disasters which had disrupted economic life and enveloped the continent in a mood of despondency. The population of Europe as a whole fell by some twenty million during the fourteenth century, and it took the whole of the fifteenth to make up this loss. Poland's population did not drop significantly during the fourteenth, and rose sharply during the fifteenth century. The gap between the populous west of Europe and underpopulated east narrowed considerably. It also narrowed in economic terms. The underdeveloped east was less seriously affected by the disruption and damage than the more sophisticated western economic structures. While stagnation set in elsewhere, Poland continued to develop, and since investment was easier and more profitable there, people and capital moved into the country in search of lucrative opportunity.

The immigrants brought with them a variety of influences reflecting their varied origin, and these were acclimatised in different ways throughout the regions of Poland. In the north, Flemish architects brought in by the Teutonic Knights left behind massive gothic monuments in the churches, town halls and city walls of Gdańsk and other Pomeranian cities. In Poznań, Warsaw and Kalisz, the Flemish style was mitigated by local styles – themselves marked by Franconian and Burgundian examples of an earlier age – to produce lighter, more delicate forms. In Kraków the most remarkable cross-breeding took place, dominated by a strong Bohemian influence.

In architecture it was this Kraków style which became most distinctive in its unashamed juxtaposition of varied elements. The magnificent church of St Mary in the market square is a good example. It was rebuilt and added to throughout the fifteenth century, acquiring its fine stellar vault, and the steeples which endow the building with a dreamy exoticism. During the same period the city walls were reinforced by fine gates and towers and finished with a delightful barbican.

Secular architecture had begun to qualify for the attention hitherto

18   The stronghold of Marienburg, headquarters of the Teutonic Knights until 1466, when it was incorporated into the Kingdom of Poland.

19   Church of St Mary in Kraków, the main church of the predominantly German merchant patriciate, rebuilt extensively until the 1480s, when it acquired its present aspect.

20   The Barbican of St Florian's Gate, Kraków, built in 1498.

21 Church of St Mary, Gdańsk, founded in 1245 by Duke Świętopełk II of Gdańsk-Pomerania. The church was extensively rebuilt in the 14th and 15th centuries, and the stellar vaulting was not finished until the 1490s.

22 The frescoes in the Chapel of the Holy Trinity in Lublin Castle, dating from 1415, show unusual Byzantine influences, which reached Poland from Russia, via Lithuania, as a result of the accession to the Polish throne of Władysław Jagiełło, pictured (*top* **23**), as one of the Three Kings on the altar of the Chapel of Our Lady of Sorrows in Kraków Cathedral, painted c. 1480 by a local painter. **24** The votive Madonna with the kneeling figure of the knight Wierzbięta of Branice, painted c. 1425, is a fine early example of the same Kraków school.

OPPOSITE PAGE **25** The figure of the sorrowful Christ in the Tryptych of Korzenna is typical of local thematic traditions, with their human representation of the Mother and Son. This was subjected in the early 15th century to the elegant Hungarian influence visible in the Crucifixion of the Sącz school, c. 1440 (**26**). By the second half of the century, the Kraków painters had gained in sophistication, as demonstrated in the Flight into Egypt by the Master of the Polyptych of the Dominican Church in Kraków, dating from 1465 (**27**). The Annunciation from the Parish Church of Cięcin (1490) is a good example of the eclecticism and self-assurance that characterise the artists of the Małopolska school (**28**).

29 The courtyard of the Collegium Maius of the Jagiellon University, which dates from the 1490s, when a number of earlier buildings were linked into a quadrangle.

30 *(Left)* Memorial to Filippo Buonaccorsi (Callimachus) of San Gimignano, secretary to King Kazimierz IV and tutor to his children, a key figure in the Polish Renaissance. The bronze plaque was projected by Veit Stoss in Kraków in 1496, and cast at the Vischer foundry in Nuremberg in 1501. It is now in the Dominican Church in Kraków, where Buonaccorsi is buried.

31 *(Above)* King Kazimierz IV. Detail from the red marble tomb in the Wawel Cathedral sculpted by Veit Stoss in 1492.

32 Gothic retained its popularity long after it had been superseded by the Renaissance style. The exuberant façade of the Church of St Anne in Wilno, built in 1508, is one of the last examples of its use in major cities, and a showpiece of architectural virtuosity. Napoleon, who saw it as he was marching through on his way to Moscow in 1812, was so enthralled that he wanted to have the building removed to Paris.

33 Gothic carried on in general use in smaller towns, and particularly in country parish churches. The church of St Lawrence in Zacharzowice in Silesia, below, dates from the 1580s, by which time even Renaissance forms were being replaced by the baroque, yet it is built in the characteristic Gothic style, with thick interlocking beamed walls and a tall vault covered in shingles. Everything, right down to the candlesticks, in such churches was usually made of wood.

accorded only to churches and monasteries. Town halls were built on principal squares, their conception and their decorated towers highly reminiscent of the *signoria* of many an Italian city.

The finest example of Polish Gothic secular architecture is the Collegium Maius of Kraków University. Built in 1494, it displays all the grace and proportions of earlier Italian building combined with the functional intimacy of an Oxford college. One of the most unusual products of Polish Gothic was the church of St Anne in Wilno, a flamboyant building dating from 1508. No less than thirty-three different kinds of moulded brick were used in the ornamentation of its west front, which thrives with a bizarre luxuriance.

The development of painting was also regional, with a Pomeranian school dominated by Flemish influence, Gdańsk by the north German, the burgeoning Silesian school almost indistinguishable from its Bohemian mentors, and, here again, the Kraków and south Polish schools showing the most catholic mixture of influences. The painters radiating from Kraków worked in Małopolska, in Sandomierz, Lublin, Lithuania and Lwów. They were among the first to follow the example of Italy, but were also open to other influences. Thus the frescoes of the Franciscan monastery in Kraków painted in 1430 show the unmistakable influence of Giotto, while those in the Lublin Castle chapel reveal a pedigree which contains ancestors in the Russian art of Pskov. In some areas a Balkan influence is detectable, while the small but sophisticated group of painters known as the Sącz school added a strong dose of Hungarian art to this mixture in the 1440s, partly the result of political connections between the two countries.

Painting was dominated by foreigners for longer than other arts owing to a limitless supply of immigrant artists, but by the mid-fifteenth century native talent was strongly in evidence. In Kraków, painters such as Marcin Czarny and Mikołaj Haberschrak left an identifiable oeuvre of exceptional quality. But it was in sculpture that indigenous talent took the most vigorous lead. Inspired by contacts with Bohemia during the reign of Kazimierz the Great, Polish artists began to produce very fine work in the last quarter of the fourteenth century, most notably the beautiful and highly characteristic wooden figures of the Madonna and Child from Toruń, Wrocław, Lubieszów, Kruźlowa, Kazimierz and elsewhere. The most remarkable secular work by a Polish sculptor is the fine marble tomb of Władysław Jagiełło in Kraków Cathedral (1431). Not far from this stands the tomb of Kazimierz IV, an exquisite monument chiselled by one of the greatest sculptors of the Middle Ages, the German Veit Stoss, who settled in Kraków in 1477. It was here that he produced his masterwork, the magnificent carved altarpiece of St Mary's Church. Indigenous sculptors could not take up this challenge, and in the next century the availability of relatively cheap Italian sculpture would push aside the less refined local talent.

An area in which the Poles maintained their ascendancy was music. The Church had set store by singing as a means of involving in its rites the religiously somnolent Poles and later the recalcitrant Lithuanians. This produced a harvest of semi-liturgical folk music and carols, and helped to raise the standard of musical expression. To sing the *Bogurodzica*, one of the earliest surviving pieces of Polish vernacular verse, a hymn to the Virgin sung by knights riding into battle, requires a degree of musical education. Its first recorded use was at the Battle of Grunwald in 1410, but it was written at least a century earlier. The first organ in Poland was built at Toruń in 1343, and by the end of the century organists in various cities were noting down their repertoire. It is not until the 1430s that a major figure appears on the Polish musical scene, the composer Mikołaj of Radom, who wrote polyphonic sacred music and some secular songs for court use.

Polish literature remained encased in the limits of medieval parochialism. Religious verse proliferated, attaining a remarkable quality of expression in works such as the deeply moving *Lament of the Virgin Under the Cross*. Written about 1450, this concentrates exclusively on the human dimension of a mother's grief for her dead son, and seems to ignore the divinity of Christ and the message of the Crucifixion. Its lyricism is absent from the lives of saints and conversations with death which make up the bulk of the period's oeuvre, and even from the extant love-poems. Another flourishing branch was political poetry, the most interesting example of which is Jędrzej Gałka of Dobczyn's *Pieśń o Wyklefie*, a panegyric to John Wycliffe.

Prose-writing also developed, from the lively and observant but naïve chronicles of Janko of Czarnków, written in the 1370s, to the wonderful annals of Jan Długosz, a church canon and tutor to the royal family, an educated, travelled and thoroughly sensible man. In 1455 he began writing his *Annales seu Cronicae Incliti Regni Poloniae*, based exclusively on primary sources. He sifted his information, paring down legend and myth, separating the true from the false with the instinct of a historian, thereby providing a most reliable source of information on the period.

Emotionally, Długosz was a creature of the Middle Ages. As he painstakingly wrote his last *Annales* in the 1460s, he seized every opportunity to carp at what he saw as newfangled and unnatural ideas or practices, the cosmopolitan spirit that was invading the venerable closes of medieval Kraków. He was not wrong to feel threatened; a revolution was indeed taking place. His successor as tutor to the royal family, Filippo Buonaccorsi, was both a leading light in and a symptom of this revolution. Buonaccorsi was a native of San Gimignano in Tuscany who had incurred the wrath of the Pope and fled to Poland, where he was guaranteed immunity and preferment. In 1472 he was given a professorship at the University of Kraków and soon became the centre of a widening circle propounding the humanist philosophy of life.

The university itself was playing an increasingly important part in the life of the nation. Although it had been founded by the Piast Kazimierz the Great and lavishly endowed by the Angevin Queen Jadwiga, who bequeathed her entire fortune to it on her death in 1399, it had come to be known as the Jagiellon University. It was under the Jagiellon dynasty that it received funds necessary for expansion and the patronage of kings who recognised its diplomatic and political potential. Foreigners from as far afield as England and Spain came to study or teach in its halls, while native graduates went abroad to widen their learning. Not all made an important mark like Maciej Kolbe of Swiebodzin, who became rector of the Paris Sorbonne in 1480, but in an age lacking in professional diplomats, travelling scholars were a useful vehicle for many a *démarche*. When it came to negotiation a team of urbane academics was invaluable, as the Council of Constance had demonstrated.

In order to rule their vast domains the Jagiellons needed administrative cadres which only such a school could furnish. During the long reign of Kazimierz IV (1446–92) some 15,000 students passed through the university, and all the major dignitaries, prelates and even soldiers of the time had a degree from Kraków, often supplemented by one from a foreign university. As it grew, however, the university moved further away from formal studies towards the speculative and humanistic fields. In 1449 a chair of classical poetry was endowed, by a woman (the German poet Conrad Celtis dubbed Poland an 'Amazon society' on account of the atypical position of women in public life). At about the same time, Marcin Król of Żurawica founded a chair of astronomy and mathematics, a field that embraced all the most progressive and speculative aspects of late medieval learning. This school enjoyed great popularity under a succession of fine teachers, and drew to itself a disproportionate number of students. Among those admitted in the year 1491 was a young boy from Toruń called Mikołaj Kopernik, who was to make Poland's most important single contribution to European civilisation. Even as he studied in Kraków, Copernicus (as he is known) began to question accepted principles and to work along lines which a few decades later were to revolutionise man's view of the universe and of himself.

More than any other centre of learning in Central and Northern Europe, Kraków had become a crucible in which the scrap of the medieval world was being alloyed with the new mentality of the Italian Renaissance. There was little or no resistance to the progress of new ideas, and the Church encouraged their dissemination. Piotr Bniński, Bishop of Kujavia, devoted his own fortune and that of his diocese to patronage of the arts, paying more attention to arranging symposia by humanist poets than to the spiritual duties of his position. Grzegorz of Sanok, Archbishop of Lwów, was animated by the same spirit. Born of plebeian stock in 1407, he went to school in Poland and then Germany. Back in Poland, he took the post of choirmaster while pursuing studies at the Jagiellon University, from which he graduated in 1433. His subsequent appointment as tutor to the children of Jan Tarnowski brought him into contact with the royal court, and took him on a journey to Italy. He stayed in Rome long enough to attract the attention of Pope Eugenius IV, but it was in Florence that he dallied longest. He made friends with a number of Florentine scholars and poets, and began collecting a library, buying or copying anything he could lay his hands on. His return to Poland in 1439 was something of a literary event. For several years Grzegorz of Sanok lectured on Graeco-Roman poetry and Italian literature at the Jagiellon University, and his nomination to the archbishopric of Lwów in 1451 provided further means with which to promote his interests. At his residence of Dunajów near Lwów he established a small court modelled on that of Urbino. He gathered around him a group of scholars and poets who led a life of intellectual refinement nurtured by a stream of visitors from Italy. It was there Buonaccorsi first came when he had to flee his native country.

Buonaccorsi later moved to the royal court in Kraków and wrote, amongst others, a set of counsels for the king, like some Polish Machiavelli. His writings, which he published under the pen-name of Callimachus, his position at the Jagiellon University, and his part in founding, along with the German poet Conrad Celtis, a sort of Polish writers' workshop, the Sodalitas Litteraria Vistulana, all contributed to make him into a key figure in the Polish Renaissance.

The Italian connection grew stronger as Poles travelled to study or to visit cities like Padua, Bologna, Florence, Mantua and Urbino at the height of their splendour. Italians of every class and trade came to Poland, bringing with them amenities and refinements, ranging from painting to postal services – which permitted Buonaccorsi to carry on a regular correspondence with Lorenzo de' Medici and Pico della Mirandola. The impact was omnipresent and lasting, nowhere more so than on the language. The first treatise on Polish orthography appeared in 1440, and the Bible was first translated in 1455, for Jagiełło's last wife, Sophia. In their search for words or expressions to describe hitherto unknown objects or sentiments, the Poles more often than not followed the simple yet melodious Italian examples. Such borrowings are found in profusion in areas such as food, clothing, furnishing and behaviour, as well as in the expression of thought. These words rapidly passed from speech into writing, and from writing into print. The year 1469 saw the first commercial use of Gutenberg's invention of moveable type, in Venice. The idea was taken up throughout Europe with breathtaking speed: printing-presses began operating in Naples, Florence and Paris in 1471; in Spain, the Netherlands and Kraków in 1473; in Wrocław, where the first book in Polish was printed in 1475; and in London in 1476.

By the end of the fifteenth century Poland had become an integral part of late medieval civilisation. Lithuania, on the other hand, was largely left out of the picture, contributing nothing and gaining little from its associa-tion with Christian Europe. The thick forests of Lithuania proper were inhabited by no more than half a million people still pagan in spirit and tribal in outlook. To the south and east, the forest landscape gave way to marshes and then to limitless expanses of rolling steppe, thinly populated with some two million Ruthenes. At the moment of Władysław Jagiełło's conversion, this vast dominion boasted five stone castles, at Wilno Kowno and Troki in Lithuania; Kamieniec and Łuck in what had been Kievan lands. The land produced little wealth and most of the population subsisted from scratching the topsoil with wooden implements, living in peat dugouts or timbered lairs. The union had little immediate impact, and there was no influx of Poles. While nothing prevented Lithuanians from doing all three in Poland, Poles were not allowed to purchase, inherit or marry land in the grand duchy.

In 1387 Władysław Jagiełło granted the Lithuanian nobles the first element of personal freedom, the right to hold property outright. In 1434 he extended the act *Neminem captivabimus* to the Grand Duchy, but it was some time before the principle of this was either understood or translated into common practice. While Poland demanded power-sharing and repre-sentation, Lithuania continued to be ruled autocratically. While Jan Ostroróg, Palatine of Poznań, Master of the Jagiellon University and Bachelor of those of Bologna and Erfurt, applied himself in 1467 to writing a treatise on the Polish system of government containing a programme for social reform, the average Lithuanian nobleman hardly knew what a political right was.

The only link between the two societies was the Jagiellon dynasty. They were a remarkable family. Władysław Jagiełło's forbears the Dukes of Lithuania were ambitious and ruthless, spending much of their time murdering each other in pursuit of the succession. They had an uncanny gift for diplomacy, and Jagiełło assumed a garb of wisdom and maturity along with the Polish crown. Although he consistently followed his own ambition and served himself and his family first, he respected every Polish custom and treated his subjects with a fairness which left them with nothing to cavil at. He rapidly shed his uncouth manners and with time achieved a certain wizened distinction.

Jagiełło's son Władysław III, killed at the Battle of Varna in 1444 in his twentieth year, never had the opportunity to show his mettle as a ruler, but the image of the chivalrous boy-king immediately passed into legend. By contrast, his younger brother Kazimierz IV reigned for forty-six years. His gentle, cultivated personality appropriately hovers over this period of prosperity and ease in the country's history. Yet it was he more than any other who was the architect of Poland's international supremacy. His reputation was as widely-travelled as his interests, and he was the only Pole, significantly, ever to wear the English Garter. His wife Elizabeth of Habsburg bore him seven daughters, who make him the ancestor of every monarch reigning in Europe today, and six sons: one saint, one cardinal, and four kings. Kazimierz was succeeded in Poland by Jan Olbracht, a young prince with a passion for reading who drank, danced and loved hard, dressed like a peacock and worshipped pleasure – a Polish Henry VIII. His brother Aleksander was a much-loved lightweight who died in 1506 having done little to be remembered or cursed for.

Jagiełło's instinctive cleverness was only partially inherited by his son Kazimierz IV, and further diluted in the next generation. While the dynasty acquired a high degree of culture and lost the ravenous instincts of their ancestors, they did not replace native cunning with the political maturity demanded by their new role. Throughout this formative century, when the magnates and the szlachta were erecting the structure of their democracy, the crown failed to define its own spheres of interest. Difficult issues such as the reorganisation of the country's defences or the reform of the fiscal system were avoided, while the mercurial Jagiellons took up other matters only to drop them again, bequeathing each other a growing number of loose ends. This was particularly true of foreign affairs, for which they had a passion.

Rather than concentrate on binding Silesia and Prussia to the Polish crown, they liked to indulge grandiose ambitions whose benefits were mixed. Kazimierz IV's policy of 'thrones for the boys' enmeshed Poland in a number of fateful, and ultimately fatal, conflicts. Turkey and Poland shared a common interest, and in 1439 an embassy from Murad II came to Kraków to negotiate an alliance against the Habsburgs of Austria, who had taken over Hungary. This failed to materialise, since the King of Poland took Hungary himself and proceeded to make war on Turkey over Moldavia, a war which cost him his life at the Battle of Varna. Some eighty years later, in 1526, Louis the Jagiellon, also King of Hungary, was to lose his life in the same way. He was trampled to death in a muddy stream at the Battle of Mohacs, fighting against Suleiman the Magnificent over a Hungary which passed to Ferdinand of Habsburg after the battle.

The feud with Muscovy was equally pointless. After the Tatar invasions, the Lithuanian dukes had started collecting the scattered shards of

Kievan Rus, heedless of any consequences. The remaining Russian princi-
palities were too weak to think of anything but survival, but with time, the
Principality of Muscovy began to nurture ambitions. After the fall of
Constantinople in 1453 the Princes of Muscovy, who were linked by
marriage to the Byzantine Emperors, declared their city to be Constanti-
nople's successor, the 'Third Rome', protector of the Eastern Catholic
Faith, and spiritual mother of all the Russias – most of which were under
Lithuanian dominion. Such bombastic pretensions uttered from the political backwater of fifteenth-century Muscovy were not to be taken seriously.
Nevertheless, the assumption of this role of 'liberator of Holy Russia' gave
Muscovy that element of political cohesion which would help to build it up
into a great power. By the time this status had been achieved a couple of
centuries later, this self-imposed mission had become deeply embedded in
the political philosophy of the rulers of Moscow, at the basis of which it still
lies today. Ideological pipedreams and holy wars have a tendency to
outlast the territorial squabbles that give birth to them, and to accommodate themselves to any political changes that may take place.

In the fifteenth century, Poland and Lithuania could afford to laugh at
this posturing. Apart from their own strength, they could count on the
Tatar Golden Horde, a powerful cat to the Muscovite mouse. In the latter
part of the century, however, the Golden Horde went into decline, and its
stranglehold over Muscovy was broken. The only other power in the area
were the Tatars of the Crimea, but these had recently become subjects of
Turkey. The number of possible allies diminished dramatically as the
whole area fell into two camps – the Muscovite and the Turkish. Jagiellon
forays against both inevitably drove them into each others' arms, and in
1498 came the unpleasant consequence – an alliance of Muscovy and
Turkey against Poland-Lithuania.

Until now, there had been a sufficient number of more or less independent units which could be juggled around in alliances to fit any situation,
but this was transformed by the new hegemony, whereby one Habsburg or
Jagiellon dominion automatically commanded the support of a string of
others. Sides had been taken, national and supranational ideologies had
set hard, and an entirely new configuration had emerged in East-Central
Europe: Turkey with its pool of Islamic allies, Muscovy with its still
embryonic Russian following, the Habsburgs with their German connections, and Poland with its awkward bedfellow Lithuania and its dubious
vassals in Prussia.

The contest for supremacy in Central and Eastern Europe opened with a
struggle between the Habsburgs and the Jagiellons over the crucial axis of
Silesia, Bohemia and Hungary. The Jagiellons won the first round in the
fifteenth century, but failed to hold on to their advantages, and in the next

century they were to lose all of them to the Habsburgs. After two more centuries of conflict and diplomacy, Poland and Turkey were to drop out, leaving only Russia and the Habsburgs, now supported by the rising power of Germany, locked in a conflict which was to start two world wars. In the twentieth century, Moscow was to achieve outright mastery over the whole area – with the help of Western Europe and the United States.

International diplomacy was the key to success, and although she was later to fail utterly in this respect, Poland did perceive this quickly enough. It is no coincidence that in 1500, when a tentative rapprochement was taking place between the Habsburgs and Muscovy, Poland made her first treaty with France. She also considered a proposed English alliance, but in 1502 the Seym rejected this on the grounds that England 'is in a state of continual revolution.' Henry VII and Henry VIII repeatedly angled for an Anglo-Polish alliance against Turkey but nothing came of this, since Poland needed the support of Turkey, with whom she signed an Eternal Peace in 1533.

In the year 1500, the combined Kingdom of Poland was the largest state in Europe, over twice the size of France. In all, about one third of the entire European mainland was ruled by two Jagiellon princes. But this power was to some extent dead power. The Jagiellon lust for dominion had dissipated itself, leaving nothing in its stead. Their lack of vigilance had allowed the authority of the crown to decline, making it difficult for their successors to resume an aggressive policy. Poland began to drift on the waves, weathering each storm in turn, without a determined long-term course.

Whatever international advantages they may have forfeited, the last two Jagiellon kings gave their subjects and their country something of inestimable value. Zygmunt I or the Old, the youngest son of Kazimierz IV, succeeded in 1506 and died in 1548. His son, Zygmunt II Augustus, became Grand Duke of Lithuania in 1522 and King of Poland after his father's death. Their combined reign from 1506 to 1572 displayed a certain continuity, even if their persons did not. The strong Solomon-like father was strikingly different from his glamorous, refined son who stands out, along with Francis I and Charles V, to whom he was often compared, as the epitome of the Renaissance monarch.

They encouraged every form of creative activity throughout the most dynamic period of Europe's artistic development, and they graciously allowed their subjects to do anything they wanted – except butcher each other in the name of religion. They institutionalised a spiritual and intellectual freedom which still lives, and they steered their country away from the storm which was blowing up on the horizon. This was to batter every other ship of the European fleet, causing untold suffering and millions of deaths. As in the case of the Black Death, only Poland was to be spared, but this time not because of a quirk of fate. It was principally owing to the efforts of the last Jagiellons that the murderous Reformation and Counter-Reformation never grew into anything more dangerous in Poland than a squabble over seating arrangements at a family wedding.

5

God and Caesar

'To wish to legislate on religion
is not Polish.' – Hugo Grotius

Religion has always been important to the Poles. They have used it to
define their identity and to construct a national mythology, projecting to
the outside world the image of a nation more bound up with its religion
than any other, devoted to its practice and motivated by its orthodoxies.
The reality is somewhat different. However deep and lasting the influence
of religion may have been on the Poles, it has never dominated their
judgments or their instincts to the extent that it has those of other nations
which hardly qualify as particularly spiritual or bigoted.

Throughout the late Middle Ages the Kingdom of Poland-Lithuania
was only nominally a daughter of Rome. The large numbers of Christian
Ruthenes living within its borders continued to practise the Orthodox rite,
acknowledging the Patriarch of Constantinople rather than the Pope.
Another group of Christians who paid no heed to Rome were the communities of Armenians to be found in the major cities of south-eastern
Poland running the trade with the East.

A significant proportion of the population was not Christian at all. The
Jewish community multiplied each time there was an anti-Semitic witch-
hunt in other countries, and its numbers soared in the decades after the
expulsions from Spain in 1492 and Portugal in 1496. If zealous prelates
were shocked to see synagogues in every Polish township, they were hardly
less so to see mosques standing on what was supposed to be Christian soil.
These belonged to the descendants of Tatars who had settled in Lithuania
in the fifteenth century and become loyal subjects of their adopted country.
Many of them had been admitted to the ranks of the szlachta, but clung to
the Islamic faith. By the mid-sixteenth century there were nearly a
hundred mosques in the Wilno, Troki and Łuck areas.

One of the conditions of the union between Poland and Lithuania in
1385 had been the immediate conversion of that country to Christianity.

34 St Stanisław, patron of Poland, blesses King Zygmunt the Old. Opposite the king is Piotr Tomicki, Bishop of Kraków, and behind him Chancellor Krzysztof Szydłowiecki. This painting (c. 1520) by Stanisław Samostrzelnik represents a spiritual a temporal supremacy of the Catholic Church which was under serious thre throughout the 16th century.

35 (Above) The monastic church of Basilian fathers at Supraśl, 1503–10, illustrates the mixture of Byzantine a Gothic styles which characterised Orthodox church architecture in the Polish lands.

36 (Below, left) The Armenian Cathedral of Lwów, built c. 1450 by a Genoese architect from Kaffa in the Crimea, is typical of earlier Armenian ecclesiastical architecture.

37 (Below) The Karaite Kenessa of Wilno, dating from the 17th century, harks back to the Eastern traditions of this Jewish Sect.

38 *(Left)* The interior of the 14th-century Synagogue of Kazimierz in Kraków testifies to the strength of the Orthodox Jewish community in the city.

39 *(Above)* The small wooden Mosque of Dobuciszki is typical of the hundred or so Islamic places of worship dotted around the Wilno and Troki area in the 16th century.

40 *(Below, left)* The Calvinist Chapel at Wodzisław typifies in its simplicity the Protestant reaction to the wealth of the Catholic Church.

41 The medal struck in 1580 by the Arians or Polish Brethren as a token of gratitude takes the fundamentalism of the Polish Protestant movement a stage further by its human representation of Christ, struck crudely in base metal.

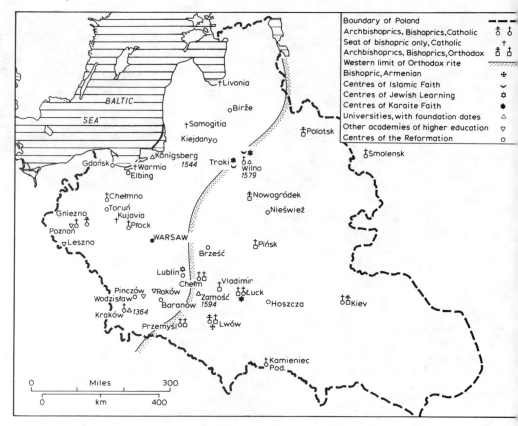

Boundary of Poland	▬ ▬ ▬
Archbishoprics, Bishoprics, Catholic	♰̇ ♰̇
Seat of bishopric only, Catholic	†
Archbishoprics, Bishoprics, Orthodox	♰̂ ♰̂
Western limit of Orthodox rite	⋯⋯
Bishopric, Armenian	✠
Centres of Islamic Faith	◡
Centres of Jewish Learning	✿
Centres of Karaite Faith	✱
Universities, with foundation dates	△
Other academies of higher education	▽
Centres of the Reformation	○

The religious debate of the sixteenth century

Formal gestures apart, little had been done to bring this about, and one
hundred and fifty years later, Grand Duke Zygmunt Augustus recorded
that 'outside Wilno . . . the unenlightened and uncivilised people generally
accord that worship which is God's due, to groves, oak-trees, streams, even
serpents, both privately and publicly making sacrifices to these.' A hundred years later, when the Germans were preparing to spend three decades
butchering each other over the consistency of a wafer, the supposedly
Catholic Poland tolerated a state of affairs described by Melchior Gedroyc
on taking over the diocese of Samogitia:

> In very extensive areas of my bishopric, one would search in vain for a
> single person who has ever been to confession or Communion in his life;
> a single person who knows how to say one prayer or make the sign of the
> Cross; a single person who has the faintest idea of the Mysteries of the
> Faith.

The Polish hierarchy had failed to impose a strict Catholic or even Christian orthodoxy on the population, largely on account of its personal and political viewpoint. The Polish Church enjoyed a unique relationship with the Vatican. Its bishops were appointed not by Rome but by the King of Poland, who submitted his candidates for Rome's approval. When this was not forthcoming it was ignored. In 1530, for instance, Pope Clement VII violently objected to the anti-Habsburg and pro-Turkish policy of the Primate Archbishop Jan Łaski, and demanded that he be cashiered. He referred to him as '*perditionis alumnus, Judae Scariothis frater, nomine archiepisco-pus, opere vero archidiabolus,*' and insisted that King Zygmunt dismiss him on pain on excommunication. Characteristically, nothing was done in response to this.

The king was guided by political considerations when appointing bishops and this led him to choose either powerful magnates whose support he needed to enlist, or, more often, trusted men of his own. These were drawn from his court, which was made up of people of motley origins and ruled by a humanistic and empirical spirit. A high proportion of his secretaries were of plebeian stock, and Zygmunt felt no compunction in ennobling those, like his banker Jan Boner, whom he favoured. This favour transcended creed as well as class. The Jew Abraham Ezofowicz, whom Zygmunt elevated to the rank of Treasurer of Lithuania, did convert to Christianity before being ennobled (the Orthodox rite), but his brother Michał remained a practising Jew when he was elevated to the szlachta in 1525 – a case without parallel anywhere in Christian Europe.

It was inevitable that this spirit would percolate through into the Church as its prelates were chosen from this milieu. The Polish clergy were no more debauched than those of other countries at this time, and possibly less so – the last quarter of the fifteenth century saw the foundation of no fewer than eighteen new fundamentalist and strict Franciscan monasteries in the provinces of Mazovia and Małopolska alone. What did set them apart was an unusual element of realism in the face of other religions and of candour with respect to corruption. Bishop Krzycki, for instance, has left a little poem concerning the gossip that surrounded a fellow-bishop caught in the act of lowering a spent girl from his bedroom window in a net. 'I fail to see what shocks everyone so,' the poet-bishop wrote, 'for no one can deny that the Gospels themselves teach us to use the Net of the Fisherman.'

Krzycki wrote much erotic verse before he became bishop, and this did not affect his career any more than it did that of another, who ended up as Prince-Bishop of Warmia. Jan Dantyszek was a good example of what the times could offer a clever man. A plebeian by birth, he entered the king's service, becoming a secretary and later a diplomatic envoy. After a life which took him round the whole of Europe and brought him into contact with Francis I of France, Henry VIII of England, assorted popes,

Ferdinand Cortes, Martin Luther, with whom he formed a close friendship, the Emperor Charles V, who tried to keep him in his service, and Copernicus, who became a close friend and protégé, Dantyszek settled down to his episcopal duties with a degree of worldly wisdom.

One searches in vain for ardent spiritual involvement or preoccupation with dogma in the Polish religious tradition. It was remarkably immune to the crises that convulsed the Church in other countries – the great heresies of the twelfth and thirteenth centuries, and the reaction to the Black Death, whose horrors seemed to negate the existence of a benevolent God and drove people towards penance and mysticism. The only major heresy that did affect Poland, the Hussite movement, did so because it was not so much a heresy as a political movement.

The conversion of Mieszko I had been an act of political wisdom. The usefulness of the Christian Church had subsequently revealed itself more than once, helping to reunite the country in the thirteenth century, and to outmanoeuvre the Teutonic Order in the fourteenth. From the outset, religion was a vital component of political health and the public good. The self-appointed guardians of the public good were the szlachta. Whether they were Catholics or not, they were keenly aware of the threats posed by the Church.

A huge institution which raked in bequests, exacted tithes, and contributed nothing in taxes to the state was bound to be unpopular. In the sixteenth century, the Church owned just over 10 per cent of all arable land in Wielkopolska, 15.5 per cent in Małopolska, and 25 per cent in Mazovia. The share owned by the crown in the same provinces was 9 per cent, 7.5 per cent and almost 5 per cent respectively. The Church wielded political power through its bishops who sat in the Senate and through its tribunals, which exercised jurisdiction over laymen on lands it owned, and kept attempting to exercise it on wider areas. This power was potentially at the disposal of Rome, a state often allied with Poland's enemies. The Church was therefore a focus for a number of the szlachta's phobias. The following is a typical complaint, uttered by a deputy during a Seym debate of the 1550s.

> The gentlemen of the clergy summon us, citing their titles and invoking some foreign, Romish law, contrary to the laws and freedoms of our Realm, attempting to extend their jurisdiction and that of their master, the Roman Pope, which jurisdiction we, not finding it in our statutes, neither can nor will bear; for we know no other jurisdiction than the supremacy of his majesty the King our master.

The tone and the sentiments expressed are characteristic of the 'national Catholicism' which was the spiritual heir of Hussitism. Many of the

Bohemian followers of Hus had traditionally taken refuge in Poland, most notably in the Lublin area. The writer Biernat of Lublin (1465–1529) was an early Polish adherent who denounced the discrepancies between the Scriptures and the practices of the Church.

In view of all this, it is not surprising that when Martin Luther nailed his famous declaration of war on the Papacy to the church door in Wittenberg in 1517 and set off a chain reaction which was to shake the whole Christian world, the seismic nature of the event was largely lost on Poland. His teachings rapidly penetrated northern and western areas, enthusiastically received by the preponderantly German population of the towns. Cities like Gdańsk were almost entirely Lutherian by the mid-1520s, but in the surrounding countryside and in other areas of the kingdom the movement for reform met with a patchier response.

Calvinism was another matter. Enhanced by its more sympathetic Francophone associations, it rapidly gained ground all over the country. The democratic spirit of Calvinism which placed the lay elder on a par with the minister could hardly fail to appeal to the instincts of the szlachta, while the absence of pomp and ceremony from its rites made it a pleasantly cheap religion to support.

By the 1550s a dominant proportion of the deputies to the Seym were Protestants, but their number is not representative, since the most ardently Catholic palatinates regularly returned Protestant deputies. By 1572 the Senate provided a similar picture. Of the 'front-bench' seats, 36 were held by Protestants, 25 by Catholics and 8 by Orthodox – an overall majority which again meant little except that many magnates had converted to Calvinism. It was they who provided the conditions for its growth in Poland. The Oleśnicki family founded a Calvinist Academy in their town of Pińczów, where they could guarantee financial security and legal immunity. It quickly became the foremost centre of Calvinist teaching and publishing in that part of Europe, referred to by the faithful as 'the Athens of the North'. Similar centres were established on a smaller scale by the Leszczyński family at Leszno, and the Radziwiłł at Nieśwież, Birże and Kiejdany.

Although they gained an ascendancy, the Calvinists never managed to control the Protestant movement in Poland. The northern cities stood by Luther; Anabaptists seeking refuge from persecution in Germany appeared in various areas of the country in the 1530s; and in 1551 Mennonites from Holland set up a colony on the lower Vistula. But the Protestant sect which produced Poland's most significant contribution to Christian philosophy were the Arians. Originally a breakaway group of Hussites practising in Bohemia until they were expelled in 1548, they settled in Poland as 'Czech Brethren', and were later known as Arians since two of their fundamental beliefs – the human nature of Christ and the rejection of the Trinity – were first voiced by Arius at the Council of Nicea in AD 235. They also came to be known variously as Anti-Trinitarians, Polish Brethren and Socinians.

Theirs was a rationalistic and fundamentalist response to the teachings of Christ, whom they believed to be a divinely inspired man. They saw his teachings as a perfect philosophy which had to be applied to the letter. They were therefore pacifists, opposed to the tenure of any civic office, to all forms of serfdom, to the possession of wealth, and to the use of money, believing as they did in the common ownership of all material goods. The word 'communist' was coined for the first time in Polish in 1569 to describe their way of life.

It was an attractive philosophy which quickly gained converts – up to about 40,000 adherents practising in some 200 temples scattered throughout the country. Their spiritual centre was Raków, where they established their own Academy, visited by students from all over Europe. It was here that the Raków Catechism was published, the work of Fausto Sozzini, a nobleman from Siena who sought refuge in Poland and became one of the leading lights of the movement. The two most prominent Polish Arians were Marcin Czechowicz and Szymon Budny, the second of whom made a fine translation of the Bible into Polish and was also responsible for a rapprochement with the Jews, which produced some curious results.

The large Jewish community in Poland had also been affected by the spirit of the times, and the expulsions from the Iberian peninsula had brought many distinguished Spanish scholars to Poland. In 1567 a Talmudic Academy was founded at Lublin, with the eminent Solomon Luria as rector. This added a new dimension to the religious debate raging throughout the country. The Jews themselves were not united, and there were still considerable colonies of Karaites – Jews who accepted only the Bible and rejected the Talmud. The Arians made many converts from the ranks of Talmudic Jews, while a number of Arians and Calvinists converted to Judaism. It was one of these converts, 'Joseph ben Mardoch' Malinowski, who played the most incongruous part in this religious interaction. It was he who put the finishing touches to the Hebrew original of *The Fortress of the Faith*, a Karaite catechism by Isaac ben Abraham of Troki, which was subsequently published in a number of countries, and was later rediscovered by Voltaire, who believed it to be the greatest demolition of the divinity of Christ ever written.

In every other country the established Church reacted with violence to the slightest departure from dogma, let alone to such wholesale rejection of the fundamental tenets of Catholicism. The reaction of the Polish hierarchy was either pragmatic or cynical, sometimes vehement, but never hysterical. Bishop Drohojowski of Kujavia, a region seriously affected on account of its large number of German-dominated towns, remained on

friendly terms with those who went over to Luther, and even went out of his
way to meet prominent heretics. With an open-mindedness rare even in
purportedly ecumenical times, he sanctioned the takeover of the Church of
St John in Gdańsk by the Lutherans, since most of the parishioners had
gone over to the heresy. He also allowed the sharing of parish churches in
his diocese by Catholics and Lutherans. He once reined in a priest who was
carried away in the pulpit calling for the rooting out of heretical weeds, by
observing that drastic weeding would only reveal how little good corn was
left standing in the diocese. Another who could not be accused of lacking in
realism was Andrzej Zebrzydowski, Bishop of Kraków. 'I don't care if you
worship a goat,' he roared at his wavering flock, 'as long as you keep
paying your tithes!'

A considerable proportion of the clergy were genuinely interested in the
reform of the Church. The Christians of the Orthodox rite had always
enjoyed three of the demands of the Protestant movement: the marriage of
priests, the use of the vernacular in the liturgy, and communion in both
kinds. The Protestant demands were therefore less shocking and novel in
Poland than in other Catholic countries. Catholic priests had often
emulated their colleagues of the Eastern Church by having common-law
wives, and they were keen to regularise their position and legalise their
broods. Stanisław Orzechowski (1513–66) actually married, but insisted
on remaining Canon of Przemyśl. He defended his behaviour in a long
debate with his bishop and with Rome, published in pamphlet form and
followed with great interest throughout the country.

Luther's revolt released passionate feelings among the clergy. Apart
from the practical demands concerning marriage and the vernacular, it
aroused a general revulsion against the medieval obscurantism of the
Church. Marcin Krowicki (1501–73) left the priesthood and published his
Defence of True Learning, a fiercely anti-clerical work in which the Papacy is
referred to as the whore of Babylon. Bishop Uchański, on the other hand,
did not forsake a career which was eventually to make him Primate of
Poland, but nevertheless penned vituperative diatribes against the practices of the Church, going so far as to compare the rule of the Papacy to the
Babylonian Captivity. In 1555 he declared himself in favour of the
marriage of priests, communion under both kinds and the use of the
vernacular. He also mooted the idea of a joint synod of all confessions in
Poland, to bring about reconciliation on common ground. When the king
promoted him to the bishopric of Kujavia the Pope refused to ratify the
appointment, but neither the king nor the Polish hierarchy took any notice.

King Zygmunt the Old (1506–48) felt that the religious debate was none
of his business. He came under considerable pressure from Rome and from
those of his own bishops who were in favour of stamping out the heresy. He
was even reproached by Henry VIII of England for not taking a more

energetic line against the Protestants. Whenever this pressure became very strong, he would take some action to satisfy the zealots, but his edicts were not worth the paper they were written on without the approval of the Seym. His attitude is summed up in his own words. 'Permit me to rule over the goats as well as the sheep,' he told one Papal envoy who was demanding arrests and executions.

In many countries the Reformation had social and political overtones. In Poland it was above all a constitutional issue. As the Papal Nuncio's secretary noted, after witnessing the debates of a Mazovian seymik, the assembly seemed staunchly Catholic when the discussion turned on the faith, the sacraments and the sacred rites, but when the talk was of the privileges of the clergy, a number of 'Protestant' voices could be heard, and when it came to the subject of the Church's immunity from taxation, the entire seymik appeared to have become fanatically Calvinist. In 1554, Bishop Czarnkowski of Poznań sentenced three burghers to death by fire for heresy, but they were rescued by a posse of mostly Catholic szlachta. The same bishop later sentenced a cobbler to the same fate, and this time over a hundred armed szlachta of all denominations, led by magnates of the Ostroróg, Tomicki and Leszczyński families, laid siege to the episcopal palace and freed the condemned man. On one or two occasions, the ecclesiastical courts managed to execute the sentence before anyone could take preventive action. In 1556 Dorota Łazewska, accused of stealing a host from a church and selling it to the Jews for alleged occult rites, was burnt at the stake in Sochaczew. The execution caused uproar, and this came in time to save the lives of the three Jews who were to be burnt on the next day. They too were saved by the intervention of Catholic as well as Protestant szlachta. As Jan Tarnowski pointed out, 'It is not a question of religion, it is a question of liberty.'

All were agreed that there would be no liberty while a single body which was independent of the parliamentary system was able to judge people and sentence them for any reason. The ecclesiastical tribunals' jurisdiction was annulled by act of the Seym in 1562. As a result, two years later Europe was treated to a unique spectacle. A young Arian, Erazm Otwinowski, was brought for trial before the Seym instead of the abolished ecclesiastical court. During a Catholic procession in Lublin earlier that year, Otwinowski had snatched the monstrance from the prelate, thrown it on the ground, and .stamped on the Blessed Sacrament, uttering obscene insults. The Seym tribunal, made up of Catholics and Calvinists, heard the case and agreed broadly with the defence, ably conducted by the poet Mikołaj Rej, who argued that if God was offended, God would punish, and as for Otwinowski, he should be ordered to pay the priest 'a shilling, so he can buy himself a new glass and a handful of flour' with which to repair the monstrance and bake a new host.

At a time when torture and death awaited anyone caught reading the wrong book in most European countries, such dispassionate adherence to the notion of human rights was extraordinary. But neither the Catholic nor the Protestant leaders were happy with this state of affairs. There was a general desire to reach consensus and to decide on a state religion. At the Seym of 1555 a majority of deputies demanded the establishment of a Church of Poland. Their demands included the introduction of the vernacular, the right of priests to marry, communion under both forms, and the investiture of all administrative control in a Polish Synod, which would rule independently of Rome. The chances of a break with the Papacy were high, but the king hesitated.

Zygmunt Augustus, the only son of Zygmunt the Old, was a melancholy figure. Painstakingly educated – some say debauched – by his mother Bona Sforza, he was dubbed 'Augustus' by her and brought up to rule accordingly. She was a forbidding creature. The first cousin of Francis I and a close relative of Charles V, she was brought up at the court of her father the Duke of Milan, which had an evil reputation for intrigue and poison. In an unprecedented move, she arranged for Zygmunt to be elected and crowned heir to the throne during his father's lifetime. But she did not contribute to his happiness, and he did not live up to her ambitions.

In 1543 he married Elizabeth of Habsburg, daughter of the Emperor Ferdinand I, who died only two years later, allegedly poisoned by Queen Bona. He then fell in love and eloped with Barbara Radziwiłł, the beautiful sister of a powerful Lithuanian magnate. Only four years after this marriage, which was opposed by virtually everyone in Poland for a variety of reasons, Barbara Radziwiłł died, and again the queen mother was suspected of using her Milanese skills. After considering at length the possibility of marrying Mary Tudor in 1553 Zygmunt married his first wife's sister, Katherine of Habsburg, widow of the Duke of Mantua. It was a disastrous marriage. The epileptic queen physically repelled him and, unlike the others, she did not die – perhaps because Queen Bona, feeling more unpopular than ever, had loaded herself up with gold and jewels and fled to Bari in Italy where, appropriately enough, she was herself eventually poisoned.

Since neither of his first two wives had borne him any children, the fact that Zygmunt Augustus refused to touch his third was a matter of some concern to his subjects. The extinction of a dynasty is always cause for alarm, and in this instance the alarm was all the greater as the Jagiellons were still the only real link between Poland and Lithuania. The Seym begged the king to attend to his wife, repulsive or not, and the Primate actually went down on his knees in the chamber to beseech the king to either possess her or cast her off, breaking with Rome if need be.

The king's behaviour at this point was crucial to both the religious and the political future of Poland, and the king lacked decision. His attitude to the Reformation was ambivalent. He never outwardly sympathised with the Protestant movement but took a great interest in the whole question of reform, avidly reading all the dissenting tracts and treatises and accepting the dedication of works by Luther and Calvin. He even sent his confessor Francesco Lismanino to Geneva and other Protestant centres to purchase the latest publications. In 1550 he issued an anti-Protestant decree in the hope of winning support from the bishops for his marriage with Barbara Radziwiłł, but this remained a dead letter like those issued by his father. A few years later he rebuked the Papal Nuncio for urging a firmer line towards the Protestants, and in effect forced him to leave Poland. When asked by his subjects which way they should lean in the religious debate, he replied: 'I am not the king of your consciences.'

Unlike Henry VIII, Zygmunt Augustus did not really want a divorce. His love for Barbara Radziwiłł had been a great passion, and her tragic end robbed him of the will to live. He continued to carry out his duties without enthusiasm, dressed entirely in black, and showed no desire to mould the future or perpetuate the dynasty. When pressed by the Seym of 1555, he took the characteristically non-committal and quite extraordinary step of referring the whole matter of the Polish Church to Rome. He sent Stanisław Maciejewski to Pope Paul IV with the four demands of the Seym. The Pope listened to them 'with great sorrow and bitterness of heart', and then rebuked Zygmunt for allowing his subjects to formulate such heretical demands. The matter of the national Church rested there, and the reformers were, for once, unaided by provocative behaviour on the part of the Pope. A few blistering attacks and excommunications would have rallied the Protestants and rekindled the ardour of the 'national Catholics'.

The principal weakness of the Protestant movement in Poland was its lack of unity, and the only candidate for its leadership spent most of his active life in England. Jan Łaski, nephew of the archbishop of the same name and a member of what was briefly a very rich and powerful family, became a Protestant while studying abroad. He stayed in Geneva with Calvin, who praised his 'erudition, integrity and other virtues'. In Rotterdam he became a close friend of Erasmus, and helped him out of financial difficulties by buying his entire library from him, but allowing him the use of it for life. He was then invited to England by Thomas Cranmer and given a pension by Edward VI who appointed him chaplain to the foreign Protestants who had taken refuge in England. Known in England as John à Lasco, he was close to Cranmer and collaborated with him on the Book of Common Prayer of 1552, but with the accession of Queen Mary he was forced to leave the country.

He reached Poland in time for the first Synod of the Calvinist Church in

1554, at which he strongly advocated greater unity and a closing of ranks by all dissenters against the Catholic hierarchy. Progress in this direction was hindered by endless quarrels over minor theological and administrative questions. Jan Łaski died in 1560, and it was not until 1570 that the Consensus of Sandomierz was finally enacted. In the event, it failed to produce the sort of Protestant front he had hoped for.

The Protestant movement enjoyed the patronage of the foremost magnates, but failed to gain the support of broad sections of the population. It never touched the peasants to any significant extent, never seriously affected those towns like Przemyśl or Lwów which had no large German population, and left much of the szlachta, particularly in poor, populous Mazovia, indifferent. Even in cases where their master went over to Calvinism the peasants clung to their old faith with surly tenacity, sometimes walking miles to the nearest Catholic church.

The Reformation in Poland was not at bottom a spiritual movement. It was a sally by the articulate classes who made use of the liberating challenge of Luther to further a process of intellectual and political emancipation which had started long before. The szlachta which had done everything to curtail the power of the crown seized eagerly on the possibilities offered by the movement for reform in order to break the power of the Church. Straightforward anticlericalism was easily confused with a desire for a return to true Christian principles, and so was another movement in Polish politics which reached a climax in the 1550s.

A purely political reformist movement had come into existence at the beginning of the century. In spirit it was very close to the Reformation, since it placed the accent not on innovation but on stricter observance of the law, on weeding out malpractice and corruption. It was known as 'the movement for the execution of the laws', or simply as the 'executionist' movement. One of its first preoccupations was that the law itself should be codified and published in clear form, and as a result much groundwork was done in the first half of the century, culminating in legal reforms passed in 1578 which fixed the legal system for the next two hundred years.

The executionists waged a war of attrition on the temporal position of the Church. It was they who gave the impetus to abolish the medieval anomaly of the diocesan courts in 1562. The Seym of the following year saw another victory, when the Church, which had always enjoyed exemption from taxation, was forced to contribute financially to the defence of the state. Much of the executionists' support stemmed from the normal person's revulsion at having to contribute to the treasury through taxation, and they were therefore keen to see that such resources as the state or the crown possessed were well run. This led them into direct conflict with the magnates, over the thorny subject of royal lands and starosties.

The crown owned estates all over the country which it did not administer itself. Some were granted to individuals for services to the crown, to favourites, and even to merchants in return for cash advances. Others were granted with the office of *starosta*. The starostas were the lynch-pin of local government, the king's officers who were in charge of law and order in a given locality. The starosties varied, but tended to be large and profitable estates which the incumbent was supposed to administer on behalf of the king, taking 20 per cent of the profit for himself as payment for the office he carried out. The rest went to the crown. All starosties and royal lands were the inalienable property of the crown, and reverted to it on the incumbent's death. In practice, things worked out differently.

The office of starosta gradually degenerated into a sinecure, while the administration of the lands, which was not subject to any verification, afforded endless scope for venality on the part of the starosta and his servants. The starosties were therefore highly sought-after by magnates who could increase their revenue without any extra effort or outlay of funds, and at the same time enjoy the prestige and power of the office. Influential families began to collect them, with the result that a magnate might have up to half a dozen important starosties, and a number of other royal estates, and his family would be understandably loath to give them up on his death. Although the lands were supposed to revert the king found it increasingly difficult not to reaward them to the son of the incumbent without alienating the whole family. If the family were powerful, this might cause problems. To all practical purposes, therefore, the starosties were becoming hereditary in the richer families.

This infuriated the szlachta, since it bolstered the position of the magnates on the one hand, and diminished the crown's financial resources on the other. Again and again the executionists clamoured for the return of these estates and the repossession by the crown of multiply-held starosties. On this issue, however, the normally executionist members of the Senate would vote with the bishops against the executionists, and the king, who by the middle of the century based his rule more and more on an alliance with the magnates, would co-operate with them. Only minimal success was achieved in 1563, when the Seym decreed a general inspection of all accounts and inventories to catch out corrupt administrators.

The executionist movement was intellectually and temperamentally the sibling of the Protestant movement, and it attracted much of the zeal which might otherwise have been concentrated on religious questions. At the same time, Catholic voters elected Calvinist deputies because they were executionists, and Catholic deputies voted with the executionist Calvinists on issues such as the demand for a national Church, on the abolition of ecclesiastical tribunals, and on the law forcing the Church to contribute financially to defence. Even at the height of the Reformation no Pole, be he a Catholic, a Lutheran, a Calvinist or an Arian, was prepared to place religious issues before constitutional and legal ones. That is why the Reformation failed in Poland. After raging and blustering in word and print for a few decades, the Protestant movement gradually burnt itself out, while the energies which had fuelled it were diverted to political matters.

The Catholic Church, which had dodged the heaviest blows and avoided confrontation, slowly went over to the offensive, as the Counter-Reformation gained strength. In Poland its progress was unsensational: no inquisition, no anathemas, no religious terrorism, no forfeitures of property, no barring from office – none of the features normally associated with the Counter-Reformation in the rest of Europe. It could hardly have been otherwise, given the spirit of legality and humanism pervading Polish society, a spirit which also burned in the breasts of the leaders of the Counter-Reformation. The greatest of these, Cardinal Stanisław Hosius, was fundamentally opposed to violence and, referring to 'Bloody' Mary, warned in 1571: 'Let Poland never become like England.'

Hosius and his principal colleague, Marcin Kromer, were unusual men by the standards of sixteenth-century Catholic prelates. Both had worked in the Royal Chancellery for the king before they went into the service of the Church. Hosius then went on to play an important role at the Council of Trent. Kromer was an historian, and in his writings he demonstrated the unifying role of the Church in the Polish state. He preferred to argue with heretics rather than condemn them. Hosius favoured a similar approach, but he made a greater and more categorical statement on the matter of religion – something the Calvinists were unable to do. His *Confessio* (1551), a lucid reaffirmation of Catholic dogma, was one of the most powerful books of the European Counter-Reformation, translated into several languages. Between 1559 and 1583, it ran to no less than thirty-seven separate editions in France alone.

In 1564 Hosius brought the Jesuits to Poland, to reconquer the hearts, and more specifically the minds, of the Poles. The most outstanding Polish Jesuit of this period was a worthy successor to Hosius in putting across the Catholic view. Piotr Skarga (1536–1612) made his mark with the publication in 1577 of a book on unity in the church and followed this up two years later with his *Lives of the Saints*, which has seldom been out of print since. Towards the end of the century he became confessor to the king and chaplain to the Seym, a position through which he exerted enormous influence.

Hosius and Skarga pinpointed the principal arguments for returning to the fold, letting time do the rest. And time was on the side of Rome. In 1570 Mikołaj Sierotka Radziwiłł, son of the man who had introduced Calvinism to Lithuania and been one of its greatest financial and political supports, went back to the Church of Rome. Others followed suit, for a variety of reasons. Even the mixed marriages which the hierarchy had fulminated against worked for Catholicism, since women had been largely left out of the religious debate and their conditioning led them to accept and stand by the old faith. Jan Firlej, Marshal of Poland, had become a Calvinist, but his wife, Zofia Boner, had not. She covertly brought his sons up to love the Catholic faith, with the result that three out of the four became Catholics when they grew up. After her death, Firlej married Barbara Mniszech, another fervent Catholic. Although their son was ostensibly brought up a Calvinist, the mother's influence prevailed, and he became Primate of Poland. As Piotr Skarga foresaw, the country would be reconquered for Rome, 'not by force or with steel, but by virtuous example, teaching, discussion, gentle intercourse and persuasion.'

As Calvin grew more strident and Protestants in various European countries began to execute not only Catholics but other Protestants, the Polish prelates cajoled and showed forbearance. They pointed out that Protestantism could be as ruthless and repressive as Catholicism. They explained that it was not only divisive, but irresponsible, and in this they were helped by the example of the Arians.

Under the influence of Sozzini, who rejected dogma and believed in the primacy of man over Christ, the Arian movement displayed a tendency to splinter into groups which argued indecorously. It became a comfortable refuge for all manner of dissenters, schismatics and general riff-raff migrating from other countries. Neither this nor the flirtations with Judaism was calculated to make the Arians popular. The Arians would turn up at seymiks and hector the szlachta: 'You should not eat bread made by the sweat of a subject's brow, but make your own. Nor should you live on estates which were granted to your forbears for spilling the blood of enemies. You must sell those estates and give the money to the poor.' Their creed of non-violence posed grave problems, since the status of the szlachta was directly and vitally tied up with the bearing of arms, and although most Arian szlachta did answer the *levée en masse* a question-mark remained. (Their Synod of 1604 allowed them to serve in the army, as long as they did not kill or wound anyone.)

With the impending extinction of the Jagiellon dynasty, Poland and Lithuania needed unity of purpose rather than dissent and refusal to take responsibility. Nevertheless, the constitutional and legal aspects of the case were still paramount. After the death of Zygmunt Augustus the Seym which met under the name of the Confederation of Warsaw to shape Poland's future in 1573 passed an Act whose most memorable clause ran as follows:

> Whereas in our Common Wealth there is no small disagreement in the matter of the Christian faith, and in order to prevent that any harmful

contention should arise from this, as we see clearly taking place in other kingdoms, we swear to each other, in our name and in that of our descendants for ever more, on our honour, our faith, our love and our consciences, that albeit we are *dissidentes in religione*, we will keep the peace between ourselves, and that we will not, for the sake of our various faith and difference of church, either shed blood or confiscate property, deny favour, imprison or banish, and that furthermore we will not aid or abet any power or office which strives to this in any way whatsoever . . .

The freedom to practise any religion without suffering discrimination or penalty was henceforth enshrined in the constitution. This law was observed rigorously by Catholic kings, Catholic Senates and an increasingly Catholic population. Some illegal executions did take place, but they were few. When no criminal offence had been committed, even acts of extreme provocation went unpunished. In 1580 the Calvinist Marcin Kreza snatched the host from a priest, spat on it, trampled it, and then fed it to a passing mongrel, for which he was reprimanded by the king and told not to do it again.

In 1572 on the other hand, after a riot which led to the burning down of the Calvinist Chapel in Kraków, five Catholics were beheaded to set an example, and the Catholic inhabitants started a subscription for rebuilding the Chapel, to which Bishop Krasiński contributed a generous sum. The Calvinist writer who chronicled the course of the Counter-Reformation in Poland, and listed every execution or sectarian killing of a Protestant between 1550 and 1650, came up with a total no higher than twelve. During the same period, over 500 people were legally executed for religious reasons in England, and nearly 900 were burnt in the Netherlands, while hundreds more suffered confiscations and attainders, which were unknown in Poland. This unique absence of violence stemmed partly from the Polish attitude to religion, partly from an obsession with legality and the principle of personal liberty, and partly from the fact that throughout this period Polish society concentrated on an attempt to build utopia on earth.

6

A Royal Republic

Zygmunt Augustus was only thirty-three years old when he married Katherine of Habsburg in 1553, but he refused to touch her. As the heirless king paced the Italianate galleries of the Royal Castle on Wawel hill dressed in mourning for his beloved Barbara, his subjects thought uneasily of the future. Like the Habsburg Empire in later centuries, the realm of the Jagiellons was a conglomerate of territories with disparate populations, differing customs and varying forms of government which coexisted within one state. The force holding this structure together was neither a feudal bond, nor a bureaucratic system, nor a military hegemony, but a broad consensus whose only physical embodiment was the Jagiellon dynasty itself. Its extinction therefore raised the question not of who would rule the country, but whether it would continue to exist in its present form.

The only thing which could prevent the realm from falling apart was an entirely new formulation of the consensus which had created it originally. But who was to formulate this? The Poles? The great regional lords? Who represented the population of this mongrel conglomerate? The answer was, of course, the szlachta, and they were not slow to point it out.

By the mid-sixteenth century the szlachta included Lithuanian and Ruthene boyars, Prussian and Baltic gentry of German origin, as well as Tatars and smaller numbers of Moldavians, Armenians, Italians, Magyars and Bohemians. It was regularly increased by intermarriage with wealthy merchants and peasants. The szlachta made up nearly ten per cent of the population. Since they extended from the top to the bottom of the economic scale, and right across the board in religion and culture, they represented a wider cross-section as well as a greater percentage of the population than any enfranchised class in any European country until the nineteenth century. To be a member of the szlachta was like being a Roman Citizen. The szlachta were the nation, the *populus Romanus*, while the rest of the people inhabiting the area were the *plebs*, who did not count politically.

While the score of patrician families and the spiritual lords of the

Church fought hard to establish government by oligarchy, the mass of the 'noble people' fought for democratic control of what they passionately felt to be their country. It was they who pressed for the execution of the laws, for a more clearly defined constitution, and for a closer relationship with the throne. They met with little support from Zygmunt the Old and Zygmunt Augustus, both of whom tended rather to support the magnates. While the executionists struggled with increasing desperation to arrive at a definition of the powers of the Seym and the role of the monarch and his ministers, the magnates stalled any such definition, since they hoped to take matters into their own hands when the time came.

The joker in the pack was Lithuania. The szlachta of the Grand Duchy had long wanted to enjoy the same rights as their colleagues in the Kingdom. In spite of being granted a Senate of their own (*Rada*) at the beginning of the century, and a Seym in 1559, the minor szlachta of Lithuania were politically immature, and their magnates told them how to vote. One Lithuanian family, the Radziwiłł, had shot to prominence at the beginning of the century. They accumulated wealth by means of marriages with Polish heiresses, and held most of the important offices in the Grand Duchy. The head of the clan, Mikołaj 'the Black', was Chancellor and Marshal of Lithuania and Palatine of Wilno, as well as the King's close friend and unofficial lieutenant in the Grand Duchy. His cousin, Mikołaj 'the Red', brother of Barbara, was Hetman (commander-in-chief) of Lithuania and Palatine of Troki, the second most important province in the Grand Duchy. In 1547, Mikołaj the Black had obtained from the Habsburgs the title of Prince of the Holy Roman Empire and as the extinction of the Jagiellons approached he dreamed of detaching the Grand Duchy from Poland and turning it into his own kingdom. In the end, it was not so much reason as fear that prevailed. Throughout the 1560s, the new Tsar of Muscovy, Ivan 'the Terrible', stormed around his territories with his notorious thugs, boiling people in oil and slaughtering whole cities for little apparent reason. Without Polish support, Lithuania would soon find itself sharing the same fate.

Reservations gradually melted away and, after one last tantrum by the Lithuanian magnates, the Senate and Seym of Lithuania and those of Poland met at Lublin on the border between the two states. On 1 July 1569 they unanimously swore a new Act of Union. At the practical level, the Union of Lublin was hardly revolutionary. It stipulated that henceforth the Seyms of both countries should meet as one, at Warsaw, a small city conveniently placed for the purpose. The combined upper house now contained 149 senators, and the lower 168 deputies. Poland and Lithuania would share one monarch, not, as had been the case hitherto, *de facto* (because the Jagiellon elected to the Kraków throne was already the hereditary Grand Duke of Lithuania) but *de jure*. The Grand Duchy was to

Polish – Lithuanian boundary after the union of 1569	
Polish boundary after the peace treaty of Jam Zapolski, 1582	
Fief of the Holy Roman Empire	
Piast duchies under Habsburg overlordship	

The Polish Commonwealth of 1569

keep its old laws drawn up in the Statutes of Lithuania in 1529, a separate treasury, and its own army. This was to be commanded by a Grand Hetman and a Field-Hetman of Lithuania. The ministers of the crown (Marshal, Chancellor, Vice-Chancellor, Treasurer and Marshal of the Court) were joined by identical officers for Lithuania. The Union was a marriage of two partners, with only the slightest hint of the dominant position of Poland. It was the expression of the wishes of the masses of the szlachta, the embodiment of their vision of a republic in which every citizen held an equal stake. The combined kingdom now formally became 'the Most Serene Commonwealth of the Two Nations', '*Serenissima Respublica Poloniae*' to foreigners.

There was an obvious paradox in the coexistence of monarchy with republicanism, yet the Poles tried hard to make a virtue out of the seeming contradiction. Stanisław Orzechowski even claimed that the Polish system was superior to all others, since it combined all the beneficent qualities of monarchy, oligarchy and democracy. The fact that it might combine all their faults as well was not thought relevant. In spite of continuous efforts by the executionists, the relationship between these three elements was never precisely defined. In principle, the Seym was the embodiment of the will of the people, and therefore the fount of legislative power; the Senate were the custodians of the law; the king was both a political unit in his own right and the mouthpiece of the Seym. While the Seym had curtailed the monarch's personal power, it wanted to invest much of its own in his person, thereby turning him into its executive. The would-be oligarchs in the Senate resisted this aim, while the last two Jagiellon kings avoided being drawn into the issue. The uncertainties attendant on the Reformation and the impending interregnum made the deputies hesitate before placing too much of their executive power in the hands of the king.

There was never any question of doing without a king. The Seym had debated what to do on the death of Zygmunt Augustus as early as 1558. Because of the stalling tactics of the Senate, nothing had been formally agreed when, on 7 July 1572, the last of the Jagiellons died. The point at issue was not whether there should be a king, what role he should play, or even who he should be, but rather how he should be chosen, and by whom. Early suggestions on procedure envisaged an enlarged Seym, where each member would have one vote. The eleven major towns were to be represented, but not the bishops, since they were technically agents of a foreign power.

When the time came, the Senate demanded the exclusive right to elect the new king, which brought an immediate and angry response from the szlachta. Someone suggested that the entire political nation should have an equal vote, an idea seized on by the bishops, who realised that an overwhelming majority of the szlachta were Catholic and therefore likely to support a Catholic candidate. The cry for universal suffrage was taken up by an ambitious young deputy to the Seym, Jan Zamoyski, the Starosta of Bełz, who rapidly captivated the masses with his rhetoric and became the undisputed tribune of the noble people. With their support, he forced the proposal through the Convocation Seym which met after the king's death, in 1573. From now on every single member of the szlachta, however poor, was a king-maker. More than that: each one carried a royal crown in his knapsack, for it was stipulated that only a Polish nobleman or member of a ruling foreign family could be a candidate to the throne of the Commonwealth.

The procedure for choosing the king crystallised in practice, with the first election of 1573. On the death of the sovereign, the Primate of Poland assumed the title of *interrex*, provisionally taking over the functions of the monarch, and summoned the Convocation Seym to Warsaw. This fixed the date of the election, restated the rules, and vetted all the proposed candidates. It also set down the terms on which the king elect was to be invited to take the throne. Then came the Election Seym, which met at Wola outside Warsaw, and to which every member of the szlachta could come. Since tens of thousands of voters might turn out, along with their servants and horses, this was often a remarkable gathering.

The centre of the Election Field was taken up by a fenced rectangular enclosure. At one end of this there was a wooden shed for the clerks and senior dignitaries, including the Marshal of the Seym, who was in charge of supervising the voting and policing the whole gathering. The electors remained outside the enclosure, on horseback and fully armed, drawn up in units according to the palatinate in which they lived. This symbolised the *levée en masse*, the obligation to fight for the country which lay at the basis of all the szlachta's privileges. It says a great deal for the restraint of the proverbially quarrelsome szlachta that the occasion did not degenerate into a pitched battle in the heat of contested elections. The bitterest arguments usually took place between the senators and the deputies on procedure and points of order. Each palatinate sent ten deputies into the enclosure, where they and the assembled senators listened to the representatives of the various candidates make an election address on behalf of their man, extolling his virtues and making glittering election pledges. The deputies would then go back to their comrades outside the enclosure and impart what they had heard. When this had been mulled over, the voting began. Every unit was given sheets of paper, each with the name of a candidate at the top, and the assembled voters signed and sealed on the sheet bearing the name of the candidate of their choice. The papers were then taken back into the enclosure, the votes counted, and the result officially proclaimed by the *interrex*. The whole procedure took no less than four days at the first election, in 1573, but subsequent elections were over in a day or two.

The szlachta were very fond of these elections. It was a great gathering of the clans, and any down-at-heel gentleman could meet the greatest dignitaries of the Commonwealth. The representatives of the various candidates set up 'hospitality tents' in which they plied the voters with food, drink and even money in the hope of gaining their vote. Rich magnates fraternised with the poorest members of the szlachta in order to gain their support for a favoured candidate. Most important, the szlachta could exercise the right to choose who would reign over them – a choice unthinkable in most European countries, and therefore a matter of tremendous pride to the man who could freely exercise it.

The king thus chosen could hardly harbour any illusions about Divine Right. To make sure that all remnant of any such idea should be banished from his mind, his prospective subjects made him swear an oath of loyalty to them and their constitution, as well as to a set of other conditions laid

Dignitaries of the Kingdom of Poland (Grand Hetman, Field-Hetman, Court Treasurer, Equerry, Steward, etc)		Dignitaries of the Grand Duchy of Lithuania (Hetman, Field-Hetman, Court Treasurer, Equerry, Steward, etc)	

KING

	1 Ab. of Gniezno	2 Ab. of Lwów	
88 C. of Sącz	4 B. of Kujavia	3 B. of Kraków	89 C. of Międzyrzec
90 C. of Wiślica	7 B. of Płock	5 B. of Wilno	91 C. of Biecz
92 C. of Rogoźno	8 B. of Warmia	6 B. of Poznań	93 C. of Radom
94 C. of Zawichost	9 B. of Łuck	18 C. of Kraków	95 C. of Ląd
96 C. of Srem	10 B. of Przemyśl	19 P. of Kraków	97 C. of Żarnów
98 C. of Małogoszcz	11 B. of Samogitia	20 P. of Poznań	99 C. of Wieluń
100 C. of Przemyśl	12 B. of Chełmno	21 P. of Wilno	101 C. of Halicz
102 C. of Sanok	13 B. of Chełm	22 P. of Sandomierz	103 C. of Chełm
104 C. of Dobrzyn	14 B. of Kiev	23 C. of Wilno	105 C. of Połaniec
106 C. of Przemęt	15 B. of Kamieniec	24 P. of Kalisz	107 C. of Krzywin
108 C. of Czchów	16 B. of Livonia	26 P. of Sieradz	109 C. of Nakło
110 C. of Rozprze	17 B. of Smolensk	28 P. of Łęczyca	111 C. of Biechów
112 C. of Bydgoszcz	25 P. of Troki	30 P of Brześć Kujawski	113 C. of Brzeziny
114 C. of Kruszwica	27 C. of Troki	31 P. of Kiev	115 C. of Oświęcim
116 C. of Kamień	29 Sta. of Samogitia	32 P. of Inowłódz	117 C. of Spicymierz
118 C. of Inowłódź	36 P. of Smolensk	33 P. of Ruthenia	119 C. of Kowal
120 C. of Santok	38 P. of Polotsk	35 P. of Podolia	121 C. of Sochaczew
122 C. of Warsaw	40 P. of Nowogródek	37 P. of Lublin	123 C. of Gostyń
124 C. of Wizna	42 P. of Vitebsk	39 P. of Bełz	125 C. of Raciąz
126 C. of Sierpc	43 P. of Mazovia	41 P. of Płock	127 C. of Wyszogród
128 C. of Rypin	45 P. of Rawa	44 P. of Podlasie	129 C. of Zakroczym
130 C. of Ciechanów	46 P. of Brześć Litewski	47 P. of Chełmno	131 C. of Liw
132 C. of Słońsk	48 P. of Mścisław	54 P. of Czernyhów	133 C. of Lubaczów
134 C.-E. of Sieradz	49 P. of Malbork	55 C. of Poznań	135 C.-E. of Łęczyca
136 C.-E. of Kujavia	50 P. of Bracław	56 C. of Sandomierz	
	51 P. of Pomerania	57 C. of Kalisz	
	52 P. of Mińsk	58 C. of Wojnicz	
	53 P. of Livonia	59 C. of Gniezno	
	60 C. of Sieradz	61 C. of Łęczyca	
	62 C. of Samogitia	63 C. of Brześć Kujawski	
	69 C. of Smolensk	64 C. of Kiev	
	71 C. of Polotsk	65 C. of Inowrocław	
	73 C. of Nowogródek	66 C. of Lwów	
	74 C. of Płock	67 C. of Volhynia	
	75 C. of Vitebsk	68 C. of Kamieniec	
	78 C. of Rawa	70 C. of Lublin	
	79 C. of Brześć Litewski	72 C. of Bełz	
	80 C. of Chełmno	76 C. of Czersk	
	81 C. of Mścisław	77 C. of Podlasie	
	82 C. of Elbląg	83 C. of Bracław	
	84 C. of Gdańsk	86 C. of Livonia	
	85 C. of Mińsk	87 C. of Czernyhów	

MINISTERS

of Lithuania   of the Crown

10 Marshal of the Court	8 Treasurer	6 Vice-Chancellor	4 Chancellor	2 Marshal	1 Grand Marshal	3 Chancellor	5 Vice-Chancellor	7 Treasurer	9 Marshal of the Court

Ab. = Archbishop

B. = Bishop

C. = Castellan

P. = Palatine

Sta. = Starosta

C.-E. = Castellan-Equerry

Fig. 5   The Senate of the Polish Commonwealth in session. The numbers denote the order of precedence among the Senators and the Ministers respectively.

down in two documents, one, the *Acta Henriciana*, immutable, the other, the *Pacta Conventa*, drawn up specifically by the Convocation Seym before every new election. In swearing to these, the king abdicated all right to a say in the election of his successor and agreed not to marry or divorce without the approval of the Seym. He undertook not to declare war, raise an army, or levy taxes without its consent, and to govern through a Council of Senators chosen by the Seym, which he had to summon at least once in every two years. If he defaulted on any of these points, his subjects were automatically released from their oath of loyalty to him – in other words, he could forfeit his throne if he did not abide by the terms of his employment.

The king was, in effect, a functionary, the chief executive of the Commonwealth. He was not by any means a powerless figurehead, but his power was not arbitrary, and he was not above the law. Although he had no aura of divinity surrounding him, the king could, and many did, build up a strong position and elicit unbounded respect and devotion from his subjects. No elected King of Poland was ever treated as Charles I or Louis XVI, however bad his behaviour.

Like every other people affected by the new learning of the Renaissance, the Poles had been fascinated by the rediscovery of the artistic and political culture of ancient Rome and the Hellenic world. The apparent similarities between some of their own institutions and those of the ancient republics tickled the national vanity considerably. Without looking too closely at the pitfalls that led to the demise of the Roman Republic, the *Senatus Populusque Polonus* drew further on this model. The Polish political vocabulary bristled with terms such as 'liberty', 'equality', 'brotherhood', 'nation', 'citizen', 'senate', 'tribune', and 'republic'. Like the makers of the French Revolution of 1789, the Poles increasingly borrowed the style, the symbolism and the concepts of the Roman Republic.

The difference between the Poles of the sixteenth century and the French revolutionary leaders, however, was that the Polish system was based almost entirely on precedent. The notion of electing a monarch, for instance, was no revolutionary concept developed by theorists or borrowed from ancient Rome: it was deeply rooted in the national tradition. It had evolved as a result of Poland's devolution into duchies, and had appeared in some form at every royal accession since then. After the death of Kazimierz IV in 1492, there had been a regular election of one of his sons, which was repeated after the death of every subsequent king. The idea of choosing a foreign prince was based on the precedent of the Kraków Lords approving the accession of Louis of Anjou, and their subsequent choice of Jagiełło. Virtually every clause in the *Acta Henriciana* and most of those in the *Pacta Conventa* were a repetition of older privileges. As in England, there was no written constitution, merely a great body of legislation written into the statute books, swelling gradually by accretion over the centuries, with

42 The Polish Parliament in session, a woodcut of 1580. The king is flanked by his officers of state and faces his ministers; the senators are seated on either side, and the deputies stand at the four corners.

43 *(Left)* The acts passed by the Seym during its session of 1557 in Warsaw. All new legislation was immediately printed in pamphlet form.

44 *(Above)* The coping-stone of Polish parliamentary democracy, the constitution of *Nihil Novi*, whereby no act could be decreed by the king without the prior approval of the deputies of all the lands of Poland, granted on 31 March 1505 by King Aleksander.

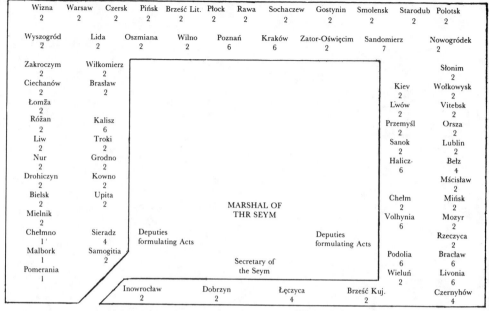

Fig. 6   *The Seym in session. The numbers denote the number of deputies returned by the respective constituencies.*

many resulting oddities, quaint exceptions and regional variants. Like the Bible, it could be read in many ways. The Poles' respect for anything enshrined in precedent and sanctified by age was, and is, almost unbounded. Roman law never supplanted, or even seriously affected, the common law of Poland.

Although the Polish constitution evolved over the centuries out of practical rather than theoretical motives, it was fashioned by a mentality which was idealistic rather than pragmatic. The parliamentary system lacked procedures for ensuring correct behaviour, and relied to an inordinate extent on the integrity of the individual deputy and senator. The Marshal of the Seym (not to be confused with the Marshals of Poland and of Lithuania, who were the king's ministers) was elected at the beginning of each session by the deputies, and it was his duty to keep order. Since he had no authority to silence a deputy or expel him from the chamber, the orderly conduct of debates depended in large measure on his skill in easing tensions and steering attention back to the point at issue. His job was made no easier by the ambiguities inherent in the mandate given to the deputies by their electors. In principle, the deputies were the representatives not merely of the seymiks which had returned them, but of the corporate electorate of the whole Commonwealth, and they were supposed to cast their votes as such. At the same time, each deputy was given a set of written instructions by the seymik before he left for Warsaw to take up his seat. These instructions varied from general guidelines to specific orders on how to vote on certain issues. The electorate's participation in government did not end with the election of a deputy, and the deputy could ill afford to disregard the injunctions of his electors, since he had to face a 'debriefing' seymik in his constituency after the end of the parliamentary session. Sometimes, deputies were instructed not to vote on any unforeseen major issue without consulting their electors first.

This practice tied the hands of the deputies and tended to reduce the value of parliamentary debate, but an intelligent and experienced deputy could still vote according to his conscience and answer for it successfully to his electors. It was not until the beginning of the next century, when the electorate began to grow suspicious of central government, that the instructions became literally binding. It was in vain that Jan Ostroróg pleaded with his fellow deputies in 1613 that 'this mandate which you have been given is not a written order from a master to his servant.' The practice helped to dent the authority of the Seym, and paved the way for factionalism and intransigence.

The Polish parliamentary system was more vulnerable than most, because of a principle whose perverted form, the *liberum veto*, was to become ridiculously famous in the eighteenth century: the principle that no legislation could be enacted without unanimity. Some such convention originally existed in virtually every parliamentary body in Europe, and survived in areas such as the English jury system. It did not mean that everyone had to vote for a measure unanimously. It originated in the twin convictions that any measure not freely assented to by all lacked full authority and that no genuinely dissenting opinion should be simply disregarded by the majority. As the saying went, votes should be weighed, not counted. Dissenting minorities were listened to, argued with and persuaded, and only when broad agreement had been reached (the word used was the Latin *consensus*) was a measure passed. In theory, a small minority, even a minority of one, could block the passage of a bill. In practice, minorities were ultimately ignored if they proved intractable.

Another curious feature of the constitution was the right of Confederation, a form of political action older than the Seym itself. It was an association of gentry and towns which came together in an emergency. Such an emergency might be thought to exist when a monarch died, when the country was invaded, or when some crisis incapacitated the organs of government. A group would form a Confederation, elect a Marshal, publish their aims and invite others to join. It was a form of plebiscite, a way of showing determination legally, and as such it could take place within a Seym where deadlock had been reached. The institution was poorly defined, and therefore open to abuse, but it was the one political forum in which strict majority voting was observed.

A weakness of the Polish parliamentary system was the under-representation of the towns, and therefore of trading interests, in the Seym. This was not so much a flaw in the constitution as a reflection of the social structure that had evolved in Poland. A number of cities, including Kraków, Lublin, Lwów, Poznań, Wilno, Gdańsk and Toruń, had the right to send deputies to every Seym, including the Election Seyms, and other towns were on occasion invited to send deputies. In theory, these had exactly the same rights in debating and voting as any other, but the reality was often different. As the writer Sebastian Petrycy put it: 'Once upon a time a donkey was asked to a wedding feast; he marvelled and licked his chops at the thought of the new unfamiliar delicacies he would be tasting, but when the day came the donkey found he was there to carry water and kindling to the kitchen for the wedding-feast.' The civic officers of Kraków, Lublin and Lwów were automatically ennobled, but whether they were members of the szlachta or not, the city deputies were usually intimidated by their noble colleagues and feared to say anything – with some reason, since it appears that in 1537 the Kraków deputies were physically attack-ed. The cities often found it easier to stay away from the Seym and put up with whatever taxes might be imposed on them in their absence, or to employ the local palatine to look after their interests.

In the fifteenth century the towns, with their predominantly foreign populations enjoying a favourable administrative status, did not bother to join in the scramble for power and thereby missed an opportunity for integrating their rights into the constitution. They had always dealt direct with the crown, which guaranteed their status, but when the crown began to abdicate its responsibilities to the Seym, the towns, like the peasants, were left undefended. The cities did not fight for their prerogatives at this stage, which meant that they were gradually excluded from the legislative process. In 1550 members of the szlachta were barred from indulging in trade (mainly at the insistence of the merchant classes), and soon the szlachta began to regulate admissions to its own ranks. In 1578 the Seym passed a law taking away from the crown and arrogating to itself the exclusive right to ennoble people (except for battlefield grants of arms by the king). In 1611 a law was passed preventing plebeians from buying landed estates, a back door to noble status. This sort of legislation was not watertight, and extremely difficult to enforce in view of the absence of any heraldic institution or register, but lines were being drawn. A merchant might join the szlachta by some means and thereby acquire voting rights, but when he did, he found himself banned from practising anything except agriculture, politics and war.

The same applied to the peasants, who had also had a direct relationship with the crown. As the judge of the supreme court of appeal, the king was the final arbiter in all their disputes with landowners. In 1518 Zygmunt the Old was persuaded to give up his right of arbitration, and in 1578 the Seym itself assumed the function of the supreme court. Since it represented almost exclusively landed interests, the peasants were unlikely to find justice there. It is perhaps worth noting here that the principles of Polish democracy were not exclusive to the Seym, and every village had its elected communal council and officers. The squire's functions within this, usually as local magistrate, were not feudal or proprietary, but elective.

Not all the drawbacks of the Polish constitution were specific to it. All democracy breeds its own problems, and one of these is the impossibility of carrying on a successful foreign policy when decision-making is hamstrung by the devolution of power and the force of public opinion. The element of secrecy was impossible to sustain since all Seym debates were open to the public and all its resolutions immediately printed. After 1572 Poland's foreign policy began to bear an uncanny resemblance to that of modern liberal democracies in its lack of consistency, its unaggressive style and its slowness of response. Defence, a natural partner of foreign policy, suffered from the same problems. No democracy likes an army, because nobody likes paying for one. In the late sixteenth century about two-thirds of the entire revenue of most European states was spent on armament, almost seventy per cent in the case of Spain. In Poland, the figure was nearer twenty per cent. In the 1480s a 'Current Defence Force' of 2,000 was set up to parry Tatar raiding, and in 1520 the Seym increased the numbers slightly. In 1563 a new system of 'Quarter Troops' was introduced, paid for out of a quarter of all revenues from starosties, but the number of men under arms remained tiny in relation to the vast area of the Commonwealth.

Clemenceau's observation that 'a Frenchman will gladly give his life for his country, but his money – never!' could apply as well here, but it was not just that the Poles did not like paying for the troops. The szlachta also liked to perpetuate the idea of the *levée en masse*, which would be unnecessary if there were an adequate standing army. More important than either of these considerations was the deep-rooted conviction that a standing army was sooner or later bound to be used by the crown to enforce absolutist government. This fear of authoritarian rule was responsible for all that is most striking about the political edifice of the Commonwealth.

The salient features of this edifice were the oath of loyalty made by the incoming monarch to his subjects, and the clause which stipulated that if he defaulted on his obligations as laid down in the *Pacta Conventa* and the *Acta Henriciana* his subjects were automatically released from their obligations to him. The latter was an obvious recipe for disaster. It amounted to a right to mutiny if the king overstepped his powers – itself a question open to highly subjective interpretation. Yet, unlike the *liberum veto*, this principle was never carried through to its logical end. In 1607 and 1665 mutinies broke out in the spirit of this clause, but neither of them led to the dethronement of the monarch. They were intended as a final rap on the royal knuckles to make the king desist from his plans.

The release clause was only a long-stop measure in the whole scheme of checks and balances erected in order to make sure that power was never concentrated in too few hands. It also proclaimed the basis of the relationship between king and subject. Ruler and ruled were bound by a bilateral contract which placed obligations on both and had to be respected by both. This notion of a contract between the throne and the people was almost entirely absent from the political mind of Europe at the time – only in England were the germs of such ideas in evidence. In Poland the contract freely entered into by both sides was the cornerstone of government.

While the Habsburgs of Austria, the Bourbons of France, the Tudors of England, and every other ruling house of Europe strove to impose centralised autocratic government, ideological unity and increasing control of the individual through a growing bureaucracy, Poland alone of all the major states took the opposite course. The Poles had made an article of faith of the principle that all government is undesirable, and strong government is strongly undesirable. This belief was not based on some kind of inherent love of chaos, but on a deeply felt conviction that one man had no right to tell another what to do, and that the quality of life was impaired by unnecessary administrative superstructure. That such ideals should be held by people who simultaneously oppressed their own subjects, the peasants, is neither novel nor exceptional. The Greek founders of modern political thought no less than the Fathers of the American Revolution applied a double standard which cannot be equated with hypocrisy.

These attitudes – the dislike of authority for its own sake, the rejection of any theory that the public good could be served by exerting pressure on the individual, and the belief in the inalienable rights and dignity of the individual – were not new in Poland. They had been in evidence throughout the Middle Ages, and they are very much in evidence at the present time. It was in the sixteenth century that they became institutionalised, in what was, by any standards, an unusual and admirable constitution.

7

The Kingdom of Erasmus

'Polonia mea est.'
Erasmus of Rotterdam to
William Warham, Archbishop of
Canterbury

In the early 1600s the Polish Commonwealth was the largest state in Europe, with 990,000 square kilometres. The nature of this vast expanse varied from the undulating landscape of Wielkopolska to the flatness of Mazovia and the dense forests of Lithuania, from the mountains of the Tatra to the swamps of Byelorussia, from the forests and lakes of Mazuria to the wild plains of Podolia rolling away into the distance, which the Poles referred to as 'Ukraina', meaning 'margin' or 'edge'. The Polish heartlands were rich and cultivated. As well as grain, they produced a variety of fruit, including peaches and nuts, figs and melons, which a contemporary claimed 'can boldly rival the fruit of Hungary and Italy.' Wine was produced from grapes grown on the sunny slopes south-east of Kraków and along the course of the Vistula. Wool and down were exported to England and Holland. Rock-salt was abundant, as well as other minerals, such as iron, lead, copper, silver and lapis lazuli.

The Mazovian plain afforded little above a livelihood for its inhabitants. Lithuania was rich in the wealth of the forest – furs, wax, honey, timber, pitch – and its woods were a haven for bears, wolves, lynxes, elks, aurochs and bison, while the coastal regions yielded quantities of amber. The plains of the Ukraine effortlessly bore bountiful harvests and fed herds of cattle which provided meat for most of southern Germany.

The population of the Commonwealth in 1600 was, at ten million, equal to that of Italy and the Iberian Peninsula, twice that of England, and two-thirds that of France. Only 40 per cent were Poles, and they were concentrated in about 20 per cent of the area. The settled peasantry was made up of three principal ethnic groups – Polish, Lithuanian and Ruthene – and its lifestyle varied considerably across the country. The free, land-owning peasantry of Wielkopolska nourished themselves 'main-ly with pork, fish and vegetables . . . mutton, veal and beef . . . both wheaten bread and wine.' The increasingly burdened rural proletariat of Mazovia ate less well, while the primitive serfs of Lithuania and Byelorussia survived on black bread, gruels, root vegetables, and whatever mushrooms and fruit they could gather.

The cities too were far from uniform. The great trading emporium of Gdańsk, almost a city-state in itself, was preponderantly German. Nearby lay the smaller but equally busy port of Elbing, which had a large colony of English and Scots. Kraków and Wilno were full of Hungarians and Italians. Lwów, a city with an individual outlook, both politically and culturally, and the only city apart from Rome to have three Christian Archbishoprics, was made up of Poles, Germans, Italians and Armenians. Almost every town also had its Jewish community. In the north, where certain cities enjoyed exemptions under medieval charters granted by the Teutonic Order, the Jews were confined to a specific quarter. In the rest of the Commonwealth they settled where they would, and there were quantities of small towns in the south and east which were almost exclusively made up of Jews. The other foreign minorities spoke Polish and Latin as well as their own languages, but the Jewish community, which accounted for nearly ten per cent of the entire population, led a life of its own, communicating almost exclusively in Hebrew or Yiddish, while the Karaite Jews spoke Tatar.

A charter of 1551 set up what was in effect a Jewish state within the state. Local Jewish communes (*Kahal*) sent deputies to a national assembly (*Vaad*) which governed the whole community. It passed its own laws, assessed its own taxes, funded and regulated its own legal system and institutions, communicating directly with the crown, not the Seym. The next hundred years saw a remarkable flourishing of this community, which grew confident and assertive. Jealous merchants in Lwów complained in 1630 of the Jews behaving 'like lords, driving in carriages, in coaches-and-six, surrounded by pages and grand music, consuming costly liquors in silver vessels, behaving publicly with pomp and ceremony.' They were rich merchants and bankers, small traders and inn-keepers, artisans and farmers, and above all they were agents, factors and doctors. Every village had one or two Jews, every little town had its community, with synagogue and ritual baths and its own private existence, rich in its own lore.

The szlachta's lifestyle also varied dramatically. The wealthiest could compare with any grandees in Europe, the poorest were the menial servants of the rich. In between, they might be wealthy landowners or humble homesteaders ploughing and harvesting with their own hands, barefoot and in rags, poorer than many a peasant. The level of education was just as variable, religious affiliation was multifarious, and everyone spoke a different language. Six were recognised for legal purposes; Polish, Latin, Ruthene, Hebrew, German and Armenian. The szlachta nevertheless evolved an exceptionally homogeneous culture and outlook. Not only was this culture highly representative of the various groups within the country, it was also imitated by the lower orders.

The outlook of the szlachta was deeply affected in the sixteenth century by two influences which might be thought mutually exclusive. The first was the discovery of ancient Rome, and the analogies increasingly made between its institutions, customs and ideology, and those of the Commonwealth. This affected the Poles' attitude to government and moulded the political edifice of the Commonwealth. It also affected styles. At the most superficial level it was responsible for the abandonment of the long hair of the late medieval period and the adoption of the 'Roman' haircut. It was instrumental in the wholesale acceptance of Renaissance forms in architecture. At the psychological level it gave the Poles a sense of belonging to a European family, based not on the Church of Rome or the Empire, but on the idea of Roman civilisation, whose legacy they now arrogated to themselves.

The second influence was more nebulous but far more pervasive. It stemmed from a theory elaborated by various writers at the beginning of the century to the effect that the Polish szlachta were not of the same Slav stock as the peasantry, but descendants of the Sarmatians, a warrior people from the Black Sea Steppe who had swept through South-Eastern Europe in the sixth century. This theory drew a neat pseudo-ethnic distinction between the political nation and the rest of the population, the plebs, and was accepted with enthusiasm by the multi-racial szlachta in spite of its illogicality. How far they really believed in it is not clear, but it was useful and appealing to this motley collection who were far more at home with the 'noble warrior' Sarmatian myth than with the image of Christian Chivalry, with all that this entailed in terms of fealty, homage, service, humility and vassalage.

In time, the Sarmatian ethic, or simply Sarmatism, supplanted others and grew into an all-embracing ideology, but in the sixteenth century its influence was visible principally in manners and tastes. As a result of contacts with Hungary and Ottoman Turkey various accoutrements of Persian origin were gradually incorporated into everyday wear and use. By the end of the century the Polish costume had come closer in style to that of the Turks than to any Western European apparel.

The szlachta did not like to put money away, and invested in things they could wear or use out in the open – clothes, jewels, arms, saddlery, horses, servants and almost anything else that could be paraded. Weapons were covered in gold, silver and precious stones. Saddles and bridles were embroidered with gold thread and sewn with sequins. It was common for a nobleman who had a number of fine horses and several caparisons to have them all harnessed and led along behind him by pages, rather than leave them at home where no one would be able to see them. The Poles were close to their horses, which were symbols of their warrior status, and looked after them with loving care. The horses were dressed in fine tack, covered in rich cloths, adorned with plumes and even wings, and, on high days and holidays, dyed. The dye was applied to the coat everywhere except for the back under the saddle, and sometimes the mane and tail would be dyed another colour for contrast. The most popular colour was cochineal, but at funerals, for instance, black and purple or green was a favourite combination.

Another area in which supposedly eastern atavisms were encouraged by Sarmatism was the love of ceremony. Hospitality was a way of showing respect and friendship, and rarely confined to providing adequate food and drink. Highly spiced with aromatic roots and herbs, the fare was not unlike Persian or north Indian cooking. A great deal of drinking accompanied this banqueting. Vodka and other spirits were never served at table or in the home, and the Poles drank wine, imported for the most part from Hungary and Moldavia, but also from France, Italy and even the Canary Islands and, in the following century, California. Beer was plentiful, and another common drink was mead, often cut with cherry or raspberry juice.

The Scots traveller Fynes Moryson noted that 'no countrey in Europe affoordes victuals at a lower rate' and marvelled at the 'strange cheapness of such necessaries'. Fortunes were nevertheless spent on extravagance and display. Where the money came from is not difficult to trace. The discovery of America flooded Europe with minerals and precious metals in the sixteenth century, and the eventual consequence of this was to raise prices of commodities such as food. Over the hundred years, the price at which Poles sold their agricultural produce went up by over 300 per cent. The actual buying power of what the szlachta had to sell went up against staple imports such as cloth, iron, wine, pepper, rice and sugar, by just over 90 per cent between 1550 and 1600. During the same period, the quantity exported more than doubled. The result was that landed Poles became a great deal richer in terms of cash to spend than their counterparts elsewhere in Europe.

This permitted increasing numbers of Poles to travel abroad. They did so primarily in order to study at foreign universities, because in the 1530s the Jagiellon University went into decline, and henceforth catered principally to burghers and clerics from the lower orders. Lutherans might send their sons to study at Wittenberg and Calvinists at Basel, for religious reasons, but the most popular universities were those of Italy. Between 1501 and 1605 Polish students consistently made up at least a quarter of the whole student body at the University of Padua. As they grew richer, they began to mix tourism with study, and by the end of the century noblemen young and old set off on a grand tour to broaden their minds. The most immediate consequence was that various models and amenities seen in Italy were brought home. The wealthy would come back loaded with pictures and sculpture, books and objects. Once home, they would set about embellishing their own surroundings along the lines observed abroad.

In 1502 Prince Zygmunt returned from his travels bringing with him an architect from Florence, Francesco Fiorentino. In 1506 Zygmunt became king, and commissioned Fiorentino to rebuild the Royal Castle on the Wawel. Keeping to the existing layout, the architect created three residential wings and one curtain wall enclosing the courtyard with three tiers of galleries. The work, started in 1507, was taken over by another Florentine, Bartolomeo Berecci. Berecci had come to Kraków in 1516 and was given the task of building a mausoleum for the king. Completed in 1531, the square, lantern-domed chapel is one of the finest pieces of Italian Renaissance architecture north of the Alps.

These two buildings were beacons which set off a chain-reaction throughout the country, providing work for three new architects from Tuscany, Filippo di Fiesole, Nicolo di Castiglione and Giovanni Cini. The Zygmunt Chapel was widely copied: Primate Łaski had a similar one built for himself at Gniezno, Bishop Krzycki at Pułtusk, and Bishop Tomicki in Kraków. The much-admired colonnades of the Wawel inspired magnates who were building new residences for themselves.

By the 1550s the Tuscan architects were joined by others. The only major one to come from Florence was Santi Gucci. Bernardino di Zanobi de Gianotis was a Roman; and so was Paulo Dominici; Giovanni Maria Padovano, Pietro di Barbona and Bernardo Morando came from Padua; Giovanni Battista Quadro was from Lugano, and Galeazzo Appiani from the Grisons. As well as local variants, they introduced the new Mannerist style. In the north of the country, Gdańsk played host to Anton van Obergen, Wilhelm van dem Blocke and Jan Vredeman de Vries, who, ably emulated by the local architect Jan Strakowski, rebuilt large areas of the city in the Dutch Mannerist style.

This diversity was compounded by local factors. One was the contribution of Polish masons such as Benedict of Sandomierz, responsible for the stonework in the Wawel of 1511–30, who introduced his own blend of Gothic and Renaissance decoration. Native architects such as Tomasz of Lwów, Jan Michałowicz, Wawrzyniec Lorek, Tomasz Grzymała and Gabriel Słoński added a variety of home-grown elements. Polish clients often insisted on the incorporation of Gothic motifs in Renaissance buildings for traditional reasons. The climate played a part as well, since

45 Courtyard of the Royal Castle on Wawel hill in Kraków, begun in 1507 by Francesco Fiorentino, completed in the 1530s by Bartolomeo Berecci. A unique feature are the tall columns of the third tier, which successfully dealt with the visual heaviness of the pitched roofs and the shadow of the overhanging eaves made necessary by the northern climate. This was the first major application of Italian Renaissance architecture in Poland, and had an immediate impact all over the country.

46 The manor house of the Grudziński family at Poddębice, built in 1610.

47 Chełmno Town Hall, 1567–70, a fine example of Polish Renaissance architecture. The windows in the second storey were pierced later; originally everything above the first coping was only decorative parapet, designed to hide the pitched roof which clashed stylistically with the Renaissance façade.

48 *(Above)* The Chapel of St Anne At Pińczów, built c. 1600 by Santi Gucci.

49 One of the granaries which lined the Vistula at Kazimierz Dolny, whence the grain was despatched by raft to Gdańsk. The fabulous profits that flowed from the grain trade are reflected in the decoration of these store-houses, which date from the first decades of the 17th century.

50 The Parish Church of Kazimierz Dolny, built 1610–13 by 'Jacobus Balin, Italus, murarius Lublinensis', as he signed himself, is one of the finest examples of the Lublin type of Renaissance-Mannerist church-building which burgeoned in the first decades of the 17th century.

51 Interior of the small Mannerist Camaldolite Church of Rytwiany, decorated in the 1620s. The paintings are by Venante da Subiaco, the plaster-work by Giovanni-Battista Falconi.

52   Baranów, built in the 1580s for Andrzej Leszczyński, probably by the Florentine architect Santi Gucci. It is a good example of the Renaissance magnate's residence, constructed on a traditional castle plan, with towers, curtain walls and a central courtyard (**53**).

the need for pitched roofs threatened to cancel out the aesthetic impact of a Renaissance façade unless they could be hidden in some way.

From this mixture evolved a distinctively Polish version of Italian Renaissance architecture, which was then re-exported to Bohemia, Muscovy and Silesia. The first major building to display the pronounced characteristics of this style was the Sukiennice, the Cloth Hall of Kraków. Reconstructed by Padovano after a fire in 1555, it was the product of many of these influences, including an additional one – recently introduced fire regulations which stipulated that all roofs in the city must be surrounded by a wall. This meant that the decorative parapet running along the top of the façade was raised. Padovano, a sculptor by training, decided to make a feature of it. The effect was so successful that the idea was widely adopted as the chief decorative feature of most secular façades, often constituting up to one third of the height of the entire elevation.

All these elements were used to great effect on the residences of magnates. The addition of colonnaded galleries around a severe medieval courtyard introduced elegance and intimacy into the building. The replacement of medieval machicolations and battlements with a decorative frieze beautified the dour walls and towers. New residences were still conceived as castles. In the 1550s Tomasz Grzymała built a country villa for Zygmunt Augustus at Niepołomice which kept to a castle plan, and in the 1580s the Calvinist magnate Andrzej Leszczyński erected a similar residence at Baranów. Krasiczyn, built for Stanisław Krasicki by Galeazzo Appiani, is another example of this juxtaposition of Gothic framework and Renaissance decoration. The castle is in the form of a square with four round corner towers and a rectangular one over the central gateway, which was approached by a drawbridge over the moat. The outer walls, pierced by many windows, are only defensive in principle, and the parapets are no more than a delicate filigree of stonework. The courtyard is more redolent of an opera-set than of a castle, with arcades, galleries and loggias breaking up the formality.

The new style also affected the smaller country houses of the wealthy szlachta, but for the most part these were constructed of wood. The only major wooden buildings of the period to have survived into this century were synagogues. Judging by the virtuosity of their architecture, wooden country houses must indeed have been, as one contemporary French traveller put it, 'the most artistically constructed bonfires one could imagine'.

In the second half of the sixteenth and the first quarter of the seventeenth centuries Poland came closest to producing its own style in architecture by selecting a number of features of different origin and developing them together in an original way. Both the selection and the development vividly illustrate the divergent influences which made up Polish taste. The same instincts that fed on Sarmatism are undoubtedly largely responsible for the extravagance and the fantasy displayed by this type of building. It also reflected an attempt to give form to some of the classical ideals that the educated szlachta had embraced. Many of the important buildings of the period are public buildings, and they embody the spirit that was responsible for constructing the Commonwealth, the Polish utopia.

Nowhere is this spirit more in evidence than in the largest, the most monumental, and the most ambitious building project of the age – the city of Zamość. Nowhere can one find a more obvious connection between ideal and practice. And few individuals offer as complete a picture of the contradictions of the age as does its creator, who was both a child of the Renaissance and a forerunner of a new baroque plutocracy, a libertarian and an autocrat, one of the creators of the constitution, who sowed some of the first seeds of its corruption.

Jan Zamoyski was born in 1542, the son of a Calvinist 'backbench' senator. As a young man he completed courses at the Sorbonne and at the new Collège de France, then at the University of Padua, of which he became Rector. While there, he published a treatise on Roman constitutional history and became a Catholic. He returned to Poland with a letter of recommendation from the Senate of Venice to Zygmunt Augustus, who employed him as a secretary. Politically ambitious, he made his mark during the first interregnum, and was the first to combine the offices of Chancellor, which he obtained in 1578, and Hetman, which he became in 1581. He married, among others, the daughter of the dynastically-minded Mikołaj Radziwiłł 'the Black', and later the niece of the second elected king of Poland. Whether he aspired to the crown himself is not clear, but he set a pattern of independence and aloofness from royal authority which was to be followed by most magnates in the next century.

In 1571 Zamoyski inherited four villages, a number of small pieces of land, and the rich Starosty of Bełz. A tough businessman, he methodically set about enlarging this estate, gradually squeezing out adjacent landowners and buying out the senior branch of his family from the seat of Zamość. By 1600 he owned 6,500 square kilometres in one block, as well as countless other estates, properties in all the major cities, and thirteen lucrative starosties. Including royal lands, his property covered 17,500 square kilometres.

In 1580 he began to build New Zamość. It was to be an ideal city, a platonic concept, laid out geometrically according to symbolic axes and points of reference, and before a stone was laid he and his architect, Bernardo Morando, had meticulously planned the whole. It was dominated at one end by his own palace, and at the centre by the town hall. Other major buildings included the guild hall, the Catholic Collegiate Church, the Franciscan Church, the Armenian Church, the Orthodox Church, the synagogue, the university, the library, the arsenal, the public baths, and the three market squares. The city was underpinned by a sophisticated sewage system and surrounded by star-shaped fortifications of the most modern type, flanked by seven bastions and pierced by five gates.

Zamość made economic sense. It was settled by large numbers of Hispanic Jews, Italians, Scotsmen, Armenians, Turks and Germans, who could provide everything from medical facilities to a cannon foundry, from jewellery to printing presses. By endowing his vast estate with a capital city, Zamoyski turned it into a self-sufficient state, and all the profits, levies and dues on commerce and industry which would otherwise have gone to the royal cities or the treasury went into his own pocket. The idea was widely copied. In 1594 the Żółkiewski family founded their administrative capital at Żółkiew, which by 1634 when it passed to the Sobieski was a flourishing centre with fifteen different guilds. Soon every magnate was building a private town for himself, a trend that contributed to the decline of the old cities of the Commonwealth.

Zamość is nevertheless unique. It is a perfect model of Polish Renaissance-Mannerist style in every function – ecclesiastical, administrative, military, palatial, sanitary and domestic. This unity did not stop at the design of the streets and the public buildings. Every merchant's house, both inside and out, echoed this perfectionism. The client worked closely with his architect. While conducting a military campaign he wrote letters to Flanders to specify themes for the tapestries he had ordered, and sent sketches as well as instructions to Domenico Tintoretto in Venice explaining how he wanted the alter-pieces painted.

The purpose was not merely to achieve beauty. In accordance with the tenets of Renaissance philosophy it was to combine functionalism with aesthetic perfection in order to create the ideal environment. Every element was of importance, and if there was one that overshadowed the others, it was probably the university, opened in 1594. More time was lavished on this project than on any other, with much thought given to what subjects should be taught, how and by whom in order to produce the ideal citizen of the Commonwealth.

This unbounded faith that science and learning could breed perfect citizens, that ideal conditions could produce political harmony, that artistic unity could physically enhance life – the belief, in a word, that utopia could be built, was fundamental to the course Poland took in the sixteenth century. It was the product of over a century of prosperity and security, of political self-confidence based on the civil liberties of the citizen, and finally of an impressive legacy of political and social thought which continued to spread and develop through the printed word. There may not have been very much awaiting publication when the first press was set up at Kraków in 1473, but by the early 1500s the widespread urge to leap into print was evidenced by the proliferation of presses in a number of provincial cities. While originally legislation demanded that all books be passed by the Rector of the Jagiellon University, the executionist movement won a notable victory in 1539 by obtaining a royal decree on the absolute freedom of the press.

Only a fraction of the existing literary heritage was in the vernacular, which was still orthographically inchoate and marked by regional variation. Atlases and geographical works published between 1500 and 1520, and works on the history of Poland that appeared in the following decades, helped to standardise the spelling of place-names. The publication of large numbers of books in Polish from the 1520s imposed uniformity of spelling and grammar. In 1534 Stefan Falimierz published the first Polish medical dictionary; in 1565 Grzepski published his technical handbook *Geometria*. The six translations of the New Testament – Königsberg (1551), Lwów (Catholic, 1561), Brześć (Calvinist, 1563), Nieśwież (Arian, 1570), Kraków (Jesuit, 1593), Gdańsk (Lutheran, 1632) – constituted an exercise in Polish semantics. In 1568 the first systematic Polish grammar was compiled by Piotr Stojeński, an Arian of French origin; in 1564 Jan Mączyński issued his Polish-Latin lexicon at Königsberg; and finally, in 1594 the writer Górnicki and the poet Kochanowski published a standard Polish orthography which regulated spelling definitively. Latin nevertheless continued in use, and predominated in religious and political literature for some time, both because it was a better tool for theoretical and philosophical writing, and because it was universal to Europe.

The most striking aspect of Polish thought at the time was its profound preoccupation with public affairs and government. The discussion on the Polish body politic was opened by Jan Ostroróg with his *Monumentum pro Reipublicae Ordinatione* (1467), which argued for a more just social and political system. This tradition was taken up by Marcin Bielski (1495–1575) and Marcin Kromer (1512–89) who used books on the history of Poland to polemicise about the rights and wrongs of the system. Stanisław Orzechowski contributed *Quincunx*, an extraordinary attempt to use geometry to establish the ideal form of government. Andrzej Frycz-Modrzewski (1503–72), a royal secretary and Zygmunt Augustus' delegate to the Council of Trent in 1545, and a close friend of Melanchthon, with whom he had studied at Wittenberg, published a treatise on the Polish legal system, and in 1554 a longer work, *De Republica Emendanda*, setting out a political utopia of striking radicalism.

Most of this literature was fervently idealistic, and, like the work of the eighteenth-century *philosophes*, pervaded by the mirage of an ideal condition. It represented existing abuses and injustice as perversions of this condition, rather than as inherent in human affairs. It singled out the ill-treatment of the peasants as an example. These writers were correct to point out that this was a relatively recent development caused by the greed of landowners, but they erroneously saw the motives as equally recent developments, rather than as elements in a stratified society. It was the notion that by curing the soul one would automatically cure the blisters on the feet, which more pragmatic schools of thought would deal with by prescribing a good pair of shoes.

The next generation of political writers applied their ideas to actual political institutions. Paprocki's *O Hetmanie* was an attempt to define the role and duty of the Hetman; Warszewicki's *De Legato* did the same for those engaged in diplomacy; Górski's *Rada Pańska*, Zamoyski's *De Senatu Romano*, and Goślicki's *De Optimo Senatore*, all lectured on the conduct of affairs of state. Although they were more practical they still clung to the belief that good government depended on good people rather than on strong institutions which would force people to be good, or at least to pretend to be good. As Jan Zamoyski said in the speech inaugurating the university he had founded: 'Republics will always be as good as the upbringing of their young men.'

Not all the political literature was as high-sounding, and many writers used more popular literary vehicles for their message. Marcin Kromer employed the classic medieval form in his *Conversation between a Soldier and a Monk*; the historian Marcin Bielski wrote versified satires such as *The Women's Seym*; Biernat of Lublin translated Aesop's *Fables*, which he prefaced with a mock life of the author, in whom he created the first of a long line of Polish Candide figures. A similar figure, the soldier Albertus, a cross between Sancho Panza and Schweik, rapidly became the stock hero in a tradition of semi-political plebeian verse and drama which flourished in the second half of the century.

More unexpected than the outburst of political polemic was the abundant literary flowering which took place at the same time. The first Polish lyric poet was Klemens Janicki (1516–43). The son of a peasant, he entered the priesthood and studied at the universities of Bologna and Padua, where he was crowned poet laureate by Cardinal Bembo, and then returned to his native land. Like some nineteenth-century Romantic, Janicki spent his youth in frivolity and what was left of his short life contemplating his unhappiness. He was self-obsessed and fascinated by the conflict between emotion and reason. With his delicacy of sentiment and his affecting imagery, Janicki was a fine poet, capable of expressing himself in simple Polish, as well as in the elegant and lucid Latin in which he composed most of his works.

Mikołaj Rej of Nagłowice (1505–69) was an entirely different sort of man, a country gentleman totally devoid of the *angst* which gripped Janicki. Not a great writer, he was more of a literary dabbler, a gossip, a moralist dominated by topicality. He rushed into print with astonishing prodigality, sometimes borrowing ideas or whole passages from classical or foreign authors in order to produce his homespun philosophy. Most of his poems and stories, written in robust Polish, are vehicles for religious, political or social polemic. With his eye for the vignette and the grotesque, Rej is often reminiscent of Rabelais, and he gives a vivid picture of the life and ways of Polish society.

There was no question of the szlachta dominating the literary scene, either as writers or as readers. By the end of the fifteenth century over 80 per cent of the 6,000 parishes in Wielkopolska and Małopolska had schools attached to them. The resultant upsurge in literacy is reflected in the range of style, as well as in the diverse origins of the authors. While the peasant Janicki poured out his scarred sensibilities the nobleman Wawrzyniec Korwin (d.1527) composed Sapphic odes. The Mayor of Lublin, Sebastian Fabian Kłonowic (1545–1602) wrote lengthy works in Latin and Polish, of which the most noteworthy is the poem *Roxolania*, a florid description of the Ukraine. Jan Rybinski, the son of a Czech Arian who moved to Gdańsk, began by writing Latin verse, but then turned to Polish, in which he wrote some beautiful poems in the 1590s. These and a host of others were overshadowed by one figure who dominated the second half of the century.

Jan Kochanowski (1530–84) was a nobleman of average means who had studied at Kraków, Königsberg and Padua. He spent some years at court considering a career in the Church, and then retired to his estate of Czarnolas to enjoy a quiet life of writing. He was a humanist who looked on everything with the philosophical wonder of the Renaissance creature. He was a natural poet, prolific and imaginative, and his use of Polish, a language he did more than any other to enrich, was masterful and refined. His lyrical verse and court poems, *Fraszki*, endure in their charm, but it was *Psałterz Dawidów*, a paraphrase of the psalms of David, which won him immediate and lasting recognition. On retiring to his beloved Czarnolas, he wrote bucolic pieces exalting the pleasures and virtues of a life close to nature.

'Others may have marble halls, and line their walls with cloth of Gold. I, Lord, would live in this family nest. But grant me health and a clear conscience,' he wrote. God responded by shattering his happiness. The poet's three-year-old daughter Urszula died suddenly, triggering a spiritual crisis which was to produce the first great work of art in the Polish language – *Treny*. Kochanowski applied the Greek form of the *threnos*, the formal lament for the great, to the diminutive subject, and this bathos lends power to his exploration of human suffering. The nineteen poems of the cycle are a progress through the various stages of the experience of loss. With its moving yet lucid analysis of human feelings, of a mind wavering between despair, reason and faith, and its total lack of self-dramatisation, this lament remains one of the finest works in Polish literature.

Kochanowski did not avoid the political subjects popular with other writers, and he could be lapidary in his social comment. His outlook was that of the middle szlachta – reformist in religion and executionist in politics – and he was preoccupied with the good of the Commonwealth. This comes out strongly in one of his most unusual works, his only sally into drama.

Although there was dramatic entertainment at court from the 1520s and a number of professional troupes active around the country, the theatre was not as popular or developed in Poland as in England and France. The repertoire consisted of adaptations of Greek drama or vigorous slapstick comedy for the lower orders, and Kochanowski's short play *The Dismissal of the Greek Envoys* is the only exception. The characters in the play are not really people, but in effect the voices of collective interests, and the play is not about their feelings, but about the fate of Troy, which is a sort of corporate character. This curious use of dramatis personae to represent the collective is seminal because it foreshadows nineteenth- and twentieth-century Polish drama, the mainstream of which is neither lyrical nor psychological, but ethical and political.

The state of mind which defined itself in the words of these writers has in more ways than one endured to the present day. The style, not only of writing, but also of thought and behaviour reflected in this literature is a curious mixture of ideological bombast, emotional sincerity, and healthy cynicism. The three seem to coexist quite happily, as do the two most pervasive themes. One is the almost obsessive feeling of responsibility for and compulsion to participate in the organic life of the Commonwealth at every level. This is evident not only in the political literature and the religious debate, but in virtually all writing which is not concentrated on specific themes such as love or death.

The other is the quest for Arcadia. If political writing rested on the myth of an 'ideal condition' which had been perverted and must be restored, the literary imagination translated this into a quest for the state of innocence as epitomised by country life. This imagery is apparent in the works of Kochanowski, but the poet who expanded and defined it was Szymon Szymonowicz (1558–1629). In 1614 he published a collection of poems in Polish entitled *Sielanki*, a word he coined to mean idylls. Although influenced by Virgil and the idylls of Theocritus, his were not the pastoral dreams of faun and nymph, but visions of a rustic Eden populated with superstitious peasants and supine squires.

The *sielanka* theme haunted Polish thought and literature, sometimes assuming the proportions of a cult. Inspired by the quest for a lost innocence, which implied a rejection of corruption, it could take many

NICOLAVS COPERNICVS

The Humanist tradition: **54** (*Top left*) Mikołaj Kopernik, student of the Jagiellon University, priest, poet, lawyer, engineer, soldier and astronomer. **55** (*top right*) Jan Kochanowski, the greatest poet of the Polish Renaissance: effigy on his tomb in the parish church of Zwoleń. **56** (*Below left*) Sebastian Petrycy (1554–1626), Professor of medicine at the Jagiellon University, deputy to the Seym and political writer. **57** (*Below right*) Stanisław Bieżanowski (1528–93) Professor of Poetry at the Jagiellon University.

forms. In the minds of the nineteenth-century Romantics, for instance, it became confused with the quest for the lost motherland, and implied a rejection of political reality. More often, it took the form of intellectual withdrawal from the world which, at its worst, could sanctify intellectual escapism and make the spirit of enquiry suspect.

There is a strong, if undefinable, connection between these states of mind and Poland's place in European culture. By the middle of the sixteenth century, the Poles were as widely travelled as any nation, and the Commonwealth saw more foreigners than most countries. It is not always easy to trace the progress of Poles abroad, when a Jan Łaski became Johannes à Lasco, a Frycz-Modrzewski, Fricius Modrevius, a Goślicki, Grimaldus, and a Nowopolski, Novicampianus, but it is known that Kochanowski knew Ronsard, that Stanisław Reszka and others were friends of Tasso, and that a considerable number of Poles, including Tomicki, Krzycki, and of course Jan Łaski, were closely associated with Erasmus of Rotterdam. Leonard Coxe, who taught at Cambridge and the Sorbonne before becoming professor at the Jagiellon University, remarked in a letter to an English friend that the Poles walked, talked, ate and slept Erasmus, beginning with King Zygmunt, who wrote to him in a familiar style usually reserved for sovereign princes.

The literature of other countries was avidly read in Poland, and it is worth noting that Kochanowski was inspired to write his *Psałterz Dawidów* by reading Buchanan's paraphrase of the Psalms of David. For those whose knowledge of languages was restricted, there was no lack of translations. Łukasz Górnicki rendered into Polish Castiglione's *Libro del Cortegiano*, the textbook of manners and thought for the Renaissance nobleman; Piotr Kochanowski, the nephew of the poet, produced fine translations of Tasso's *Orlando Furioso* and *Gerusalemme Liberata*; and a number of lesser figures published hundreds of translations or paraphrases of foreign texts in cheap editions.

Polish poetry may not have been read widely in other countries, but the political and religious works penetrated everywhere. Modrzewski's *De Republica Emendanda* was available in Latin, French, Italian, Spanish and Russian. Goślicki's *De Optimo Senatore* was published in Venice, Basel and London. Kromer's *Confessio* ran into several dozen editions of the original Latin text in various countries, and was translated into Polish, Czech, German, Dutch, French and English. Technical works such as Grzepski's *Geometria* were reissued abroad as contributions to scientific knowledge, and finally there was the man whom Melanchthon referred to as 'the Sarmatian astronomer who moves the Earth and stops the Sun', and Luther simply called 'that fool' – Copernicus.

Mikołaj Kopernik was born at Toruń in 1473, the son of a merchant. He enrolled at the Jagiellon University in 1491 to study astronomy, and later joined the priesthood, which permitted him to travel and pursue his studies at the universities of Bologna, Ferrara and Padua. After returning home, he became administrator of the bishopric of Warmia, but also worked as a lawyer, doctor, architect, and even soldier, commanding a fortress in the last clash with the Teutonic Order in 1520. He built himself an observatory and continued to work on the great discovery he had made, that the sun and not the earth was the centre of the planetary system. The results, published in 1543, the year of his death, under the title *De Revolutionibus Orbium Coelestium*, produced shock-waves the length and breadth of Europe.

It is true that in the plastic arts Poland like many others was overshadowed by Italy and the Netherlands, and that home-grown painters and sculptors contributed nothing of original value to the legacy of the age, but there was an exception in the field of music. Zygmunt I was a liberal patron and made musicians welcome at his court. In 1540 he established the Capella Rorantistarum, renowned as one of the best male choirs in Europe, and by the next decade Kraków had become an important musical centre, attracting many foreign composers. Among those who stayed for longer periods were Marenzio of Brescia, the famous organist of St Mark's in Venice, Claudio Merulo, and the Hungarian lutenist Valentine Bakfark, who published his best works there in 1565. Among Polish composers were Sebastyan of Felsztyn, Mikołaj of Kraków, Cyprian Bazylik and Wacław of Szamotuły, who wrote religious music, dances and songs. In the 1540s Jan of Lublin compiled two organ tablatures which are treasures of Renaissance music, and a couple of decades later Wojciech Długoraj produced a volume of music for the lute. The second half of the century was dominated by Marcin Leopolita, appointed Compositor Cantus by the king in 1560, whose Easter Mass is an outstanding work; and Mikołaj Gomółka (1539–1609), the greatest Polish composer of the Renaissance. Many of his works have not survived, but perhaps the most original one is *Melodye na Psałterz Polski*, written in 1580, which set Kochanowski's psalms to music in an idiom perfectly suited to their mood.

The works of these composers have been found as far away as England and Spain, and the artists also travelled. One who achieved international fame in Paris was the lutenist Jakub Polak, sometimes known as Jacob de Reys (1545–1605). The same is true of the foremost composer of the early baroque, Mikołaj Zieleński (1551–1615), who was Kapellmeister to Primate Baranowski at Łowicz before setting off on his travels. He came under the influence of Gabrielli while in Venice, where he published two volumes of vocal works and fantasies for harpsichord and strings in 1611.

Erasmus was prompted to 'congratulate the Polish nation . . . which . . . can now compete with the foremost and most cultivated in the world.' But this could very well serve as an epitaph, for a highwater mark had been reached in terms of Polish participation in the cultural life of Europe. A crucial role in this was played by language. For centuries the native tongue had been supplemented by Latin, which enjoyed the twin benefit of being a developed instrument of communication and an international medium without which the Poles would have been utterly isolated. As Fynes Moryson noted in 1593, 'there is not a ragged boy, nor a smith that shooes your horse, but he can speake Latten readily.' During the sixteenth century the first of these benefits dwindled as Polish rapidly evolved into a lucid, harmonious language as efficient as Latin for the expression of ideas. The second benefit of Latin also began to wane, as a general drift throughout Europe towards the vernacular began to restrict its international usefulness. The same was true within the Commonwealth itself; the city dwellers of Flemish or German origin, the Scotsmen of Elbing and other minorities tended more and more to speak Polish, while the Lithuanian and Ruthene inhabitants of the eastern areas were more easily reached by Polish, having never had Latin even in their liturgy. In the 1530s the sermons given in St Mary's, the chief place of worship of the rich German merchants of Kraków, began to be given in Polish. From 1543 the decisions of the Seym were published in Polish not Latin, and the same went for legal documents. As Polish became the language of state and the language of literature, Polish thought became increasingly inaccessible to Western Europe. On the other hand, the use of the vernacular enhanced its influence in other areas.

In a poem he wrote to Erasmus, Bishop Krzycki assured him that the Poles were not only reading all his works, but also passing them on 'across the Don'. The Russian world, which never had the Latin lifeline, was almost entirely dependent on Poland for access to classical and contemporary European literature. It was from Kochanowski's translations of Tasso, for example, that the first Russian translations were made. Poland had become to Muscovy what Germany had for centuries been to Poland – a cultural broker. This permeated every facet of life: what in Poland, as in England, was known as 'the French disease' was known in Muscovy as 'the Polish disease'.

The Commonwealth was the disseminator of things Western and the printing house of Eastern Europe. The first book, a Bible, to be printed in Ruthene (the language mid-way between Polish and Russian spoken by the population of Byelorussia and the Ukraine) was published in Wilno in 1517. The first book in Lithuanian was printed at Königsberg in 1547. More surprisingly, the first printed work in Romanian was published in Kraków, from which also came quantities of books in Hungarian. By the end of the century the printers of Wilno, Kraków and Lublin were making small fortunes from supplying Eastern European markets. The Polish presses also printed all the Hebrew religious texts for the European diaspora, and published the Jewish theological debates of this important period.

The Polish szlachta continued to learn Latin for two more centuries, partly for symbolic reasons. Italian, too, was widely known, but German, which had been highly useful until the end of the Middle Ages, was gradually dropped. The issue of language complemented broader developments. Partly as a result of the Reformation, Germany's importance as a source of culture declined for Poland. France and Spain were in the grip of the Counter-Reformation and increasingly absolutist government, which made them unattractive to the Poles. Direct links had been forged with Italy, and Poland itself had acquired most of the amenities for which it had in the past been dependent on others. If the fifteenth-century Pole had seen himself as living on the edge of a flat earth whose centre was somewhere far away to the West, his counterpart in the late sixteenth had a very different view. He saw Poland not as peripheral to Europe, but as central to its own world.

The East had never had much to offer except for Tatar raids and Muscovite maraudings, but in the course of the sixteenth century a new world came into view beyond these nuisances. Persian and Ottoman culture began to exert a strong fascination for Polish society. Apart from owning Turkish artefacts, Stanisław Lubomirski, Palatine of Kraków, also kept three eminent orientalists in his permanent entourage. Tomasz Zamoyski, son of the Chancellor and Hetman, was learning four languages at the age of eight; Latin, Greek, Turkish and Polish. By the time he had completed his early studies, he was fluent in not only Turkish, but also Tatar and Arabic. The Polish Commonwealth was turning into a hybrid synthesis of East and West, a melting-pot of different races, religions and cultures. As it withdrew more and more into this world it had created, Polish society appeared increasingly exotic to other Europeans, as incomprehensible, and seemingly absurd, as Turkey itself.

8

Democracy in Crisis

There was nothing oriental about the man the Poles chose as their new king in 1573. Nor was he the most likely candidate for the throne of the multi-denominational Commonwealth. A few months before the Seym passed its act on religious freedom, Henri de Valois, younger brother of Charles IX of France, took an enthusiastic part in the St Bartholomew's Day Massacre, personally taking potshots at fleeing Protestants.

The first election went remarkably smoothly. At the news of Zygmunt Augustus's death the szlachta was placed on full military alert to keep the peace within and discourage invasion from without, while the Convocation Seym gathered to thrash out the details. The tensions between Protestant and Catholic, szlachta and magnates, were eased in a spirit of compromise and restraint.

The pace livened when the candidates were announced and their agents arrived to press their respective suits. The candidates were Ernest of Habsburg, Henri de Valois, Ivan IV of Muscovy, and the two outsiders John III of Sweden and Stephen Bathory of Transylvania. A key figure was the late king's sister, Anna, universally respected as the last surviving member of the Jagiellon dynasty. Many took it as read that the successful candidate would marry her, thereby cementing his position on the throne and emulating the precedent set by Jagiełło himself, an assumption which she did much to further by her own influence. Others, including the majority of the Senate, suspected her ambition and saw her as an obstacle to establishing a new dynasty. Apart from being no beauty, Anna Jagiellon was well over fifty years old.

This did not stand in the way of the cunning agent of Henri de Valois, Jean de Monluc, Bishop of Valence, who quickly divined the princess's value and laid Gallic siege to her affections on behalf of his master. He assured her that the valiant prince, twenty-eight years her junior, was consumed with passion for her, caring but little for the Polish crown. The Habsburgs also tried subtlety, but it backfired. They sent two Czechs on the assumption that they would be more acceptable to their Slav cousins than a German. One started warning the Poles against the designs of the Habsburgs, and the other was suggested by a group of szlachta as a candidate for the throne himself.

The Muscovite candidature had been suggested on the grounds that the rising power of Muscovy might best be rendered harmless in the same way as that of Lithuania had been. If Poland could tame the fur-clad Jagiełło, then perhaps the Commonwealth could do the same with the Tsar. But Ivan the Terrible was not an alluring prospect, and even the most sanguine supporters of the idea had to admit that it was unrealistic.

With the Muscovite ruled out and the Habsburg rejected by the majority of the szlachta, the Frenchman emerged as the favourite, endorsed by the reticent yet unmistakable approval of Anna Jagiellon, whose vanity had been aroused. Over 50,000 szlachta turned up outside Warsaw to vote, accompanied by as many servants and attendants, all armed to the teeth. To the astonishment of the foreign observers present, no shot was fired or steel blooded in spite of the contentious issues involved. Henri de Valois was elected by an overwhelming majority, and a delegation was despatched to Paris.

Henri received the news as he was laying siege to the Protestants of La Rochelle, and hurried back to Paris to meet the delegation of eleven dignitaries and 150 szlachta who arrived from Warsaw on 19 August 1573. They were not there in such force just to impress the Parisians, which they did with their exotic clothes, their jewellery and their painted horses. Henri de Valois had to be fully acquainted with the conditions of his employment and obliged to accept them before he placed a foot on Polish soil. At a ceremony in Notre Dame on 10 September attended by the entire French court, he swore to observe the *Acta Henriciana*, named after him, laying down the constitutional obligations of the monarch, and the *Pacta Conventa*, which listed his personal undertakings.

The ceremony went perfectly until he came to the article in the *Henriciana* concerning religious freedom. He tried to mumble his way through, missing out the clause in question. The Poles, who had been alert to such a contingency, drew his attention politely to the fact that he had overlooked a clause. He demurred, but Jan Zborowski stepped forward, booming: 'Si non iurabis, non regnabis!' Henri swore. The French royal family were not going to let an oath stand in their way and Charles IX was even prepared to listen to the so-called *Postulata Polonica*, in which the Seym lectured him on his treatment of French Protestants.

Henri de Valois travelled to Poland overland and arrived in the middle of an exceptionally cold winter. The tight hose and light jerkins of the Frenchmen were no match for the climate, and by the time the royal party reached Kraków they were frozen and depressed by the sight of the snowy wastes. The king and his new subjects were in many respects ill-matched.

The mincing, scented young man, with his cascading earrings and his tight cod-piece, came as something of a shock to the robust Poles. In spite of this, and although he showed unwillingness to be bound by the *Pacta Conventa*, he was not unpopular. He was gallant towards Anna Jagiellon, though he made no move in the direction of marriage, and went out of his way to charm and captivate those he saw as the most important figures. But suddenly fate took a hand. On 30 May 1574 Charles IX died unexpectedly aged only twenty-four, and Henri became King of France.

His intention was to keep both crowns, a course of action favoured by some magnates, who could foresee that they would be free to rule in his absence. It was agreed that he would set off for France in the autumn, but Henri made his own plans. On the night of 18 June he slipped out of the Wawel and rode hard for the frontier. He was caught up with in Silesia by Jan Tenczyński, who begged him to return at once, but Henri dismissed him with vague promises.

The Poles felt deeply wounded by the behaviour of the king, and when the shock died away, a new question arose: was there or was there not an interregnum? It was a nice question, to which precedent afforded no answer. In the autumn letters were despatched to the newly-crowned Henri III of France, one from the Polish senators and deputies, one from the Lithuanians. The Poles gave an ultimatum – if he did not present himself in Kraków by 12 May 1575 the throne would be declared vacant. The Lithuanians merely pleaded for his return. Henri replied that he had every intention of keeping the Polish throne, and suggested sending his younger brother the Duc d'Alençon as Viceroy.

The Poles would have none of it, and called a new election. The bitter experience of the first had considerably dampened the optimism of the voters, and the magnates saw an opportunity of settling the question themselves as they had always aspired to do. The Senate conducted its own election and chose the Emperor Maximilian II, but as they gathered in Warsaw Cathedral to sing the *Te Deum*, in his name, the szlachta howled in protest. It was then that a minor candidate at the first election, Stephen Bathory, Duke of Transylvania, was suggested, and on 14 December 1575 he was acclaimed king by the szlachta. Bathory reached Kraków on 23 April of the following year, and was married to Anna Jagiellon and crowned on 1 May. He arrived in Poland without finery, accompanied only by a couple of regiments of Hungarian infantry. He bedded Anna dutifully, making it clear that he did not take the Polish throne lightly. A forthright man and an able general, he knew how to command, and one of his greatest assets was his intuitive gift for picking men who would serve him well. He appointed a new Chancellor, Piotr Wolski, and a new Vice-Chancellor, Jan Zamoyski, who was to become a close partner in all his enterprises and a mainstay of his rule.

The new king was in a difficult position, as Maximilian arranged an alliance with Muscovy and succeeded in getting the city of Gdańsk to declare itself for him. Stephen Bathory was not easily cowed, and he marched north to Gdańsk. On his way he called the Seym to Toruń, where he announced his intention of putting the country in order. Although he defeated the army sent out by Gdańsk, the prospect of a long siege was not alluring. Ivan the Terrible had invaded from the east, and the international situation was looking ugly. The king therefore seduced Gdańsk back to the fold with a number of trading concessions, and switched his attention to problems that had been brewing unchecked for decades while the Poles had been absorbed by their religious and political debates.

Dramatic shifts in power had been taking place all around Poland since 1515, when King Zygmunt the Old, the Emperor Maximilian I, and the Jagiellon King Louis of Hungary and Bohemia had met at Pressburg to discuss the future of East Central Europe. The two Jagiellons were then in possession of the areas coveted by the Habsburgs, but the still young Louis had no heir, and it was in order to avoid a war that the three met. The issue was settled amicably. It was agreed that Hungary and Bohemia would pass to the Habsburgs if Louis produced no heir, in return for which the Habsburgs bound themselves to eschew their traditional policy of supporting the Teutonic Knights and other enemies of Poland.

It was a measure of his apathy that Zygmunt did not press his case for areas which the Habsburgs could hardly have disputed. The last Slav prince of Szczecin-Pomerania, the heirless Bogusław X, wished to switch his vassalage from the Empire to King Zygmunt. Nothing was done, and when he died the Duchy reverted to the Empire. There was a similar situation in Silesia, where the towns and much of the gentry were German, but the rural population Polish. The area was still ruled by Piast princes, some of whom, like Jan III of Opole, spoke no German. They were vassals of the Bohemian crown, worn by Louis Jagiellon. When Louis was unexpectedly killed in 1526 at the battle of Mohacs his crown passed to the Habsburgs, so that when Jan III died in 1532 his principality automatically reverted to the Empire. Although several of the Piast dynasties in Silesia survived to the end of the following century, 1515 was the logical moment and the last opportunity for the obscure bonds of an outdated vassalage to be cut in favour of a more nationally-oriented arrangement.

Zygmunt displayed a similar attitude with regard to the Teutonic Knights. Monastic orders were seminally affected by Luther's teachings, and the Teutonic Knights were no exception. Grand Master Albrecht von Hohenzollern (who was King Zygmunt's nephew) and most of his knights came under Luther's spell just as Poland defeated them again, in 1520. Since the Vatican and the Empire had cast the Protestant knights adrift, there was nothing to prevent Poland from winding up the bankrupt crusading state. Instead, Zygmunt sanctioned its transformation into a secular duchy hereditary in the Hohenzollern family, who became vassals of the Polish crown. On 24 February 1525 Albrecht von Hohenzollern went down on his knees in the market square of Kraków and paid formal homage to Zygmunt as Duke of Prussia. Many Poles were unimpressed by the sight of the kneeling German. Cardinal Hosius called the king 'a madman who, being in a position to crush the vanquished, prefers instead to show mercy'. Even the court fool Stańczyk taunted the king on his folly, taunts which were fully justified two hundred and fifty years later.

The Livonian branch of the Knights also secularised, but their independence was under threat from the start. Denmark, which had long-standing interests in the area, dreamt of turning it into a colony, a dream shared by Sweden, while Muscovy saw a chance of gaining a coastline on the Baltic. Faced by this concert of rival interests, the Livonians could see no way of guaranteeing their continued existence other than by becoming vassals of the Commonwealth, which they duly did in 1561.

Livonia's adhesion to Poland only deepened a conflict with Muscovy which had begun in 1512. In that year the Tsar had made alliances with the Teutonic Order and the Empire, which enabled him to field a more modern army and contributed directly to his capture of Smolensk, the easternmost Polish bastion. Although a Polish army under Hetman Ostrogski gave his forces a drubbing at the battle of Orsza in 1514, the threat from the east would not go away. Throughout the 1550s and 1560s Ivan the Terrible made repeated attempts to slice through Lithuania to the sea.

In 1577 Ivan invaded Livonia once more, and while Lithuanian detachments managed to contain the invasion, Stephen Bathory decided that a conclusive war was called for. He made his preparations and in 1579 declared war on Muscovy. Having concentrated his forces near Wilno under Hetmans Mikołaj Mielecki of Poland and Mikołaj Radziwiłł of Lithuania, he moved on Polotsk, which he quickly captured. In the following year Stephen collected an army of 30,000, which moved out in three corps, one commanded by himself, the other two by Mikołaj Radziwiłł and Jan Zamoyski. The Poles took Vielikie Luki and other fortresses. In the following year, 1581, the Polish army besieged Pskov, which was ably defended by the brothers Ivan and Vasily Shuysky. As a terrible winter set in, King Stephen returned to Poland, leaving Zamoyski in command outside Pskov. Meanwhile negotiations had begun through the dubious good offices of the Jesuit Antonio Possevino, acting on instructions from Rome.

Although these campaigns have been glorified by nineteenth-century historians as national and religious crusades, the negotiators in this instance were an Italian Jesuit on behalf of Muscovy, and three Orthodox

– a Lithuanian, a Byelorussian and a Ukrainian – on behalf of the Polish Commonwealth. As the Polish army was freezing to death outside Pskov, the treaty of Jam Zapolski was finally signed on 15 January 1582, leaving the whole of Livonia as well as Polotsk and other areas under Polish rule.

The systematic way in which he and his trusted men carried through the Muscovite campaigns is characteristic of Stephen's reign as a whole. He abided by the constitution, but did not hesitate to use the powers it left him. He proved something of a disappointment to the executionists, who were instrumental in his election, by failing to reinforce the role of the Seym and rejecting their demands for reform. As he declared to the Toruń Seym at the beginning of his reign, he was '*rex non fictus necque pictus*' – a king, not a statue or a painting. In 1580 he even imposed censorship on political literature. This did not endear him to the deputies, but it helped to re-establish royal authority and respect for the crown. Unfortunately for the Commonwealth, Stephen Bathory died suddenly in December 1586, after a reign of only ten years.

The Commonwealth faced its third interregnum in the space of fourteen years, which fostered a feeling of impermanence and did nothing to contribute to the orderly conduct of the next election. Although the candidates included the late king's nephew and the new Tsar of Muscovy, the contest was essentially between Archduke Maximilian Habsburg and Zygmunt Vasa of Sweden. The Habsburg faction included all those disgruntled by the firm application of law under King Stephen and was strongly supported by the influence of Rome and the money of Philip II of Spain. With the great Armada about to sail against England, the Habsburgs were at the height of their aspirations to dominate Europe.

The anti-Habsburg camp lent their support to the only other likely candidate, Zygmunt Vasa, son of King John III of Sweden and Catherine Jagiellon, second sister of Zygmunt Augustus. The pro-Habsburg party attempted to force through their candidate, but they failed in the face of multitudes of impassive szlachta, and on 19 August 1587 Zygmunt Vasa was elected to rule as Zygmunt III. Three days later Maximilian invaded at the head of an army and laid siege to Kraków, but he was defeated by Hetman Zamoyski, who pursued him back into Silesia, routed him again, and took him prisoner.

When Zygmunt arrived in Kraków to take up his throne he enjoyed the accumulated popularity of his Jagiellon forbears and sealed this by his excellent command of the Polish language. The delight of the Poles was short-lived. The twenty-two-year-old king's difficult childhood had marked his character and his outlook indelibly. He was born in a dungeon where his parents had been imprisoned by the then king of Sweden. The only ray of light in this dismal incarceration had been brought by Polish Jesuit priests who had devoted themselves to his education. The results of this formation were that he was obsessively mistrustful and secretive, and a religious fanatic. The mention of religious toleration nauseated him. As the Papal Legate Annibale di Capua noted: 'King Stephen was good to soldiers, this one will be good to priests.'

The king's religious ideas quickly began to tell. His first appointments made it clear that Catholics were more likely to get the best offices. The Seym of 1589, which wanted to redraft the religious clauses of the Act of the Confederation of Warsaw in order to make them more binding, was overruled by the king and his supporters. A noble casualty of this bigotry was the Chancellor's project for tightening up election procedure. He proposed limiting the interregnum to a maximum of eight weeks, introducing voting by delegation from the seymiks (i.e. abolishing the universal vote) and, perhaps most important of all in view of later events, the rigorous enforcement of majority voting. At the king's insistence, the Primate introduced the *sine qua non* that all candidates to the throne must be Catholic, which guaranteed uproar in the Seym and rejection of the scheme. The king saw the causes of parliamentary reform and of religious liberty as being synonymous, and he made every attempt to sabotage any project which smacked of either.

He had been elected for anti-Habsburg reasons, and the attempt by Maximilian to usurp his throne seemed to underline this. Yet Zygmunt wasted little time in freeing the Archduke, marrying a Habsburg, and signing an 'eternal peace' with Vienna whose benefits for the Commonwealth were not apparent. His intentions were locked away behind a countenance of frigid reserve, and only the coterie of Jesuits perpetually in attendance were privy to them. With time, they began to reveal themselves. Zygmunt had been reared by his religious mentors as the future leader of the Counter-Reformation in Sweden, and therefore regarded the Polish throne as a means to an end. It seems he was prepared to hand over Poland to the Habsburgs in return for their support in reclaiming Sweden for himself and Catholicism, a Sweden enlarged by Polish provinces on the Baltic such as Livonia.

The Chancellor uncovered evidence of the king's machinations and in 1592 led the Seym in a formal inquisition into and indictment of the king's behaviour. Zygmunt had blatantly broken the *Pacta Conventa* and the *Acta Henriciana*. He was given a dressing-down and a stern warning. He apologised to his subjects and solemnly promised to behave correctly in the future, so no drastic action was taken. His subjects remained suspicious, and Zygmunt became even more secretive than before.

In the same year his father the King of Sweden died, and Zygmunt was determined to take up his inheritance. The Seym allowed him to go, on condition that he returned within a year. If he had failed to make himself popular with the Poles he did no better with his own countrymen. They heaved a sigh of relief when he took ship for Poland leaving his uncle, Charles of Södermannland, as regent. The inevitable followed: uncle Charles ruled Sweden as his own to the growing annoyance of his nephew, who went over in 1598 to reaffirm his authority, only to be humiliated. In the following year the Parliament in Stockholm deposed Zygmunt, adding the proviso that his son Władysław could accede if he became a Lutheran.

Zygmunt started a war which rapidly culminated in the loss of Livonia. In 1601 the Poles regained it, but in 1605 his uncle, now Charles IX, invaded once again. The whole province would have fallen to Sweden had it not been for the brilliant Hetman of Lithuania Jan Karol Chodkiewicz. With a skeletal army of 4,000 men Chodkiewicz took on Charles at Kircholm and worsted him in the space of three hours, strewing the field with 9,000 Swedish dead. Hostilities continued sporadically until 1609 when Chodkiewicz undertook a decisive winter campaign with an even smaller army and captured Riga. The Swedish defeat seemed to be compounded by the death in 1611 of Charles IX, but it was to be only a lull. The king was succeeded by the under-age Gustavus Adolphus, who was to prove an immeasurably superior general, while the Chancellor appointed to rule during his minority was Axel Oxenstierna, one of the most brilliant statesmen of seventeenth-century Europe. He exploited Sweden's peripheral situation during the Thirty Years' War which broke out in 1618, by joining in against the Catholic-Habsburg camp when there was something tangible to be gained, and keeping out when there was not. Although Poland had declared its neutrality, King Zygmunt privately sent the Habsburgs a reinforcement of 10,000 cavalry, which contributed to their victory at the Battle of the White Mountain against the 'Winter King' of Bohemia. Sweden therefore disregarded Poland's official neutrality and invaded Livonia and Pomerania. In 1627 Hetman Koniecpolski defeated the army of Gustavus Adolphus on land and the Polish navy defeated the Swedish fleet at sea. Peace was eventually signed at Stumsdorf in 1635, restoring Poland's provinces, but even that did not mark the end of the conflict. The Polish Vasas' claim to the Swedish throne would cause more bloodshed yet.

The Commonwealth had no part in these wars, and no reason for fighting them. The Seym had lost control over the king's conduct in foreign affairs, but retained a strong negative influence on its outcome, since it could refuse funds and troops at the crucial stage. Once the king's actions had provoked foreign invasion, however, the Commonwealth had no choice but to defend itself. Thus Polish foreign policy under the three Vasa kings, Zygmunt III (1587–1632) and his sons Władysław IV (1632–48) and Jan Kazimierz (1648–68), largely took the form of elaborate plans which foundered either shortly before or shortly after being put into effect,

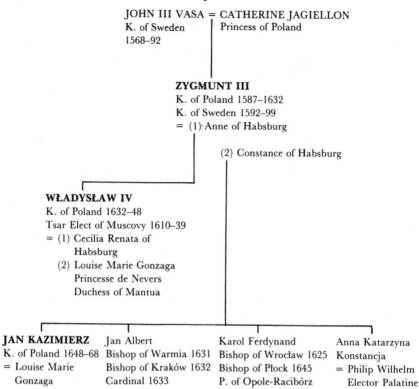

JOHN III VASA = CATHERINE JAGIELLON
K. of Sweden | Princess of Poland
1568–92

ZYGMUNT III
K. of Poland 1587–1632
K. of Sweden 1592–99
= (1) Anne of Habsburg

(2) Constance of Habsburg

WŁADYSŁAW IV
K. of Poland 1632–48
Tsar Elect of Muscovy 1610–39
= (1) Cecilia Renata of
      Habsburg
  (2) Louise Marie Gonzaga
      Princesse de Nevers
      Duchess of Mantua

JAN KAZIMIERZ	Jan Albert	Karol Ferdynand	Anna Katarzyna
K. of Poland 1648–68	Bishop of Warmia 1631	Bishop of Wrocław 1625	Konstancja
= Louise Marie	Bishop of Kraków 1632	Bishop of Płock 1645	= Philip Wilhelm
Gonzaga	Cardinal 1633	P. of Opole-Racibórz	Elector Palatine

Fig. 7   The Vasa Kings of Poland

since it usually pursued objectives for which there was no enthusiasm in the Seym.

Notwithstanding his apologies to the Inquisition Seym of 1592, Zygmunt continued on his own course, breaking the pledges he had made in the *Acta Henriciana* on at least three counts: contracting a marriage (twice, to a Habsburg), carrying on secret diplomatic negotiations and embarking on foreign wars, without the approval of the Seym. His attitude seemed to be that the Polish constitution was a tiresome obstacle-course which had to be circumvented or bulldozed, and the szlachta's discontent was brought to a head in 1605 by his attempts to do the latter.

The programme he presented to the Seym that year included the imposition of a permanent annual tax in lieu of those voted by the Seym; the introduction of a larger standing army; the reduction of the Senate; and the abolition of the lower chamber altogether. The spokesmen of the opposition, Chancellor Zamoyski, Marek Sobieski and Field-Hetman

Żółkiewski, pointed out that this was unrealistic, whereupon the king in a fit of pique refused to ratify the other business of the Seym and dismissed it. In the last speech he ever made, the old Chancellor told the king that he would have the absolute loyalty of his people, all the taxes he wanted and greater power if only he could bring himself to identify with the interests of his subjects and his kingdom. It was a last appeal on behalf of the szlachta's right to participate in the making of policy, and a warning for Zygmunt to abandon his international schemes.

The warning and the appeal went unheeded, and when the Chancellor had been laid in his grave that summer, Zygmunt called a second Seym in the hope of having a freer hand. Another vociferous leader of the opposition, Mikołaj Zebrzydowski, Palatine of Kraków, called a rival assembly of the szlachta which threatened the king with dire consequences if he did not abide by the constitution. The Seym sitting at Warsaw tried to hammer out a compromise, but this was scuppered by the king and his Jesuit advisers, who demanded the repeal of the Act of the Confederation of Warsaw, which guaranteed religious freedom. More and more szlachta and some magnates such as Janusz Radziwiłł joined Zebrzydowski at Sandomierz, and with the king persisting in his demands, they voted his dethronement in accordance with the last clause of the *Acta Henriciana*. It was a critical moment. Zebrzydowski's case was constitutionally watertight, but while few people sided with the king, most were reluctant to raise arms against him and what he stood for. After some hesitation, the two Hetmans Chodkiewicz and Żółkiewski decided to stand by the monarch. They assembled the royal troops and defeated, or rather dispersed, the rebellion at Guzów.

Nobody was penalised for having taken part in the rebellion, which reflected the hazy way in which the issues on both sides had been presented. Zebrzydowski was no intellectual, and his revolt had not been raised on clearly formulated grounds of principle. It merely joined together a selection of magnates and szlachta in a vaguely anti-absolutist and anti-clerical coalition. Had the constitutional issues been clearly spelled out the king would no doubt have been overwhelmed. As it was, he was given the sullen support of the majority who felt it their duty to stand by him even if he had broken his pledges. All the republican talk apart, the Poles were still monarchists with a deep respect for the kingship.

The affair had a detrimental effect on the political system of the Commonwealth. On the one hand the szlachta had tried and failed to invoke its rights according to the constitution, which revealed how academic these rights really were. On the other hand the king had been defied with armed rebellion, and as it was not ruthlessly crushed it would probably happen again. The rebellion had highlighted a number of faults in the constitution which should have been corrected in the natural process of evolution. The long interregna and the rapid succession of kings had interrupted this. By the time it might have been resumed – in 1589 with the Chancellor's project of reform – King Zygmunt was on the throne, and he had his own ideas. Opposition to these could be voiced in the Seym, but it could not be converted into political action. Power had been dispersed so successfully that neither the king, nor the Senate, and least of all the lower chamber of the Seym, could act without the full support of at least one of the other two.

The king was the catalyst which made the parliamentary process function, since he was the only source of executive power. Zygmunt failed to understand the workings of the system, and his suspicious nature prevented him from taking the advice of his senior ministers. As a result, he had fallen into the trap of thinking that the crown had no constitutional power. It did not require a Pole to see how wrong he was. The Papal Nuncio Malaspina noted in 1598: 'Great is the power of the Senate and the nobility, for without their agreement no measure can have binding force, but the greater is the power of the king, for he has bread, and he can give it to whom he pleases.' Or, as the Italian Giovanni Botero observed in 1592, 'The king has as much power as he is allowed by his own skill and intelligence.' Stephen Bathory had lacked neither, and he was never thwarted in his plans. The mulish Zygmunt possessed neither, and the result was a succession of fruitless and damaging collisions with the institutions of the Commonwealth.

The source of the king's power was the right to appoint the senior officers of the Commonwealth, and all the palatines and castellans who made up the Senate. His influence was based on the right to grant the lucrative and prestigious starosties. He was free to appoint whomever he wished, and was under no obligation to favour the rich or powerful. Under the last two Jagiellons most of the senior officers, senators and bishops were the king's men, many of whom had been groomed and tested in the royal chancellery. This had desirable consequences for the crown in that it had a supply of capable and loyal men to place in key positions, and that talent and ambition were drawn towards the royal court as an ante-room to power.

Although Stephen Bathory appointed capable professionals rather than grandees, it was inevitable that elected monarchs would be driven by a sense of insecurity to seek the support of the more influential. Zygmunt III consistently favoured members of the richest families, and while some did their questionable best to support him, they soon outgrew the need to bow to his wishes. Wealth and power meant independence, and both were being accumulated on an unprecedented scale.

Between 1550 and 1650 a new magnate class emerged. The Firlej, Tarnowski, Tenczyński and other great houses of the Jagiellon era disappeared or declined into obscurity, making way for an oligarchy which was to dominate the life of the Commonwealth over the next three centuries – families such as the Potocki, which produced no less than thirty-five senators, three Hetmans and one Field-Hetman in less than two hundred years; or the Lubomirski, who shot to prominence, aided by the favour of Zygmunt III. In 1581 Sebastian Lubomirski owned four villages and a couple of homesteads. By 1629 his son Stanisław owned ninety-one villages, parts of sixteen others, and one town. He also held eighteen villages and two towns on lease from the crown, and a valuable starosty of five villages. With his two great castles of Łańcut and Wiśnicz, his Palatinate of Kraków, and his two Imperial titles, the Prince-Palatine no longer needed the king.

The crown was powerless in the face of such independence. Any attempt to curb a magnate would be sure to provoke widespread opposition, even from the poorest szlachta, who saw it as an attack on personal liberty. There was also the matter of the magnates' very real physical power. Most of them had numerous retinues, and some maintained regular regiments of foreign mercenaries as well as bodyguards of landless szlachta and a pool of supporters and clients. When the Koniecpolski and Wiśniowiecki families quarrelled over an estate in the Ukraine, each decided to call out its troops and supporters to intimidate the other. The combined strength of the two bodies confronting each other came to over 10,000 men.

The factors that contributed to the wealth of the magnates overlapped those that furnished them with manpower. This period saw enormous fluctuations in the supply of and demand for agricultural produce. A bumper harvest in 1618 coincided with high prices on the export market, while 1619 yielded a tiny crop accompanied by low prices and a European financial crisis. Small estates benefited only marginally from a good year and suffered cruelly in a bad one, often going bankrupt for lack of financial reserves. Increasing numbers of minor szlachta were forced to sell out to the local magnate, who always had capital at his disposal. The birthrate of the minor szlachta soared in the sixteenth century owing to improved hygiene and medical care, and the resulting numerous families only compounded the slide into poverty. A sort of noble *lumpenproletariat* came into being, with nothing to offer except a vote and a sword. As they could not indulge in trade, they were obliged to take service. Since there was no large royal army or administration which could absorb them, they sought employment from the magnates, as agents, courtiers or soldiers. A pattern of clientage evolved, and the courts of the magnates gradually took over the social functions of the royal court. Some of the magnates created what were in fact small states, with their own economic arrangements, their own administrations, their own armies, and, of course, their own monarchs.

The pattern varied around the Commonwealth. In Wielkopolska a higher percentage of szlachta managed to hang on to productive estates,

58   The Castle of Wiśnicz, built 1615–21 by
Matteo Trapola for Stanisław Lubomirski,
Palatine of Kraków and Prince of the Holy
Roman Empire. Inside is a magnificent baroque
palace which housed a court of over 200 people,
a vast staff, including 30 musicians, and a
permanent garrison of 600. Wiśnicz epitomises
the outlook of a new class of magnates.

60   Stanisław's sister Katarzyna, portrayed by
a Kraków painter in all the trappings of her
wealth, married Prince Janusz Ostrogski, a
Ruthene magnate. Typically, the inscription
claims that she was also the daughter of the
Castellan of Kraków, whereas in fact her father,
Sebastian Lubomirski (1539–1613) made the
family fortune as commissioner for the
Wieliczka salt-mines in the 1580s, but never rose
beyond the back-bench Castellany of Wojnicz.

59   Ornamental drinking-cup made of
coconut, silver-gilt and rubies. Kraków, first
quarter of the 17th century.

61 The castle of Krzyžtopór at Ujazd, built between 1631 and 1644 by Lorenzo de Sent for Krzysztof Ossoliński. It was said that the grand dining-hall had a glass ceiling which was the bottom of a huge fish-tank, but the splendours of the castle did not survive its destruction by the Swedish invaders in 1655.

62 Some of the camels which made up the suite of Jerzy Ossoliński on his embassy to Rome, depicted by Stefano Della Bella.

thereby not only maintaining their own financial independence, but also thwarting the accumulation of vast latifundia. No such princely states developed there, even if the real wealth of the magnates was on a par with that of those in Lithuania or the Ukraine who owned areas the size of a small country. It was here, in the eastern areas of the Commonwealth, that the great magnates were a law unto themselves. Their ambitions and priorities were of no interest to the rest of the country, but their ability to carry on a semi-independent policy dragged the whole country into disaster on more than one occasion. Possibly the most spectacular of these was a private jaunt which developed into years of full-scale war with Muscovy and left relations between the two countries in shreds. Its beginnings were disreputable and its end bloody and humiliating for both sides.

Ivan the Terrible had died in 1584 leaving two sons, Fyodor who took the throne, and Dmitry who became a monk. Fyodor died in 1591, and his younger brother was assassinated, probably by Boris Godunov who became Tsar. In 1601 Muscovy was racked by severe famine, giving rise to unrest and rebellion, and dark rumours began to circulate about Boris, about his bloody deeds, and about divine retribution.

In 1603 a runaway monk appeared at the court of Prince Konstanty Wiśniowiecki, Palatine of Ruthenia, claiming to be Ivan's son Dmitry. He spun a yarn about his miraculous escape from Boris Godunov's cutthroats in 1591, and although this was taken with a pinch of salt, his potential usefulness was quickly perceived by Jerzy Mniszech, Palatine of Sandomierz, a man whose personal ambition was exceeded only by the fortune he had made out of salt-mines. He had married off one daughter to Wiśniowiecki, and was now seeking a match for his second, Maryna. The False Dmitry agreed to marry her in return for financial and political backing. Dmitry went to Kraków and converted to Catholicism. This earned him the support of the Jesuits, who persuaded the Papal Nuncio himself to introduce him to King Zygmunt. The king received him graciously, granted him a pension, and permitted him to canvass support and raise an army. The impostor then tried to persuade the Chancellor and the Hetmans to back him, without success, but there was no lack of adventurers willing to follow him.

In September 1604 Dmitry set off at the head of an army of 3,000 men, paid for by the Mniszech fortune. His progress was facilitated by the chaos reigning in Muscovy. Cities surrendered to him and many boyars joined his ranks. In April 1605 Boris Godunov died suddenly in Moscow, and Dmitry entered the city without a fight. He was crowned Tsar, and Maryna Mniszech arrived to take her throne beside his. In May 1606 there was a rising in Moscow, and Dmitry was killed. His Polish followers were put to the sword, his wife was locked up, and his corpse was dragged by the

63 The ruins of the fortress at Kamieniec Podolski, the south-eastern bastion of Polish rule, which eventually fell to Sultan Mehmet IV in 1672.

64 Silver medal by Sebastian Dadler of Gdańsk commemorating the relief of Smolensk by Władysław IV in 1634, in which the Muscovite commanders are shown begging for mercy.

65 Contemporary woodcut of Piotr Sahajdaczny, 'Hetman of His Royal Majesty's Zaporozhian Army', who commanded the Cossack contingent during Prince Władysław's siege of Moscow in 1618, and played an important part in the defence of Chocim against the Turks two years later.

genitals to Lobnoye Mesto, where it was cut up, burnt, stuffed into a cannon, and shot off westwards, whence he had come.

Vasily Shuysky was elected to rule in his place, but that was not the end of the story. In July 1607 an even more disreputable impostor claiming to be the miraculously surviving Dmitry gained a following. The freed Maryna Mniszech 'recognised' him (her Jesuit confessor made them go through a second marriage ceremony just in case), and he became the rallying-point for disgruntled Muscovites and Poles who had followed his earlier namesake. They were joined by a number of Lithuanian magnates, including Samuel Tyszkiewicz and Jan Piotr Sapieha, nephew of the Chancellor of Lithuania. The Sapieha lands were scattered on both sides of the border, hence their interest in eastern conquest.

So far, the whole war had been a private affair, not involving the Commonwealth officially. In 1609, however, Tsar Shuysky made a defensive alliance with King Charles of Sweden, who had been waiting for an excuse to invade Livonia. This was a bugle-call to Zygmunt III, who could see all his enemies combining in their heretical wickedness. The Seym sent Chodkiewicz to oust Charles from Livonia, but refused to countenance intervention in Muscovy. Ignoring it, Zygmunt asked for and received full crusading status from Pope Paul V (anyone taking part got full remission of sins, and anyone killed went straight to Heaven), and marched out at the head of his own army. He laid siege to Smolensk and soon got bogged down. The pseudo-Dmitry was besieging Moscow with an army made up of Polish adventurers, Cossacks, and Russian boyars. With the intervention of Zygmunt III, most of the Poles left him in order to join their king, with the result that the impostor had to fall back on Kaluga and, in effect, drop out of a rapidly changing picture.

Early in 1610 the Tsar's brother Dmitry Shuysky set off to relieve Smolensk. Hetman Żółkiewski made a forced march and surprised Shuysky's army at Klushino. He won a resounding victory and pursued the fleeing remnants to Moscow, where the boyars deposed their Tsar and elected in his place Władysław, the eldest son of King Zygmunt. At last an honourable way out had been found. But when Żółkiewski returned to Smolensk and recommended that the fifteen-year-old Władysław be despatched to Moscow, he found Zygmunt sour and obstinate. Such a diplomatic solution did not fit in with his plan of bringing the Catholic Faith to Moscow on the tip of his sword. He continued to besiege Smolensk, the boyars waited for the arrival of Władysław, and the small Polish garrison in the Kremlin lived on borrowed time. Since they had not been paid for months, the soldiers offered the Muscovite crown jewels for sale, touting them round Europe by letter. As there were no takers, they divided them up amongst themselves.

On 13 June 1611 Smolensk surrendered to Zygmunt. He felt strong and refused to negotiate with the boyars, adamantly insisting that the whole of Muscovy must go over to Catholicism before he would consider allowing Władysław to become Tsar. There were several risings against the Polish garrison in Moscow, which retaliated by burning large areas of the city. Eventually, in November 1612, the Poles capitulated and left the Kremlin.

In February 1613 the boyars elected a new Tsar, Mikhail Fyodorovich Romanov, son of the Metropolitan Bishop of Rostov, an associate of the false Dmitry. As the new Tsar was crowned (with a minor coronet found in the baggage of a slaughtered Polish soldier), the situation remained confused. His father was a prisoner in Poland. Maryna Mniszech and her three-year-old son were entrenched in southern Russia, supported by the Don Cossacks, and, in 1618, Władysław set off at the head of an army to claim his throne, having at last gained the approval of his father. He failed to take Moscow, and in 1619 a peace was signed which returned Smolensk and other areas to Poland, and permitted Władysław to style himself 'Tsar elect of Muscovy'.

The matter was not allowed to rest there. Taking advantage of the death of Zygmunt III in 1632, the Muscovites invaded and laid siege to Smolensk, which was only saved through repeated relief of the garrison by Krzysztof Radziwiłł. In September 1633 King Władysław reached Smolensk with a large army and defeated the Muscovites. In the following year peace was signed, and one of the principal demands of the Muscovites was that the document of Władysław's election by the boyars in 1610 be handed back to them. Since the document itself could not be found in the archives, Władysław agreed to a solemn church ceremony in Warsaw, during which he abdicated all his titles and pretensions to the Muscovite throne before a delegation of boyars.

Symbols were immensely important, and they could be very telling. As King Zygmunt III lay dying only two years previously, after the longest and possibly most incompetent reign in Poland's history, he had called his son to his bedside. With the last strength of his trembling arm he placed on Władysław's brow the royal crown of Sweden. He himself lay in state wearing the crown of Muscovy. The only crown which was his to wear, the crown of Poland, had never figured in his scheme of things.

9

Soldiers of the Virgin

When the tower of Kraków's Town Hall had been rebuilt in 1556 a copy of Erasmus' New Testament was immured in the brickwork. When the same tower was repaired in 1611 the book was replaced by a Catholic New Testament, along with a picture and a relic of the first Polish Jesuit to be canonised, St Stanisław Kostka. The symbols could hardly have been more apt. One vision of life was replaced by another, the spirit of enquiry by one of piety, humanist principles by post-Tridentine conformism, and if Erasmus was the beacon for all thinking Poles in the 1550s, the Jesuits were the mentors of their grandchildren.

The Church of Rome could not launch an all-out offensive in Poland, as the battle-lines criss-crossed society in the most confusing way. When Cardinal Aldobrandini, the future Pope Clement VIII, visited Wilno in 1588, he was astonished at a dinner given by a Catholic canon that the principal guest was a Calvinist, Judge Teodor Jewłaszewski of Nowogródek, whose father was the Orthodox Bishop of Pińsk, and whose son was brought up as an Arian. In such situations it was not feasible to be rigorist. Even the bigoted Zygmunt III grudgingly had to allow his Protestant sister Anna to install a Lutheran Chapel on the Wawel.

Even fervent Catholics tended to feel that they were, as the saying went, 'born noble, not Catholic', and this would emerge whenever the Church's activities grazed a public issue. The political solidarity of the szlachta far outweighed religious loyalties. In 1627 the king was persuaded to have a Protestant book seized, but this caused immediate uproar throughout the country. The distinguished Arian Samuel Przypkowski voiced the proto-Orwellian sentiments of the majority of the szlachta when he raged: 'The next move will be to institute torture for having thoughts . . . Our cause is bound to the cause of common freedom by a knot so tight that the one cannot be separated from the other.'

In this climate, the progress of the Counter-Reformation proved slow. It was not until 1658 that the Arians were banished, for having refused to bear arms at a time of national peril. In 1660 the Quakers were expelled from the area of Gdańsk, whence they set sail for America (many of the religious communities of the United States, particularly the Unitarian churches, can trace their pedigrees back to Poland). In 1668 the Seym ruled that nobody could convert from Catholicism to any other church on pain of exile, and in 1673 admittance to the szlachta was barred to non-Catholics. None of these measures actually prevented anyone from practising the faith of his choice, and there was furthermore a twilight zone between what the Seym decreed and what even the most rabidly zealous Catholic officer of the law was prepared to implement against a fellow citizen.

Nevertheless, time was on the side of Rome. The overall Protestant majority in the Senate in 1569 shrank to a handful by 1600. The number of Protestant chapels dwindled by about two-thirds during the same period. The fact that a fervently Catholic king favoured those of his faith when making appointments was undoubtedly one of the reasons. The drift back to Rome was, however, linked more closely with states of mind than with cynical considerations. It was intimately connected with a change of intellectual climate attendant on the loss of the humanist vision, and this change of climate was not confined to Poland. The pragmatic optimism of the early sixteenth century had abandoned society, giving way to a more agonising search for absolutes, for a vision of man in the world based on spiritual rather than rational values.

The first metaphysical note in Polish literature was struck by Mikołaj Sęp-Szarzyński. He died in 1581 while Kochanowski was still writing, and he stands out from his contemporaries by his religious fervour and asceticism. In his *Dumy*, whose elegiac verses glorify wars with the Tatars as a struggle of good against evil, he introduced a perception typical to the following century. His anxieties were mirrored in a religious revival, of which the spectacular resurgence of monasticism was an eloquent symptom. The Dominican Order, for instance, numbered no more than 300 brothers in 40 communities at its lowest point in 1579. Twenty years later there were 900 brothers, and by 1648 there were 110 large communities. Between 1572 and 1648 the total number of monasteries in the Commonwealth rose from 220 to 565. The same period saw the foundation of new contemplative or ascetic orders such as the Benedictine nuns of Chełmno and the Barefoot Carmelites, starting a mystical tradition in Polish religious life which had seldom been in evidence before.

A concomitant decline in the standard of learning and the quality of thought, both of which can be detected in public life and political debate, was perhaps the most important factor at work, since it played into the hands of the more causal features of post-Tridentine Catholicism. The poet Kacper Twardowski (1592–1641) was a typical Renaissance figure writing elegant courtly verse, until he fell seriously ill. He saw this as a warning from God, and spent the rest of his life feverishly rewriting his entire oeuvre, paraphrasing all the erotic pieces into ascetic religious verse. Chancellor Wolski saw the light as he lay on his death-bed in 1630 and ordered that his collection of Italian paintings, one of the largest and best in Poland, be burnt as a rejection of earthly vanity and an offering to the Almighty.

The idea of life as a series of rewards and punishments meted out by God was taken up by the Polish Bossuet, the Jesuit Piotr Skarga, who extended it to political affairs, using the style and rhetoric of the Prophets to threaten the Poles with impending catastrophe if they did not mend their ways. Skarga did more than any other to formulate the political outlook of the Polish Church, and he put it across with force.

The principal vehicle used by the Jesuits to reconquer the soul of Poland were the colleges they established all over the Commonwealth, of which there were nearly forty by the mid-seventeenth century. They were free, they accepted Arians, Calvinists and Orthodox as readily as Catholics, and the teaching was of a high standard. The Spanish, Italian, Portuguese, English and French priests who accounted for most of the teachers added an element of cosmopolitanism which the poorer szlachta appreciated. In 1587, twenty-three years after the first Jesuit had set foot in Poland, the Jesuit College of Wilno had some sixty priests and novices teaching over 700 pupils. 'There have always been and there still are in the classes of this college very numerous sons of heretics and schismatics,' explained the Rector, Garcias Alabiano; 'Their parents send them to our schools solely to learn the Arts, and not to be taught the Catholic Faith. However, by the Grace of God, not one of them has to this day left without abjuring his parents' errors and embracing the Catholic Faith.' The sons of humble country squires were no match for the Jesuits, whose mastery of psychology was remarkable.

Two years later the college was elevated to the status of university by Stephen Bathory, and its influence increased accordingly. By the 1620s, with the Jagiellon University sinking into clerical sophistry and that of Zamość lapsing into provincialism, Wilno had only two rivals: the Arian Academies of Raków and Leszno. Raków, founded under the spiritual aegis of Fausto Sozzini (Socinius) and the patronage of the magnate Jan Sienieński, had become the principal centre of Arian thought in the early 1600s, attracting teachers and students from all over Europe. During the next decades it gave rise to a whole library of Socinian literature which was disseminated throughout the world. Spinoza and Locke are among those thought to have been influenced by the deist writings of the Polish Brethren. In 1638 two students of the Academy desecrated a Catholic wayside shrine, and this was built up into a major scandal, as a result of which the Senate ordered the closure of the Academy and its press. The

Brethren simply moved these to the nearby estate of another Arian magnate, but they were gradually undermined by continual legal harassment by the Catholic hierarchy. The Arian College of Leszno, founded in the previous century by the Leszczyński family, was enhanced in 1620 when the Czech philosopher Jan Amos Komensky (Commenius) became rector. His teachings were particularly influential in Holland and England, which he visited under Cromwell's Protectorate (it was during this visit that he was invited to preside over the new college in New England known as Harvard). Leszno was sacked during the Swedish war of 1655, just three years before the banishment of the Arians, so that by the second half of the century the Jesuit University of Wilno had no serious rival.

Between the arrival of the Jesuits in 1564 and the end of the century, no less than 344 separate books by Jesuits were published in Poland. This literature, much of it on subjects of general interest, subtly promoted a definite political stance. The Jesuits ranged themselves behind the crown, particularly after the accession of their ally Zygmunt III in 1588, and displayed marked hostility towards the szlachta. The hostility stemmed not only from the Jesuits' genuine sympathy for the peasantry, but also from the incisive realisation that the real foe of Catholic absolutism were not so much the Arians or the Calvinists, the Jews or the Muslims, but the 'democratic Catholics' who made up such a large proportion of the szlachta.

The constitution of the Commonwealth stood in the way of the Counter-Reformation and the szlachta were the guardians of the constitution. Little could be achieved through the power of the crown, so the Jesuits looked for other weapons. They even began to use the pulpit to incite the downtrodden to raise their heads: the spectre of a nationwide peasants' revolt in support of the king and the Church was not a pleasant prospect for the szlachta. It never came to that. The Zebrzydowski rebellion, which voiced some unequivocal intentions where the Jesuits were concerned, frightened them. It also revealed the fact that the lower chamber of the Seym was becoming increasingly powerless to do anything except register opposition. As the Jesuit Order attracted more and more minor szlachta into its own ranks, it learnt to operate more adroitly within the system, while opposition to it melted away under the influence of its educational activities. Its schools turned out thousands of young szlachta imbued with a ready-made set of religious, social and political principles, replacing reason and knowledge as the guides to behaviour. Although it would be dangerous to suggest that they managed to indoctrinate people, it is impossible to ignore the Jesuits' influence on thought and behaviour, and this had a drastic long-term effect on the course of Polish history, for the way in which the constitution was used depended on the rational integrity of the whole body politic. The minor szlachta were the first to fall back into bigotry, but the magnates also showed a marked decline from the standards of their fathers and grandfathers.

The magnates collected wealth and office with single-minded egoism and often behaved like petty tyrants. Yet they entertained an idealised view of themselves as pillars of the democratic constitution. They were fond of likening their families to the senatorial houses of ancient Rome – to the extent, in the case of the Lubomirski, of claiming descent from Drusus (the Radziwiłł, not to be outdone, actually published a family tree showing Hector of Troy as their ancestor). Such posturing could not hope to clothe the naked ambition lurking behind it, but neither entirely cancelled out a genuine sense of duty which, when combined with a good brain and an education, produced admirable leaders of the nation. This was true of the sixteenth century and it was very true of the end of the eighteenth. In the seventeenth, however, the decline in education affected even the greatest of them.

A characteristic figure in this respect was Jerzy Ossoliński, born in 1595 into an old family of substance which his generation carried into the top league. After a Jesuit education, he set off on a grand tour through Holland, England, France, Italy and Austria. He distinguished himself as a soldier at the siege of Moscow in 1618, and subsequently as a diplomat before embarking on a parliamentary career. In 1631 he was elected Marshal of the Seym, an opportunity he used to put forward a project for reform of voting procedures. In 1636 he entered the Senate as Palatine of Sandomierz, two years later he was appointed Vice-Chancellor, and in 1642 Chancellor of Poland. An intelligent statesman, he was the first Chancellor for forty years to take full control of foreign affairs. He inspired respect for himself and the king he served by his strong yet moderate approach, but his attitude to religious issues was tinged with the new fanaticism. His Jesuit upbringing showed whenever there was talk of religious toleration, and he was instrumental in the closing down of the Raków Academy.

Ossoliński was a great patron, but he lacked the civic vision of his predecessors, and created little more than monuments to himself. In 1635 he built a grand residence at Ossolin, in 1643 the magnificent Church of St George at Klimontów, and then a fine Palladian palace in Warsaw. It was his elder brother Krzysztof who encapsulated the spirit that guided them both in one of the greatest pieces of self-advertisement by any Polish family – the astonishing castle of Krzyżtopór. Built on a spectacular ground-plan consisting of a number of courtyards of different sizes radiating from a central *cour d'honneur* superimposed on a mass of star-shaped fortifications, it looks for all the world like a beached ocean-liner. The windows were ornamented with marble plaques inscribed in Latin to the praise of various real and invented forbears.

Such ostentation and vanity were characteristic of Ossoliński and other contemporaries. His embassy to Rome was an excuse to show off. He pawned and mortgaged in order to cover his servants in gold and to caparison his horses and camels in pearls for the occasion. He accepted the title of Duke from the Pope, and one of Prince from the Emperor in 1634, titles which only caused the bearer embarrassment in the Commonwealth and whose sole purpose was the gratification of vanity. The cornerstone of the constitution was the absolute formal equality of the szlachta, and as such no titles were recognised – with the exception of those accorded at the Union of Lublin to Lithuanian and Ruthene families of Jagiellon or Rurik descent, such as the Czartoryski, Sanguszko, Zbaraski, Zasławski and others. Poles travelling abroad often assumed titles commensurate with their status but there was widespread resentment against those like the Radziwiłł and Lubomirski who paraded at home titles they had obtained from the Emperor, and in 1638 the Seym forbade their acceptance.

Ossoliński's political career coincided with a period which witnessed a gradual abandonment of the concepts on which the Polish system rested. In 1632, when Władysław IV had to swear the *Acta Henriciana*, a Jesuit confessor explained to him that an oath taken under duress without full intention was invalid in the eyes of God. To his credit, Władysław refused to see it that way. The very fact that a senior representative of an order which virtually controlled higher education in the country could suggest that a solemn oath made in church before Senate and Seym could be wriggled out of with a bit of casuistry was hardly encouraging for the political, not to say moral, health of the Commonwealth. In the event, the original text, based on the Act of the Confederation of Warsaw, in which the inhabitants of the Commonwealth pledged, as equals, to respect each other's religious beliefs and practices, was amended. The new text 'graciously permitted' others to practise a different faith, but the Catholic Faith was, in Ossoliński's words, 'mistress in her own house', while the Protestants were no more than tolerated guests. The equation of Protestantism with 'foreignness' was a Jesuit habit, and it caught on. The notion was fostered that to be Polish was to be Catholic, and while there was no objection to ethnic minorities practising different rites or the Livonian szlachta remaining Protestant, Poles who were Protestants began to be viewed as eccentric, even suspicious. A psychological connection had been made between Catholicism and patriotism, a patriotism made increasingly vital by the succession of wars in the first half of the century. Since these were fought against Protestant Swedes and Orthodox Russians, Jesuit and other writers began to picture the Poles as defenders of Catholicism. When the Turks and Tatars took over as the enemy in the following decades, it was a short step to turn the Poles into the defenders of Christendom. A

powerful myth grew up of Poland as the predestined Bulwark of Christendom, the *Antemurale Christianitatis*, a phrase first applied to it by
Machiavelli. 'Lord, you were once called the God of Israel,' Jakub Sobieski
prayed in the 1650s: 'on bended knee we now call You the God of Poland,
our motherland, the God of our armies and the Lord of our hosts.'

In spite of growing chauvinism, Poland was still open to outside influences,
and Poles continued to travel abroad in pursuit of culture. Translations of
French, Italian, Spanish, Turkish and Persian works were published with
little delay, and plays by Shakespeare were performed in Poland as early as
1609. Zygmunt III kept an Italian *commedia dell'arte* at his court, supplemented in the 1620s by an English troupe. He also kept about sixty
musicians and singers, and during the first half of the century few courts
had such good music. Warsaw was the first place outside Italy in which the
new art of opera flourished. In 1633 Władysław IV set up a royal opera
company, and Piotr Elert wrote the first Polish opera in the late 1630s.
Adam Jarzębski, who started his career at the court of the Elector of
Brandenburg and in 1620 joined the royal music in Warsaw as first violin,
was an architect as well as a composer, so he was able to design sets for the
opera. Marcin Mielczewski, director of the royal music from 1638 to 1644,
and later of the orchestra of the Bishop of Płock, left over fifty works,
including the first Polish compositions in the *concertato* style. Bartłomiej
Pękiel, royal organist from 1632, and director of the royal music from 1649,
was the author of an oratorio and the *Missa Pulcherrima* (1669), his last
work. They are only the most outstanding of a string of composers,
including Stanisław Szarżyński, Grzegorz Górczycki, Damian Stacho-
wicz, Jacek Różycki, Jan Podbielski and Frescobaldi's pupil Andrzej
Niżankowski, who testify to a continuous tradition of artistic
refinement.

It is only fair to say that while the Jesuits contributed to the stifling of
thought and the ossification of society, their artistic patronage is responsible
for much of the best building and painting of the period. They also contributed some remarkable individuals, including the greatest lyric poet of the
Polish Baroque, Maciej Kazimierz Sarbiewski (1595–1640). A member of
the minor szlachta, Sarbiewski was educated by the Jesuits and joined the
Order. In Rome he was crowned Poet Laureate by Pope Urban VIII. On
his return to Poland he became a lecturer at the University of Wilno, and
later chaplain to Władysław IV. He wrote lyrical odes in which religious
and bucolic themes are treated with a baroque sensuality in a Latin which
is both musical and colourful. His *Liricorum Libri*, published in 1626 under
the pseudonym of 'Casimir', ran into more than sixty editions. Samuel
Taylor Coleridge, who began to translate the collection, declared that,
with the exception of Lucretius, 'no Latin poet ancient or modern, could be

said to equal Casimire in boldness of conception, opulence of fancy, or beauty of versification'.

In terms of poetic talent and spiritual honesty Sarbiewski was a lone beacon in a dark night. Most of his contemporaries churned out verse endowed with neither vision nor freshness, and what substance there was tended to be obscured by verbiage and bombast. While some, like Szymon Zimorowicz (1608–29), indulged in pastoral lyrics, most of them preferred the heroic subject of war. A typical figure is Jan Zabczyc (d.1629), whose epic about the Muscovite wars is one huge acrostic, the first letter of each line read vertically spelling out the name and all the titles of the impostor Dmitry. Although the wars involved only a fraction of the population, they gave rise to a tradition of heroic and pathetic verse, a latter-day *chanson de geste* inspired by the unique conditions and atmosphere in which they were fought, particularly in the case of operations against the Turks and Tatars. In the Ukraine, in the Wild Plains, in Moldavia, tiny Polish forces would operate in a vast and empty theatre whose landmarks were rivers with haunting names and legendary battlefields cleared only by wolves and buzzards. The enemy was wild, cunning and alien. The odds were almost invariably heavily on his side. These conditions engendered a psychology and a lore which complemented the religious and chivalric element. Companies of Polish knights with the image of the Blessed Virgin on their breastplates and the words of the *Bogurodzica* on their lips faced the Infidel in contests which tested human mettle more than military logistics.

'Do not disturb yourself, most beloved wife, for God watches over us,' Hetman Żółkiewski wrote from his camp at Cecora in Moldavia on the night of 6 October 1620: 'and if I should perish it will be because I am old and of no further use to the Commonwealth, and the Almighty will grant that our son may take up his father's sword, temper it on the necks of pagans and, if it should come to pass as I said, avenge the blood of his father.' On the morrow his army was defeated and his body hacked to pieces by janissaries. His head was sent to Istanbul, where it was displayed on a pike.

Such images gripped the imagination. They were retold and glorified by poets such as Samuel Twardowski (1600–61) and Wacław Potocki (1621–96) in long epic works. Twardowski served in several campaigns, but Potocki never fought. He was an Arian landowner from Małopolska (no relation to the great Potocki family). None of his work was printed in his lifetime (about a quarter of a million lines have been published to date, representing a fraction of his output), yet he was widely read in manuscript copies. His greatest and most popular work is *The Chocim War*, a lengthy epic about the Polish stand against the Ottoman army in 1621, a wonderful mixture of highblown heroic narrative and down-to-earth detail. It is rich in fine passages and gives a valuable insight into the mind of the Pole of

Potocki's generation, who was 'born in a camp, bathed in blood, and lulled by the sound of musket-fire', or at least liked to believe he was.

Wespazjan Kochowski (1633–1700), a small landowner from Sandomierz who had served many years as a soldier before taking up the pen, took this a stage further. In *A Polish Psalmody* (1695), he produced a modern equivalent of the Psalms and solved a problem that had beset Polish writers. The heroes of antiquity fought against tremendous odds, usually in the shape of the gods, and from this unequal match stemmed the epic quality of the combat. The heroes of Polish epic poetry, on the other hand, were Christians fighting the Tatars or Muscovites. When Christians fight infidels God is on their side. There is therefore nothing epic in their victory, whatever the physical odds. Kochowski found a way out of this dilemma. By transposing the whole narrative into a quasi-biblical context he turned the hero into an instrument of Heaven, a champion of the Lord. This also implied, as had Piotr Skarga, that Poland had a special part to play in God's scheme, a divine mission. This notion deeply marked the seventeenth-century Pole's attitude to war. There were elements in it of biblical messianism, of the hellenic epos and of the ascetic violence of the medieval crusades, compounded with a dose of arrogance, for warfare was still the preserve of the szlachta.

Like other states, the Commonwealth employed mercenaries – German, Scottish or French infantry and dragoons drilled on standard European lines. It could also count in the hour of need on the private armies of magnates. The core of its armed forces, however, was made up of volunteers. The infantry consisted of peasants, some of whom were levies, raised and paid for by twenty-five per cent of revenue from the starosties and royal lands, and therefore known as 'quarter troops'. In 1579 Stephen Bathory instituted a new system under which peasants from royal lands could volunteer to become reserve soldiers, freed from all servage and dues in return for their regular training and readiness to fight, and paid when on active service. This type of infantry, known as the Piechota Wybraniecka, was higly effective on account of its regular training in peacetime and its good morale.

The cavalry was based on the chivalric pattern of the knight and his squires. The szlachta who fought in the front line were known as *towarzysze*, or 'companions'. Each companion would bring with him as many men as he could afford to equip, most of them poor szlachta, to make up the second and third ranks, and these were known as *pocztowi*, literally 'retainers'. Hetman Tarnowski's own regiment during the Obertyn campaign of 1531, for example, consisted of some two hundred men: Hieronim Szafraniec, Starosta of Chęciny, with thirty retainers; Zbigniew Sienieński with twenty; Jan Gamrat with twenty; Stanisław Spytek Tarnowski with

66 A group of light cavalry. The officer carries the *buzdygan*, the baton of command, and the troopers are armed with sabre, bow-and-arrows, and the all-purpose *czekan* or *obuch*. Detail from the *Entry of the Polish Embassy into Paris*, by Stefano Della Bella.

67 17th-century bow- and arrow-quivers.

68,68A 17th-century *buzdygan*, and a short *obuch*.

69 A regular-issue Polish cavalry sabre dating from the end of the 16th century, based on a Hungarian adaptation of the eastern sabre.

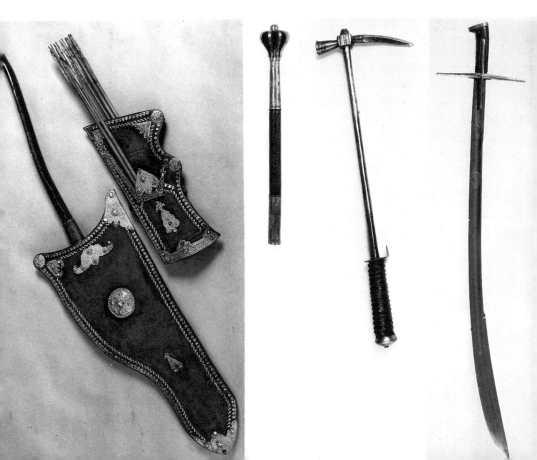

sixteen; Auctus Ligęza with sixteen; Jan Ossoliński with ten; Mikołaj Koła with eight; and another twenty or so companions with two or three retainers apiece. Companions equipped themselves and their retainers at their own expense, but received soldier's pay when on active service.

The presence in the ranks of large numbers of volunteers, and particularly of szlachta who were fighting not for the cause of some king but for their own Commonwealth, gave them the same edge over their enemies as that enjoyed by the soldiers of revolutionary France in the 1790s. The gentleman-trooper carried the szlachta's democratic principles in his saddle-bag and thought of his commander and the Hetman as elder brothers. Because of the importance of timing and manoeuvre in Polish cavalry tactics, it was customary for all the companions to be given a run-down of the plan before an engagement, further enhancing the element of participation.

Polish armies were called upon to operate in a variety of terrain and climatic conditions, ranging from baking plains in the south to freezing bogs and forests in the north; from wilderness to heavily built-up areas. The foe varied from lumbering Swedish pikemen and musketeers to nimble Tatar warriors and Spahis. The fighting was usually far from home without any ancillary services. The accent of all military thinking was therefore on mobility, adaptability and self-sufficiency.

The father of Polish military science was Hetman Jan Tarnowski, who published his *Consilium Rationis Bellicae* in 1558. He elaborated the old Hussite tactic of forming a gigantic square, a mobile fortress which could save a small army caught out in the open field, and this became standard practice in all operations against Tatars and Turks. Tarnowski also developed the traditional features of Polish strategy, most of which were unique. The high degree of mobility and the need to live off the land were both reasons for Polish armies operating in divisions, while most European armies marched in a great mass until the end of the eighteenth century. Another peculiar feature was the tradition of the deep cavalry raid sweeping out ahead of the main army, sometimes covering over a thousand miles in a great arc behind enemy lines. The crux of any battle was the cavalry charge. This was not the same as the heavy massed armoured attack which had come to grief on the battlefields of the Hundred Years' War in France. It was an elaborate manoeuvre of probing charges by light cavalry supported by artillery leading up to the decisive charge by heavy cavalry deployed in a chequerboard pattern and not a single mass. Each troop had space on all sides, so the bringing down of one rank or section did not affect the others.

The Poles set great store by artillery, and in this they were in advance of their enemies until the eighteenth century. They preferred lighter cannon to heavy pieces, purposeful direction to saturation bombardment and mobility to numbers. At Kircholm in 1605, Chodkiewicz defeated the Swedes with only four cannon, at Klushino in 1610 Żółkiewski had only two. From the Turks the Poles learnt much about incendiary and explosive shells, and they themselves developed rocketry to great effect. They had a number of good theoreticians, most notably Kazimierz Siemienowicz, whose influential treatise on milti-stage rocketry was published in 1650; and outstanding commanders, such as Marcin Kątski, who alone of all the allied generals managed to bring his guns to bear at the relief of Vienna in 1683.

Similar principles obtained in the infantry. Lightly dressed, without helmets or armour, the soldiers were armed with a musket, short sword and hatchet. Only one man in eight carried a pike. In the 1550s, a Polish regiment of 200 men could deliver 150 shots in five minutes, while contemporary Spanish brigades of 10,000 men operating in the Netherlands could only deliver 750 in the same time. Polish infantry possessed ten times greater fire-power on a man-to-man basis than standard European infantries.

Cavalry made up the backbone of the Commonwealth's military power, and outnumbered the infantry by about three to one. The Poles crossed horses from Turkey with a number of European breeds, without any apparent method but with an instinct for speed and endurance. They rode on eastern saddles, which place less strain on the horse. These two factors explain their ability to cover tremendous distances (up to 120 kilometres a day over several days) without killing their mounts. Their ability to fight for long hours without exhausting themselves stemmed from the fact that their sabre was probably the finest cutting weapon ever in use in a European army. It was the curved eastern sabre, modified by the Hungarians and further adapted by the Poles in the sixteenth century until it reached a combination of length, weight and curve which gave it an uniquely high ratio of cutting-power to effort expended.

The pride and glory of the Polish cavalry, its mailed fist, was the Husaria, the winged cavalry. This operated in regiments of about three hundred men highly skilled and armed to the teeth. The companions of the front rank carried an astonishing lance of up to twenty feet in length, which outreached infantry pikes, allowing the Husaria to cut straight through a square. Having planted his lance in the chest of an enemy pikeman, the companion then drew either his sabre or another weapon peculiar to the Poles, a rapier with a six-foot blade which doubled as a short lance. Each companion also carried a pair of pistols, a short carbine; a bow and arrows; and a variety of other weapons, the most lethal of which was the *czekan*, a long steel hammer which could go through heads and helmets like butter.

The retainers carried much the same arsenal without the long lance, while the rear rank often led spare mounts into the charge. The bow they carried was the small, curved eastern type, more quick-firing than any musket, accurate at longer ranges and easier to fire from a moving horse.

The Husaria wore helmets, thick steel breastplates and shoulder and arm guards, or eastern scale armour. The companions also wore wooden arcs bristling with eagle feathers rising over their heads like two wings from attachments on the back of the saddle or the shoulders. Over one shoulder they wore the skin of a tiger or leopard as a cloak. These served to frighten the enemy's horses, and indeed the enemy himself, and the wings had the added advantage of preventing Tatars eager for ransom from lassoing the Polish riders in a mêlée. But the main purpose of these accoutrements was to give an impression of splendour. The companions in the Husaria were young noblemen who liked to show off their wealth. Helmets and breastplates were chased or studded with gold and often set with semi-precious stones. Harnesses, saddles and horse-cloths were embroidered and embellished with gold and gems. The long lance was painted like a stick of rock and decorated with a five-foot-long silk pennant which made a frightful noise at the charge.

For over a century, the Husaria were the lords of the battlefield. Kircholm (1605), where 4,000 Poles under Chodkiewicz accounted for 14,000 Swedes, was little more than one long cavalry manoeuvre ending in the Husaria's charge. Klushino (1610), where Żółkiewski with 6,000 Poles, of whom only 200 were infantry, defeated 30,000 Muscovites and 5,000 German and Scottish mercenaries, was a Husaria victory, as was the battle of Gniew (1656), in which 5,500 Polish cavalry defeated 13,000 Swedes. In many other battles, from Byczyna (1588) and Trzciana (1629) to the relief of Vienna (1683), the Husaria dealt the decisive blow.

Though hardly a maritime nation, the Poles did have a navy for a while. In 1560 Zygmunt Augustus copied the English practice and licensed a total of thirty privateers to sail under the Polish ensign. He established a Maritime Commission and in 1569 launched a galleon and a frigate of the Polish navy. In 1620 Zygmunt III had a further twenty warships built and in 1627 the Polish navy fought its only sea-battle when it defeated the Swedish fleet off Oliwa. If the Poles did not like paying for an army, they liked digging into their pockets even less for a navy, which seemed an unnecessary luxury since cordial relations with England and Holland meant that Poland had maritime friends in the Baltic. The navy dwindled, and the only sailor of talent Poland produced, Krzysztof Arciszewski, became an admiral in the Dutch navy.

Victory was repeatedly achieved at low cost and with little apparent effort, and this had a pernicious effect. Increasingly, when money was needed for defence, voices were raised in the Seym and the seymiks to the effect that 'they're scaring us with Turks and Tatars just to get money out of us', in the belief that if any real threat materialised it could be parried easily by the noble Polish knight, armed with the superiority of his political freedom and inspired by God. There was much truth in this, but times were changing.

10

The Deluge

'Poland is like a spectator who stands safely on the sea shore, calmly looking on at the tempest raging before him,' wrote Krzysztof Opaliński, Palatine of Poznań, in the 1630s. Most of Central Europe was absorbed by the self-perpetuating butchery of the Thirty Years' War; France, divided by the Fronde, was poised on the brink of open civil war; other states were rent by profound internal disorders or religious and political repression. By contrast, Poland's wars were fought by small armies on the confines of the Commonwealth, and by 1635 peace had been obtained in all areas.

Although the wisdom of hindsight reveals germs of later disease in the political system, there was nothing palpably sickly about it, and it continued to work remarkably smoothly. When Zygmunt III died in 1632, his eldest son Władysław was elected king unanimously in the space of half-an-hour. (An occasion enlivened only by the fact that during the Coronation Seym one of the queen's more comely ladies-in-waiting leant too far over the balustrade of the spectators' gallery, which gave way; luckily for her, part of her dress caught on a nail, and after much ripping and tearing her naked form came to rest held only by a single strand of clothing about her waist, suspended in mid-air above the admiring body politic of the Commonwealth.) The Commonwealth's prestige soared, and Władysław IV was in a position to mediate on behalf of other states caught up in the Thirty Years' War. France repeatedly urged him to take the Imperial crown after the death of the ailing Ferdinand II, offering the necessary funds and military as well as diplomatic support. When his wife died, no less than sixteen portraits of various princesses were sent by foreign courts offering advantageous arrangements. In 1641, after the Prussian line of the Hohenzollerns had died out, their cousin Frederick William of Brandenburg, known as the Great Elector, knelt in homage before Władysław at Warsaw Castle to receive the tenure of the Duchy of Prussia. Nobody suspected that this would be the last such act of homage. Indeed, nobody suspected that within fifteen years the Commonwealth would have virtually disintegrated.

A closer look reveals that although what appeared to be favourable treaties had been signed, none of them represented more than a lull in hostilities which were bound to break out again. Poland could afford to relax its vigilance only because the Habsburgs, Brandenburg and Sweden were absorbed by the Thirty Years' War, because the new Romanov dynasty was still consolidating its power in Muscovy, and because the Porte was busy elsewhere. The situation changed drastically when the war came to an end in 1648, the very year in which the Commonwealth was shaken to its foundations by the explosion of formidable internal tensions that had been building up for fifty years.

The Commonwealth of Two Nations set up by the Union of Lublin in 1569 had one great flaw – it contained three nations, not two. Leaving aside the various minorities, the Commonwealth was inhabited by three principal ethnic and cultural groups: Poles, Lithuanians and Ruthenes. The Ruthenes had originally been absorbed into the Grand Duchy of Lithuania, whose old aristocracy they had replaced. The majority of the magnates of Lithuania were Orthodox Ruthenes but thought of themselves as Lithuanians and were proud of their separate status within the Commonwealth. The same could not be said for the inhabitants of the Ukraine, the great expanse which had once been the Kievan principality of Rus, had then been absorbed by Lithuania and, in 1569, was administratively tacked on to Poland.

The inhabitants of this area were in no sense a nation, but over the century following the Union of Lublin a mixture of religious strife, class tensions, cultural deprivation and simple regionalism contrived to turn them into one. The original Ruthene population had been diluted by the intrusion of Lithuanians, then Poles, Muscovites, and lesser contingents of Tatars, Moldavians and other Southern European migrants. Like the American West in the nineteenth century, the underpopulated but fertile Ukraine acted as a magnet for the most unlikely elements.

There was a fundamental conflict from the start between those, both indigenous and immigrant, who sought the freedom of the steppe, and those with more settled interests. Both the Ruthene boyars and the immigrant Polish and Lithuanian szlachta wanted to cultivate land, develop amenities and establish order. Polish administration was closely followed by Catholic clergy and large numbers of Jews, mostly brought in by the masters of large estates to act as middlemen, agents, rent-collectors and inn-keepers – all of which made them particularly odious to the local peasants.

The Ukraine had its own nobility, some of whom, like the Ostrogski and Zasławski, were descended from the Rurik rulers of Kiev; others, like the Zbaraski and Wiśniowiecki, from other Ruthene princely families. These were well equipped to stand at the head of their people, both by their ancient lineage and by their immense personal power. Prince Konstanty Ostrogski owned a hundred towns and 1,300 villages. Prince Jarema Michał Wiśniowiecki owned 38,000 homesteads, inhabited by some 230,000 of his subjects. But these princes became separated from their people by the lure of Polish culture and Western civilisation. A classic pattern of alienation evolved: it was with the best intentions that Prince Zbaraski travelled in the West and spent three years studying under Galileo, returning to the Ukraine to build, fortify and improve, but his people resented the improvements, and came to see him as a traitor.

With the great lords of the area failing to take responsibility, the only influence that could have stabilised this turbulent society and given its various elements a corporate identity was religion. The hierarchy of the Orthodox Church, which had been seriously shaken by the fall of Constantinople and the subsequent Ottoman expansion in the Balkans, was still in a state of disarray at the end of the sixteenth century. In 1588 the Patriarch of Constantinople paid a pastoral visit to his flock in the Commonwealth and held two synods, at Wilno and Kamieniec Podolski. The Chancellor of Poland put forward the suggestion that the Patriarch should settle in Kiev and turn it into the centre of the Orthodox Church. Jesuit influence prevented this, and several years later the Patriarch was invited by Tsar Boris Godunov to Moscow.

Before leaving Poland, the Patriarch had appointed Bishop Terlecki of Łuck to represent him in Poland. Terlecki started negotiations with his counterpart the Catholic Bishop of Łuck in the hope of achieving greater formal and political recognition of his own hierarchy. These moves played into the hands of the Jesuits, particularly of Piotr Skarga. Rome was amenable to any arrangements the Jesuits might recommend, and negotiations quickly came to a head. In 1595 an Act of Union was signed at Brześć between the Orthodox and the Catholic bishops. In return for their acceptance of the Pope instead of the Patriarch as their spiritual head, the Orthodox, henceforth known as Uniates, were allowed to keep their old Slavonic liturgy, the marriage of priests and communion under both forms.

The Jesuits congratulated themselves on having brought millions of wayward sheep into the fold, but many Orthodox priests and their flocks felt indignant at not having been consulted, and refused to adhere to the Union. Prince Ostrogski, head of the staunchest Orthodox family in the Ukraine, even called for an Orthodox-Protestant alliance to combat it. Since the Uniate bishops had failed to bring over their whole flock, there were now in effect three and not two Churches – Roman, Uniate and Orthodox. While the Roman and Uniate looked to the West, the Orthodox looked elsewhere. The Union had been designed to bind the Orthodox population of the Ukraine to Poland. In fact it had bound half of them to Moscow.

The Uniate bishops, disappointed because the seats in the Senate they had expected never materialised, still tried to force the Union on their flocks. They cajoled and bullied, but this only created tensions which were increasingly seen in a nationalist, or at least regionalist light. The organisation of the Uniate Church proceeded slowly. It was not until the 1630s that Metropolitan bishops were installed at Kiev and Polotsk, and by then the whole matter was coming under discussion once again. Władysław IV was keen to revise the arrangement within the framework of an entirely new formulation of religious freedom. He wanted to replace the toleration of differing religions as enshrined in the Act of the Confederation of Warsaw (1573) by some form of oecumenical consensus on religious diversity. After much preparation, he managed to hold a congress at Toruń in 1645, in which Catholics, Lutherans and Calvinists discussed their differences for a month before adjourning. The congress was inconclusive, but, as the king himself put it, 'at least nobody insulted each other'. A similar congress between the Catholic, Orthodox and Uniate Churches was planned for 1648. Meanwhile Metropolitan Mohila of Kiev was in the process of renegotiating the Union of Brześć with Rome.

These efforts to repair the shoddy work came too late. As Lew Saphieha, Chancellor of Lithuania, a supporter of the principle of the Union, had written to one of the Uniate bishops: 'Your dear Union has brought so much bitterness that we wish it had never been thought of, for we have only trouble and tears from it.' In fact, much of the bitterness stemmed from more tangible social and political factors. The drift of the Ruthene nobility towards Western culture was reflected in their choice of religion. Catholicism was a direct bridge to that civilisation, and more and more Ruthene lords crossed it. In 1632 Jarema Wiśniowiecki, the last of the great Ruthene princes to live entirely in the Ukraine and to cling tenaciously to the language, culture and traditions of Kievan Rus, converted to the Church of Rome. Orthodoxy had become the religion of the peasants. It was inevitable that the peasants would eventually see in it a rallying-point and a weapon.

Not that religion was on the face of it all that important to the inhabitants of the Ukraine. It was a turbulent place, where morality was in no great evidence and church-going confined to the more settled fringes. Frontier provinces often have a lore of their own, and in the case of the Ukraine a specific pattern was set by the most identifiable element in the local jigsaw – the Cossacks.

The Cossacks were not a people, they were a way of life. The very name 'Cossack' derives from a Turkish-Tatar word denoting a free soldier. While their skill with long-boats has suggested Viking traditions, it is now generally accepted that they were originally a breakaway group of Tatars, joined over the centuries by kindred spirits, including such unlikely ones as

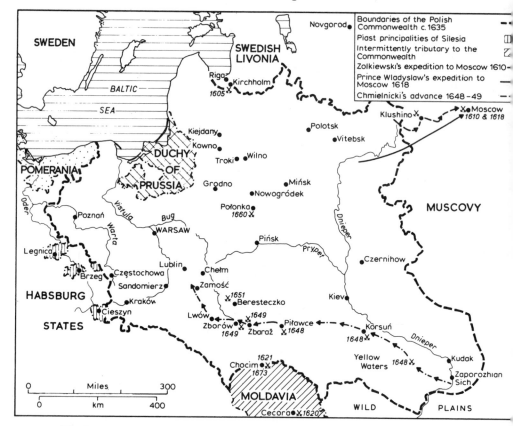

The Commonwealth in the mid-seventeenth century

Germans, Scandinavians, Jews and Spaniards. If their origins were mysterious and varied, their attitude and culture were simple. Their headquarters, the *Sich*, which lay on the Zaporozhe, the islands in the rapids of the
river Dnieper, was a commune in which elected elders held office. The
population of the *Sich* was highly variable, and almost anyone in the
Ukraine could be a Cossack if he wished. Much was written in the
nineteenth century about the national and cultural unity of the Cossacks,
with the accent on Romantic notions of the noble savage. Cossack leaders
were cast as either knights of Orthodoxy crusading against the Jewish and
Jesuit interloper, or as folk heroes dreaming of liberation from under the
Polish lord's boot. Such interpretation largely ignored the facts. The
Cossack leader Sulima, who led a rebellion in the 1630s, turns out to have
been a man of substance, and a creditor of no less a person than Prince
Wiśniowiecki himself. Sulima's friend Pavluk led his rebellion in the name

of the King of Poland, and his first action was to massacre the elders of the *Sich*. In the 1660s, Ivan Bruchowiecki, the leader of the Muscovite-inspired rising purporting to be on behalf of the Orthodox faith, was in fact a Polish Jew. The greatest of the Cossack heroes, Bohdan Chmielnicki, was a Jesuit-educated member of the Lithuanian landed szlachta, whose loyalties – to Poland, to the Cossacks, to the Porte, to Muscovy, and ultimately to himself – could hardly be construed as adhering to any nationalist or religious code.

The crux of the matter was the legal status and military role of the Cossacks. The area they inhabited marched with two highly threatening states. One was the Principality of Moldavia, whose rulers owed allegiance alternately to Poland, Turkey and Hungary. The other was the Khanate of the Krim Tatars, with its capital at Bakhchisaray in the Crimea, separated from the Commonwealth by a broad stretch of no-man's-land known as the Wild Plains. The Tatars were nominally subjects of Turkey. Every spring their raiding-parties or *tchambouls* set off along three trails running north into Muscovy, north-west into Poland, and west into the Ukraine respectively. They would debouch unexpectedly from the Wild Plains and scatter into smaller parties which scoured the countryside, burning and looting as they went. They took chattels and herds, and above all people, leaving behind only the old or infirm. As soon as their hands were full they would drive the booty back to the Crimea whence the wealthy would be ransomed and the rest shipped to the slave-markets of Istanbul.

Although the Tatars were a nuisance, they never represented a serious threat on their own. The threat lay in the fact that they could, and sometimes did, join up with an Ottoman army marching up through Moldavia, thereby effectively outflanking any Polish defence. Ever since the 1520s, when the Turks had ousted Venice and the Knights of St John from the eastern Mediterranean and taken over much of the Balkans, Moldavia and the Ukraine were the obvious theatre of their future expansion. The Commonwealth was directly threatened, and responded with two moves. In 1593 a Polish expedition placed a friendly vassal on the Moldavian throne and a *pax polonica* was imposed on the area, affording some security to the south-eastern reaches of the Commonwealth.

The other measure taken in the 1590s was the transformation of the Cossack community of the Zaporozhe *Sich* into an army. It was a sensible solution to what was on the one hand a problem of law and order in this frontier province, and on the other a need to create a defence force for the Commonwealth. The Cossacks were to play the same role in their area as the Knights of Malta in the Mediterranean. The Seym set a 'register' of serving Cossacks which defined their number and their pay, but while 'His Majesty's Zaporozhian Army' wore the title with pride, it did not quite fulfil the role expected of it. Instead of parrying Tatar raids, the Cossacks preferred to conduct their own. They would push into the Crimea or else climb into long-boats, sail down the Dnieper, and molest Turkish cities on the Black Sea. In 1606 they raided Kilia, Akerman and Varna. In 1608 they captured Perekop. In 1617 they sacked Trebizond. Their most spectacular achievement was in 1615, when they attacked Istanbul itself.

Relations between the Commonwealth and the Porte grew increasingly sour, and in 1620 Iskander Pasha invaded Moldavia. A small Polish force under Hetman Żółkiewski set off in support of the vassal prince. The Poles were defeated, Żółkiewski was killed and Field-Hetman Koniecpolski was taken prisoner. Tatar *tchambouls* swarmed into Poland as far as Lwow, in the rear of a second Polish army which had dug in at Chocim to hold off the Turks. Although the Poles managed to drive the Ottoman forces back then and on a similar occasion ten years later, the whole area remained vulnerable.

Nor had the creation of the Zaporozhian Army solved the internal problems of the Ukraine. The Cossacks saw themselves as loyal subjects of the king, and they had a particular affection for Władysław IV. But they were constantly at loggerheads with local authorities, the landed szlachta and the agents of large estates who kept trying to pin non-register Cossacks down to their official peasant status. In 1630 the register was raised to 8,000, but this proved to be the high-point of Polish concessions to the Zaporozhians. The Poles were wary of letting the Cossacks grow too strong, and at the same time they failed to understand the curious mixture of loyalty and mutiny that motivated them. Political discontent was quickly translated into mutinies which were an excuse for organised banditry. In 1637, after Pavluk's mutiny had been suppressed by Mikołaj Potocki, the register was reduced to 6,000. A fortress was built at Kudak on the bend in the Dnieper, from which a Polish garrison kept an eye on movements in the *Sich*.

Instead of being admitted as the third 'nation' of the Commonwealth, the Ukraine was treated, by its own élite as well as by the Poles, as a sort of colony, and the resultant sense of deprivation was a cause of profound bitterness. It was these simmering tensions that boiled over in the late 1640s, triggering off a series of events that finally shattered all the dreams of Ukrainian nationhood, broke the Commonwealth's power decisively, and benefited Turkey and above all Muscovy beyond its wildest expectations.

In 1640, and again in 1644, uncommonly large Tatar *tchambouls* ravaged Podolia and Volynia. Hetman Koniecpolski managed to defeat them, but not before they had carried off multitudes into slavery. In the winter of 1645 the Tatars sent their *tchambouls* into Muscovy in even larger numbers and this time Field-Hetman Mikołaj Potocki was dispatched with a Polish army to help the Muscovites, the result of a rapprochement which had taken place between Warsaw and Moscow. This gave rise to a plan for a joint Polish-Muscovite offensive into the Crimea, which Muscovy would then incorporate into its own boundaries, followed by a similar expedition into Moldavia, which would be incorporated into the Commonwealth. Two unexpected factors shattered this plan. One was that Hetman Koniecpolski, now approaching his sixtieth year, absented himself to marry for the third time. His bride, Zofia Opalińska, was not only a great heiress but also a vivacious girl of sixteen. After a brief honeymoon which the Hetman described to a friend in ecstatic terms, he died of exhaustion on 10 March 1646.

The other surprise came in May, when King Władysław announced that he was going to lead a crusade to recover Constantinople. Like many idle yet vain people, Władysław IV was forever entertaining dreams of military glory. His projects of conquering Muscovy and Sweden, his diplomatic initiatives in Central Europe, and almost every enterprise he had undertaken had come to nothing. Now a new chimera appeared to his fancy, cleverly exploited by the ambassador of the Venetian Republic, which badly needed a diversion against the Turks. The Seym was in uproar, and Chancellor Ossoliński quashed the project. But Władysław had already secretly given the Cossacks money, and told them to double the register to 12,000 and start building long-boats. The Cossacks had set to work in high spirits. Their anger was all the greater when news reached them that the Seym had stymied the king's plans. The agreed Crimean and Moldavian campaigns were less attractive to them than a royal licence to take to their boats and rampage around the southern shores of the Black Sea. As sometimes happens at such moments, one man and his personal grievances stumbled on to the scene and brought about an explosion. His name was Bohdan Chmielnicki.

Chmielnicki was a member of the landed szlachta, and although he was Orthodox, he had been educated by the Jesuits. He took part in the 1620 Moldavian campaign, and was taken prisoner by the Turks at the battle of Cecora along with Koniecpolski. When they recovered their freedom, Koniecpolski obtained for him the post of Secretary to the Zaporozhian Army. Chmielnicki was not an attractive individual. He waged a personal vendetta with a no less unsavoury Lithuanian neighbour who finally killed his son. Failing to get justice from the local court, Chmielnicki went to the *Sich*, where he stirred the already indignant Cossacks into a frenzy and started negotiating with the Tatars.

The situation was not critical. The king was personally due in the Ukraine, Polish forces were concentrating, and the Muscovite army had started moving south to link up with them. Hetman Potocki, however, decided that a show of strength was required and in April 1648 he dispatched his twenty-four-year-old son Stefan with 3,500 men, half of them Cossacks, towards the *Sich*. At the end of the month he reached the Yellow Waters, where he was surrounded by the Zaporozhian Army under Chmielnicki. For three weeks he held out in his fortified camp, but when his own Cossacks deserted he attempted to retreat. He and his army were quickly cut to pieces. His bibulous father, who had been making a leisurely march to his assistance, was ambushed at Korsuń. Only a couple of cavalry regiments managed to escape, while he and Field-Hetman Kalinowski fell into the hands of the Cossacks.

The consecutive defeats came as a rude shock to Poland and greatly enhanced Chmielnicki's prestige. Cossacks and peasants flocked to his banner from all over the Ukraine. At this point, the situation turned critical. Władysław IV, the only man in a position to placate the Cossacks, died unexpectedly on his way from Wilno to Warsaw. With a whole province in revolt and the two commanders of the Polish forces in captivity, the last thing the Commonwealth needed was an election. The Muscovites realised that plans would have to be shelved. Their army, moving down the Dnieper towards the prearranged meeting with the Poles, halted and then gradually withdrew.

It was fortunate for the Commonwealth that both the Primate and *interrex*, Maciej Łubieński, and the Chancellor, Jerzy Ossoliński, were sagacious men. They arranged a ceasefire through Adam Kisiel, Palatine of Kiev, the only Orthodox member of the Senate. Having secured a provisional truce, Kisiel went on to negotiate a broader settlement, but hopes of an amicable resolution were dashed by Prince Wiśniowiecki, who led his own private army into the field against the Cossacks. The greatest Ruthene lord of the Ukraine was not interested in Ukrainian autonomy, but in restoring order and putting down the rabble. This strengthened the hand of those in the Cossack camp who wanted war rather than negotiation, and Chmielnicki bowed to the pressure.

A large Polish army had assembled, including detachments of the *levée en masse* from the threatened areas, but since the two Hetmans were still alive in Cossack hands, it was commanded by a committee of three. The *levée en masse* fled after a short skirmish at Piławce, and the rest of the army was precipitated into a disorderly retreat. It was an appalling display. 'These were not the Poles we knew, the victors over Turks and Muscovites, of Tatars and Germans,' one Cossack colonel said, 'but cowards and rabbits, children clad in steel. They died of fright when they saw us.' The news of Piławce spread like wildfire, and the whole of the Ukraine rose. The beleaguered garrison of Kudak capitulated and with it vanished the last semblance of Polish order in the Ukraine. Huge numbers of peasants joined the Cossacks, and, aided by Chmielnicki's Tatar allies, they scoured the country with fire and sword. Szlachta, whether Ruthene or Polish, were murdered, along with priests and nuns, and Jews were massacred in their thousands. The Tatars were merciless, and taught their Cossack allies many a refinement. The Moldavian custom of impaling alive caught on, and was practised with relish by Cossacks and Poles alike. Decades of tension erupted into mindless cruelty. Chmielnicki was no longer master of the situation, any more than Ossoliński on the Polish side. Leading the crusade against the rabble were Prince Wiśniowiecki and Janusz Radziwiłł, Field-Hetman of Lithuania, both acting independently.

Rid of the mixed blessing of the *levée en masse*, the Polish army had dug in at Zbaraż, where it held off the Cossack and Tatar army. Then came the first Polish success, at the Battle of Zborów, after which negotiations were reopened and a basic agreement quickly reached. The three Palatinates of Kiev, Bracław and Czernyhów were to be declared Cossack territory, into which no Polish troops, Jews or Jesuits would be allowed. All dignitaries and officials in the area were to be Orthodox Ruthene szlachta, and the register was to stand at 40,000 men.

Ossoliński and his more reasonable counterparts had managed to pour oil on the water once again, and the Ukraine quietened down. It was not to last. In 1650 Jerzy Ossoliński died, leaving the camp of moderation seriously weakened. In the same year, Chmielnicki accepted the over-lordship of the Sultan, who named him vassal Prince of the Ukraine. Polish forces moved into the Ukraine and in the three-day Battle of Beresteczko routed the Cossack army and its Tatar allies. A new peace was signed at Biała Cerkiew annulling all the previous Polish concessions, but while one Polish army set about pacifying the Ukraine, another which had gone to Moldavia to head off Chmielnicki's Turkish allies was defeated and massacred at Batoh.

While a plague ravaged the country, discontent simmered in many quarters. Władysław IV had been succeeded by his younger brother, Jan Kazimierz, a complex and not very inspiring figure. He had spent some of his life as a soldier and some of it as a Jesuit priest. He was intelligent and resourceful, but he suffered from fits of depression and listlessness which hindered a consistent policy. His lack of charm did not help him to gain the confidence of the szlachta, while many magnates felt an intense dislike for him. They also distrusted the queen, Louise Marie de Gonzague, Duchesse de Nevers, Princess of Mantua, who ruled the king, or, as the French ambassador, de Béziers, put it, 'gets everything she wants out of him, by exhausting rather than convincing him.'

Her grandfather, a friend and collaborator of Marie de Médicis, had come to Poland with Henri de Valois, and her father, the last Gonzaga Duke of Mantua, had also spent some time in Warsaw. She herself was brought up entirely at the French court, and was at one time groomed to marry Gaston d'Orléans, but spoiled her chances by her affair with the notorious Cinq Mars, beheaded by Richelieu. In 1645, as a result of a rapprochement between Poland and France, she married Władysław IV, and after his death, his younger brother Jan Kazimierz. He was then forty, and she thirty-eight.

She was brought up in the intellectual atmosphere of the Paris salons, frequented Port-Royal, and surrounded herself with mathematicians and scientists. She brought this love of the arts and sciences with her to Poland. She took an active interest in everything from astrology (supporting the Gdańsk astronomer Hevelius) to flying machines (paying for the development of a flying dragon invented by one of the king's secretaries which caused a stir among the savants). She had also brought in her wake a bevy of young French ladies who quickly made good matches in Polish society. They introduced French court culture to Poland, but their real importance, and that of the queen herself, was that they were part of a plan hatched by Mazarin to bring the Commonwealth within the French orbit, and if possible, place a Bourbon on its throne. As they set to work laying the foundations for this, they aroused Polish suspicions.

The fumbling way in which the Cossack mutiny had been handled and the embarrassing defeats suffered by Polish arms gave many the impression that the Commonwealth was sick. At least one faction among the magnates, including the Radziwiłł and Lubomirski families, felt that the best cure would be the removal of Jan Kazimierz, and they began to plot accordingly. In the case of the Radziwiłł, it went further. The family had thought of themselves as quasi-royal for the last century, and their dream of assuming the throne of a separate Lithuania had grown into something of an obsession with Janusz Radziwiłł, who hated Jan Kazimierz.

In 1654, Bohdan Chmielnicki, who had developed dynastic aspirations quite as extravagant as those of the Radziwiłł, negotiated the Treaty of Piereyaslav, placing himself under the protection of Muscovy in return for military assistance against the Commonwealth. Tsar Alexey began to style himself 'Tsar of Great and Little Russia'. There were protests from some of the Cossacks, and the Orthodox Metropolitan of Kiev announced that he for one was still a subject of the King of Poland. Nevertheless, Alexey invaded Lithuania while the Cossacks advanced into Poland. He defeated Janusz Radziwiłł and took Polotsk, Smolensk, Vitebsk and Mohilev, while the Cossacks reached Lublin. In the following spring Alexey took Wilno, and titled himself 'Grand Duke of Lithuania, Byelorussia and Podolia'. Far from getting Lithuania for themselves the Radziwiłł were now in imminent peril of becoming Muscovite subjects, and they reacted quickly. They appealed for help to the King of Sweden.

Charles X Gustavus had just ascended the throne. His country was bankrupt after the Thirty Years' War, its only asset a huge and now redundant army. In spite of the twenty years of peace with the Commonwealth, the Swedes still dreamed of extending their possessions on the Baltic. The discontent of many Polish magnates, the confusion attendant on the Cossack and Muscovite invasions, and finally the appeal from the Radziwiłł, all paved the way for an invasion, which took place at the beginning of 1655.

The Swedes rapidly made themselves masters of Pomerania and advanced into Wielkopolska. A Polish army barred their way, but was made to capitulate by Krzysztof Opaliński, Palatine of Poznań, and his colleague the Palatine of Kalisz, who officially transferred their provinces to Swedish overlordship. The enemies of Jan Kazimierz all over the country announced his dethronement in favour of Charles X. With three enemy armies operating in the country confusion reigned. Disoriented by a false rumour that Jan Kazimierz had abdicated, Hetman Stanisław Rewera Potocki capitulated. Isolated groups of szlachta and small bodies of troops on their way to join the army either capitulated or dispersed.

Jan Kazimierz advanced to face the enemy with a small army commanded by Stefan Czarniecki, Castellan of Kiev. In September 1655 they were defeated at Żarnowiec and fell back on Kraków. The king then took refuge in Silesia, while Czarniecki tried unsuccessfully to hold Kraków. On 22 October Janusz Radziwiłł signed an agreement at Kiejdany detaching Lithuania from Poland and placing it under the protection of Sweden. Swedish troops appeared in every province, often accompanied by magnates or szlachta who supported Charles. Since there was little to choose between one Vasa king and another many accepted what appeared to be a fait accompli. The structure of the Commonwealth seemed to have fallen apart like a house of cards.

A few centres of resistance remained. Gdańsk held out stoutly for Jan Kazimierz; Lwów, under the command of Krzysztof Grodzicki, the one-eyed defender of Kudak, held off the Cossacks; Piotr Potocki, Palatine of Bracław, was holding Kamieniec; the fortress of Zamość defied a siege laid by Charles himself; and the fortified monastery of Częstochowa fought off a siege in a manner which has passed far beyond history into legend. Even in Lithuania, one member of the Radziwiłł family and a number of szlachta led by one of the Sapieha clan defiantly refused to bow to the new arrangement. The Tatars were prescient enough to see that if the Commonwealth were defeated it would only be a matter of time before Muscovy and the Cossacks would devastate the Crimea, and Mehmet Girey therefore signed an alliance with Jan Kazimierz, immediately followed up by the despatch of several thousand warriors to the Polish army.

The majority of the population of the Commonwealth was quite prepared to accept Charles as king, but he was only interested in keeping Pomerania and Livonia, and treated the rest of Poland as occupied territory. He and his generals immediately began exporting everything they could lay hands on – pictures, sculpture, furniture, entire libraries. The Protestant Swedes also took to burning down churches, having first emptied them of everything portable, and this sacrilege incensed the peasants, who were hardly concerned as to who sat on the throne. They began to massacre lone soldiers, then lone detachments. A guerilla war developed, with bands of loyal szlachta and peasants making life very unpleasant for the Swedes. In January 1656, the king took the offensive at the head of the army he had rallied. Although they managed to win the three-day battle of Warsaw in July, the situation began to swing against the Swedes. Denmark and Holland joined the Polish alliance, and in June a Dutch fleet broke the Swedish blockade and sailed in to relieve Gdańsk. The Swedes made an alliance with the Elector of Brandenburg and the Prince of Transylvania, and briefly managed to reoccupy Warsaw in 1657, but they and their allies were decisively beaten in the following year. In 1660 peace was signed on the basis of a return to the *status quo ante*.

The death of Chmielnicki in 1657 had ended the Cossack threat. He was succeeded by Jan Wyhowski, a moderate and a realist, who quickly brought negotiations to a head. On 16 Setpember 1658 the Union of Hadziacz turned the Commonwealth of Two Nations into a Commonwealth of Three Nations. The Ukraine was to have its own Chancellor, Treasurer, Marshal and Hetman, chosen by the king from candidates proposed by the Cossacks. It was to have its own courts, its own mint, and of course its own army. Several hundred Cossacks were ennobled, and the Metropolitan of Kiev and the Orthodox bishops of Lwów, Przemyśl, Chełm, Łuck and Mścisław were to have seats in the Senate. No Polish or Lithuanian troops were allowed to enter the three Palatinates, in which only Orthodox Ruthenes were to hold office. The Ukraine was to be given two Ruthene universities and a number of schools, paid for by the Commonwealth.

This project came to nothing. At the end of 1659 Wyhowski was toppled by Chmielnicki's son, who emulated his father by swearing allegiance to both the King of Poland and the Tsar of Muscovy at the same time. Muscovite forces invaded in support of the Cossacks, but both they and the Cossacks were beaten by Polish armies at Cudnów and Połonka in 1660. Having pacified the Ukraine, Jan Kazimierz invaded Muscovy, but he was soon forced to withdraw: Poland was devastated and exhausted, and the Ottoman armies hovered in the south.

Strategically, the position had shifted in favour of Muscovy, whose ambition to become the sole and undisputed focus for the future of Russia had been realised. Ivan the Terrible had crushed Novgorod. Pskov and every other Russian political unit beside Moscow, which left only Kiev and the Ukraine, but the Cossacks had put paid to any hopes of creating an independent Russian centre there. They had started out by changing

70 The Sarmatian warrior: Stefan Czarniecki, Field-Hetman of Poland and Palatine of Kiev, from a portrait by B. Matthisen. He remained faithful to King Jan Kazimierz throughout the Swedish wars, and although he suffered some crushing defeats in 1655, he rallied the forces of resistance and eventually carried the war through Denmark into Swedish territory. Note the *Bułava*, the Hetman's baton of command.

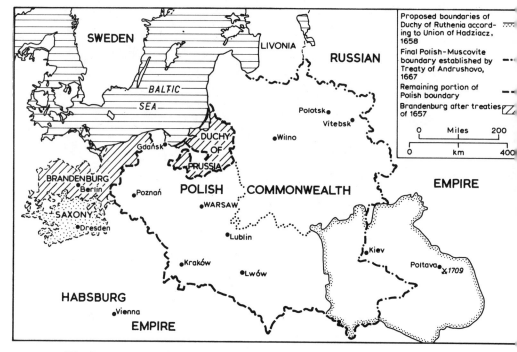

Proposed boundaries of Duchy of Ruthenia according to Union of Hadziacz, 1658	
Final Polish-Muscovite boundary established by Treaty of Andrushovo, 1667	
Remaining portion of Polish boundary	
Brandenburg after treaties of 1657	

The Commonwealth in decline

allegiance in order to force the Commonwealth into concessions, but this tactic had turned into a bad habit. By the time the concessions had been wrung from the Commonwealth by the Union of Hadziacz, the Cossacks were changing sides every few months and fighting among themselves. Chmielnicki had been so successful in demonstrating to everyone that the Ukraine was a vital strategic area that he turned it into a Balkans. None of the interested parties – the Commonwealth, Muscovy, the Habsburgs, the Porte – could countenance its independence. Certainly, none of them could countenance its remaining entirely under another state's domination. By the Treaty of Andruszowo in 1667, Poland and Muscovy divided the Ukraine between themselves along the Dnieper.

No less a personage than Leibniz pointed out, in a pamphlet written a couple of years later, that the Treaty of Andruszowo was strategically disastrous for the Commonwealth. It was not the loss of territory that mattered. The Ukraine, a potential partner and ally against both Muscovy and Turkey, had ceased to exist. What remained in Polish hands now formed a sort of promontory surrounded on three sides by enemies. Not being a distinct partner in the Commonwealth, the area was little more than a colony, inevitably discontented and liable to be subverted by Muscovy. With the Ukraine cancelled out, Muscovy no longer needed to fear Poland in the military sense, while Poland was now in a weaker position with regard to both Turkey and Muscovy. It was a nail in the coffin of the Commonwealth's Great Power status.

11

Anatomy of Decay

Polish diplomatic missions were famous in seventeenth-century Europe. They were carried out in the manner of a Roman triumph, and the show made by Prince Zbaraski as he entered Istanbul in 1622 is typical:

> At the front marched two regiments of Hungarian infantry, followed by a hundred laden waggons decked in the arms of the Zbaraski, then a group of servants, and two troops of light cavalry. Behind these rode ten picked youths, dripping with gold and gems. Their mounts, harnessed with pearls, covered in embroidered cloths, with coloured horse-tails at their chins, foamed at the mouth as they champed at their golden bits. Behind them came the sons, relatives and friends of the Zbaraski, all in velvet embroidered with silver and gold thread. The envoy himself wore a cloak of cloth of gold and a fur cap with a beautiful diamond jewel clasping a tall plume. Six handsome footmen in velvet jerkins led his bravely prancing steed. Behind him rode twenty page-boys in Circassian dress, with helmets, shields and quivers. These were followed by fifty young men in Roumelian costume, with curved bows hanging from gold sashes, a troop of Cossacks and a hundred servants of the Prince, all in silk. The rear was brought up by forty mounted musketeers of the Prince's bodyguard, their horses wearing ostrich-plumes, silver breast-plates, and silver rings which jangled on their harness.

In 1633 Rome was treated to the carnival of Jerzy Ossoliński's embassy, consisting of some three hundred riders and ten camels decked out in feathers, gold caparisons and pearls, which Stefano Della Bella captured in a set of engravings. The same artist happened to be in Paris in 1645 when Rafał Leszczyński's cavalcade entered the city. This time he needed thirteen long plates to contain the multitude of riders, most of whose horses were intentionally loosely-shod, so that they scattered the cobbles of the Faubourg Saint-Antoine with solid gold horse-shoes as a gesture to the populace of the city. Both camels and gold horse-shoes became *de rigueur* in subsequent embassies, and numbers went up as well. In 1676 Prince Michał Czartoryski took no less than 1,500 retainers on his embassy to Moscow. In the following year Jan Gniński strained the arrangements made by his Turkish hosts, one of whom quipped that he had brought too many to sign a peace, and too few to fight a war.

Both as a measure of Poland's wealth and as a symbol of its diplomatic ascendancy, these displays were highly misleading. They obscured the fact that the Commonwealth had no regular diplomatic organisation, no central chancellery which could coordinate one, and no coherent foreign policy. They were more successful in giving the impression that Poland was a country of immense wealth, distorting the economic realities. The Commonwealth's economy had suffered from the twenty years of war, but these only aggravated a situation induced by unfavourable patterns which had been defined long before.

While the sixteenth century saw the beginnings of capitalism take root in the West, Eastern Europe had drifted into what might best be described as industrial agriculture. Poland exported foodstuffs, cattle, wax, hemp, timber, flax, charcoal, pitch, iron and other raw materials, and only a few low-quality finished products, such as beer, rope and cloth. It imported products of every description and a quantity of colonial goods. It was essentially the sort of trading pattern that places third-world countries at the mercy of the industrialised nations today. This was pointed out as early as 1543 by the Polish economist Andrzej Glaber and by foreign travellers, who saw the extreme cheapness of food in Poland as a sign of an unhealthy economy. The carriage of goods was predominantly in foreign hands, which meant that a large part of the profit was made outside the country. Of the ships leaving Gdańsk with Polish exports in 1585, for instance, 52 per cent were Dutch, 24 per cent Frisian, and 12 per cent English. The real market-place for Polish grain was not Gdańsk but Amsterdam, whence it was re-exported to Spain and other countries.

This trade began to decline in importance quite early. By 1625 Hamburg had overtaken Gdańsk as the busiest port in the North. Prices of grain on Western markets fell steadily as smaller countries like England and the Netherlands learnt to grow more intensively and to feed themselves with colonial products, such as rice and eventually the potato. This was further aggravated by Muscovy beginning to export the same products as Poland.

The most dramatic effect on this trade was produced by the twenty years of war in the middle of the century. Grain exports through Gdańsk in the early 1600s averaged 200,000 tonnes per annum, reaching some 250,000 tonnes in the bumper year of 1618. The figure for 1651, after three years of Cossack unrest, was only 100,000 and two years later this had fallen to 60,000, which remained the average yearly figure for the rest of the century. The import of 'colonial' goods (spices, rice, sugar, dyes, silks) through Gdańsk went up by 10 per cent between 1615 and 1635, and then shot up by 50 per cent between 1635 and 1690. Only in the case of Gdańsk are such comprehensive figures available, and it is impossible to ascertain the position for other ports like Elbing, or for overland trade with Germany and Muscovy, where the balance was more favourable. Nevertheless these figures are a good pointer to general trends.

The mid-century wars were disastrous in other respects. The casualties were not in themselves remarkable, except in the south-eastern areas where the butcheries of Jews and clergy took place. The Tatars led many thousands off into slavery and Tsar Alexey deported huge numbers of people from Byelorussia to colonise newly conquered areas of Siberia, but the most destructive were the Swedes. The wholesale razing of crops, the burning of villages and towns, and the removal of cattle brought about famine, compounded by a plague. The results were devastating. Between 1600, when the population of the Commonwealth stood at over 10 million, and 1650, there was an increase of 23 per cent, but in the ten years between 1650 and 1660, it fell by at least 25 per cent, to below the original 10 million mark. With war and famine destroying their villages, people wandered the countryside in search of less badly affected areas. As a result, production of food fell to disastrous levels. By 1668, when the situation had stabilised, 58 per cent of arable land on szlachta estates was lying fallow, while the figures for Church estates and royal lands were 82 per cent and 86 per cent respectively.

The greatest casualties were the towns. At the beginning of the century, Gdańsk was still by far the largest, with 70,000 inhabitants, followed by Warsaw (30,000), Kraków (28,000), Poznań and Lwów (20,000), Elbing (18,000), Toruń (12,000) and Lublin (10,000). Of the other 900 or so townships throughout the Commonwealth, most had between 500 and 2,000 inhabitants. In all, about a quarter of the population lived in towns. The Swedish army took a heavy toll of the cities it entered, and only Gdańsk and Lwów managed to keep the enemy outside the walls. After the ravages of war came the food shortages. The result was that between 1650 and 1660, the urban population of the Commonwealth declined by up to 70 per cent.

The major cities had long been under pressure from private towns belonging to magnates or the Church. Places like Lublin, Sandomierz and even Kraków were losing much of their business as agents for the produce of the country and as providers of finished goods to the locality. They were poorly represented and heavily taxed. After the wars, which destroyed much of Warsaw, Kraków, Poznań, Lublin and Wilno – the latter was put to fire and sword for seventeen days by Tsar Alexey in 1655 – they found it difficult to rebuild. Such investment as was forthcoming was lavished on the private towns by their solicitous owners. But these private towns could not replace the older cities in one crucial respect. They were functionally limited to the exploitation and the provision of essentials to a given area, and there was little scope for enterprise or investment by individual merchants or manufacturers. They never grew into centres of finance and credit, generating their own wealth and industry, while the older towns were in no position to carry on this function as before. Only the magnates, the Church and the crown could promote industrial development, and although they did do so to some extent, this was hardly sufficient.

Elective monarchs tended to regard the Commonwealth not as part of their patrimony, to be cared for and enriched on behalf of their descendants, but rather as a sinecure which should be enjoyed while it lasted. They tended to use their position either to enhance their own glory or further the cause of their dynasty, which was why they were more active in foreign policy than in home affairs. It was only when it had become clear to Zygmunt III that his son was going to succeed him that he began to care for the internal health of the Commonwealth. In 1624 he set up new steelworks at Bobra and Samsonów, and a few years later modernised the mines under royal control. Władysław IV, who felt dynastically attached to Poland, took an active part in industrial development, but even where the will existed, the means often did not.

The fiscal arrangements of the Commonwealth had always been based on minimalist principles, as it was widely felt that taxes generated spending and yet more taxes. Moreover, the burden of taxation was very unevenly and unprofitably laden on the economy. The greatest areas of economic activity were the landowning szlachta's home and export sales, which were exempt from taxation; the large Jewish community in Poland, which assessed, collected and paid in its own taxes without outside supervision, with predictable results; and the greatest financial centre of the Commonwealth, the city of Gdańsk, which had for long benefited from extensive immunities (which is why it was so consistently patriotic in the face of foreign invasion and the threat of incorporation into a less accommodating state). In a word, the greatest areas of financial activity in the country were hardly taxed at all.

The main body of Treasury revenue was from a plethora of taxes inherited from medieval times – land tax, property tax, poll-tax, customs and port dues, mining concessions, hearth tax, and so on – which were unproductive and complicated to collect. The crown's income from royal lands and starosties was susceptible to venality on the part of administrators and beneficiaries. All special taxes or surcharges, as well as the rates at which existing taxes were assessed, had to be voted on a one-off basis by the national Seym. The result was that in the first half of the century the Commonwealth's revenue was only slightly higher than that of the tiny state of Bavaria, and about one-tenth of the revenues of France.

The Commonwealth was caught in a vicious circle. The available resources could not be adequately taxed and used to repair the economy without a measure of political reform. This could not be achieved in a situation where the crown lacked the resources to adopt a vigorous policy, the state was penniless, and the majority of the electorate financially dependent on the magnates, who for obvious reasons opposed any such reform.

The crisis of 1648–68 had revealed that whereas the human fabric of the Commonwealth was resilient and difficult to demolish, the structural element of the state was desperately flimsy. In place of the institutions and procedures which constitute the beams and girders of most political edifices, the Commonwealth had only moral concepts and hazy traditions. The crown was an ill-defined institution, without the usual dynastic buttressing. The king inherited his predecessor's problems without any of the personal advantages or popularity his predecessor might have gained. Since the reigning monarch was only a temporary incumbent, loyalty to the crown did not necessarily mean loyalty to the king. Each one had to build up his own following and his own power-base, which were highly sensitive to the fortunes of politics.

There was no administrative body in the Commonwealth able to guarantee continuity and provide a new king with organs of power. Even the army had slipped away from under the crown's control. The Hetmans and the Regimentaries (who were the paymasters of the foreign mercenaries) made all decisions and provisions with complete independence. The extremely damaging Slav habit of life tenure of office, which had crept into practice at the end of the sixteenth century, meant that an incoming monarch had to wait for years before he could place men he trusted in important posts. As well as representing his only method of exerting control, the king's right of appointment was his main source of influence. With the rise of the oligarchy of magnates, however, it grew increasingly difficult for him to exercise this freely. Jan Kazimierz found it impossible to promote his ablest soldier, Stefan Czarniecki, to the rank of Field-Hetman when this fell vacant, because it was coveted by the powerful Jerzy Lubomirski.

The Seym had lost most of its executive power long before, but by the middle of the century it had also lost its coherence, largely because the nation whose mouthpiece it was had lost its sense of purpose. In principle, the szlachta were equal and united. These twin principles were expressed symbolically in the fact that a penniless gentleman addressed a magnate as 'brother', and that multifarious origins were submerged in the political identity of the Polish 'nation'. A baptised Jew from Volhynia would sign himself *'gente Ruthenus, Natione Polonus, origine Judaeus'*. In many ways, the Commonwealth resembled a modern one-party state. Membership of the

'Party' was more important than wealth or personal attributes, and position within the 'Party' was most important of all. Contemporary diaries and letters refer to people not by their names, but by their offices. It is not unusual to find an account of the doings of a Palatine of Kraków, his meeting with the Castellan of Rawa, the Starosta of Kaniów, the Field-Hetman of the Crown, the Marshal of the Court or the Grand Equerry of Lithuania, without a name being mentioned.

The only real bond uniting the szlachta was the community of shared privileges, the 'Golden Freedoms' which guaranteed the same immunity to all. Nobody could tell even the humblest member of the szlachta what to do, and no power could lock him up or punish him, whatever he said or did within the law. That was no small thing in the context of seventeenth-century Europe. Absolutism and centralised government were gaining ground in all but a few of the smaller states of the continent, and the szlachta felt that their freedoms could easily be trampled if their vigilance lapsed. They feared that even the slightest tampering with the constitution might undermine their position, and therefore saw any talk of reform as a direct attack on their sacred inheritance – their only inheritance in the case of the poorest. Nothing could unite them like a programme for reform, not even foreign invasion.

In effect, their community of interest was largely fictitious by this stage. The gap between the richest and the poorest had grown immense, destroying the 'co-operative' element in the Commonwealth. The magnates owned the country, while some two-thirds of the szlachta, the *bene nati sed non possessionati*, had no material stake in it. The szlachta was also growing increasingly mongrelised. The legislation aimed at preventing the upward mobility of other classes was almost impossible to enforce, and barriers never became impermeable to infiltration. Plebeians continued to marry or assimilate into the szlachta with little difficulty. The king ennobled Polish and foreign soldiers, particularly Scots and Frenchmen. Another significant source of intake into the szlachta was a clause in the Statutes of Lithuania of 1588 according to which any Jew who converted to Catholicism was automatically ennobled. The attendant differences of outlook were compounded by the sheer size of the Commonwealth. The fear of Tatar raids felt by someone who lived east of Lwów seemed overstated to an inhabitant of Wielkopolska; the Livonian's anxiety about Muscovite intentions was of little concern to a landowner from Mazovia; and a soldier from Podolia felt more out of place in Gdańsk than if he had gone to Istanbul. The szlachta were the only administrative cement holding these disparate provinces together, but because they were the political body of the nation as well as the administrative force, divergent political outlooks could affect the administrative unity of the state. The Palatine of Poznań or Hetman of Lithuania who went over to the Swedish

71 The Polish way with horses: they were caparisoned in silk and velvet embroidered with silver and gold, pearls and precious stones, and, on high days and holidays, dyed in a variety of colours.

72 Wincenty Gosiewski, Field-Hetman of Lithuania, who fought successfully against the Swedes in 1655, but was defeated and captured by the Muscovites. While in captivity, he translated the *Maximes* of Pierre de la Serre, and was later pensioned by Louis XIV for his efforts to bring about the election of the Duc d'Enghien to the Polish throne. His francophilia did not prevent him from affecting the Sarmatian style, as can be seen from his coat of eastern mail, his cap of pearls and his Turkish-style shield.

73 Part of a silver coffee-service made in Lwów in the second half of the 17th century. Ottoman taste was not limited to armour and horse-tack.

side did not see themselves as traitors, for they were acting as political units while making their choice, rather than as officers of the king. At a less dramatic level, regional political viewpoints held by factions in the Seym frequently obstructed the smooth passage of legislation of national benefit.

The political culture of the electorate and its deputies was no longer up to handling the machinery of government, with its subtle blend of regional autonomy with centralism and individual freedom with ideological conformism. The regionalism had turned into parish-pump politics, and individual freedom into bad behaviour. The humanist vision of the previous century was replaced by religious superstition and political dogmatism. Safe in its near-monopoly, Jesuit schooling had declined considerably, and now confined itself to inculcating into its pupils a religious, social and political catechism, and teaching them enough Latin and Rhetoric to enable them to drone on for hours at political meetings. Foreign travel, the panacea of the sixteenth-century Poles, became less common and its purpose less salutary. Those who had gone abroad in the 1550s had returned with an education and a collection of books. Those who travelled in the 1650s brought back pictures and venereal disease. Gradually, the whole exercise came to be seen as pointless and pernicious, while foreigners and their ways were viewed as suspect. Even Polish cities, being full of imported manners, were widely regarded as dens of wickedness and depravity – as well as being the preserve of moneyed plebeians.

From such feelings a siege philosophy was born, a bumpkin mentality which soon took over a large proportion of the minor szlachta, and was given voice by a profusion of local bards. From their humble but comfortable wooden manor houses hung with portraits of ancestors and captured Turkish weapons, manor houses which they represented as repositories of virtue and Sarmatian values, these members of the szlachta propounded a gospel of mediocrity. They suggested that a life in the country was a life close to God, and drew all their experience from Nature. The observation that Nature survives all calamities, that land laid waste by the invader flowers again in the spring, bred the particularly damaging wisdom that somehow the Commonwealth would survive. Combined with the blind faith that God would not let His people down, this encouraged an attitude of optimistic fatalism with regard to politics.

The contrast between the purity of country life and the vanity and wickedness of the court is a recurring theme in European thought and literature. In Poland it was woven into political life as well, and sixteenth-century writers sought to transfer the utopian ideal of the Commonwealth into the local unit of the manor in order to create Arcadia. By the middle of the seventeenth century, this train of thought had been turned on its head. The perfect complacency of a life of self-sufficient idleness in the country was idealised for its own sake and projected on to the public life of the state.

The only extra-mural activities accorded a place in this canon were the szlachta's right and duty to cast its vote and defend the country. Local seymiks, which were not hard to get to and afforded all the entertainment of fashionable race-meetings, continued to be well and vociferously attended. Royal elections, which demanded the cost and inconvenience of a journey to Warsaw, drew fewer and fewer voters as time went by. As for military service in defence of the Commonwealth, the szlachta contributed more lines of verse to its glories than soldiers to its ranks during the course of the seventeenth century. The less they served, the more they believed in the myth of their chivalric role. The less they participated in government, the more indispensable to it they believed themselves to be. The less it functioned, the more they extolled the perfections of the Commonwealth and its constitution.

This precarious balance between a dogmatic belief in a set of myths and shibboleths and a fundamentally cynical grasp of reality is characteristic of the szlachta of this period, as it is of many a society in decline. A good illustration of this state of mind is to be found in the memoirs of Jan Chrysostom Pasek (1636–1701), one of the most colourful literary creations of the seventeenth century. Through the pages of his memoirs this typical minor noble from Mazovia reveals himself as a brave, ignorant, pious, cunning, superstitious, drunken, litigious, xenophobic, and yet remarkably endearing personality. The book narrates with honesty and verve his life of soldiering in Poland and Denmark, and his retirement to the country, where he partakes fully of the excitements of local scandals, seymiks, lawsuits, hunting, and all the other activities of the szlachta. Pasek no doubt thought himself a good man and a religious one, but as in the case of Pepys, it is the fundamental amorality of the author that makes the memoirs such an authentic and entertaining source.

Such attitudes were politically disastrous in a state where everything depended on the wisdom and goodwill of the electorate. Sensible debate was ruled out by ignorance and bigotry, and consensus was no longer possible in a society divided by conflicting interests. The absence of any modern sense of service to the state meant that there was nothing to put in its place. The delicate structure built up over the centuries by the Poles on the principle of respect for a decision freely reached by the community was now being operated by a society of insufficient political sophistication. This was partly the consequence of the Union of Lublin itself.

In 1569, the Polish Seym doubled in numbers to admit the deputies and senators of Lithuania, and there was an immediate impact on the standard of parliamentary behaviour. The Lithuanian deputies were mostly placemen elected by docile seymiks in the presence of the local magnate's armed gangs. The Lithuanian magnates were so powerful that they tended to be humoured by successive kings, and the result was that by the middle of the seventeenth century their position was unassailable. It then became virtually impossible to deny a small group of families all the offices they wanted. The pattern of increasing oligarchy developing in Poland was only a pale reflection of the situation in Lithuania. In Poland, certain families felt one of the offices to be their preserve, but they did not simultaneously covet the others. The Lubomirski family obtained the staff of Marshal four times and the baton of Hetman once. The Zamoyski managed three Chancellors and one Hetman, the Leszczyński three Chancellors, the Potocki four Hetmans. In Lithuania, the magnates had the whole country sewn up. Between 1500 and 1795 the Radziwiłł held the Marshalcy five times, the Chancellorship eight times, the baton of Hetman six times, the Palatinate of Wilno twelve times, and the second most important Palatinate in Lithuania, Troki, six times. Such people had no time for the niceties of the Polish constitution, and all too often reduced the system to absurdity, using its technicalities to trip up its functioning and betray its intention.

The most infamous example of this occurred in Warsaw on the evening of 9 March 1652, as the Seym agreed to prolong its statutory session in order to deal with pressing business. Władysław Siciński, the deputy for Upita in Lithuania, stood up and registered his personal veto of the prolongation, after which he walked out of the chamber and disappeared. It dawned on the deputies, and on the Marshal, Andrzej Fredro, that the Seym could not prolong its session in the face of the formal veto of one of its members. Horrified and angry but obsessed with legality, the deputies dispersed. Since it was only on the very last day of the session of a Seym that the legislation passed actually became law, the dissolution of the session at this point effectively annulled all the decisions taken so far. The reason for Siciński's veto was not hard to find. He was the placeman of the Field-Hetman of Lithuania, Janusz Radziwiłł, who was piqued with Jan Kazimierz for not giving him the senior baton and therefore ordered Siciński to disrupt the Seym so that the king could not collect any taxes or pursue any policy until the next session. It was the first time that the old principle of unanimity had been invoked as a technicality, but it was not to be the last.

From the 1580s hardly a decade passed without some project for streamlining the system being put forward. The earlier projects tended to have the support of the Seym. They were sunk either by the Church hierarchy, which would manage to tie in clauses limiting religious freedom, or by the crown, which would make them conditional on an increase in its own powers, leading inevitably to their rejection by the Seym. In the late 1650s Jan Kazimierz prepared a fresh project for constitutional reform, thinking that the crisis of the Swedish wars might predispose the szlachta to accept a strengthening of state power. Since Jan Kazimierz had no heir, the interregnum after his death was bound to be critical and possibly dangerous. The queen, who was behind the policy of the court party, proposed that his successor should be elected in his lifetime. The szlachta abhorred the idea. The free election of the king was one of the cornerstones of the constitution, and any election carried out during the lifetime of a reigning monarch suggested an inevitable bias in favour of his favourite candidate. In this particular instance it meant, as the queen fully intended, that the French candidate nominated by the court would win. The szlachta were suspicious of the queen's influence, and the Habsburgs, who were alarmed at the idea of the Bourbons establishing themselves in Warsaw, did everything they could to whip up feeling against her and the court party.

The project for parliamentary reform, which included earlier suggestions on voting by two-thirds majority, the removal of the seymiks' control on the deputy they had elected, a permanent basic annual tax, as well as the project for electing a successor *vivente rege*, came up before the Seym of 1658. It foundered mainly on minor points. The court party continued to press the issue in the following years, but two factors militated against a compromise. One was that the queen, who believed that if all else failed something of a coup d'état might be staged, was placing Frenchmen in key posts in the army. The other was that Marshal Jerzy Lubomirski, who happened to be on excellent financial terms with Vienna, began to threaten rebellion if the court party persisted. An attempt was made to impeach him in the Seym, whereupon he rallied part of the unpaid army and groups of discontented szlachta and, in 1665, staged a rebellion in the manner of Zebrzydowski. The court party decided to fight it out, and their troops were soundly routed at Mątwy in 1666.

Not long afterwards, Jerzy Lubomirski came and begged the king's pardon, which was duly granted. The whole affair had been just as pointless as the Zebrzydowski rebellion, and it was a blow to the prestige of the crown and of Jan Kazimierz himself. Louise-Marie died in 1667, and with his principal moral support gone, the ailing king abdicated his throne. Shortly after, he left for France, where he ended his days as Abbot of St Germain-des-Prés.

The election which followed was the first at which disturbances took place. The two principal candidates were Philip Wilhelm Prince of Neuburg, the Habsburg favourite, and Charles de Bourbon, Duc de Longueville. The szlachta who assembled at Warsaw were in no mood for 'foreign autocrats', and overwhelmingly voted for a Polish nonentity, Michał Korybut Wiśniowiecki, son of the fire-eating scourge of the Cossacks, Prince Jarema. It was a slap in the face of the court party which had spent mountains of gold to put a Bourbon on the throne, and an insult to the magnates who had backed the Habsburg candidate. These 'malcontents' immediately began plotting Michał's overthrow, but soon desisted.

Michał, openly referred to as '*le singe*' by the malcontents, was of too little consequence. His only accomplishment was that he could speak eight languages, but he had nothing intelligent to say in any of them, and he quickly settled down to a minimum of ruling. After twenty years of war and strife, the country was only too happy to sink into a stupor and let things take care of themselves.

Large Tatar *tchambouls* hunted unmolested over the Ukraine. The Seym ignored alarming reports reaching it from Hetman Jan Sobieski, who was doing his best to police the area. It felt justified in ignoring his calls for reinforcement by the fact that in the following year he managed to defeat the Tatar army at Podhajce with the meagre forces at his disposal.

In 1672 Sultan Mehmet IV invaded at the head of a substantial army, and the Commonwealth was rudely awakened from its slumbers when the seemingly impregnable fortress of Kamieniec fell to his assault. It had been defended by no more than two hundred infantry and a troop of horse, and most of its large array of heavy cannon had remained silent, since there were only four gunners. This level of neglect was symptomatic. There was no army with which to stem the progress of the Turkish host, and Poland could do nothing but sue for peace. The Sultan imposed the humiliating treaty of Buczacz, which detached Kamieniec with the whole of the Ukraine and Podolia from the Commonwealth, and demanded a yearly tribute. This stirred the Seym to vote money for a new army, but it failed to alter the course of policy or to galvanise society into action. Michał's reign muddled on to its dismal end, which came in November 1673, as another huge Ottoman army under the Grand Vizir, Hussein Pasha of Silistria, advanced towards Poland.

As King Michał lay dying in Warsaw Castle, Hussein Pasha's janissaries prepared to cross the Dniester into Poland. With the chaos of an election looming, the situation looked grim. The king expired on 10 November 1673, and on that very same evening Hetman Jan Sobieski drew up his troops outside the Turkish camp at Chocim. He watched all night and on the morrow attacked and completely annihilated the Ottoman army in a brilliantly executed action, news of which travelled rapidly back to the capital. The principal candidates for the throne, Charles of Lorraine, François Louis de Bourbon, Prince de Conti, and James Stuart, Duke of York (the future James II of England), were eclipsed by the aura of glory surrounding the returning hero. The szlachta assembled on the election field voted overwhelmingly for him.

Jan Sobieski, who ascended the throne as Jan III in May 1674, was an energetic man of forty-five. From his close-cropped head and his jewelled fur cap to his soft yellow boots with their silver heels he was every inch the Sarmatian magnate, and he had all the virtues and vices that implied. Since his baptism of fire at Beresteczko in 1651 he had seen service against each of Poland's enemies in turn. Although he had commanded a 3,000-strong *tchamboul* of Tatar allies against the Swedes in 1656, it was the Tatars and the Turks who were his most constant and savage foes. His uncle Żółkiewski had been slain at Cecora, his elder brother had fallen in the massacre at Batoh. The crusade against the Infidel was part of his life. Yet he spoke Tatar and Turkish and loved the amenities of the East. The banners, tents, carpets, horse-cloths and weapons he took as booty were not mere trophies, they were objects whose aesthetic value he appraised like a Turk.

At the same time he built himself an Italianate palace and collected European works of art with discrimination. He was well read in Italian and French literature, and he was one of Poland's best letter-writers. He wrote to his French wife, Marie Casimire de la Grange d'Arquien, every day or two for twenty years, whether he was at home or campaigning – his first action after saving Vienna was to sit down and pen a letter to her. These letters are colourful and full of verve, as well as gallantry, and he wrote of himself as 'Céladon' and addressed his wife as 'Astrée' or some other heroine of French literature. This Sarmatian *galant* was a curious mixture: he was pious in religion, almost superstitiously so, and managed to combine this with a strong dose of cynicism. Like so many of his fellow magnates, he was greedy and not always scrupulous in his private affairs, but faultlessly correct in public life. He was as ambitious and dynastically-minded as most fellow magnates – there is a portrait of his son (who was not christened Konstanty for nothing) wearing Roman costume and leaning on a classical shield bearing the Sobieski arms, inscribed with the words *In hoc signo Vinces*. Yet he was not ruthless in the pursuit of his aims, perhaps unfortunately for Poland, and he was a chivalrous man much loved by his fellow soldiers. Charles of Lorraine, who had been a rival for the throne of Poland at the election of 1673, and who could have aspired to command the allied army marching to relieve Vienna ten years later, gladly put himself under Sobieski's orders, served him with devotion, and on one occasion risked his neck to save the king's life.

Sobieski was a brilliant soldier, combining personal bravery and dash with tactical skill and a good strategic mind. He was strong and agile, quite capable of spending days in the saddle and nights under the stars, in spite of the obesity which came with age. In politics too he lacked neither enterprise nor vision. He calculated that the way to win the necessary authority to deal with internal questions lay through a successful foreign policy. He believed that before the Commonwealth could deal with the Ottoman threat it must check the recent rise in the power of Muscovy and bring Prussia back into its fold. The Hohenzollern Elector of Brandenburg had chosen the crisis of the Swedish wars to detach this province from the Commonwealth, and Sobieski had personal as well as national reasons for wishing to reoccupy it. Like many people, he believed that Poland should have a Polish dynasty. Yet no Pole could hope to rule effectively without a power-base which would put him above the other magnates. Sobieski's intention was to establish his son as Duke of Prussia, thereby assuring him that power-base.

In 1675 Sobieski signed the treaty of Jaworów with France, which offered to finance an invasion of Prussia while her other ally, Sweden, invaded Brandenburg. France undertook to neutralise the Habsburgs and persuade the Ottoman Porte to give back Kamieniec and other lands taken from the Commonwealth by the treaty of Buczacz. It was a neat plan which benefited Poland most of all, since it would have removed the Brandenburg-Prussia threat to the Baltic coast forever. Sweden duly went into action against Brandenburg, but the Polish forces were not able to invade Prussia because Turkey not only refused to give back Kamieniec, but launched a new offensive into Poland. The large army which had been collected was used not against Prussia but against the Turks, who were defeated at Żurawno in 1676. By the time this operation was complete, Sweden had made peace with Brandenburg, and the favourable opportunity had passed.

The failure of the Jaworów plan was a blow to Sobieski, who had to wait until the next opportunity for international action presented itself. In the following decade, the Sultan proclaimed a new *jihad* and a large Ottoman army advanced into Europe. It took over Hungary and, in the summer of 1683, laid siege to Vienna. France wanted the Poles to stand by and watch the destruction of the Habsburgs. But the Commonwealth could under no circumstances consider allowing Ottoman power to appropriate half of Eastern Europe and take up a threatening position along the whole of its southern frontier. As the Grand Vizir approached Vienna Sobieski signed a treaty with the Emperor, and the Seym readily voted a levy of 36,000 troops in Poland and 12,000 in Lithuania (which never turned up, since Hetman Sapieha had no intention of helping Sobieski). At the end of August the fifty-four-year-old Sobieski set out at the head of his army, at the beginning of September he met up with and took command of the allied troops from various parts of the Empire, and on 12 September he relieved Vienna.

The Turks fled in disorder, but the campaign was by no means over, and Sobieski continued the war. The majority of Hungarians had gone over to the Ottoman camp for anti-Habsburg reasons, and Sobieski perceived an opportunity of detaching Hungary from Austria. On 7 October he lost the first battle of his life, at Parkany. Although he defeated the Turks two days later, it proved difficult to conclude the campaign. Meanwhile, opposition to his policies was mounting at home. Once again the king, now beginning to feel his age and suffering from gallstones, had to give up his plans.

He had never managed to make the magnates forget that he was one of them, and their jealous suspicions dogged his every move. In Lithuania, the Sapieha and Pac families had supplanted the Radziwiłł as the principal trouble-makers, and they raised the old spectre of secession from the Commonwealth. Sobieski's popularity with the szlachta was of little help to him, since it could not be translated into concerted political action. Persistent failure had a demoralising effect on the king, who gradually began to accept the immutability of the status quo. He was still capable of energy and went on campaign as late as 1691, but illness and apathy prevented him from pursuing active policies, and the ship of state began to drift helplessly before his death in 1696.

12

Oriental Baroque

The decline of great nations is as baffling as it is fascinating. It is generally held that the Polish Commonwealth entered the critical stage in the year 1648, and it is not difficult to trace it earlier, to the Zebrzydowski rebellion, for instance. Yet the earlier one deems the decline to have set in, the more inexplicable the whole process becomes. How was it possible for the most administratively lax and politically unorganised state in Europe to go on steadily declining for nearly two centuries without falling apart? How was it possible for the country with the smallest army and the worst geographical position on the continent to ward off rapacious and efficient neighbours for so long? How indeed was it possible for a backward economy which had been ravaged and bankrupted to go on functioning at all?

It is not difficult to find contradictions to the accepted view of the country's condition. While it might be concluded that the position of the king had become one of the most frustrating, dangerous and unenviable in Europe, Bernard Connor, a sober English doctor who spent ten years at the Polish court, insists that:

> As for the Kings of Poland, they may rest in security in the bosom of their country, even amidst the noise of arms, either within or without their dominions . . . For what contributes chiefly to the happiness of these princes is the loyal observance and voluntary obedience paid them by those who are at liberty to do the contrary. I have often heard Monsieur de Polignac, the French Ambassador, say at Warsaw, that he thought a King of Poland more happy in his person and condition than a King of France.

And Polignac was the ambassador of Louis XIV.

Statistics can prove that the economy had slumped, but lavish new buildings kept rising from the ruins of war; cities which had been burnt, plundered and depopulated still manufactured exquisite artefacts; an atrophied educational system and a climate of philistinism continued to produce refined taste and give birth to thought. The transition from the power, wealth and cultural life of the Renaissance to the weakness, poverty and stagnation that eventually engulfed the Commonwealth was not only slow, but very uneven. Culturally, this was bound to be so in a huge and thinly-populated country and a society that rejected conformity. What might appear to be entirely contradictory currents of thought and behaviour ran alongside each other, occasionally mingling only to flow apart again.

Epic poetry in the manner of Potocki and Kochowski continued to glorify the crusading role of the Commonwealth, but in the second half of the century pacifist poets who spoke for the landed szlachta dwelt at tedious length on the pleasures of country life, producing concoctions which the Romantic poet Adam Mickiewicz later summed up as 'a thousand lines about planting peas'. Their devout, often bigoted minds did not feel any need to question or examine. Their verse was couched in a macaronic language which mixed Polish with Latin and gave Polish words Latin endings or vice-versa. This, as well as a tendency to plunder the classics for references and mythological allusions, was highly characteristic of the age in every field of expression, reflecting inner confusion. It occasionally produced extravagantly baroque effects, but little in the way of arresting thought.

Amid this parochial complacency, poets like Szymon Starowolski (1588–1656) wrote lucid pieces begging for the renewal of the Commonwealth, and the intellectual traditions of the sixteenth century lingered in the works of writers such as the Opaliński brothers. There was nothing parochial about Krzysztof Opaliński (1609–55), who was educated at the universities of Louvain, Padua and Orléans before embarking on a political career as one of the leading opponents of Jan Kazimierz. In 1650 he published a book of acerbic satires which criticised the condition of Poland, denouncing political attitudes and abuses, and castigating the szlachta for their poor treatment of the peasants. He was one of the first to join the Swedes in 1655, partly out of a belief that Charles X would whip the country into line.

His brother Łukasz (1612–62) wrote tracts on politics, religion, poetry and even architecture. In 1641 he published an important work advocating the reform of parliamentary procedures and collaborated with the court party to that end, providing it with useful propaganda through his satires on people and attitudes. In 1650 he became Marshal of Poland, and stood by Jan Kazimierz throughout the Swedish war. In 1661 he helped to found the first Polish newspaper, the *Polish Mercury*, which reported international affairs and trade information.

By the second half of the century the last shreds of idealism had given way to scepticism. Jan Andrzej Morsztyn (1620–93), the most gifted writer of the period, could not be accused of wasting ink on the state of the Commonwealth. A courtier by nature, he gained the office of Treasurer with the favour of Louise Marie de Gonzague. He effortlessly penned short erotic poems and aphorisms for her amusement. He also wrote some religious and lyrical verse, and made fine translations of Corneille and Tasso. Under Jan Sobieski he was impeached and banished for plotting with the French to prevent the relief of Vienna, whereupon he and his Scots wife moved to France, where he was pensioned by Louis XIV.

A man even more revealing of the mood of the times, both as a writer and a political figure, is Stanisław Herakliusz Lubomirski (1642–1702). The son of Jerzy Lubomirski, the rebellious Marshal and Hetman, Stanisław was brought up to great things by one of the richest and most influential families in the Commonwealth. He spent two years on a grand tour before starting on a political career which was to culminate in his appointment to the office of Marshal by Jan Sobieski in 1676. He was a brave soldier and a talented man, yet he never managed to break out of the mould into which he had been born, that of the self-willed magnate who knows no bounds. It was almost inevitable that having started out as a friend and supporter of Jan Sobieski he would eventually drift into surly opposition.

Lubomirski was a discriminating patron of the arts, and in 1668 he married Zofia Opalińska, a bluestocking with a passion for music and mathematics: together they covered every conceivable interest from engineering to astrology. He wrote Italianate comedies as well as some of the best seventeenth-century religious verse in Polish. He wrote dissertations on current affairs, and a treatise on literary taste and form. He translated a number of foreign works, and then wrote his last and most famous book, *De Vanitate Consiliorum*, in Latin. This work, which ran into sixteen editions, shows the influence of Lubomirski's favourite writers, Bacon, Montaigne and Lipsius, and, at bottom, the lack of a strong intellectual personality in the author himself. As a statement of social and political values it lacks conviction, and as an attempt to develop an ethical code it can offer little more than tired scepticism. In the late 1670s Lubomirski had commissioned his architect to build an extensive 'Arcadia' at Mokotów, now a district of Warsaw, and this delightful playground was dominated by a central kiosk, which bore the inscription, composed in verse by Lubomirski himself: 'I wish not for God; I seek not Heaven: I know not other lands; I understand not other people; I know not myself.'

A striking feature of this mood of scepticism is that it went hand-in-hand with exuberant and constructive patronage of the arts. The inescapable paradox is that while historians can prove Poland to have been bankrupt as well as intellectually stagnant, neither the philistinism nor the ravages of war and economic ruin could be deduced by looking at the heritage of the age in the plastic arts. The only thing it has in common with the political life of the country is its lack of logical development and its haphazard accommodation of often discrepant elements.

The first Renaissance building in Poland dates from 1502, the last from 1670; the first baroque building from 1584, the last from 1799. The overlap was enormous. In 1588, chronologically right in the middle of the Renaissance span, one Baroque church had already been built at Nieśwież, and one Gothic one was just being started at Przasnysz. The situation was further complicated by religious questions. In the 1520s, over ninety per cent of the parish churches in the diocese of Gniezno were medieval wooden structures ripe for rebuilding, but the Reformation delayed this by seventy years. The first major church in the Renaissance style was Morando's Collegiate Church in Zamość, started in 1587. This was followed by a burst of building in Lwów, where Paulo Romano and Pietro di Barbona set an individual style with their Bernardine and Moldavian churches, which incorporated Byzantine and even Ottoman elements.

The Counter-Reformation generated a need for new and larger churches, and between 1600 and the 1650s the countryside was dotted with quantities of churches in a characteristic Polish Renaissance-Mannerist style. Some were rebuildings of older structures, but even where this was not the case precedent exerted an influence. In most countries the Renaissance style succeeded an airy late Gothic, but in Poland it came on the tail of an earlier monumental Gothic. Something of the massive simplicity of this was incorporated into the typical Polish Renaissance churches, which usually consist of a barrel-vaulted single nave ending in a small rounded apse, and a flat Mannerist front with ornamentation but no towers. The Zamość church was the first of this type, and its most beautiful example is the parish church of Kazimierz.

The first Baroque architect in Poland was Giovanni Maria Bernardone of Como, who built a church for Mikołaj Radziwiłł at Nieśwież in 1584, and a few years later began the church of Saints Peter and Paul in Kraków for the Jesuits, which went so far wrong that it had to be rebuilt entirely by Giovanni Trevano of Lugano, the king's architect. When Zygmunt III decided to move the capital from Kraków to Warsaw in 1597, he gave Trevano the job of building a royal residence on the site of the small medieval castle. Work started in 1599 and was not finished until 1619 by Matteo Castelli. The new castle was strikingly severe in contrast to the Wawel and other Renaissance residences. There were no decorated parapets, no loggias or colonnades. The pentagonal building was massive in aspect, the only decorative feature being the clock-tower with its Baroque spire. In the 1620s Castelli built a summer residence for Zygmunt III at Ujazdów, equally massive in character and only lightened by a couple of loggias and the flamboyant spires on the four towers.

This style was copied by Matteo Trapola who rebuilt the castles of

Wiśnicz and Łańcut for Stanisław Lubomirski in the 1620s. While Wiśnicz has a galleried courtyard in the earlier style, Łańcut resembles the Warsaw castle, the proportions of the façades and the Baroque spires contributing most of the decoration. If the great residences of the Renaissance conformed to a harmonious pattern reflecting the ideas of their masters, those of the seventeenth century reveal the magpie mentality of theirs. In 1637 Tomasso Poncino built a palace for the Bishop of Kraków at Kielce, in which Baroque forms jostle with Renaissance arcades and loggias to create a curiously hybrid effect. Podhorce, a summer residence built for Hetman Stanisław Koniecpolski between 1635 and 1640, is a magnificent palace designed jointly by the two foremost military architects in Poland at the time: Andrea dell'Aqua from Italy, and Guilleaume Levasseur de Beuplan from Normandy. The result, part fortress, part palazzo, has little in common with other buildings of the age. In the second half of the century French influences were strongly in evidence in new palaces such as Otwock, built for the Bieliński family, while a very 'Polish' Baroque was created specially for King Jan Sobieski.

Warsaw had suffered from the Swedish wars more than most cities and virtually all the fine buildings, including the Royal Castle, were destroyed. In 1677 Jan Sobieski commissioned a residence just outside the city at Wilanów (Villa Nuova). He chose an architect of Italian descent born in Poland, Augustyn Locci, and instructed him to build a cross between a Polish gentleman's country manor and an Italian villa. The result is both homely and grand, simple and lavish, and although it was subsequently enlarged it has not lost its original flavour. The most important figure in the rebuilding of Warsaw was Tylman van Gameren, who came to Poland from Utrecht in the mid-1660s at the invitation of Jerzy Lubomirski. Gamerski, as he began calling himself, developed a personal, somewhat severe Palladian style, and soon became the most sought-after architect as Warsaw rose from the ruins of war.

The Church was hardly more consistent in its choice of style. It was not until the second half of the century, when new buildings were needed to replace churches burnt down by the Swedes, that Baroque forms were adopted definitively. The resulting architecture was far from uniform, however, but settled into two main styles. The Kraków style was set by the Church of Saints Peter and Paul, which was modelled on *Il Gesu*, and influenced by the Borromini churches of Rome. The churches in the Kraków style were sober single-nave constructions, normally without towers, robust and monumental. A good example is the Camaldolite Monastery of Bielany by Andrea Spezza; better still the Jesuit church in Poznań, built in 1698 by Giovanni Catenaci and Bartołomiej Wąsowski.

The second style, known as Wilno Baroque, developed towards the end of the seventeenth and the beginning of the eighteenth century. It was the

74 The country retreat of Wilanów outside Warsaw, built in 1681–2 by Augustyn Locci for King Jan Sobieski, is less typical of the dynastic and imperial aspirations nurtured by the king than the portrait (**75**) by one of his court painters c. 1690. The king's warrior status is accentuated by his campaigning haircut and the shield suspended behind him. This also strikes an Imperial Roman note, which is echoed in the Roman armour worn by his son Aleksander (second from left). His other sons, Konstanty and Jakub, wear 'Sarmatian' and French armour respectively. The trio thus symbolise the East, the West, and Classical Antiquity. The queen, born Marie-Casimire de la Grange d'Arquien, holds the hand of her grand-daughter Maria Leopoldina, who is held by her mother (Jakub's wife), Hedwig Elizabeth Amalia, daughter of Philip Wilhelm Neuburg-Wittelsbach, Elector Palatine. Their third daughter, not yet born when the picture was painted, was Maria Clementina, who later married the Old Pretender, James III.

77 (*Right*) The fine Roman Baroque of the Kraków type in the Jesuit Church of St Mary Magdalen in Poznań, built between 1677 and 1701 by Giovanni Catenaci and Bartłomiej Wąsowski.

76 (*Left*) The more sensual forms of the style known as Wilno Baroque are in evidence in the façade of the Church of the Basilian Fathers at Berezwecz, dating from the mid-18th century, with its rippling juxtaposition of concave and convex surfaces.

78 Silver salver made in Kraków in the middle years of the 17th century.

product of a greater mixture of influences, with Polish architects predominating, and is in many ways closer to the Austrian Baroque than the Italian. The churches are taller, thinner, more graceful and more richly decorated than those of the Kraków style. With their abundance of curling and chasing, they are more obviously sensual. Although it is not entirely typical, the finest example is the church of Saints Peter and Paul in Wilno, built by Jan Zaor between 1668 and 1675.

Some of the most destructive elements in Polish public life – the Counter-Reformation, the megalomania of the magnates and the mythologising tendencies of Sarmatism – are responsible for the revival of painting in Poland. The flourishing guild painting of the fifteenth and early sixteenth centuries had been robbed of its most lucrative commissions by the Reformation and the fashion for buying pictures in Italy. It was not until the beginning of the seventeenth century that a new demand made itself felt – for realistic and often lurid religious scenes on the one hand and for great historical canvasses depicting the exploits of some real or imaginary forefather of a magnate on the other.

The man who set the style was a Venetian, Tomasso Dolabella, who spent the years 1600 to 1650 in Poland as court painter. He specialised in monumental pictures, both religious and historical, and was soon being copied by bevies of local artists (upwards of 250 have been identified working in Kraków alone). This sort of Italian religious painting remained popular in Poland long after it had died out elsewhere, with artists such as Szymon Czechowicz (1689–1775) and Tadeusz Konicz (1733–93) continuing to produce vast Baroque works well into the second half of the eighteenth century (the latter principally in Rome, where he worked in the Palazzo Borghese and for Cardinal Stuart).

With the arrival in Poland in the 1640s of Peter Claes van Soutman, a pupil of Rubens, and Romeyn de Hooghe, Flemish portrait-painting became fashionable. These artists were emulated by Franciszek Lekszycki and Daniel Freher of Kraków, and Bartłomiej Strobel and Jerzy Daniel Schultz of Gdańsk. With time, the taste for the grandiose and the panegyric took over portraiture as well, and this was satisfied by Jerzy Eleuter Siemiginowski of Lwów and Jan Tretka of Kraków, whose many apotheoses of Jan Sobieski are typical. At a humbler level, this taste gave rise to a new tradition of 'Sarmatian portraits'. Originally just the head and shoulders painted on a small hexagonal piece of tin to be affixed to a coffin, this type of likeness became popular in its own right. Usually a two-dimensional and primitive depiction of the subject with coats-of-arms and symbols of office introduced unceremoniously, it was iconography rather than art. The rendering of the face was usually highly expressive, contrasting sharply with the flatness of the rest of the picture. These portraits enjoyed popularity with the middle szlachta, whose manor-houses were packed with galleries of such likenesses.

If Renaissance architecture suited the style and thought of the Poles of the sixteenth century, the Baroque might have been invented for the Sarmatians of the seventeenth. It awakened a degree of sensual appreciation of form, ornament and luxury which found immediate satisfaction in and complemented the increasing contact with the East. This fed on war just as well as on peacetime trade. Ottoman armies believed in comfort and splendour, and as a result the booty could be quite spectacular. 'The tents and all the waggons have fallen into my hands, *et mille autres galanteries fort jolies et fort riches, mais fort riches,* and I haven't looked through all of it yet,' wrote a triumphant Jan Sobieski to his wife from the Turkish camp outside Vienna a few hours after the battle, adding that it was all of higher quality than what he had captured at Chocim ten years earlier.

By the early 1600s the Polish cavalry had adopted most of the weapons used by the Turks as well as many of their tactics. The Hetmans used the Turkish baton for command, and the horse-tails which denoted the highest rank among the Turks were born aloft behind them too. The Poles also dressed more and more like their foe, and even the Tatar habit of shaving the head was widely practised on campaign. So much so that on the eve of the Battle of Vienna the king had to order all Polish troops to wear a straw cockade so that their European allies should not take them for Turks, from whom they were virtually indistinguishable. With Sobieski's accession to the throne, military fashion invaded the court and became institutionalised. This 'Sarmatian' costume had the advantage of being non-partisan, while French or German clothes were equated with foreign intrigue. The growing complex vis-à-vis Western Europe meant that it was the advanced West and not the still obscure (though physically more dangerous) East whose influence was feared. The Sarmatian costume became a symbol of healthy, straightforward patriotic 'Polishness'.

The Poles also had a feeling for the beauty of Islamic art, which was not appreciated in Western Europe. They prized the design and craftsmanship of the weaponry and the horse-tack, and relished the art and the luxury of Ottoman textiles. Eastern hangings replaced Flemish tapestries and arms joined pictures on the walls of manor-houses. At the Battle of Chocim, Jan Sobieski captured a silk embroidery studded with 'two thousand emeralds and rubies' from Hussein Pasha which he thought so beautiful that he wore it as a horse-cloth for his coronation. A few years later he gave it as the richest gift he could think of to the Grand Duke of Tuscany, who put it away and wrote it down in his inventory as *'una cosa del barbaro lusso'*.

Turkish clothes suited Baroque architecture, and servants were dressed up accordingly. Wealthy szlachta and magnates often kept captive Tatars or janissaries at their courts, but they also dressed their Polish pages as

Arabs and bodyguards as Circassian warriors. This taste was carried so far that religious music was provided in Karol Radziwiłł's Baroque chapel at Nieśwież by a Jewish orchestra dressed as janissaries, which might have been considered sacrilegious in other societies, not to say tasteless.

The luxury of Ottoman taste suited the Sarmatian love of extravagance and ritual in everyday life. There had never been any sumptuary laws in Poland and the tendency to show off was unrestrained. Money still had no investment role in the minds of most Poles and all surplus went into movable property of the most demonstrative kind. In this respect, inventories made on the death of members of the szlachta are illuminating. A poor gentleman would be found to possess a horse or two, fine caparisons and horse-cloths, saddles, arms and armour, a small number of rich clothes, jewellery, perhaps some personal table-silver, a few furs and lengths of cloth, and little in the way of money. Inventories of country houses and castles reveal the same pattern. Jewellery, clothes, silver, saddlery, arms and armour, cannon, uniforms for the castle guard, furs, lengths of cloth, Turkish, Persian and Chinese hangings, banners, tents, horsecloths, rugs and kilims, Flemish tapestries and pictures are listed. Furniture hardly figures, except where it is made of silver. The chattels of a Polish nobleman therefore differed in quite specific ways from those of his equivalent in England or France, where clothes, jewels, paintings and tapestries tended to be only the tip of the iceberg of wealth. The Polish magnate's only remotely productive investment was his land. The rest of his wealth was invested in belongings. A rich man's coat was a tradeable item, so stiff was it with gold thread. Every button was a jewel, the clasp at his throat and the aigrette on his fur cap were works of art. The French traveller Verdum noted that Jan Sobieski wore 200,000 thalers' worth of jewels on a normal day, and that on a great occasion his attire would be worth a considerable proportion of his (by no means negligible) weight in gold. Urszula Sieniawska, whose inheritance was being disputed by a number of relatives in 1640, left no less than 5,000 diamonds, rubies, emeralds and sapphires in her jewel-case. Maryanna Stadnicka, wife of the Palatine of Bełz, left 8,760 pearls. The same degree of opulence went for other items. Pictures, statuary and tapestries suffered badly from looting, particularly during the Swedish wars. In 1655 no less than 150 carts of booty left the Lubomirskis' Wiśnicz. Many collections were so vast, however, that the looting made only a slight impression. The inventory of Żółkiew, one of the Sobieski family seats, drawn up after Peter the Great had personally looted it in 1707, still lists upwards of 700 oil paintings in the castle.

These castles were also full of people, on the principle that the more there were surrounding a man, the more important he was. Poor relatives and landless friends, the sons of less wealthy henchmen and clients of one sort or another would form a court around a magnate. On top of this, he would employ teachers for his children, musicians, whole corps de ballet, jesters and dwarfs, a quantity of chaplains, secretaries, managers and other officers. Such a court needed marshalling, and Stanisław Lubomirski had two marshals of the court, one more than the king. After that came all the servants, stable-staff, kitchen-staff, falconers, huntsmen, organists, castrati, trumpeters, units of cavalry, infantry and artillery. The fashion for show-attendants meant that there were dozens of *hajduks*, wearing Hungarian dress, *pajuks*, in Turkish janissary costume, and *laufers* in what looked like something out of Italian opera, covered in ostrich-feathers. These attendants had no purpose beyond standing about or running in front of the master when he rode out. The numbers were impressive. When Rafał Leszczyński's wife died in 1635, he had to provide mourning dress for just over 2,000 servants – and neither cooks nor kitchen-maids were included as they were not seen. Karol Radziwiłł's army alone amounted to 6,000 regular troops.

The heads of great houses took themselves seriously, and much of this splendour was indulged in out of a feeling of self-importance and dignity. When Karol Radziwiłł's intendant commented that he lived better than the king, the characteristic reply was – 'I live like a Radziwiłł – the king can do what he likes.' Every major event in the life of the family was treated with gravity and ceremonies were constructed round it. When a child was born, the artillery fired salutes and special operas were staged. When the master returned from the wars, triumphal arches were erected and fire-works let off. Any occasion served as an excuse and no move was made by a great man without pomp. This reached its apex in the last quarter of the seventeenth and the first of the eighteenth centuries, but even as late as the 1760s, the Palatine of Podolia, Prince Adam Czartoryski, could not afford to travel discreetly when visiting other parts of the country, as one of his courtiers relates.

The convoy was made up of two kitchen waggons, a third with the larder, a fourth for the bakers, a fifth with the cellar, carrying drink and vessels, the sixth with the pastry-cooks, a seventh with the confection-ers, the eighth with the coffee-makers, a ninth with the buttery and other supplies, the tenth with the physician and his dispensary, the eleventh with the tableware, the twelfth with the smith and the wheelwright, the thirteenth and fourteenth with the bakery, the fifteenth and sixteenth carried the trunks and belongings of the courtiers who rode in the Prince's carriages, the seventeenth the Prince's garberobe, and the eighteenth the tents. Each was a covered waggon drawn by seven horses; the coachmen and foreriders were dressed in traditional Polish manner, with long coats and topcoats, tall fur caps and embroidered belts. An equerry and two uhlans rode with the waggons. Behind them three mounted stable-boys, dressed in the Turkish style, led six camels covered in beautiful drapes of worked cloth, bearing large chests which contained the library. Behind this caravan, which would depart early, came two or three large carriages, and a number of lighter ones, in which rode: Doctor Goltz, two chaplains, Father Dąbrowski, Soszkiewicz, General Orłowski, Ciesielski, Rembielinski, Kniaźnin, the Swiss Master Lubitz, the Englishman Tayler, chamberlain Szymanowski, Captain Brzostowski, General Zdrojecki, the military commissioner Witosławski, Janusz Tyszkiewicz, Ksawery Brzostowski, Majors Bitner, Kayserling and Börken. Finally at eight o'clock the Prince himself would depart, often on horseback, attended by: Börken, Orłowski, Niemcewicz Julian, his adjutants: Jan Swiętorzecki, Józef and Dionizy Hrebnicki, Łaski, Przysiecki, Sichen, Wisogierd, Kublicki, Sadowski, his courtiers: Paszkowski and Soroka, cavalry ensigns, all on horseback. In addition, the marshal of the court Borzecki, the secretary for foreign correspondence Skowroński, the secretary for Podolian affairs Witoszyński, the secretary for Lithuanian matters Zdzitowiecki, the secretary for current affairs Karpiński, and the secretary for Mazovian business Zaleski, rode in either their own or the Prince's carriages. At least eight spare horses were led along for the Prince by an equerry and a stable-hand. There were also two Hungarian Leib-Hussars, Janos and Ferenc: a Negro and a Turk who made up and offered pipes from their horses; the pages Romanowicz, Podwiński, Oranowski, Kimbar and Krupinski, dressed in green jackets, with cartridge-cases, swords and quivers with bow and arrows. When the Prince rode a horse, he was followed by a light buggy with a change of clothes, in which rode his valet and barber Rosinski, who carried a soaping-dish and razors in his cartridge-case. As a guard for the convoy there were fifty cossacks from the Ukrainian estate of Granów armed with pistols, carbine, sword and lance.

It was more than mere show – it was a style of behaviour which introduced ritual into every action and translated its significance into visible activity. It shared affinities with the behaviour of contemporary grandees in Spain and Sicily, and of German ruling princes, but probably the closest parallel to a Polish magnate's way of life at this time is to be found in that of an Indian maharaja. Yet there were many aspects of this style of behaviour which were specific to the Polish Commonwealth. Nowhere is this more obvious than in the practice of religion as it developed in the seventeenth century, partly under the influence of the taste of the faithful, partly as a result of the Church's continuing policy of bringing every aspect of the life of the Commonwealth within its own orbit, if not actually under its control.

Control was not something that could be effectively exerted over the likes of Karol Radziwiłł, who summed up his attitude in a letter to Anna Jabłonowska in 1764: 'I praise the Lord, believe not in the Devil, respect the law, know no king, because I am a nobleman with a free voice.' A man whose ideal was the cult of unbounded liberty did not take easily to having, for instance, his sexual freedom restricted by laws even more nebulous than those of the Commonwealth. The hold on society which the Church did have was based on a juxtaposition of life and ritual which succeeded in making religion into an integral part of every person's regular activities. The leaders of the Counter-Reformation insisted on the inseparability of the Church as an institution from the Commonwealth as an institution, of piety from patriotism. They were largely successful in that they bred the notion in the average Pole that the Catholic Church 'belonged' to him in much the same way as the Commonwealth did. Churches were used for seymiks and for the sessions of local tribunals. National commemorations and holidays were fused with religious feasts. The priesthood became for the poorer nobility much what the civil service or army were in other countries – the only noble profession and a refuge for upper-class mediocrity.

Outward signs of the Faith were encouraged in every way. The cult of the Virgin and of the Saints, which had died away during the Reformation, made a come-back. Every town, village, institution, guild and confraternity was provided with a patron. Pictures of the Virgin before which miracles allegedly took place were 'crowned' and declared to be miraculous. The solemn coronation of the Black Madonna of Częstochowa took place on 8 September 1717 before 150,000 faithful. By 1772, there were a staggering four hundred officially designated 'miraculous' pictures of the Virgin within the Commonwealth, each one a centre of pilgrimage and a recipient of votive offerings of jewellery, money, tablets and symbolic limbs. Other popular centres of pilgrimage were the very Polish phenomenon of Calvaries. The first of these, Kalwaria Zebrzydowska, was built between 1603 and 1609 by the leader of the rebellion against Zygmunt III. He sent a man to Jerusalem to establish the layout of all the places which relate to the stations of the Cross – Pilate's Palace, Golgotha, the Tomb – and to measure the distances between them. Zebrzydowski's Dutch architect, P. Baudarth, then built an open-air Way of the Cross, with a chapel in a different style for each of the fourteen stations.

Physical expressions of religious intention were encouraged, including processions, penances and even flagellation. Just as in everyday life, the accent was in translating feeling and purpose into action and ritual. Nowhere was this more pronounced than where public life and religion came together, at funerals. A magnate would have a huge architectural folly, a *castrum doloris*, built as a canopy for his coffin, and this would be

In 1595 a vision of three crosses was seen on a hill on the estate of Mikołaj
Zebrzydowski, Palatine of Kraków, who sent one of his courtiers to Jerusalem to get
drawings, measurements and plaster models of the Holy Places. In 1600 he started
building a vast open-air Way of the Cross, with a chapel in a different style for each
station. **80** (*Top right*), Herod's Palace. **81** (*Bottom right*) the House of Caiaphas. **82**
(*Bottom left*) Golgotha. **79** (*Top left*) the fifth station.

83 This picture of the Virgin in the parish church of Chodyszew was only one of four
hundred pictures in Poland officially recognised as miraculous by the Church. Each
was a centre of worship and a recipient of votive tablets, limbs and jewellery.

84,85 Coffin-portraits of Barbara Domicela Lubomirska, (d. 1676), and of Stanisław Woysza, Steward of Smolensk, (d. 1677). Painted on tin or copper, these were affixed to the coffin and sometimes hung in churches after the funeral.

86 The *castrum doloris* erected for Anna Radziwiłł at Nieśwież in 1747. Humbler mortals could expect more frugal constructions, but only the lowliest were sent off decorated with symbols of his office and wealth, his portrait and coat-of-arms, and with elaborate inscriptions in his honour. Lengthy panegyrics were commissioned from the best poets, and printed in large editions. The ritual included the old Polish custom of breaking up the dead man's symbols of office and, if he were the last of his family, shattering his coat-of-arms. Neighbours, friends, family, servants and soldiers would pay their last respects in more or less theatrical ways, while congregations of monks and nuns sang dirges and recited litanies. The funeral of Hetman Józef Potocki in 1751 took two weeks, for six days of which 120 pieces of cannon saluted continuously (using up a total of 4,700 measures of powder). Over a dozen senators, hundreds of relatives and entire regiments congregated in Stanisławów to pay their last respects in the church which was entirely draped in black damask, before a huge catafalque of crimson velvet dripping with gold tassels, decorated with lamps, candelabra, Potocki's portrait, captured standards, pyramids of weapons and other symbols of his office and achievements. Then came the high point of the ritual, as the poet Karpiński describes it:

> One after the other, chosen horsemen rode into the church at a gallop, and one would shatter the lance before the coat-of-arms at the foot of the Hetman's coffin, another broke the sabre, another the rapier, another the arrows, another the standards, and so on. Each one, having broken his instrument and thrown it down at the foot of the coffin, would then leap from his horse and fall at the foot of the coffin himself, as it were showing his grief. Two of these heroes failed miserably to break the lance and the standard, and only managed to scatter the candles standing round the catafalque, but they did better with the falling and the grief, because they were both quite drunk.

The Sarmatian lifestyle was a unique growth, produced by cross-pollenation between Catholic high Baroque and Ottoman culture at its zenith, which could only flourish in the ethnically diverse soil of the Commonwealth. It was a natural East-West synthesis, perfectly suited to the need for expression of the Poles. Everything about it was theatrical, declamatory and buxom. It was radically inimical to the bourgeois ethic of thrift, investment, self-improvement and discipline which was beginning to dominate the behaviour of Western Europe, and as a result it was often condemned as ridiculous and primitive, even by Poles of later centuries. At its worst, Sarmatism was absurd and destructive, encouraging as it did outrageous behaviour and an attitude that bred delusion. By its very exuberance, however, it defused passions and allowed what was possibly an irreconcilable collection of peoples to reach a kind of harmony. As Doctor Connor commented: 'It is certain had we in England but the third part of their liberty, we could not live together without cutting one another's throats.'

The hybrid culture of Sarmatism suited not only the Poles and the Lithuanians. It seeped into Hungary, Moldavia and the Balkans, into Prussia and the Baltic provinces, and into Russia, where distinctly Polish features can be detected in contemporary church architecture. Similarly, Polish became the *lingua franca* in these areas. It was widely spoken in Muscovy, and in the 1680s under Peter the Great's half-sister, the regent Sophia, it became the court language of the Kremlin, since it represented a life-line to other nations. In 1697, for instance, Boris Sheremetev's embassy to Vienna conducted its negotiations with the Austrians exclusively in Polish. The appeal of Sarmatism was not dependent on the Commonwealth's political power any more than it was limited by its frontiers. It was a congenial way of life, and probably the closest that part of Europe has ever come to producing a distinctive and all-embracing culture of its own.

13

The Reign of Anarchy

'Future generations will wonder in astonishment,' King Jan III said to the Senate in March 1688: 'that after such resounding victories, such international triumph and glory, we now face, alas, eternal shame and irreversible loss, for we now find ourselves without resources, helpless, and seemingly incapable of government,' Future generations have indeed wondered, and wonder still. The spectacle of a society galloping towards its own destruction is incomprehensible and irritating to the modern mind conditioned by the orthodoxies of nationalism and progress. The very existence of the *liberum veto*, that most powerful symbol of the Commonwealth's political decay, leads many to conclude that the Poles had parted with their senses.

The single deputy's power to veto was an illogical application of the old principle of consensus: it was technically legal even though it was contradictory to the spirit of the law. The szlachta never used it honestly in their own interest and mostly deplored its consequences. Its first use in 1652 set the pattern for the future – the technicality was invoked, in bad faith, by a deputy who was in the pay or the power of one of the magnates. Those who cast the veto were on the whole obscure creatures from Lithuania and the Ukraine, where minor nobles were more subservient to local magnates than in Wielkopolska, for instance. A similar analysis of those who stood behind them shows the Potocki family as leaders, closely followed by the Sapieha and Lubomirski. The Commonwealth's neighbours soon caught on to the fact that they too could use the veto. If Brandenburg did not like the idea of Poland making a treaty with the Habsburgs, its diplomatic agents in Warsaw could offer thousands of ducats to any backwoods deputy who was prepared to stand up and veto the treaty as it was being ratified by the Seym. This was so convenient to the Commonwealth's neighbours that they clubbed together to make sure the Poles did not close the loop-hole. In 1667 Brandenburg and Sweden agreed to go to war if necessary 'in defence of Polish freedoms' (i.e. to stop the Poles from abolishing the veto). Over the next hundred years the same clause was contained in virtually every treaty made between Russia, Austria, Brandenburg and

Sweden. The Seym became a sort of diplomatic market-place. Although vast sums were paid out to deputies in the process, the whole business involved less cynicism than might be expected. It would appear that most of those who cast a veto had convinced themselves that they were doing the right thing. At the end of the century the Marquis de Vitry reported from Warsaw to Louis XIV that while the agent of Brandenburg had plenty of client deputies, he himself could not find a single one who would act in the French interest for all the louis d'or in the world.

The phenomenon of the veto was by no means simple. It was widely perceived to be detrimental and evil in practice, yet it was endowed with the respect of custom. During the Reformation ardent Catholics had refused to allow the persecution of people guilty of the worst acts of sacrilege; now people convinced of the iniquity of the veto were not prepared to take drastic action. The right to cast a veto grew into a fetish, particularly among the minor szlachta who saw it as a symbol of their personal involvement in the Commonwealth, as well as the ultimate guarantee of their freedoms. Any attack on it was therefore equated with an assault on these freedoms and on the constitution.

The veto itself was merely the most obvious symptom of a political disease which went far deeper. The first veto was not repeated for seventeen years, the second not for another ten. It was not until the period between 1696 and 1733 that it became endemic to parliamentary life. The first was cast at a moment when Polish society had lost its consensus, a fact eloquently demonstrated three years later by the collapse in the face of Swedish invasion. The last was registered in 1763 by a deputy in Russian pay, who was laughed out of the Seym. The power of veto had existed for well over a hundred years before it was first used, and it continued to exist for thirty after it was last invoked. The disease was not in the constitution, but in the mind of the people who abused it. It took hold gradually, with only a few isolated rashes visible at first, reached the moment of crisis in the 1720s and 1730s, and, having failed to kill the patient, retreated rapidly.

The sickness manifested itself fully after the death of Jan III in 1696. The election that followed was one of the most dismal episodes in Polish parliamentary history. The principal candidates were the king's son Jakub; François Louis de Bourbon, Prince de Conti; and Friedrich Augustus Wettin, Elector of Saxony. Jakub Sobieski was in Silesia at the time of his father's death, and was immediately seized by Saxon troops. On 27 June 1697 the szlachta assembled on the election field voted overwhelmingly for the Prince de Conti and the Primate proclaimed him king. On the same evening a small group of malcontents 'elected' Friedrich Augustus, who marched into Poland at the head of a Saxon army. On 15 September, as the Prince de Conti, escorted by a French squadron under Jean Bart, was sailing through the Sound, Friedrich Augustus was crowned in Kraków by the Bishop of Kujavia as Augustus II of Poland. At the end of the month the Prince de Conti came ashore only to discover that he had been pipped at the post. His supporters were not keen to start a civil war, so he re-embarked and sailed back to France. It was the first time that a deceased monarch's son had not been elected to succeed him; that the rightful candidate had been debarred from the throne by military force; and that the Poles had acquired a German king, which went against a long tradition of keeping German hegemony at arm's length.

The twenty-seven-year-old Augustus was nothing if not picturesque. Universally known as Augustus the Strong and described by one of his subjects as 'half bull, half cock', he could break horseshoes with one hand, shoot with incredible accuracy, drink almost anyone under the table, and fornicate on a scale which would be hardly believable if he had not left regiments of bastards to prove it. He was not a stupid man, and he intended to turn the Commonwealth into a centralised monarchical state. Like Sobieski, he saw war as the surest way to gain prestige and a free hand to carry out his plans. In 1698 he met Peter the Great, who was on his way back to Russia from Western Europe, and in the course of an all-night drinking-bout the two men planned a joint war against Sweden. In 1699 an agreement was signed between Peter the Great, the King of Denmark and Augustus. Augustus was not allowed to enter into such treaties as King of Poland. It was therefore an alliance of Muscovy, Saxony and Denmark which went to war on Sweden the following year.

The allies had made a mistake in thinking that they could easily defeat the eighteen-year-old Swedish King, Charles XII. This callow youth who preferred to sleep in a stable rather than in a bed and despised refinement of any sort was endowed with inhuman energy, reckless bravery and a faith in his own destiny that was soon echoed in the popular myth that he was invulnerable. He made short shrift of the Danes, beat off the Saxon army attempting to take Riga, and then turned on the Russians, whom he drubbed at the battle of Narva. Augustus decided it was time to sue for peace.

Charles XII would have none of it and demanded that Poland dethrone Augustus if it did not wish to be invaded. The Commonwealth was not at war with anyone, but almost everyone in the Commonwealth was at loggerheads with someone else. In 1702 the Sapieha family placed Lithuania under Swedish protection, and in April Charles XII entered Wilno. The Lithuanian rivals of the Sapieha, mainly the lesser szlachta, appealed to the Tsar. Muscovite troops moved into the Grand Duchy in support, which they could easily do, since Charles XII had already moved into Poland in pursuit of Augustus. Incensed at the Swedish invasion, the szlachta of Małopolska began to feel a rising loyalty towards Augustus, and the rump Seym which met at Lublin in 1703 called for war with

Sweden. The following year 'Poland' joined the Muscovite alliance against Sweden, partly in order to keep pace with Lithuania, which had already done so. At this point Charles XII met Stanisław Leszczyński, Palatine of Poznań, a refined and intelligent young man of twenty-seven for whom he developed a great esteem. Without further ado, Charles arranged for Leszczyński to be 'elected' by eight hundred assembled szlachta and proclaimed King of Poland. The situation had now reached farcical dimensions. Two kings of Poland, neither of them with much of a following and little in the way of Polish troops, were being swept along by Peter the Great and Charles XII respectively in a *contredanse* which took them twin-stepping around the Commonwealth, until Charles had the good idea of invading Saxony. There he finally pinned down Augustus and extorted his abdication of the Polish throne. Stanisław I was king.

Charles decided that the time had now come to take on Peter the Great. He laid his plans with Stanisław and with Ivan Mazepa (originally Jan Kołodyński), once a page to Jan Kazimierz and now Ataman of the Cossacks on the Russian side of the Dnieper. Their independence was being eroded by Muscovite rule and they dreamt of reuniting the Ukraine. An alliance against Russia was formed, on the basis of an independent future for the Ukraine in alliance with Poland. On 8 July 1709 Charles XII and Mazepa were routed by Peter the Great at Poltava.

The war was over, and Augustus reascended the Polish throne, a little wiser but incomparably worse off for the events of the last ten years. When he and Peter had planned the Northern War on that night in 1698, he had been the stronger partner. After ten years of bungling he was little more than the Tsar's client, dependent on his support and protection. There was no clear way out of the predicament for him or for the Commonwealth, as the power-balance in Eastern Europe had altered dramatically during those ten years.

On 18 January 1701 Frederick III, Elector of Brandenburg and Duke of Prussia, had dubbed himself 'Frederick I, King in Prussia', a title which could in no way be reconciled with the fact that the Duchy of Prussia was at that time still a vassal of the Commonwealth. The Hohenzollerns had ably exploited every opportunity to upgrade the real and formal standing of their dominions, and dreamed of achieving Great-Power status, necessarily at the expense of Poland. This had become a real possibility, as a number of other states ceased to compete for influence in that part of Europe. Turkey was decisively defeated (Hetman Feliks Potocki's victory at Podhajce in 1698 was the last Polish-Tatar battle), a defeat sealed by the Treaty of Karlowitz in January 1699, by which the Commonwealth regained Kamieniec and the whole of left-bank Ukraine. Sweden, which had erupted into international affairs only a hundred years before and grown into a serious threat for the Hohenzollerns in particular, was wiped out at the battle of Poltava. France, robbed of its allies in the East – Turkey, Sweden and Poland – shifted its theatre of confrontation with the Habsburgs to Spain and Italy. Distracted by the War of the Spanish Succession, the Habsburgs had failed to take advantage of the Northern War, and henceforth assumed a secondary role in Polish affairs. On the other hand, Muscovy had taken full advantage of the situation and grown into the greatest power in Eastern Europe. In 1721 Peter took the title of Emperor of All Russia, having first successfully put into effect a new strategy which introduced an element into diplomacy that is still the cornerstone of Russian power in Europe. It was the strategy of domination through 'protection', an elaborate system of ascendancy by meticulous hypocrisy.

The Seym of 1712 reached deadlock on various reforms put forward by Augustus, whereupon he brought in troops from Saxony. This had the effect of rallying the opposition, which in 1715 formed a Confederation. It was at this point that Russia offered to mediate. The offer was accepted by both sides with some reluctance, and a Russian envoy arrived in Warsaw – accompanied by 18,000 troops which were to keep order. The ensuing Seym of 1717 was known as the Dumb Seym. It sat in a chamber surrounded by Russian troops, the deputies were forbidden to speak, and the Russian mediator forced his solution on it, couched in the Treaty of Warsaw. This laid down, amongst other things, that Augustus could keep no more than 1,200 Saxon Guards in Poland. The Polish army was fixed at a maximum of 12,000 men, a figure quite sufficient since Moscow arrogated to itself the role of protector, and promised to leave a large number of Russian troops in the Commonwealth on a basis of 'friendly cooperation'. The fact that over two hundred and fifty years later the whole of Eastern Europe is still infested with these 'friendly protectors' testifies to the brilliance of Tsar Peter's policy. A few years later Augustus, who wanted these troops out at any cost, secretly offered Peter various border areas in exchange for a withdrawal. A lesser man might have accepted, but Peter grandly refused and went on to publish Augustus's proposals with feigned indignation and horror, as befitted the scrupulous protector of the Commonwealth's territorial integrity.

Poland's internal and external affairs were now the business of Russia, and to a lesser extent of Prussia and Austria, since Poland had to be kept isolated. The three neighbouring powers looked on her territory more and more as a sort of no-man's-land. Russia moved her troops about the Commonwealth as though it were a training-ground, while Prussian and Austrian armies took short cuts, in times of war even setting up depots and garrisons in convenient Polish towns. Poland had become, as the saying went, 'a wayside inn for foreign armies'.

On 1 February 1733 Augustus II died of alcohol poisoning in Warsaw.

His last words were: 'My whole life has been one uninterrupted sin. God have mercy on me.' He had hoped to ensure the succession of his son Augustus to the Polish throne, but this seemed unlikely since Stanisław Leszczyński, whose daughter had married Louis XV of France, was expected to stand for election and win easily on account of his popularity. Russia, Prussia and Austria signed an agreement to throw in their combined strength behind the young Saxon, who had already promised to cede Livonia to Russia if elected.

The 13,000 electors who turned up voted unanimously for Leszcyzński, who had travelled to Warsaw incognito. In Paris Voltaire composed an ode of joy for the occasion, but Russian troops were already on the move. On 5 October 20,000 of them assembled 1,000 szlachta outside Warsaw and forced them to elect Augustus of Saxony. Five days later France declared war on Austria and started the War of the Polish Succession. King Stanisław's supporters gathered in confederations all over the country and the city of Gdańsk raised a sizeable army on his behalf. Two years of sporadic fighting ensued, but France made peace, having got what she wanted from Austria in Italy. Stanisław was given the Duchy of Lorraine as a consolation prize by his son-in-law, and Augustus III ascended the Polish throne.

The Commonwealth effectively ceased being a sovereign state in 1718 with the imposition of the Russian 'protectorate'. It had also virtually ceased to function as a political organism. The Seym was not summoned between 1703 and 1710, the years of the Northern War, which meant that no legislation was passed and no taxes could be levied. When the Seym did sit again, it was hardly more effective. Of the eighteen sessions called under Augustus II, ten were broken up by the use of the veto. The king tried to impose stronger government, but his policies were poorly thought out. He had an unfortunate conviction that a show of strength by the Saxon army was a desirable prelude to any change, and this had the immediate effect of provoking the opposition of those who would otherwise have agreed with him. In the last years of his reign he did manage to gain the support of a reformist faction among the magnates and szlachta, but their programme for reform was cut short by his death in 1733.

His son Augustus, Poland's new monarch, was obese, indolent and virtually incapable of thought. He would spend his days cutting out bits of paper with a pair of scissors or else sitting by the window taking potshots at stray dogs with a pistol. He also drank like a fish. The extremes of drunkenness usually put down to Slavic barbarism were introduced by the only two representatives of that proverbially sober nation, the Germans, to sit on the Polish throne. Augustus II had been the first to elevate drinking marathons and duels to cult proportions, and his porcine son was a worthy successor.

Augustus III reigned for thirty years. He spent only twenty-four months of that time in Poland, since he felt more at home in Saxony. Yet he was not as unpopular with the szlachta as might have been expected – he was the first king who never made the slightest attempt to curtail their prerogatives and increase his own. The tiny army dwindled to half its theoretical size, since nobody sought to prevent the officers from indulging in the usual habit of pocketing the pay meant for their troops. Apart from the legal system, which had never been dependent on central authority, there were no visible signs of a nationwide administration. The country seemed to run itself solely on the momentum of its own inertia.

This state of affairs favoured the magnates, or rather the dozen or so men who stood at the pinnacle of wealth and power, who had turned into something approaching sovereign princes. It was to the courts of the leading families and not to the royal court at Warsaw or Dresden that foreign powers sent envoys and money. The Potocki, Radziwiłł and similar families involved half of Europe in their affairs and managed to harness the forces of great Powers in the service of their own family interests. Their activities were monitored at Versailles and Potsdam, at Petersburg and Caserta. The marital intentions of the young Zofia Sieniawska were a case in point. The only daughter of Adam Mikołaj Sieniawski, Hetman and Castellan of Kraków, and of Elżbieta Lubomirska, she was a great heiress. She married Stanisław Doenhoff, Palatine of Polotsk, no pauper and also the last of his line, who died, leaving her everything. Every family in Poland produced a suitor in the hope of coffering the fabulous fortune. Louis XV was quick to realise what was at stake, and the young widow was begged to come to Versailles, where it was hoped she could be married to the Comte de Charolais, a Bourbon in search of a throne; Augustus II tried to monitor her suitors; the Duke of Holstein wanted her for himself; the Habsburgs threw in their influence behind the Duke of Braganza, for whom they had royal ambitions; and Petersburg sent ambassadors and money to influence her choice in their direction. The interest in the widow was well-founded. In 1731 she settled for the poorest of all her suitors, Prince August Czartoryski, turning his family into the most powerful in Poland over the next hundred years.

The power of these families rested on a combination of wealth and control of their lesser peers, and reflected a growing disparity between rich and poor. The figures for the Palatinate of Lublin provide an example of the dramatic change in the distribution of land over the previous two hundred years. In the 1550s, 54 per cent of all land owned by the szlachta was in holdings of under 1,500 hectares, but by the 1750s only 10 per cent was in such medium holdings. In the 1550s only 16 per cent was in large estates of over 7,500 hectares, but by the 1750s over 50 per cent was accounted for by larger estates. The large estates grew larger, the small ones smaller, with the result that by the mid-eighteenth century about a dozen families owned huge tracts of land, another three hundred or so possessed lands equivalent to those of the greatest English or German landlords, and as many as 120,000 szlachta families owned no land at all. The remainder owned small estates which provided little more than subsistence for the family and its dependents.

The Northern War had devastated the country, and the population of cities like Poznań had dropped to no more than 2,000 by 1710, one tenth of what it had been a hundred years earlier. In the countryside the ravages of war only compounded the decay that resulted from the continuous downward trend in agricultural prices. Szlachta and peasant farmers squeezed every available bushel out of the land and every drop of sweat from the workforce as their holdings became less and less profitable. Between 1500 and 1800 average yields per acre increased by 200 per cent in England and the Netherlands, by 100 per cent France, and by only 25 per cent in Poland. Inventories dating from this period show that even in such well-ordered areas as Wielkopolska small estates were in a condition of decrepitude, with buildings falling down, implements worn out and livestock depleted. Those worst affected were the landless peasants, but the habitual clichés about their condition need to be qualified.

Historians have a tendency to dwell on the supposed misery of the peasants, which is dangerous since the very term 'peasant' in Poland covers every non-noble inhabitant of the countryside. It includes the significant proportion of freeholding landed peasants who were economically better off than about 40 per cent of the szlachta, and the efficient tenants on large estates who could afford to employ others to fulfil their labour-rents, as well as the landless rural proletariat. There was technically no such thing as a serf in the Commonwealth – not in the sense of the European serf of the Middle Ages or the Russian serf before 1861. No peasant belonged to anyone; he was his master's subject only insofar as he had contracted to be in return for a house and/or rent-free land. Every peasant, however abject, was an independent entity enjoying the right to enter into any legal transaction with a freedom unthinkable in most countries at the time. Since, however, all the local organs of justice were controlled by the landowners, his rights often turned out to be academic. By the seventeenth century the landowners in effect exercised the power of life and death over their tenantry. How far they were inclined or allowed to abuse this right varied greatly from area to area, depending on the morality of the master rather less than on the level of education and determination of the peasant. Foreign travellers were often struck by the misery of the peasants and described with indignation the inhuman treatment meted out by their masters, but their accounts are contradictory. For every Abbé Vautrin who lamented 'the miseries of serfdom', there is a Dr Connor who claimed that 'the peasants in Poland live well satisfied and contented.' Unlike almost everywhere else in Europe, there were no peasant revolts in Poland after the Middle Ages, and this supports the evidence that confrontation with the landlord took place in the courts.

There is no doubt that the overall standard of living of the peasantry went down with a fair degree of consistency between 1500 and 1700, as did that of the majority of the szlachta and indeed of all the less wealthy inhabitants of the Commonwealth. The diet of the peasants declined in terms of quality and variation from the relatively high standards of the sixteenth century. They now consumed less meat and fish, and fewer varieties of vegetables. Yet the staple diet of cereals, vegetables (mostly peas and cabbage), and occasional meat, supplemented by mushrooms, nuts and fruit, looks positively healthy when compared with the sort of misery experienced, for instance, by their Irish counterparts in the nineteenth century. Nevertheless, the peasant of the 1700s was caught in a poverty trap which seriously impaired his ability to stand up for whatever theoretical rights he had, and he was a poor successor to his forebears.

The most pauperised segment of the population were the Jews, whose hopes for a peaceful future had been grievously shaken by the terrible massacres at the hands of the Cossacks in 1648 and of the Russians a few years later. The Jewish communities found it difficult to revive their economic position in a climate of mercantile stagnation which also exacerbated conflicts with Christian merchants. They underwent the same slide into parochialism as the rest of Polish society, which permitted the Rabbinate to re-establish a medieval grip over their lives, while their institutions ceased to function properly. The palatines who supervised the finances of the *kahals* in their provinces had done so only sporadically during the decades of war and unrest, with the result that venality and nepotism became characteristic features of their affairs. When a royal commission did eventually look into the *kahal* finances, it was discovered that they had been indulging in eccentric banking operations with the Jesuits, and that most of them were on the point of bankruptcy as a result of massive embezzlement. The whole Jewish 'state within a state' had to be wound up in 1764 as a result.

The masses of Polish Jewry lived in desperate poverty, in an increasingly hostile environment, and it was out of this hopeless misery that Hasidism was born. This was a mystical ecstatic cult, rejecting painful realities and offering a spiritual palliative that attracted vast numbers of the poorest Jews in the teeming provincial *shtetls* of the Commonwealth. It was founded in Podolia by Izrael ben Eliezer (1700–60) as a reaction to abstruse rabbinical learning, and it drew the ire of the orthodox Rabbinate. The Rabbinate also had to contend with the heresy of Shabbetai Zevi, who had proclaimed himself to be the Messiah in the 1660s, and acquired a

87 Interior of the synagogue at Przedbórz, dating from about 1760. None of the wooden synagogues survived the last war, and existing photographs and drawings can only hint at the ambitious structure and elegance of execution that characterised wooden building in Poland.

great following. It was the son of one of his disciples who caused the greatest ructions of all in the Jewish community. Jakub Frank in turn proclaimed himself Messiah and decreed that Poland was the Promised Land. His following grew rapidly. One of Frank's theories was that evil could be destroyed through indulgence in it, which led to some spectacular orgiastic rites. The Rabbinate invoked the law to curb the heresy, which turned it into a public issue. The Bishop of Lwów staged a public debate between the Talmudic experts nominated by the Rabbinate and the Frankists, with the Jesuits as adjudicators. To the delight of the Jesuits, Frank succeeded in tying the orthodox experts in knots and then announced that he and his sect would convert to Catholicism. Frank was baptised in 1759 with the king himself standing godfather, and all the converts were ennobled.

These outbursts of fervour stemmed from the psychological and material Babylon from which there seemed to be no possibility of escape. The depressed *shtetls* and the stinking Jewish slums of the larger towns were an eyesore which struck all foreign travellers. Yet they were only the darkest spots on a grim landscape of decrepitude and poverty, a poverty made all the more stark by the occasional evidence of fabulous wealth, and by the quantity of new building on a spectacular scale.

The only redeeming feature of Augustus III was a love for beauty inherited from his father, who had made Dresden one of the artistic centres of Europe. Augustus II had entertained great ideas for rebuilding Warsaw, and brought architects from Dresden to draw up plans. The only one put into effect was that of the great 'Saxon Palace' and Gardens. With the accession of Augustus III a new wing was added to the Royal Castle, which was refurbished throughout. The Italian inspiration of previous centuries was superseded by the French style and Dresden Rococo. A fine example of French classicism is the 'tin-roofed' palace built in Warsaw in 1720 for Jan Lubomirski. Other French-inspired buildings were the Bieliński Palace at Kozłówka and the Potocki at Radzyń, both by the father-and-son partnership of Józef and Jakub Fontana, descendants of an Italian architect who had settled in Poland over a century before. Like the Huguenots in England, these Italians established dynasties of architects, sculptors and painters who continued to dominate the artistic scene, even when Italian influences waned. The finest exponent of Rococo architecture in Poland was just such a man. Bernard Meretyn (Meretino) was active in south-eastern Poland in the 1740s, and his outstanding works include the Cathedral of St George in Lwów and the Town Hall of Buczacz. The most grandiose of the private commissions was the residence built in 1730 for Hetman Jan Klemens Branicki by Sigismund Deybel at Białystok, which was often called 'the Versailles of the North'. The layout of these country residences tended to conform to the French pattern, with wings or pavilions forming a horseshoe, a form which was to remain the basis of much East European country architecture.

The new houses needed to be furnished, as so much of the older chattels had perished or been looted, and craftsmen like Boule, Meissonier, Caffiéri and Riesener in Paris were flooded with orders from Poland. But this magnificence and patronage did not correspond to any deeper artistic or intellectual revival. These buildings were an incidental excrescence, not connected to any broader movement in society. Much of the patronage was born of idleness and wealth rather than taste or vision. The Branicki Palace at Białystok contained a theatre with 400 seats, equipped with one Polish and one French troupe of actors and a corps de ballet, but the only attention Hetman Branicki paid to this impressive establishment was to have the younger ballerinas read fairy-tales to him in his dotage. The stables contained 200 horses, the library 170 books.

Inside the magnificent Palace of Nieśwież lived Karol Radziwiłł, universally known as 'My Dear', since that was how he addressed everyone he met, a man who combined in himself all the most depressing features of the age and carried them to barely believable excess. He was affable and very popular, but when in his cups he could be a dangerous neighbour at dinner. 'It was nothing to him to shoot a man down like a dog, but' as the conscientious diarist Kitowicz remarks, 'such behaviour could be considered quite ordinary in the house and family of Radziwiłł. His uncles and brothers were just as quick-tempered, and the only exception was his father the Hetman of Lithuania, who, drunk or sober, was exceptionally slow-witted.' Having shot or otherwise harmed someone, he would endow a church or give away an estate and spend days in penance in church. Life was a series of impulses unchecked by any social, judicial or political influence. Backed by vast wealth, a court of hundreds and a private army of 6,000 troops, such impulses could be carried to frightening extremes.

The Commonwealth had become the Sick Man of Europe, a laughing-stock to foreigners who believed in progress and efficient government. It had lost the will as well as the ability to conduct a policy or to defend itself. Its parlous condition was not the result of its having been defeated or subjugated. It was the consequence of what can only be called deliberate choice on the part of the Poles themselves. Not a conscious choice perhaps, but nevertheless a wholesale acceptance of a set of attitudes and acquiescence in a set of circumstances.

Token political activities were ceremoniously indulged in with the cosy certainty that nothing real would come of them. Life went on as before whether the Seym was broken up or not. The less government there was, the more the Poles came to realise its dispensability. People began to believe that anarchy, in its literal sense of 'no government', was something

88 Augustus III, Elector of Saxony and King of Poland, portrayed by Louis de Silvestre in Polish costume and wearing the Order of the White Eagle founded by his father, was the most lumpish of Polish monarchs. **89** Karol Radziwiłł, painted in 1785 by Konstanty Alexandrowicz, was a worthy subject of his in every respect. Apart from drinking himself into a stupor, the king's favourite activity was shooting at flying Bison which had been catapulted into the air for the purpose. Radziwiłł favoured great banquets and drinking-bouts which usually ended with his killing someone, after which he would stumble into his private chapel and bawl himself back to sobriety by singing hymns. Between them, these two epitomise the abysmal condition into which Poland had sunk in the first half of the 18th century. The king's only redeeming feature was his love of the arts, and he endowed Warsaw with fine buildings.

90 One of the projects, by Johann Kärchner, for the rebuilding of the Royal Castle in Warsaw.

91 (*Above*) The palace built for Hetman Jan Klemens Branicki at Białystok by Johann Sigismund Deybel in 1730.

92 (*Below*) The Orthodox Cathedral of St George in Lwów, built between 1748 and 1764 by Bernard Meretyn, who combined elements of Catholic and Orthodox layout when producing this fine example of his Rococo style.

Apart from the usual rural pursuits, the country
gentleman's life revolved round going to church and
attending frenetic and explosive seymiks in order to elect
deputies who would go to Warsaw and break up the
national Seym before it could pass any legislation.

93 A seymik taking place in a church, as they often
did in inclement weather, a drawing by J.P. Norblin.

94 St Joseph's at Baborów, dating from 1700, a typical
baroque village church.

95 The baroque manor-house at Koszuty in
Wielkopolska, mid-18th Century.

of an ideal state, the ultimate in political freedom, the crowning achievement of all the old ideals of the Commonwealth.

Such delusions could only be entertained by a very sick society. In effect, all the ideals that had fired the founding fathers of the Commonwealth back in the 1550s had been travestied and trampled. The real democratic freedom of the citizen had evaporated, to be replaced by demagoguery which could not hide the fact that a poor member of the szlachta was entirely at the mercy of a magnate. The religious freedoms had gone too. The Convocation Seym of 1733 debarred non-Catholics from holding office, from being judges and from standing for the Seym, an act that finally brought the noble tradition of toleration to an end, and Poland into line with the other countries of Europe. The szlachta's sense of duty towards their Commonwealth had been an early casualty. The last time the *levée en masse* was proclaimed was in 1667, yet the szlachta's obligation to fight was regularly invoked as the basis for its exemption from taxation and its other prerogatives. Toleration of ethnic diversity had also receded, and in 1697 the use of Ruthene for legal and administrative purposes was brought to an end. After generations of Jesuit schooling, the szlachta which had set such store by university education and foreign travel was dominated by a virtually illiterate majority. Xenophobia, bigotry and sheer ignorance combined to create an attitude which extolled anarchy and substituted drink for thought. For several decades Polish society went into a state of suspension. To most observers the country appeared to be quite moribund. Yet the sick and insensate body did not actually die, because somewhere deep within it something still stirred.

14

Stanisław the Last

'Happy Prince, worthy to begin
with splendour, or to close with
glory, a race of patriots and kings.'
Edmund Burke, *Appeal from the New
to the Old Whigs*

In the 1750s the Polish Commonwealth was the most chaotic and backward state in Europe, the butt of universal raillery. Forty years later it was
the most progressive, its king the toast of French revolutionaries, its
constitution held up as an example by liberals at Westminster and
Washington. Few people could have suspected the possibility of such a
transformation during the last years of the fat Augustus's reign.

Even when the condition of anarchy was blessed with the approval of the
electoral masses, political tracts suggesting cures proliferated. The most
famous of these was *A Free Voice* published in 1749 as the work of Stanisław
Leszczyński, the *roi bienfaisant* of Lorraine, although it seems to have been
written in the 1730s by Mateusz Białłozór. It suggests sensible but hardly
revolutionary reforms, and reveals the same naïvety that characterised the
philosopher-king's polemics with Rousseau and earned him the epithet of
le Candide couronné. Perhaps the most interesting thing about it is that by
restating the cardinal principle of Polish sixteenth-century political
thought – that the Commonwealth was a political fatherland, defined
neither by its ruler nor its ethnic distinction nor its geographical frontiers
– it introduced a novel concept into the thinking of the French political
philosophers who were moving towards a new vision of *patrie*.

In Poland the desire for reform was first translated into action by
Stanisław Konarski (1700–73), a Piarist priest who had studied in Paris
and Turin. With the backing of Bishop Andrzej Załuski he began publishing all the legislation passed since the fourteenth century in a compen-
dium entitled *Volumina Legum*, the first tome of which appeared in 1732. It
was his belief that the electorate must be acquainted with the letter of the

constitution before it could be persuaded to reform it. In 1740 Konarski founded the Collegium Nobilium, a public school which isolated young noblemen from their family background and prejudices in order to imbue them with the ideals of the Enlightenment. Konarski's next move was to reform the twenty Piarist schools in the Commonwealth, and this had far-reaching consequences. The Jesuits perceived that this modernisation of rival establishments might relegate their own colleges. Within a year they transformed these by bringing in good teachers and altering the curriculum to include such subjects as physics and chemistry.

Konarski's friend Bishop Załuski created another landmark in cultural history. He was an avid collector of books and manuscripts, a taste he shared with his brother Józef, a priest who resided at Leszczyński's court in Lunéville. In 1747 the two pooled their collections, bought a palace in Warsaw, and donated to the nation the first public reference library on the European mainland. Its original holding of 180,000 books and over 10,000 manuscripts quickly grew, aided by the Seym's decree of 1780 obliging printers to donate the first copy of any book to designated public libraries. When it was looted by the Russians in 1795, this library consisted of over 500,000 volumes.

Konarski and Załuski were not missionaries working in a cultural wilderness. Horace Walpole's friend Sir Charles Hanbury-Williams sojourned in Poland in 1746 and declared: 'One meets quantities of brilliant people with whom it is a pleasure to converse and there is a great number of houses belonging to the nobility which are always open to you. I could have mentioned five or six where the style of living is better and more agreeable than anywhere else in Europe. The women are beautiful and have the most charming manners; their carriage is noble, and they are the most accomplished persons I have ever met anywhere.' Women were assuming a dominant role in society. The most interesting poet of the first half of the century was Elżbieta Drużbacka, the daughter of a poor nobleman, who retired to a cloister after an unhappy youth and devoted herself to writing. She was not afraid of making strong points about the treatment of women, particularly in the matter or arranged marriages. Another remarkable poet whose work is too little known was Konstancja Benisławska.

The resources and influence of a number of women strongly moulded the course of Polish history over the first half of the century. The first was Izabela Morsztyn, a daughter of the poet who was exiled. It was in Paris that she met and married in 1693 Prince Kazimierz Czartoryski, a penniless descendant of the Jagiellons. Bolstered with her considerable fortune, he brought her to Warsaw, where she started a literary and political salon. She bore the prince a son who became a bishop, a daughter who became an abbess, and three other children: Michał, August and

Konstancja. Michał was the most intelligent, but it was August who in 1731 managed to marry the heiress Zofia Sieniawska. In contrast, Konstancja married a man of humble szlachta descent, Stanisław Poniatowski. A fine soldier and diplomat, one-time Swedish general and close friend of Charles XII, he was a man known only by his qualities. These were appreciated by, amongst others, Louis XV and Voltaire.

The whole family was united by an urgent desire, not devoid of personal ambition, to improve the condition of the Commonwealth, and they worked as a team. 'Michał does the thinking, August provides the finance, and Stanisław does the job,' the saying went. They were generally referred to simply as 'the family', *Familia*, a term that came to embrace not only the close relations, but also their supporters. As well as being perhaps the wealthiest faction, the Czartoryski were also the most influential, having a large following of people convinced that they represented the best hope for saving the Commonwealth. There was talk of August standing as a candidate at the royal election of 1733, but this was scotched by the appearance of Stanisław Leszczyński, whom the Familia supported. It was while they were holding Gdańsk for Leszczyński in the hopeless war of 1734 that August had a son, Adam Kazimierz. A medal was struck to announce that the young prince would be brought up with royal pretensions. He was, after all, the descendant of Władysław Jagiełło's brother, and therefore of royal blood.

Two years before the birth of Prince Adam Kazimierz, the Familia had produced another child, Stanisław Antoni Poniatowski. Although she could hardly entertain royal aspirations for him, his mother Konstancja Czartoryska did take enormous care with his upbringing, and he was sent abroad to complete his education. He travelled through Vienna, Dresden and Holland on his way to England, to which he took an immediate liking. He was fascinated by its politics, its theatre and its taste, all of which he later introduced to Poland. He then spent some time in Paris, in the care of Madame Geoffrin, who introduced him to Montesquieu and d'Alembert. By the time he returned to Poland aged twenty, he was fluent in six languages, and had developed an equally wide range of tastes and interests. This made it all the more trying for him when he stood for election to the Seym of 1750. 'For several days at the seymik one had to talk nonsense with the rabble,' he complained, 'express admiration for their ludicrous arguments, delight in their shallow concepts, and, worst of all, embrace their dirty, wretched persons.' In 1755 he went to St Petersburg to stay with the British ambassador, Sir Charles Hanbury-Williams, with whom he had struck up an intimate friendship. The ambassador introduced his young friend to a person of growing influence at the Russian court who seemed to be in need of a new lover, the twenty-six-year-old Sofia Augusta Friderika of Anhalt-Zerbst, Grand Duchess Catherine

Alekseyevna. The over-sentimental Stanisław Antoni not only obliged, but fell in love with the grand duchess, whose official lover he became.

This development was to weigh heavily on events. The Familia had been preparing to overthrow Augustus III, but they had to contend with the probability that the 'Saxon Party' led by the Mniszech family and a group of politically incoherent but stubborn defenders of the state of anarchy, including Hetman Branicki, Franciszek Potocki and Karol Radziwiłł, would oppose this and harness the support of the Russian troops stationed in the Commonwealth. They therefore bided their time while Stanisław Antoni kept them informed from St Petersburg.

In 1762 a coup d'état placed the Grand Duchess Catherine on the imperial throne, and the Familia could count on Russian support for their plans. The following year Augustus III died, and there was nothing to stop them from putting their man on the throne. But their man, Prince Adam Kazimierz, had grown up without ambition, a gentle, cultivated figure who preferred books to politics and was happier corresponding in Sanskrit with English orientalists than following international affairs. Meanwhile, the Empress Catherine let it be known that she would look kindly on her ex-lover Poniatowski as King of Poland.

Accordingly, Stanisław Antoni Poniatowski was elected on 6 September 1764, taking the name of Stanisław II Augustus. With this election a new era dawned in Poland. Winds of change were already whistling through the Convocation Seym, sitting under the Marshalcy of Adam Kazimierz Czartoryski. The Seym was Confederated, which meant that it could pass legislation by majority vote. After hearing a visionary speech from Chancellor Andrzej Zamoyski decrying the dismal political, social and economic landscape, the Seym passed a number of measures on the Familia's programme. Majority voting was made statutory for seymiks, a small but important step towards abolishing the veto altogether. Fiscal and military commissions were established. All proposals put forward by the fiscal commission were subject to approval by the Seym, but with no right of veto. A national customs tariff was established, and a project for municipal reform was commissioned from the Chancellor. In addition, the king put into action several ideas of his own. In 1765 he founded the Szkoła Rycerska, literally 'College of Chivalry', the first entirely secular state-run academy for the training of military and administrative cadres. The very first intake of pupils included names which were to shine later, most notably that of nineteen-year-old Tadeusz Kościuszko.

In the following year, Chancellor Zamoyski laid before the Seym his project for constitutional reform which included the abolition of the veto. This elicited an immediate response from St Petersburg and Berlin, both of which threatened war if it were not withdrawn and if the Confederated Seym were not immediately dissolved. There was nothing for it but to comply. Alarmed at the renewal taking place in Poland, Catherine and Frederick decided to start a hare which would embarrass the Commonwealth internationally, revive the conservative anarchist elements, and generally foul up the political scene. They seized on the fact that in Poland (as in every other country in Europe, including Russia and Prussia) members of religious minorities did not have full civic rights. Russia demanded that all the Orthodox be granted the same rights to hold office as Catholics, and Prussia demanded the same for Lutherans.

The granting of such rights lay within the spirit of the king's and the Familia's programme. It was their conservative opponents who were against them. Yet the way in which the matter was raised turned the whole issue on its head. The progressives were opposed to granting rights to dissenters at this stage, since they knew it would provoke the ire of the conservatives. The conservatives were for the dissenters in this instance, because the issue compromised the king and his reforms. As a result, most progressives found themselves ranged against emancipation, and most of the arch-conservative bigots for it. Russian troops moved in to support two Confederations, one of Lutherans at Toruń, and one of Orthodox at Łuck. With Russia and Prussia firmly ranged on one side, many patriots, whether conservative or progressive, ranged themselves on the other. It was a muddle, meaningless but passionate, calculated to bring out the worst in everyone.

The king and his supporters had little room for manoeuvre. In October 1767 the Seym assembled in a capital full of Russian troops and deliberated under the eye of the Russian ambassador who sat in the visitors' gallery. A couple of bishops and the Hetman objected strongly to the emancipation of the dissenters. They were dragged from their beds that night and packed off to Russia under military escort. The only course was to bow to Russian demands, which included the acceptance by the Seym of five 'eternal and invariable' principles which Catherine then solemnly vowed to protect in the name of Poland's liberties. These principles (the free election of kings; the absolute rule of the veto; the right to renounce allegiance to the king; the szlachta's right exclusively to hold office and land; the landowner's power of life and death over his peasants) were an effective barricade against any possibility of reform.

Polish society had awoken from the pacifist slumber of the Saxon era, and many refused to follow the 'reasonable' course favoured by the king. At the same time a number of magnates were prepared to do almost anything to get rid of 'the upstart' Poniatowski. On 29 February 1768 a Confederation was formed in the little town of Bar in the Ukraine by the brothers Jósef and Kazimierz Puławski and Adam Krasiński, Bishop of Kamieniec. It lacked leadership of serious calibre and its programme consisted of windy phrases about the faith and national freedom. The Russians put pressure on the king to declare himself against the Confederation, but he prevaricated, hoping to avoid further polarisation on the issue. At this point, France intervened by sending money to the Confederates and encouraging Turkey to declare war on Russia, which duly broke out in October 1768. The Confederation was now joined by several magnates opposed to the king, including members of the Pac, Sapieha and Potocki families, and the greatest troublemaker of all, Karol Radziwiłł. The whole affair began to escalate out of all proportion. France sent Colonel Dumouriez, the future victor of Valmy, as military adviser to the Confederates. A provisional government was set up and Dumouriez advised it to take a more definite stance. People like Karol Radziwiłł needed little prompting, and in October 1770 the Confederation of Bar declared the dethronement of Stanisław Augustus.

The king, who had been trying at all costs to avoid civil war, was left with no choice. The forces of the crown joined the Russian troops under the young general Suvorov who defeated the Confederates at the Battle of Lanckorona. Inevitably, Russian intervention provoked more sympathy for the cause, and a guerilla war started all over south-eastern Poland. On the night of 3 November 1771, a group of Confederates surrounded the king's carriage in the middle of Warsaw and abducted him. The plan was as ill-executed as it was ill-conceived. The kidnappers lost their way, one of them changed his mind and allowed the king to escape, and by next morning Stanisław Augustus was back in his palace. The impression made all over Europe by this absurd behaviour gave substance to the Russo-Prussian propaganda that the Poles were ungovernable and dangerous, and paved the way for the final act of the dismal affair.

The Confederates were mopped up by the Russian armies, and only one pocket of resistance at Częstochowa held out until 1772. The magnates who had joined the Confederation went into exile, but over 5,000 captured szlachta were sent to Siberia. It was an inglorious end to a messy business. But if the movement itself was reactionary, its appeal to the young was patriotic and revolutionary. Both Rousseau and Mably had perceived this, which is why they supported the Confederation. People found themselves fighting for the wrong cause, but the experience radicalised them. Kazimierz Pułaski started out by fighting against the emancipation of dissenters, and died a few years later for American Independence at the Battle of Savannah.

For the Commonwealth, the Confederation of Bar could hardly have come at a worse moment. Under the ministry of Choiseul, France was straining to bring a Franco-Turkish-Austrian-Saxon alliance to bear against Russia and Prussia. Hence the French interest in the Confederation. Russia wanted to keep Poland docile, but Prussia was interested in one thing only: Frederick the Great had already announced his intention of

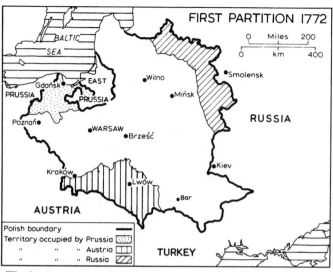

The first partition of Poland, 1772

eating up various Polish provinces 'like an artichoke, leaf by leaf.' The sudden fall of Choiseul in 1772 brought an end to French schemes in the area. Frederick had already worked out a plan for weaning Austria away from France and for binding her to Russia and Prussia – by dragging her into a tripartite despoliation of Poland. He had opened negotiations with Russia on the subject in 1771, and signed an agreement with her in February 1772. Both powers then approached Austria. The Empress Maria Teresa was at first reluctant, but then complied, and on 5 August 1772 the first partition of Poland was agreed. Prussia took 36,000 square kilometres with 580,000 inhabitants; Austria 83,000 square kilometres with 2,650,000 inhabitants; and Russia 92,000 square kilometres with 1,300,000 inhabitants. Prussia's share was the most valuable, since it included the most developed areas, linked up the two halves of the Prussian kingdom, and gave her control of the Vistula, Poland's life-line to the outside world.

The map of Central Europe had been redrawn, enlarging Prussia by an important fraction, and reducing Poland, which lost 30 per cent of its territory and 35 per cent of its population, to the same size as France. News of the partition caused alarm in many quarters. It also shocked public opinion throughout Europe. The Polish Commonwealth was in alliance with Russia and was not at war with either of the other two Powers when the whole arrangement was made. Moreover Russia never let an opportunity pass of informing the world that she was the guarantor of Polish independence and the protector of Polish territorial integrity. International politics were certainly not dictated by morality in the eighteenth century, but it was generally held that they ought to demonstrate at least a semblance of principle, and none was discernible in this case.

The three Powers determined to carry out some window-dressing, and insisted that the Polish Seym ratify the partition treaties. Some of the most depressing people in Poland were sought out, including malcontents who had done well under the Saxons and magnates whose estates were now suddenly in Russia or Austria, and a Confederated Seym was called under the Marshalcy of Adam Poniński. Prearranged deputies were elected at seymiks surrounded by foreign troops. Even so, many delegates raised havoc in the Seym, refusing to allow the ratification to proceed. The king and the Familia resorted to stalling tactics, meanwhile pulling every available diplomatic string to exert pressure on the three Powers. Alarmed by the Prussian predominance in the Baltic, Britain protested strongly, but there was little that could be done. Russia and Prussia threatened to seize even more territory, so the Seym had no alternative but to ratify the treaties of partition on 30 September 1773. Prussia took the opportunity to foist a trade agreement on Poland which took the form of draconian duties on Polish corn shipped down the Vistula.

The loss of territory would have been a fair price to pay if it had bought freedom of action. But the five 'eternal principles' dictated to the Seym by Russia excluded all possibility of constitutional reform, and neither Russia nor Prussia allowed their interest in what was happening in Poland to wane for an instant. Nevertheless, the next twenty years were to see a complete transformation. From 1772 the country was ruled by a Permanent Council, in effect the first proper ministerial government in Poland. The Council had five departments, which managed to carry out far-reaching improvements. The army, which could not be increased, was modernised. The Treasury began to function as a proper administrative body. The Police department enforced legislation, reorganised the administration of towns, and made its mark on everything from roads to prisons.

In 1776 the king commissioned Andrzej Zamoyski to produce a new legal code for the Commonwealth. Zamoyski picked a small group of collaborators, the most important of whom was Józef Wybicki, a gifted political writer. They set to work with such speed that the whole task, from inception to the publication of the two weighty tomes, took just under two years. Zamoyski's *Code of Laws* was a back-door project for political reform, a proto-constitution. It took Polish law back to its root and restated or reinterpreted it with reference to eighteenth-century conditions. The *Code* affirmed royal power, made all officials answerable to the Seym, placed the clergy and their finances under a measure of state supervision, shored up the rights of cities and of the peasants and, most controversially, deprived the landless szlachta of many of their legal immunities and political prerogatives. Its publication in 1778 induced sabre-rattling in the minor szlachta and apoplexy in the clergy. Józef Wybicki was nearly hacked to pieces at the hustings of the Sroda seymik. With feeling running high, the *Code* was held back by the reformers until the Seym of 1780, but its passage was doomed by a combination of clerical bigotry and Prussian intrigue. It was nevertheless an important document, widely accepted amongst progressives as the basis for future political reform.

An extraordinary renewal was taking place in public life, a second Renaissance which wiped the dust of the last two centuries from the whole surface of the Commonwealth. Unlike the first Renaissance, however, this was not a natural evolution, a process of ideas spreading gradually through print, by word of mouth, or by example. It was the result of a concerted effort, a war on obscurantism declared by a relatively small group whose aim was the social and political regeneration of the state, based on the re-education of society, in the spirit of Helvétius's maxim '*l'éducation peut tout*'. In 1773 the king appointed a Commission for National Education, in effect a ministry of education, the first of its kind in Europe. This comprised a selection of enlightened aristocrats – Bishop Ignacy Massalski, Joachim Chreptowicz, Ignacy Potocki, Adam Kazimierz Czartoryski, Andrzej Zamoyski – and its first secretary was the French physiocrat Dupont de Nemours. It was endowed with a part of the wealth of the Jesuit order, abolished by the Pope in 1771, and was put in control of every single school in Poland, regardless of which religious order or institution owned and ran it. It laid down curricula, chose and published textbooks, and supervised standards and teachers. With its extensive powers and resources, the Commission was able to tackle the reform of the Jagiellon University and the University of Wilno.

The accent on education as the fount of all promise was reflected in the remarkable resurgence of literary activity, the overwhelming majority of which was didactic in its inspiration. It was not the literary outburst of an exuberant society nor the poetic hedonism of idle sophisticates. It was a literature of national self-improvement, evidently political. The inspiration came from abroad. The luminaries were Voltaire, Rousseau, Diderot, d'Alembert and the Encyclopedists, whose political and social comment seemed particularly relevant to the stultified Commonwealth. To the majority of minor szlachta, ignorant, xenophobic and convinced that Polish was best, the very fact that progressives dressed in the French style (effeminate), quoted foreign writers (freemasons all), and spoke foreign languages (unpatriotic), militated against them. The sort of argument which raged in Russia a hundred years later between 'Westerners' and 'Slavophiles', between those who felt that all progress needed to be imported and those who felt that foreign influences were corrupting the purity of the ethnic genius, began to develop in Poland in the mid-eighteenth century. While the progressives attempted to apply logic and reason, jingoism and stupidity came together in defence of such hallowed 'national institutions' as the Polish costume, drunkenness and the veto. It was a brave man who would appear at a seymik in Volhynia dressed in stockings, breeches and a French coat.

The situation demanded commitment from writers, and their purpose suggested satire as the most effective weapon. The necessity of getting this across encouraged two hitherto little used forms: the periodical and the stage. In 1765 Stanisław Augustus founded the weekly *Monitor*, modelled on Addison's *Spectator*. Similar digests proliferated, and circulation figures reveal that by 1792 every forty-fifth inhabitant of the Commonwealth was a subscriber, and every twentieth a reader of one or other of these.

The editor of *Monitor*, Franciszek Bohomolec, also played a pioneering role in the theatre. As a Jesuit he wrote plays for performance in schools, and later for the National Theatre founded by Stanisław Augustus in 1765. His lead was taken up by the poet Franciszek Zabłocki, who wrote some sixty comedies, and by many others, including magnates such as Adam Kazimierz Czartoryski and Wacław Rzewuski, who wrote for their own court theatres. These plays were imitative of works by Molière, Voltaire, Marivaux and Sheridan, and mostly served to convey a moral through satire on subjects like Sarmatian obscurantism or oppression of the lower orders. Though often fresh and amusing, few are memorable, with the exception of Julian Ursyn Niemcewicz's *The Return of the Deputy* (1790), an incisive picture of conflicting political outlooks within one family.

The second Renaissance contributed only one great poet, Ignacy Krasicki (1735–1801), Prince-Bishop of Warmia, a fief in which the spiritual shepherd was also the temporal ruler. A creature of the Enlightenment, Krasicki despised stupidity and ignorance above all. He was a great raconteur, an avid reader, and a passionate gardener. He wrote articles, essays, biographies, historical works, treatises, novels, plays and poetry. His prose is clear and forceful, his poetry combines elegance of form and rhythm with beauty of language. His best-known works are his short impressionistic *Fables* (1779) and two mock-heroic epics: *The Mousiad* (1775), the tale of a war between mice and cats which can be read on several levels, and *The War of the Monks* (1778), in which the Dominicans challenge the Carmelites to a theological dispute which turns into a drinking-duel. His novels include *The Adventures of Mikolaj Doświadczyński* (1776), the Polish *Candide*, which shows the influence of Rousseau's didacticism as well as Swift's hyperbole.

No other poet of the age measures up to Krasicki, but he had many talented contemporaries. In terms of style and manner they seem to belong to different countries and periods, so uneven and varied is their output. This was largely because the literary development of the eighteenth century was crammed into a period of some thirty years in Poland. During

97 Stanisław Augustus, the last king of Poland (1764–95), seen here in a sketch for his coronation portrait by Marcello Bacciarelli, sought to bring about a renewal in Poland not merely by political means, but also through the arts.

96 Tureen and two dishes by Teodor Pawłowicz, one of the best silversmiths working in Warsaw in the last two decades of the century.

98 Plate of the 'Sultan's service' made in the faience factory established by the king in the 1770s at Belweder.

99 Wall-hanging produced in one of the factories established by magnates in the middle of the century.

100 The northern façade of Stanislaw Augustus's palace on the water at Łazienki completed in 1788. The king toiled for more than a decade with his architect, Dominik Merlini, and other artists to convert the former Lubomirski bath-house into one of the most magnificent yet restrained royal residences in Europe, and at the same time to make an aesthetic statement which was to have an enduring effect on Polish architecture.

101 The dining-room of the Little White House, a tiny retreat built by the king in the Łazienki park in 1776. The decoration of the interior is the work of Jan Bogumił Plersch.

102 (*Top*) The country residence of Młynow in Volhynia, built in the late 1780s by Efraim Szreger, who had previously worked for the king on the Royal Castle in Warsaw. Even in this pitiful state just after the Russian revolution of 1917, the stuccoed façade displays all the elegance of the early Stanislavian style.

103 The more Palladian classicism of Lubostroń in Wielkopolska, built in 1800 by Stanisław Zawadzki, one of a group of architects trained by the king, reflects the later move towards an English concept of house-and-gardens.

the Renaissance the Poles had taken what they wanted from abroad, rejecting anything that did not suit them, and eventually created a synthesis which was quintessentially Polish. In the eighteenth century they woke up to what was happening in Europe relatively late and assimilated foreign influences so rapidly that no such synthesis evolved. They were less self-assured and more obviously imitative. They devoured Boileau and Lafontaine in the same mouthful as Molière and Voltaire, Rousseau, Diderot and Mably; they discovered Shakespeare at the same time as they discovered Pope, Swift, and the novels of Richardson and Fielding. Consequently, late baroque sentimental styles jostle with crisp political satire, Sarmatian rhetoric with Voltairean brevity, and classical elegy with proto-Romantic sentiment.

The most consistent, as well as one of the best of these poets, was Stanisław Trembecki (1735–1812). He had spent part of his youth in Paris where he gambled, fornicated and duelled on an epic scale, and where he met Voltaire, Rousseau, and several of the Encyclopedists. He became a courtier and devoted friend to Stanisław Augustus, with whom he remained to the end. An element of coldness and affectation mars Trembecki's work, but his lyrics, fables and descriptive poems are nevertheless very fine, and they possess a unity of style not met with in the work of contemporaries such as, for instance, Franciszek Karpiński.

Karpiński (1741–1825) was marked by the ideas of the Enlightenment, but retained much of his Sarmatian upbringing, including a strong religious streak. He wrote *Sielanki*, amongst which are some of the most beautiful love-poems of Polish literature, as well as a collection of *Songs of Piety*. These religious poems penetrated beneath many a thatched roof, in some cases becoming Christmas Carols, one of them, *Bóg Się Rodzi*, the most popular in the Polish repertoire. Towards the end of his life he fused the love of countryside with a proto-Romantic love of country. *The Sarmatian's Lament* (1802), an ode to the deceased Commonwealth, is one of the first to bring sentimentality into love of the motherland. A similar note was struck by Adam Naruszewicz, Bishop of Smolensk, a favourite of King Stanisław Augustus who in 1774 commissioned him to write *The History of the Polish Nation*. While working on this, Naruszewicz composed an elegy on Poland's past containing several elements which were to characterise the nationalist poetry of the Romantic period.

One who seems to belong more to the nineteenth century than to the eighteenth was Julian Ursyn Niemcewicz (1757–1841), who started his career as an aide to Adam Kazimierz Czartoryski and then, after travelling widely throughout Europe and America, became a public figure in his own right. He was a prolific author of satirical and didactic poetry, drama, essays and even novels, as well as being the founding editor of the *National and Foreign Gazette* in the 1790s. Virtually all his literary activity was political in inspiration, and his most lyrical work, the *Historical Cantos*, not published until 1816, was a collection of heroic elegies on figures and deeds of the past. A man of integrity, intelligence and feeling, Niemcewicz became for the first generation of Romantic poets a symbol of all that was finest in the Commonwealth, a guardian of old Polish values who by virtue of his longevity could relay them to much younger generations of artists.

The thread that runs through the work of all these writers is the urgency they felt with regard to rescuing the Commonwealth from the trough into which it had fallen. The same urge was felt by intelligent people through-out the country, even those of a naturally flippant bent. Izabela Czartory-ska, a literary hostess and patroness of the arts, was as amorously flighty as any eighteenth-century grande dame, and created a world of extraordin-ary erotic frivolity in her lavishy designed 'Arcadia' at Powązki outside Warsaw, complete with classical ruins, shepherds' huts and temples of love, yet she gave away fortunes to the national cause, she wrote the first Polish history textbook for elementary schools, and founded the first public historical museum. If she enjoyed whiling away her time at Versailles, she was no less keen to visit her poorer tenantry in their stinking homes in order to persuade them to send their children to one of her village schools.

The king himself was an unlikely combination of seemingly contradic-tory characteristics. He was certainly vain and pleasure-loving, and at crucial moments he failed to display the sort of picturesque courage that would have made him popular with nineteenth-century historians. He has generally been represented as a peruked nonentity, a pathetic symbol, and possibly one of the main causes, of Poland's terminal impotence. He was certainly no hero, but behind the languid frivolity lurked a strong sense of purpose and a profound love of his country, and if he did not go down fighting, he served it with devotion to the bitter end.

Stanisław Augustus had no personal wealth and no distinguished ancestry. He was widely despised as an upstart who had reached the throne via the bed of the Empress Catherine, who preferred the company of women to that of hard drinking men, and who rejected Sarmatian manners for foreign clothes and taste. He ascended the throne of a state which had all but ceased to function at a moment when two powerful neighbours were preparing to cancel it out altogether. Yet he was deter-mined to rule effectively, halt the decline, and restore the country to a position of power. Although he could initially count on the resources of the Familia, these were withdrawn during the 1770s and turned into the mainstay of a powerful opposition party including members of the Potocki and Lubomirski families, which forced him into greater dependence on Russian support. His only assets were his great personal charm, his intelligence and his patience. He had been a deputy six times, and was therefore familiar with the workings of the Seym and the attitudes that prevailed in it. He was also aware as no other elected monarch had been of the considerable influence and powers still at the disposal of the crown. Having no private fortune, he was entirely dependent on these and used them to the full in pursuit of his aims. A skilful diplomatist, he was prepared to compromise and bide his time on one project in order to further another.

His was not so much a policy as a vision. From his youth, he dreamt of a total 're-creation of the Polish world' to·use his own words, involving a return to the ideals of the Commonwealth on the one hand, and turning the Sarmatians into a European nation on the other. From his reading and his travels, particularly in England, he had derived an appreciation of the importance of the state as an institution, a concept hitherto absent from Polish political thought. Quite apart from carrying out constitutional reform, he therefore aimed to alter the relationship of Polish society to the state. When political reforms were cancelled out by the Russo-Prussian intervention of 1772, he concentrated on this second tier of his programme. This could only be carried out by opening the minds of the Poles and breaking down ossified patterns of thought and behaviour.

He was not a lone gladiator taking on the whole of Polish society, and in the field of education he was following in the footsteps of Konarski and the Załuski brothers. Even when he began to diverge from the political plans of the Familia, he could still rely on its individual members to back his educational cultural initiatives, and to complement them with their own. An impressive number of enlightened magnates – Stanisław Lubomirski, Ignacy Potocki, Andrzej Zamoyski, Stanisław Małachowski and Adam Kazimierz Czartoryski, to mention only the most important – devoted their fortunes and their influence to the same cause, while less exalted figures, including many of the clergy, worked assiduously to put plans into action.

In the 1780s this handful of people turned into a national movement. By then two generations had passed through the reformed schools and been exposed to the thought of the Enlightenment, giving rise to a new phenomenon in Polish life, the *intelligentsia*. This term, only coined later, is used to describe an identifiable group which transcended class barriers – without in any way removing them – and was united by a common educational background and political vision, which might differ in details but accepted the service of society as its fundamental moral obligation. They were in effect the eighteenth-century version of the traditional concept of the 'political nation', and represented the first attempt at transforming the basis of the szlachta's right to lead the country from noble descent to personal achievement (the king ennobled artists, functionaries and tradesmen at every opportunity).

The first signs of the emergence of this new class could be read in the new political alignments which showed magnates reaching an understanding with tradesmen on issues of national significance, and in the gradual disappearance of the old battle-lines of Sarmatism and obscurantism versus Westernism and education. These connotations had previously meant that anyone who liked tradition was obliged to dislike education and that anyone who was educated had to dislike the sight of the Polish costume, the *kontusz*. In 1788, Jan Potocki, a typical young magnate brought up to speak eight languages, sent to military school in Vienna, then to serve and fight as a Knight of Malta in the Mediterranean; a man who wrote (in French) fascinating accounts of travels in the Near East, who was to become the first serious Polish archaeologist, who wrote *The Manuscript Found in Saragossa*, a fantastic gothic tale which has become a minor classic of French literature, and who was the first Pole to go up in a balloon in Warsaw (with a parrot and a dog) – this man, who could hardly be called xenophobic or Sarmatian in outlook, made a sensation and started a fashion by relaunching the *kontusz* as court wear. For the young men of his generation it had been purged of its evil associations. Backwoods demagogues would no longer be able to curry support by invoking Sarmatian values. The confusion of the Confederation of Bar, in which young idealists and patriots found themselves unwittingly fighting for clerical bigotry and Russian interests, would never occur again. The lines had been redrawn. It was possible to be a patriot and wear stockings and breeches; it was possible to be a progressive and wear a *kontusz*.

The erosion of long-held prejudice had an immediate impact on economic life, and the unfavourable balance of trade resulting from the lack of manufacturing industry began to be reversed. During the 1730s and 1740s a number of magnates decided to remedy the situation and profit from it. The Radziwiłł established glass-foundries at Naliboki and Urzecz; a furniture factory at Łachwa: a cannon-foundry at Urzecz; and workshops producing cloth, carpets and articles of clothing at their main seat of Nieśwież. The range reflects a lack of specialisation which meant that the products were often not of high quality. The same was true of the factories set up by Ludwik Plater at Krasław near Vitebsk, producing velvet, damask, carpets, carriages, swords and rifles. The Potocki factories at Brody and Buczacz specialised in high-quality carpets, kilims, tents, hangings, sashes and cloth. During the same period the Bishopric of Kraków, which owned large areas of what has since become the industrial heartland of Poland, built several new iron foundries.

With the death of Augustus III the process of economic regeneration gathered momentum. The Convocation Seym of 1764 was revolutionary not only in its political attitudes – the speech by the Chancellor which heralded so many political reforms also hectored the deputies that 'to sell raw materials and buy finished goods makes one poor; to buy raw materials and sell finished goods makes one rich.' The point was taken, and the next twenty years saw a remarkable development of mercantile and capitalist activity among the magnates and szlachta. In 1773 the Seym repealed the law forbidding the szlachta to engage in commerce. Between 1764 and 1766, a royal mint was established at Warsaw, the currency was stabilised, weights and measures were standardised, and a state postal service was founded. In 1771 a canal was dug connecting the Vistula to the Warta; in 1775 the king launched a project for one between the Bug and the Pripet; in 1765 Prince Michał Ogiński began digging a canal linking the Niemen and the Dnieper, thereby making it possible to navigate from the Baltic to the Black Sea, which opened up alternative markets for exports.

Much of the industrial activity went hand-in-hand with a resurgence in the decorative arts. In 1768 the king founded the Belweder ceramic factory which produced high-quality vases and tableware; the Czartoryskis started a porcelain factory at Korzec which employed up to 1,000 workers in the 1790s in the production of more functional items of quality under the supervision of experts brought from Sèvres. The same was true of the new furniture centre of Kolbuszowa. But there was also a certain amount of purely industrial enterprise. The state built an ordnance factory outside Warsaw and a large cloth-mill geared particularly to supplying the army. In 1767 a joint-stock Wool Manufacturing Company was floated. The Treasurer of Lithuania, Antoni Tyzenhaus, launched a formidable programme of industrialisation in Grodno as part of an energetic fiscal reorganisation of the Grand Duchy. The most business-minded of all the magnates, Antoni Protazy Potocki, established banks in major Polish cities, factories in various parts of the Commonwealth, and a trading-house at Kherson from which he operated a merchant fleet on the Black Sea and the Mediterranean.

Much of the manufacturing was based on small towns or large estates; peasants were often used as cheap labour, so there was little attendant growth in the urban proletariat. The only exception was Warsaw, which grew from 30,000 inhabitants in 1760 to some 150,000 in 1792, and began to resemble contemporary European capitals, not least politically. It had a large and vociferous artisan class and an increasingly influential patriciate, including such figures as the Mayor, Jan Dekert, and the brilliant banker and entrepreneur Piotr Tepper, who were to play an important role in the last decades of the eighteenth century.

The fabric of the Commonwealth was undergoing improvement and modernisation, moving by leaps and bounds to make up for lost time. The idealism of the sixteenth century resurfaced, impelling people towards the goal of a new utopia. Fired by the spirit of the European Enlightenment and by the example of the states of North America, people began to restructure their relationships to other social groups. Already in 1766

Chancellor Andrzej Zamoyski had freed the peasants on his estates from all labour-rents and dues, and turned all tenancies into financial transactions. Other landowners followed suit, most notably Anna Jabłonowska and Joachim Chreptowicz. Some went further. Scibor Marchocki turned his estate into a peasant co-operative, while Paweł Brzostowski founded the Peasant Commonwealth of Pawłów in 1769, a self-governing village with its own school, hospital and citizen's militia.

The king's personal contribution to this revolution is not always obvious, but his moral role in encouraging its spirit was immense. He kept abreast of everything that was being written and done abroad. He encouraged Poles to travel and foreigners to come to Poland, often by taking them into his own service. These attempts at fostering international contacts were not limited to Europe: it was with his approbation that Kościuszko and other Poles took part in the American Revolution, and it was in his service that Americans such as Louis Littlepage and Washington's General Charles Lee sojourned in Poland.

The most spectacular personal contribution made by Stanisław Augustus was, ironically, viewed after his death as evidence of his frivolity: his exorbitant patronage of the arts. It began conventionally enough. In his youth he had admired the architecture of France and shown interest in the excavations being carried out at Herculanum, even writing in 1762 to the King of Naples to send him drawings and books on the subject. When he ascended the throne in 1764, Stanisław Augustus decided to rebuild the Royal Castle extensively and commissioned Victor Louis, subsequent architect of the Palais-Royal, and several craftsmen to submit projects for the building, the interiors and the furniture. While the remodelling of the exterior was soon abandoned as being too ambitious, the designs for the interiors were adopted, and the bronzes, furniture and panelling ordered. By 1767, however, Stanisław Augustus had run into political problems, and financial ones were not far behind, so the project was discontinued.

When the king resumed his building plans, the French style was abandoned in favour of the Italian. Dominik Merlini (1730–97), a pupil of Jakub Fontana (1710–73), was appointed royal architect and teamed with Jan Kamsetzer (1753–95), a talented designer of interiors whom the king had sent to study in England, France and Italy for several years. They worked together under the king's close supervision and constant participation over the next two decades, producing a hybrid of Italian architecture with some French and English influence. In the early 1780s they completed the new interiors of the Royal Castle, which are a monument to the king's taste, and rebuilt the old Lubomirski bath-house at Łazienki, keeping only the original bath-room by Tylman Gamerski as the central point for a small palace which is one of the jewels of eighteenth-century architecture.

This return of the Italian as the dominant influence and the incorporation of English and French elements was to be a characteristic feature of the architecture of the Stanislavian period. The only Italian architect proper to work in Poland was Giacomo Quarenghi, who was commissioned by Helena Radziwiłł to rebuild her country seat at Nieborów. Yet Italian models dominated in the construction of houses in and around Warsaw. Little palaces in the *casino* manner were built by Merlini at Jabłonna for the king's brother, and by Szymon Bogumił Zug (1733–1807) at Natolin for August Czartoryski. Their interiors proclaim their Italian and French pedigree, while the exteriors and their relationship to the landscape are redolent of English Palladian architecture. This is particularly true of the last house built in the style, in 1800, by Stanisław Zawadzki at Lubostroń in Wielkopolska.

Stanisław Kostka Potocki, the first Polish writer on ancient art, spent much time in Italy drawing classical remains and directing a number of digs: in 1786 he and the young architect Piotr Aigner (1756–1841) made a new plan of Pompeii. Aigner was just one of a number of architects sent to Italy on scholarships from the king which included Wawrzyniec Gucewicz, Szymon Bogumił Zug, Stanisław Zawadzki and Jakub Kubicki. These were the men who would create the Polish classical style which flourished over the next four decades. Gucewicz (1753–98) returned from his travels fired by an enthusiasm which found expression in severe and massive buildings such as his town hall of Wilno (c.1780). Zawadzki (1743–1806) worked for a time as military architect to the king, and then moved on to build a series of country houses. Kubicki (1758–1833) worked on similar buildings and came to dominate Polish architecture in the early decades of the nineteenth century. The neo-classical country houses created by these architects dictated a style for much of East European and Russian country architecture.

There was hardly an area which the king neglected in his determination to refine the minds of his subjects, and it was largely his patronage that turned Warsaw into an important musical centre once more. He invited foreign composers such as Paisiello and Cimarosa, and commissioned works from them. His example was taken up by others. Michał Kazimierz Ogiński presided over a thriving musical centre at Słonim, and Marcin Lubomirski began to use his large private orchestra for regular public concerts in Warsaw. Native composers began producing chamber music of a national style, of which forms like the Polonaise were the mainstay. Although this vintage yielded no great musicians, composers such as Maciej Kamieński, Michal Kleofas Ogiński, W.F. Lessel and Jan Dawid Holland created a musical scene which flourished in the first decades of the next century.

The king was equally instrumental in reviving painting in Poland. He

The Reformers: **104** (*Top left*) Hugo Kołłątaj, who helped to frame the Constitution of 3 May 1791 and played a prominent role in the Insurrection of 1794, by J. Peszka. **105** (*Top right*) Joachim Chreptowicz, member of the Commission for National Education and Vice-Chancellor of Lithuania from 1793, by Anna Bacciarelli. **106** (*Bottom left*) Stanisław Małachowski, Marshal of the Great Seym of 1788 and co-author of the Constitution of 3 May, by J. Peszka. **107** (*Bottom right*) Ignacy Potocki, member of the Commission for National Education, co-author of the Constitution of 3 May, member of the Insurrectionary Government of 1794.

The Idealists: **108** (*Left*) Kazimierz Pułaski, one of the founders of the Confederation of Bar (1768), who died fighting for the American Revolution at the Battle of Savannah; engraving by James Hopwood. **109** (*right*) Tadeusz Kościuszko, who served with George Washington and fortified West Point, commanded a corps against the Russians in 1792, and led the Insurrection against them in 1794. His edicts enfranchised all peasants who fought for Poland. He freed the black slaves given to him by the US Congress and sold all his lands in America to pay for the freedom of others; portrait by Józef Kosiński. **110** Paweł Brzostowski, a wealthy landowner who had established the self-governing 'peasant republic' of Pawłów, mourns its destruction on the orders of Catherine the Great in 1792. The bas-relief on the base of the column shows him granting his peasants the constitution of the 'republic'. In the background Russian troops can be seen burning down the village; painting by François Xavier Fabre.

employed Italians such as the court painter Marcello Bacciarelli, Bernardo Belotto and others for his architectural and personal needs, and both he and the Polish aristocracy continued to lend their patronage to foreign portrait painters, particularly Angelica Kaufman, Elizabeth-Louise Vigée-Lebrun, Giuseppe Grassi and Giovanni Battista Lampi. But the king also encouraged native talent by sending young men to study abroad or putting them to work alongside the foreigners. One such apprentice, Franciszek Smuglewicz (1745–1807), went on to become a painter of historical and genre pictures and worked successfully in England for a time. Aleksander Kucharski (1741–1819) managed to establish himself as a portrait-painter in Paris. Kazimierz Wojniakowski (1772–1812) and Józef Kosiński grew into fine portrait-painters and miniaturists. The most interesting foreign arrival was Jean Pierre Norblin de la Gourdaine (1745–1830), brought from Paris by Adam Kazimierz Czartoryski, who developed an idiosyncratic impressionistic style in which he covered almost every aspect of Polish life. One of his pupils, another protégé of the Czartoryski, was Aleksander Orłowski (1777–1832), a remarkable artist who later settled in St Petersburg. Both his style and his love of mythical and chivalric themes foreshadow the Romantic painters of the nineteenth century.

Stanisław Augustus spent fortunes on the arts, running up vast debts in a number of countries, but he was not merely a spendthrift aesthete. He believed passionately in the educational role of the arts, and hoped to improve those exposed to them. But he was also trying to put across a message and to leave a legacy. Detailed correspondence between him and his artists reveals that he participated intimately in the whole process of creation. He gave an astonishing amount of thought to the thematic aspects of every building and painting he commissioned. While planning the Sala Rycerska, the Senators' Hall of the Royal Castle, he meant to turn it into a sort of Polish hall of fame, and spent years on deciding which great figures of the past should be represented, which of them should be in oil, which in marble, which in bronze, and in what relationship to each other they should be placed. As he confided to Adam Naruszewicz, he was building for the future, attempting to leave to posterity a statement on the Polish past which would serve to inspire generations to come. It was all part of his vision of a Poland regenerated intellectually and refurbished materially. There was to be a new university in Warsaw, a *Museum Polonicum*, an Academy of Sciences, and an Academy of Arts (for which some of the paintings were actually collected in London, and now hang in the Dulwich Picture Gallery). Only a fraction of his plans ever saw the light of day, yet he did succeed at the very last moment of the Commonwealth's life in recapitulating and holding up its merits and its achievements in a form which would make their memory endure.

15

A Gentle Revolution

In the spring of 1787 Catherine the Great of Russia set off on an imperial progress through her southern dominions. As the Empress drifted down the Dnieper like some latter-day Semiramis, greeted with decorations, fireworks and crowds of happy subjects lined up along the banks by her lover and minister Potyomkin, King Stanisław Augustus left Warsaw to intercept her on the Polish stretch of the river's bank. On 6 May the imperial galley tied up at Kaniów, and the Polish king came aboard. The two monarchs had last met as lovers nearly thirty years before, and after the usual formalities of greeting they retired together for a *tête-à-tête*.

They emerged after only half an hour, and the slight embarrassment they displayed was immediately picked up by the assembled courtiers and diplomats. The empress entertained the king lavishly, but declined to go ashore in Poland for a ball he had arranged in her honour. Stanisław Augustus was mortified. He had weightier reasons for disappointment than spurned feelings. He had come to Kaniów to strike a bargain. He proposed an alliance in Russia's forthcoming war against Turkey. Poland would contribute a substantial army and at the same time fend off belligerent moves by Prussia and Sweden, in return for which she would acquire Moldavia and a Black Sea port. Apart from permitting the Commonwealth to raise and test an army of its own, this alliance would have eased some of the tensions building up in Warsaw, and strengthened the king's hand at home.

Catherine's rejection of the plan left Stanisław Augustus without a policy at a critical moment and played into the hands of his political opponents. While the king had bowed to the conditions imposed by Russia after the first partition in 1772, pressures had been building up against such a docile acceptance of the situation. By the late 1780s there was a widespread feeling that the time had come to shrug off the protection and restrictions imposed by Russia, and to follow a more independent policy of reform. A group of magnates, including the Czartoryski Familia, Ignacy Potocki, Stanisław Małachowski, Michał Kazimierz Ogiński. Stanisław

Potocki and Karol Radziwiłł, who became known as the 'Patriotic Party', began to steer the country in this direction. Prussia, which had just entered into an alliance with England and Holland aimed at checking Russian expansion, made it clear that the Commonwealth could count on support if it severed the Russian connection. With Russia tied down by wars against Turkey and Sweden, and with Prussia making friendly noises towards Poland and striking hostile attitudes towards Russia and Austria, it looked as though the concert of Poland's menacing neighbours had at last fallen into discord.

The Seym which assembled in 1788 under the Marshalcy of Stanisław Małachowski, known as the Great Seym, took matters into its own hands. It voted an increase of the army and vested control of it in a Seym Commission. It placed the conduct of foreign policy in the hands of another Seym Commission. In January 1789 the Seym abolished the Permanent Council which had been ruling the country since 1772 and prolonged its own session indefinitely. In March it imposed a tax on income from lands of 10 per cent for the szlachta and 20 per cent for the Church, the first direct taxation ever to have been imposed on either.

The opposition was split between Russian toadies and chauvinistic reactionaries. Neither could voice any coherent argument and both were taken aback by events. They were also unsettled by the ferment taking place in Paris, whose heady emanations could be felt on the banks of the Vistula. On the night of 25 November 1789 Warsaw was illuminated for the anniversary of the coronation of Stanisław Augustus, which the reactionaries feared might act as a provocation to the mob. Hetman Branicki stayed up all night, a pair of loaded pistols at his side, while Kazimierz Nestor Sapieha decided to spend the night in the guard-room of the town hall. 'I don't want to hang,' he explained. There was no mob baying for blood but revolutionary clouds nevertheless hung over the capital. While the rabble in the streets confined itself to demonstrating its likes and dislikes with lampoons, a real revolution was being prepared in other quarters. In September 1789 the Seym had appointed a Commission under the chairmanship of Ignacy Potocki to prepare a written constitution for the Commonwealth.

Debate on the question of reform had grown progressively more radical and was now dominated by two of the greatest political thinkers Poland has produced, Stanisław Staszic and Hugo Kołłątaj. Stanisław Staszic (1755–1826) was one of Poland's finest sons, noble-minded, patriotic and highly intelligent. After completing a high school in Poznań he entered the priesthood, mainly to please his devout mother. He travelled through Germany, and spent some time in Paris and Rome. In Paris he became a friend of Buffon, whose *Histoire Naturelle* he translated and published in Poland. In Rome he lost his faith completely. On his return to Poland he devoted his energies to political writing. Later, in 1808, he founded the Society of Friends of Learning with a fortune he had built up in business. In 1815 he published a seminal work on the geological formation of the Carpathian Mountains, while working on a verse translation of the *Iliad*.

In 1785 he published his *Remarks on the Life of Jan Zamoyski* and five years later his *Warning to Poland*, in which he expounded his political philosophy. He was a committed republican and believed in the sovereignty of the Seym, but realised that a nation surrounded by despotic states must have a strong executive and he therefore argued for a hereditary monarchy. He intertwined political, social and economic recommendations in a way which was both practical and convincing. He saw Polish society as a 'moral entity' consisting of all the citizens of the Commonwealth, whether they were szlachta or peasants, townspeople or Jews, and in so doing laid the foundations of Poland's survival in the following century.

A very different character, and one who exerted stronger immediate influence, was Hugo Kołłątaj (1750–1812), an ambitious man and an incisive thinker with a Jacobin bent. He studied at the Jagiellon University and in Italy, where he became a priest, and was later an active member of the Commission for National Education. He showed his organisational skills when he was given the task of reforming the Jagiellon University, whose Rector he became in 1782.

He influenced the Great Seym by starting a political pressure-group known as 'the Forge', in which he combined the progressive and articulate into a powerful lobby for reform of the whole system, for a 'gentle revolution', as he put it. In *A Few Anonymous Letters to Stanisław Małachowski* (1788) he addressed the Marshal and the assembling Seym. 'What then is Poland?' he taunted them: 'It is a poor, useless machine which cannot be worked by one man alone, which will not be worked by all men together, and which can be stopped by a single person.' Like Staszic, he demanded a strong hereditary monarchy, the supremacy of the Seym and extension of the franchise to other classes. He made his points forcefully. It was he who composed the text of the memorandum presented to the king by the representatives of 141 towns, dressed in black like the États Généraux in Paris the previous year and led by Jan Dekert, on 2 December 1789. 'The slave will violently tear his bonds asunder if his ruler stifles all the Rights of Man and of the Citizen,' it warned. King and Seym took notice. A commission was set up to devise a system of representation for the towns, and in the meantime several hundred tradesmen were ennobled. In the following year Kołłątaj published his *Political Law of the Polish Nation*, which encapsulated his programme for reform. The moment was not far off when its theoretical skeleton would be given flesh and blood.

King Stanisław Augustus, who could display remarkable political flair on occasion, soon emerged from the isolation in which his abortive Kaniów plan had landed him. He invited Ignacy Potocki, Hugo Kołłątaj and Stanisław Małachowski to join him in drawing up the new constitution. They worked in secret, thrashing out differences of opinion in camera while the king's secretary Scipione Piattoli prepared the drafts. When the basic document was ready a wider group of dedicated reformers were invited to discuss it before the final version was fixed. At the same time it was decided that it would have to be passed through the Seym by stealth. The ground was prepared carefully. The allegiance of the Warsaw populace was assured by a municipal law of 18 April 1791 giving seats in the Seym to 22 representatives of major towns. Another law passed at the same time excluded landless szlachta from taking part in seymiks.

A date was chosen when many deputies and senators would still be on their way back to the capital after the Easter recess, unsuspecting of any important business, and warning was given to the citizens of Warsaw on the night before. On 3 May 1791, 182 deputies were present in the chamber, 100 of them in the secret. Outside, half of Warsaw surrounded the royal castle expectantly. The proposed constitution was read out and passed overwhelmingly, after which the King was carried shoulder-high by the populace to the cathedral, where the *Te Deum* was sung.

The document which became law on 3 May 1791 was the first written constitution in Europe. It was a satisfactory compromise between the republicanism of Ignacy Potocki, the radicalism of Kołłątaj and the monarchism of the king. The opening clauses were purposely anodyne. Catholicism was enshrined as the religion of the state, although every citizen was free to practise another without prejudice; the szlachta was declared to be the backbone of the nation; the peasantry was piously acknowledged as its lifeblood; all the privileges bestowed by Piast and Jagiellon kings remained inviolate. Hidden deeper in the thicket of print lay the substance. The throne was to be dynastically elective as it was under the Jagiellons, and since Stanisław Augustus had no children, Frederick Augustus of Saxony was named as the founder of the new dynasty. The Seym became the chief legislative and executive power in the Commonwealth, and voting was to be conducted by strict majority. Both the veto and the right of Confederation were abolished. The government of the country was vested in the king and a Royal Council under the nomenclature of the Custodians of the National Laws. This was to include the Primate of Poland, five ministers and two secretaries, all appointed by the king for a period of two years. The king could direct policy, but nothing could leave his hands without the signature of at least one of the ministers, and the whole Council was answerable directly to the Seym.

The Constitution was hardly revolutionary in itself: it was the commissions and other organs it set up which were to carry through the real reforms. Under the slogan 'The King with the People, the People with the

King', and aided by a barrage of propaganda emanating from Kołłątaj's 'Forge', they started work on a social and economic package. The most important element was an economic constitution, which was to cover property relationships, the protection of labour, investment, the establishment of a national bank and the issue of a paper currency. Kołłątaj began work on plans to turn all labour-rents into money rents for the peasants, while the king and Piattoli began discussions with the elders of the Jewish community with a view to integrating and emancipating its members.

The events in Poland were hailed all over the world. Political clubs in Paris voted to make Stanisław Augustus an honorary member. Condorcet and Thomas Paine acclaimed the Constitution as a breakthrough, while Edmund Burke called it 'this great good', and went on: 'so far as it had gone, it probably is the most pure and defecated public good which ever has been conferred on mankind.' The Prussian minister Herzberg was convinced that 'the Poles have given the *coup de grâce* to the Prussian monarchy by voting a constitution much better than the English. I think that Poland will, sooner or later, regain West Prussia, and perhaps also East Prussia. How can we defend our state, open from Memel to Teschen, against a numerous and well-governed nation?' Poland in 1792 contained nine million inhabitants. If the country were allowed time to pull itself together, it would become a Power once more. Prussia would be cut down to size, Austria would eventually have to give back its Polish provinces, which it had euphoniously renamed Galicia and Lodomeria, and Russia's rapidly increasing power would be checked.

Events in Poland assumed alarming significance in the light of the political situation in Europe. The fall of the Bastille caused fear at Petersburg, Potsdam and Vienna, and the fact that a second beacon of revolution had ignited in Warsaw did little to assuage this. They began to feel threatened by the 'revolutionary' presence in their midst, as a steady trickle of peasants from all three countries flowed into Poland in search of new freedoms.

A year before the passing of the Constitution, in March 1790, the Seym had signed a treaty with Prussia, where Frederick the Great had been succeeded by Frederick William II. The immediate object was to make common war on Austria, from which Poland intended to recapture Galicia, but it also guaranteed Prussian military support if Poland were attacked by her eastern neighbour. Prussia then demanded that Poland give up Gdańsk, which was already cut off from the rest of the country by a Prussian corridor, in return for which Polish traffic on the Vistula would be granted customs-free passage. Britain, which was behind the Polish-Prussian alliance, and whose fleet was expected in the Baltic in the autumn, urged Poland to agree, but there was opposition in the Seym. In February 1791 the Emperor Joseph II was succeeded by Leopold II, who took a conciliatory line towards Prussia, but the international situation nevertheless remained favourable to Poland. Leopold and his Chancellor Kaunitz both believed that the passing of the Constitution, far from being a threat, would probably prevent revolution in Central Europe.

Before the Constitution was a year old, however, the international situation changed once more. On 7 January 1792 Russia signed the peace of Jassy with Turkey and began to pull troops back from the southern front. On 14 February, at the first general election since its passing, the seymiks throughout Poland voted overwhelmingly to endorse the Constitution, much to the fury of Catherine who had paid out fortunes in bribes to persuade them to reject it. In March she began moving her troops towards Poland. At the beginning of the month the Emperor Leopold died and was succeeded by Francis II. In April, revolutionary France went to war against Prussia. A few days later, on 27 April 1792, Catherine sought out a number of her old placemen in Poland, most notably Seweryn Rzewuski, Feliks Potocki and Ksawery Branicki, and made them set up a Confederation in Petersburg. It was not formally declared until 14 May in the border town of Targowica, under the slogan of defence of Polish 'golden freedoms' against the 'monarchical and democratic revolution of 3 May 1791'. Four days later the confederates crossed the border at the head of, or rather dragged along in the baggage of, 97,000 Russian troops.

Against these seasoned veterans of the Turkish wars, the Commonwealth could field only 37,000 untried recruits. Frederick William of Prussia, who had written Stanisław Augustus a gushing letter in May 1791 professing his 'eagerness . . . to contribute to the support of the liberty and independence of Poland', refused the appeal for help in June 1792, 'the state of things being entirely changed since the alliance that I contracted with the Commonwealth.' The Polish forces went into action alone and acquitted themselves valiantly. One corps, under the king's nephew Józef Poniatowski, won a battle at Zieleńce, another under the American revolutionary general Tadeusz Kościuszko fought a fine rearguard action at Dubienka. But there could be no hope of victory. The Lithuanian regiments were deftly marched away from any action by their commander Prince Ludwig of Württemberg (the husband of one of the Czartoryski girls who was a natural daughter of Stanisław Augustus), who had been bribed by Catherine.

Stanisław Augustus tried to negotiate directly with Catherine. In June he wrote her a personal letter offering to replace Poland within the Russian hegemony and to cede his throne to her grandson Constantine. The letter shows that he understood Russian *raison d'état* at this moment possibly better than Catherine herself, who paid no attention and indeed demanded that he join the Confederation of Targowica instead of resisting it. The king and his closest advisers were desperate to find a way out which would guarantee the integrity of the Commonwealth and the survival of the Constitution. At a meeting of the Royal Council on 23 July, with no options remaining, Kołłątaj proposed that the king should accede to the Confederation. Ignacy Potocki and Stanisław Sołtan wanted to fight to the bitter end, by calling the whole nation to arms in the French manner, but they were overruled. The king duly announced that he was joining the Confederation. Kołłątaj, Potocki and Małachowski quietly left the country, and Generals Poniatowski and Kościuszko resigned their commissions.

Stanisław Augustus's act of humility was of little avail. In November, after the defeat of his armies by the French at Valmy, the King of Prussia demanded areas of Poland as compensation for his efforts to contain revolutionary France. A second partition was agreed between Russia and Prussia, and signed in Petersburg on 23 January 1793. Catherine helped herself to 250,000 square kilometres, and Frederick William to 58,000. The Commonwealth now consisted of no more than 212,000 square kilometres, the size of Britain, with a population of four million. What was left was not so much a skeleton as a wasted limb. The whole of Wielkopolska and most of Małopolska, the ethnic and historic heartlands of Poland, had gone, leaving a strange, elongated, utterly illogical and uneconomic rump. Even this rump, however, was not to be more than a buffer state with a puppet king and a Russian garrison.

In emulation of the first partition, Catherine insisted that the arrangement be ratified by the Seym, to be held at Grodno in Lithuania rather than in the populous and potentially explosive Warsaw. Russian soldiers and Polish traitors were regularly beaten up in the streets of the capital, whose walls were plastered with posters and graffiti of extraordinary defiance and ribaldry, and the mob seethed with a fury that only needed a catalyst. At first Stanisław Augustus refused to leave his capital, thereby making it impossible to hold the Seym in Grodno. He was eventually browbeaten and blackmailed into going, and as he left his capital all hope and will to fight deserted him.

The Russians selected candidates for the Seym from the dregs of Polish society and shamelessly rigged and bullied the seymiks to ensure their election. Even so, there were apparently not enough people in the Commonwealth quite as abject as required. A typical deputy was Dionizy Mikorski, a petty criminal whose membership of the szlachta was at best dubious and who was delighted to take the money offered by the Russians. But even he refused to vote approval of the partition, in spite of the presence of Russian troops in the chamber who would drag out recalcitrant deputies and beat them up in the courtyard, and he finished in jail. In its own way the Grodno Seym was not devoid of a heroic quality, with the very worst elements in the nation being pushed into a corner in which even they found a grain of self-respect. At one stage, a battery of guns was trained on

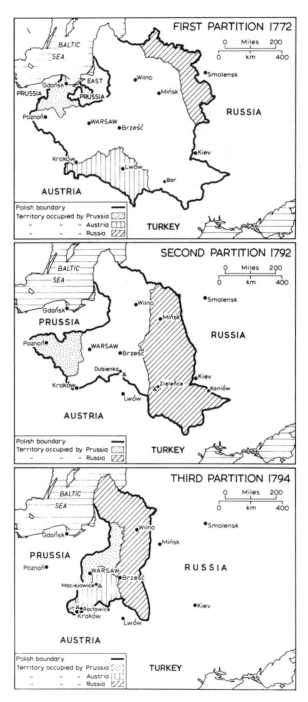

The three partitions of Poland

the building, while confiscation of property, beatings and imprisonment were meted out to anyone who raised his voice against ratifying the partitions. After three months of spectacular stubbornness on one side and ruthless barbarity on the other, the Seym decided it had made its point and voted the inevitable ratification.

The king returned to Warsaw where he technically ruled. In fact, the Russian embassy was the source of all policy and a large Russian garrison policed the country. There was no possibility for action by patriots and most of them went into voluntary exile, some to Vienna, Italy and Saxony, others to Paris. Kościuszko was hatching·a plan based on French victory against Prussia and Austria. Kołłątaj and Ignacy Potocki were thinking in terms of a national rising by the masses.

Meanwhile, Catherine herself was unconsciously creating the perfect conditions for a revolution. She started by reducing the Polish army to 12,000 and disbanding the rest. Some 30,000 able-bodied fighting men were made redundant and desperate, and these patriotic vagrants were drawn to Warsaw, automatically creating the 'revolutionary rabble' which every upheaval depends on. The way in which Poland had been carved up virtually precluded what was left of it from supporting itself. Cities had been removed, leaving their agricultural hinterland, and agricultural areas had been lopped off, leaving starving cities. Economic activity came to a virtual standstill and in 1793 the six largest Warsaw banks declared insolvency. The country had to support a 40,000 strong Russian garrison and pay whatever customs dues the whims of Frederick William might dictate. Thousands of unemployed cluttered Warsaw and watched the men of Targowica, bloated on Russian bribes, living it up grandly. The army was the focal point of discontent. Made up of a mixture of landless szlachta and emancipated peasants or townspeople, it was patriotic, revolutionary and hungry for action. When on 21 February 1794 the Russians ordered a further reduction of the army and the arrest of people suspected of subversive activity, revolution became inevitable.

On 12 March General Madaliński ordered his brigade into the field and marched on Kraków, while émigrés from all over Europe flocked back to Poland. On 23 March Kościuszko arrived in Kraków. On the following day he took command and proclaimed the Act of Insurrection in the great square. He assumed dictatorial powers, delegating the conduct of affairs to a Supreme National Council with emergency powers. He issued a provisional constitution which granted freedom to all peasants and ownership of land to all who fought in the mass levy. When the Insurrection was over all power was to be handed back to the Seym.

From Kraków Kościuszko marched north. At Racławice on 4 April he defeated a Russian army with a force of 4,000 regulars and 2,000 peasants armed with scythes. On 17 April the Warsaw cobbler Jan Kiliński raised

111 This painting by Kazimierz Wojniakowski depicts the scene in the Senate Chamber of Warsaw Castle on 3 May 1791, when the Seym voted the new Constitution. This turned Poland into a progressive constitutional monarchy and provoked the hostile reaction of Russia, Prussia and Austria, which felt obliged to stamp out this hotbed of Liberalism in their midst and partition the country between them.

112 A satirical French engraving, entitled 'The Royal Cake', showing the Empress Catherine of Russia, Frederick the Great of Prussia, and Joseph II of Austria haggling over the map of Poland, while King Stanisław Augustus clutches in desperation at his crown.

113 Kościuszko's peasant-volunteers, armed with scythes, capture the Russian guns at the Battle of Racławice in 1794; drawing by Aleksander Orłowski. The red four-cornered caps of these peasants from the Kraków region were adopted by the National Cavalry, and later worn by the Polish regiments in Napoleon's army, after which they became traditional wear for lancer units in all European armies.

114 An officer of the National Cavalry in 1794, engraving by Bellenger.

115 Members of the Jewish regiment of the Warsaw National Guard, in 1794 commanded by Berek Joselewicz, the first Jewish military formation since Biblical times.

the standard of Insurrection in the capital. After twenty-four hours of fighting the Russian troops abandoned the city, leaving 4,000 dead on the streets. On the night of 22 April the city of Wilno rose under the leadership of Colonel Jakub Jasiński, a fervent Jacobin. In Wilno and in Warsaw some of the traitors of Targowica were lynched but this ceased with the arrival of Kościuszko in the capital. While Jasiński wrote to Kościuszko that he would prefer 'to hang a hundred people, and save six million', the dictator would have none of it. Like all Polish revolutions, this one was virtually bloodless. When the Russian troops retreated from the capital, the punch-drunk mob which dragged out and hanged the handful of traitors never thought of raising a hand against the king, who sat alone and desolate in the unguarded castle.

Kościuszko, now joined in Warsaw by figures such as Kołłątaj and Ignacy Potocki, was beset by enormous problems. The Insurrection could hardly arouse optimism, and there was a measure of uncertainty as to its real political nature, as a selection of extremist Jacobins waited in the wings to seize control. Some magnates joined the Insurrection and the King donated all his table-silver, but the majority of the szlachta were cautious. As a result, it failed to benefit from the mass participation which alone could have made it succeed, and the decrees concerning the levy of peasants to its ranks were frequently frustrated by landowners. On the other hand, the Jewish community formed up and equipped a special regiment of its own under the command of Colonel Berek Joselewicz, the first Jewish military formation since Biblical times.

In spite of widespread chaos and food shortages, the Insurrectionary government achieved remarkable results. Kołłątaj, who took over the Treasury, introduced graded taxation, confiscated Church property, and issued silver currency and banknotes. He also commandeered all factories and supervised production. Cannon were produced in sufficient quantity, but there was no rifle-factory able to deal with the demand. As a result, the Poles evolved an idiosyncratic tactic of artillery bombardment combined with cavalry charge and mass attack by peasant scythemen.

Kościuszko, who had marched out to meet the advancing Prussian army under Frederick William himself, was outnumbered and defeated at Szczekociny on 6 May. On 15 June the Prussians entered Kraków. In July a combined Russo-Prussian army of 40,000 besieged Warsaw, but Kościuszko used a combination of earthworks and artillery with such skill that after two months of siege the allies withdrew. Wilno fell to the Russians in mid-August, but a week later the Insurrection broke out in Wielkopolska and a corps under General Dąbrowski set off from Warsaw in support. He defeated one Prussian army near Bydgoszcz and then marched into Prussia.

While Polish armies could achieve minor successes, the situation was growing hopeless as Austrian forces joined those of Prussia and Russia. Having extracted a pledge of neutrality from Turkey, Catherine ordered Suvorov's army to move against Poland from the south-east. Kościuszko marched out to head him off, but was isolated from his supporting column and beaten at Maciejowice on 10 October. His defeat would have been no great blow in itself, but he was badly wounded and captured, along with some of the best Polish generals.

The loss of Kościuszko induced political instability. The need for compromise badly affected the choice of his successor as commander-in-chief, which eventually fell on a Tomasz Wawrzecki, an undistinguished soldier. The Russians, who had been intending to retire to winter quarters, now decided to push home their advantage and on 4 November Suvorov attacked Warsaw. He had little difficulty in taking the east-bank suburb of Praga. Only 400 of the 1,400 defenders survived, while the mainly Jewish population was butchered as a warning to Warsaw itself. The warning carried weight, and the army withdrew, allowing Warsaw to capitulate. On 16 November, Wawrzecki was surrounded and captured, and the Insurrection effectively came to an end.

Russian troops once again entered Warsaw, soon to be relieved by Prussians, as the three Powers had decided to divide what was left of Poland between them and the capital fell to the Prussian share. A new treaty of partition was signed in 1795, wiping what was left of Poland off the map. The king was forced to abdicate, bundled into a carriage and sent off to Petersburg, and the foreign diplomats accredited to the Polish court were told to leave. The Papal Nuncio, the British minister and the chargés d'affaires of Holland, Sweden and Saxony all refused as a sign of protest against the unceremonious liquidation of one of the states of Christian Europe. Their embassies were also crammed with fugitives seeking asylum. It took the three Powers more than two years to sort out the tangles involved, and it was not until January 1797 that they were able to agree to a treaty finally liquidating the debts of the king and the Commonwealth, after which they signed a protocol binding themselves to excise the name of Poland from all future documents, to remove any reference to it from diplomatic business and to strive by every means for its oblivion. These sanguine hopes that the name of Poland would never be uttered again were quickly ridiculed by the way in which it became an element of every major diplomatic exchange and confrontation in the future. Nor were the Powers always consistent on the subject themselves. Mainly out of spite to the memory of his mother, Tsar Paul celebrated Catherine's death in 1797 by freeing Kościuszko, and all the Polish prisoners. Over the next months the Tsar spent many hours with the ailing Stanisław Augustus discussing a plan to resurrect the Polish Commonwealth, and when the king died on 12 February 1798 Paul gave him a state funeral and personally led the mourning.

It was not, however, the cranky behaviour of Paul that ensured the survival of the Polish cause. Stanisław Staszic had written that 'even a great nation may fall, but only a contemptible one can be destroyed', and the Poles did not see themselves as contemptible. Against all the arguments being put forward by Prussian propaganda that they were incapable of governing themselves, the Poles needed only to brandish one document, the last great act of the dying Commonwealth, its political testament – the Constitution of 3 May. It was a legacy which gave the orphans of the Commonwealth an inalienable right to the esteem of other nations. Many decades later, when European thought had gone far beyond the values enshrined in it, it was still a unique monument to the Polish state, as Karl Marx pointed out:

> With all its faults, this constitution seems to be the only act of freedom which Eastern Europe has undertaken in the midst of Prussian, Russian and Austrian barbarism. It was, moreover, initiated exclusively by the privileged classes, the nobility. The history of the world knows no other example of similar noble conduct by the nobility.

16

Heroic Years

The treaty signed by the three Powers in 1797 according to which Poland would never exist again in any form was a piece of wishful thinking. Russia, Austria and Prussia perpetrated their act of cynical surgery just at the moment when European thought gave birth to the Romantic movement. They began carving up and absorbing a major nation just as the age of nationalism was dawning. They carried out one of the most disreputable examples of ancien-régime intrigue and skulduggery as the powerful new force of socialism came into being.

In 1797 the situation looked bleak. For all their moral conviction, the Poles were helpless. For all the sympathy their cause aroused, they had no allies. Nevertheless, they could not reconcile themselves to the elimination of their state, and before the ink had dried on the treaty of partition they were back in the field against the three Powers. From Paris Józef Wybicki was planning a rising in Poland in connection with a French attack on Austria. A secret confederation was formed in Kraków, and in 1796 Colonel Denisko assembled a force of 1,000 men in Moldavia under the covert protection of the Porte which he led into action against the Austrians. In 1797 a regular Polish army was formed under French aegis.

After the collapse of the Insurrection, thousands of Poles had offered their services to revolutionary France. They were used throughout the French army, but clamoured to be allowed to serve in specific Polish units. Weight was added to this argument when it emerged that many of the prisoners taken in the Italian campaign were in fact Poles drafted by the Austrians in Galicia. In 1797 a Polish Legion was formed in Milan under the Command of Jan Henryk Dąbrowski. They wore Polish uniforms, Italian epaulettes and French cockades, and marched to a song written by Józef Wybicki which in the twentieth century became the Polish National Anthem. In 1798 a second Polish Legion was formed in Italy under General Zajączek and in 1800 a third on the Danube under General Kniaziewicz, but they suffered heavy losses, particularly at the battles of Marengo and Hohenlinden.

The Poles who fought in the legions believed that after liberating Italy from Austrian and Bourbon rule they would march through Hungary into Galicia, from where they would launch an insurrection in Poland. But after the Treaties of Campo Formio (1797) and Lunéville (1801), in which France made peace with Austria and other members of the coalition, the legions became an inconvenient embarrassment. Dąbrowski's temporarily became the army of the new state of Lombardy, some of the Polish units were disbanded, others were scattered throughout the French army, and one contingent 6,000 strong was sent to subjugate Toussaint Louverture in Santo Domingo. Those that did not perish from yellow fever eventually joined the black cause.

Many felt let down by Bonaparte and betrayed by France, but this was not to be the end of the Polish Napoleonic dream. The partitions had deprived the intelligentsia and the landless szlachta of their one remaining possession – their status and privileges – and thereby turned them into revolutionaries vowed to the destruction of what they saw as an unjust European order. The young war-lord Bonaparte, wiping out the frontiers of Europe with the perukes of mummified kings, could not fail to capture the imagination of these men, tens of thousands of whom would answer his call again and follow him despite his repeated callous betrayal of their cause.

Although the image of the legions fighting bravely in faraway lands haunted the young, for those who were left behind at home to carry on the business of living, Russia was ultimately the key to the problem of Poland's future. At one point this key was within the reach of one of the greatest Poles of his generation, Prince Adam Czartoryski, son of Adam Kazimierz. After the 1794 Insurrection, in which he took part, the young prince was sent by his family to St Petersburg as a hostage for their good behaviour. There he developed an intimate friendship with his contemporary the Grand Duke Alexander. The future Tsar spent hours in the company of a small group of friends – Paul Stroganov, Nikolay Novosiltsev, and Adam Czartoryski – dreaming of the day when he would be able to put into practice the ideas with which his tutor La Harpe had imbued him. When the day came, in 1801, Alexander nominated a 'Committee for Public Salvation', consisting of Stroganov, Novosiltsev, Czartoryski and Kochubey, which was to transform Russia into a modern constitutional monarchy. Czartoryski was appointed Minister for Foreign Affairs, and placed in charge of education in the former Polish territories, the eight 'Western Gubernias' of the Empire.

Czartoryski fuelled Alexander's dislike of Prussia in the belief that sooner or later Russia would reconquer the parts of Poland taken by Prussia, add them to her own share, and re-establish a Polish state. It was, however, Napoleon who beat Prussia, in 1806. After the battles of Jena and

Auerstadt his armies entered Poznan, led by a Polish corps under Dąbrowski. Napoleon allowed Dąbrowski to issue a call for insurrection, adding his taunt: 'I want to see whether the Poles deserve to be a nation.' While many were cautious, large numbers of enthusiastic volunteers came forward. On 28 November Murat marched into Warsaw and a few weeks later Napoleon himself entered the capital, greeted with triumphal arches and delirious crowds. The Poles did not disappoint Napoleon, who wrote to Cambacérès on 1 December 1806: 'It is hard to conceive the strength of the national movement in this country. The most ardent are the rich. Priests, nobles, peasants; all are of one mind.' People gave their plate and jewellery to help raise a Polish army.

For Napoleon, the Polish question was but an element in a diplomatic policy whose aim was to force Russia to join France in alliance against Britain, Austria and Prussia. Although in January 1807 he sanctioned the formation of a provisional national administration in Warsaw and the recruitment of an army, he was unwilling to commit himself further pending his forthcoming meeting with Alexander at Tilsit. There the two emperors agreed to the formation of a Polish state, but both were wary as to its extent: every step in its reconstruction committed them more deeply in relation to each other and complicated the future relations of each with Austria and Prussia. They therefore settled on a compromise which left doors open.

The Prussian share of the second partition of the Commonwealth was recognised as the Duchy of Warsaw, with Frederick Augustus of Saxony (who had been proposed as king by the Constitution of 3 May 1791) as Duke. The Duchy was not large, but it was a start. Those who had been wary of Napoleon's intentions agreed to serve in its government, including Małachowski and Stanisław Potocki. The last king's nephew, Józef Poniatowski, became commander-in-chief and Minister for War. Before leaving Warsaw Napoleon dictated a constitution for the Duchy and granted it the *Code Napoléon*.

Napoleon blatantly exploited the Duchy. Property and land confiscated by Prussia in 1792 was now sold back to the Duchy by France at exorbitant rates. The economy could hardly flourish while Napoleon's European blockade bankrupted the grain trade, and while the Duchy was expected to pay for a standing army rising to 60,000 men. In addition, Napoleon required for his Spanish campaign six regiments of foot and two of horse, some 10,000 men in all, as well as a regiment for the Imperial Guard, the famous Chevaux-Légers. When the Duchy went bankrupt, France lent money and collected the interest in cannonfodder.

The Duchy of Warsaw never rose above the status of a pawn in Napoleon's schemes. It was invaded by Austria in 1809. Poniatowski counterattacked and eventually captured Kraków and Galicia. When

116 Napoleon granting a constitution to the Duc
Warsaw in 1807; painting by Marcello Bacciarelli.
Standing from left to right are: Walenty Sobolewsk
former deputy to the Great Seym; Ksawery Działy:
Piotr Bieliński, Secretary of the Permanent Counci
deputy to the Great Seym; Ludwik Gutakowski,
President of the Council of State of the Duchy of
Warsaw; Jan Paweł Łuszczewski, Minister of the
Interior of the Duchy; Stanisław Małachowski, Ma
of the Great Seym, 1788–92 and one of the architec
the Constitution of 3 May 1791; Talleyrand; Mare
Stanisław Kostka Potocki; and Józef Wybicki.

117 An officer of the Chevaux-Légers Polonais o
Imperial Guard, a regiment which came to embod
Polish military prowess all over Europe; watercolo
Piotr Michałowski.

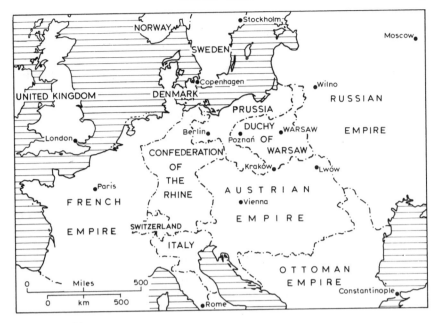

Napoleonic Europe

peace was made between France and Austria at the treaty of Schönbrunn the Poles had to give most of it back to Austria. In the following year, when Napoleon wanted to marry Alexander's sister, he made it clear that he was prepared to cede the whole Duchy of Warsaw to Russia. His attitude was best illustrated in 1812, during what he called his 'second Polish war'.

Napoleon's intention was not to conquer Russia but to cow Alexander into submission. He was therefore prepared to use the re-establishment of a strong Poland as a threat, but meant to keep his options open were Alexander to give in. So while he whipped up Polish hopes, he bypassed a Warsaw full of delegations from the provinces of the old Commonwealth. In Wilno he called the Lithuanians to arms, but refused to be drawn on the question of independence for Lithuania.

As a result, wise men sat on the fence. Nevertheless, thousands did join him, and Poles accounted for 98,000 men of the Grande Armée which marched into Russia, by far the largest non-French contingent. They also played a disproportionate role in the operations. Polish lancers were the first to swim the Niemen and carry the tricolor onto Russian territory: Umiński's dragoons were the first into Moscow; Poniatowski's Fifth Corps played a crucial role at Borodino: the Chevaux-Légers saved Napoleon's life from a pack of marauding Cossacks; Poniatowski covered the whole retreat and defended the Berezina crossings. Polish units were the first in and the last out of Russia; 72,000 never returned, and many more died of wounds or typhus in the following months. Yet they did not abandon a single field-gun or standard to the enemy in the whole retreat.

As the remnants of the Grande Armée streamed westwards and Napoleon rushed to Paris, the Duchy of Warsaw was left defenceless. Dąbrowski's division followed the French army into Germany, but Poniatowski fell back on Kraków with 16,000 men. Alexander was not vindictive and understood the predicament of the Poles who had fought against him. Throughout the spring and summer of 1813 those who had remained on the Russian side tried to induce Poniatowski and his army to cast off their loyalty to Napoleon and place themselves at Alexander's disposal. Poniatowski had the strictest sense of personal honour. He rejected the Russian proposals and led his army off to rejoin Napoleon in Germany. On 19 October, the last day of the Battle of the Nations at Leipzig, the heavily wounded prince died while trying to swim the river Elster when the French, whose retreat he was covering, blew up the bridges. The Poles continued to follow Napoleon. When he went into exile on the island of Elba, half of the symbolic guard he was allowed were Polish Chevaux-Légers.

Napoleon's treatment of Polish aspirations had been cynical from the start, and the whole episode had been of no benefit whatsoever to the Polish cause. Yet the Napoleonic wars are very important to the Poles. Since the relief of Vienna in 1683, military glory was something whole generations could only read about. Between 1797 and 1815 they were able to demonstrate their bravery, loyalty and indomitable spirit to other nations on battlefields all over Europe. Feats of valour such as the charge of the Polish Chevaux-Légers through the defile of Somo Sierra on 30 November 1808 (when a single squadron of 125 men cleared 9,000 entrenched infantry and four batteries from the defile, capturing 10 standards and 16 guns in the space of seven minutes at the cost of 83 dead) have gone down in legend. Countless other exploits earned them the respect of enemies, from the Peninsula, where the Spaniards of General Palafox spoke with awe of the *'infernales picadores'* (the Lancers of the Vistula) to the depths of Russia, where General Colbert in command of the Guard Cavalry ordered all French units to borrow the capes and caps of Polish lancers before going on picket duty, to keep Cossacks at a respectful distance.

These heroics gave generations which would not be able to fight for their own country a measure of sustenance, and Napoleon's figure recurs in art and literature well into the twentieth century as a focus for dreams of glory. The fall of Napoleon, which showed that even the greatest can be brought down by an alliance of lesser figures, was a source of consolation to the Poles, who had similarly been brought down by circumstance and cunning

The Congress Kingdom, 1815—31

collusion. The Romantic vision of Leviathan in chains could cover up a multitude of unpleasant realities.

In his act of abdication Napoleon committed his Polish troops to the clemency of the victorious Tsar, and Alexander was neither vengeful nor blind to the opportunities of the Polish question. Czartoryski believed that Alexander's paramount position in 1814 would enable him to reunite most of the Commonwealth as a kingdom under his own sceptre. Such a solution seemed probable when the ministers met at the Congress of Vienna in 1814. The obvious snag was that Prussia and Austria had no intention of giving up large sections of what they had begun to regard as their own territory, in order to recreate a Poland linked with Russia. Castlereagh's response was to suggest an independent Poland. On 12 January 1815 he made the British position clear in a circular which concluded: 'Experience has proved, that it is not by counteracting all their habits and usages as a people, that either the happiness of the Poles, or the peace of that important portion of Europe, can be preserved.'

Russia could not accept an independent Poland which would push her off the European stage she had just ascended. As Alexander pointed out to Castlereagh: 'I conquered the Duchy and I have 480,000 men to keep it with.' Talks nearly broke down, but Napoleon's escape from Elba brought the Allies to their senses and a realisation of their mutual interests. They settled on a compromise which satisfied no one and did little credit to the men who believed they were ordering Europe. A Kingdom of Poland consisting of 127,000 square kilometres with a population of 3.3 million was carved out of all three partitions. In addition, Kraków and a tiny area around the city was turned into a Republic. The Tsar of Russia was the King of Poland, and all three partitioning powers were the protectors of the Republic of Kraków. The rest of the Polish lands were signed away to their respective conquerors with many a pious clause about good treatment of the natives and respect for their institutions.

It may have been small and deprived of sovereignty, but there was at least a Polish state. The constitution, drawn up by Czartoryski, was the most liberal in Central Europe. Foreign policy and the police were both run from St Petersburg; Alexander's brother Constantine was installed in Warsaw as commander-in-chief of the Polish army; the former legionary general Zajączek was Alexander's viceroy; and Nikolay Novosiltsev was Alexander's commissioner in the government of the Kingdom. There were no other limits to the sovereignty of the Seym and Senate.

There was something unnatural about the close association between huge autocratic Russia and the tiny liberal Congress Kingdom. It was perhaps inevitable that either Poland would act as a sort of Piedmont in the liberalisation of Russia or that Russia would gradually swallow up and digest its small satellite. At first, the former seemed the more likely. The Tsar was still pursuing liberal ideals, and Russian society had come under strong Western liberal influences as a result of the Napoleonic wars. In his speech at the opening of the Polish Seym in April 1818, Alexander held out a succulent carrot to the Poles. 'Live up to your duties,' he exhorted them: 'The results of your labours will show me whether I shall be able to abide by my intention of expanding the concessions I have already made to you.'

The honeymoon did not last long. Alexander's enthusiasm for Western liberalism waned, while Novosiltsev, who had no time for Polish aspirations and did not like Czartoryski, did all he could to undermine Polish autonomy. He ably exploited the incipient conflicts between Alexander and Constantine, and between both of them and various Polish statesmen, promoting the view, which gradually gained acceptance in Russia, that the Poles were not grateful for the favours they had been given. When the Seym began to function in a normal manner with deputies expressing forthright views, Alexander grew angry and, in 1820, dissolved it. The next ten years saw a gradual erosion of all the theoretical liberties of the Kingdom, but conditions were not as repressive as they might have been.

The violence done to the territory of the Commonwealth between 1792 and 1815, and the succession of governments to which its various parts had been subjected in the same period, had surprisingly little impact on the life of the nation. The frontiers themselves figured only as administrative impediments in the minds of most Poles, who referred to them as 'the Austrian cordon' or 'the Prussian cordon'. A Pole travelling from Warsaw to Poznań or Wilno in the 1820s crossed into a different country, but as far as he or his hosts were concerned, he was merely travelling around his own. Those who had found themselves fighting on opposing sides continued to communicate and sat together in the Seym and Senate. Even the country's new masters seemed prepared to let bygones be bygones. It was symptomatic that the man who was Alexander's viceroy in Poland had started out as a Jacobin, had fought in Kościuszko's army in 1794, had commanded a Polish Legion in Italy, and had been wounded fighting for Napoleon at Borodino. The highest authority in the Prussian-occupied Grand Duchy of Posen was the governor, Antoni Radziwiłł, who was married to a Hohenzollern princess. Prince Adam Czartoryski, who had fought with Kościuszko before siding with Alexander, was one of the pillars of the Congress Kingdom, although his father had presided over the provisional government set up by Napoleon. Stanisław Potocki, a prominent member of the reformist party of the 1780s and 1790s, had sided with Napoleon but was made Minister for Religious Denominations and Public Education in 1816. Stanisław Staszic had founded his Society of Friends of Learning in 1808 with the approval of Napoleon and in 1816 became director of the government's Department of Industry. Julian Ursyn Niemcewicz, who had been locked up in the Petropavlovsky Fortress with Kościuszko, and subsequently settled in the United States, was back as a prominent figure, in spite of his uncompromising views. Even the chief censor appointed in 1819, Józef Kalasanty Szaniawski, was a Jacobin of 1794. A typically Polish compromise seemed to be in the making. The Commonwealth continued to exist in defiance of boundaries. Its traditions continued to flourish in spite of the imposition of successive political regimes.

The urge to protect and transmit all that was finest in the country's past continued to absorb the zeal of people at every level and helped to create a congenial cultural climate. The University of Wilno flourished under the direction of Adam Czartoryski and took over as the centre of academic life. New institutions such as the Krezemieniec High School, founded by Tadeusz Czacki, provided a very high standard of education. The Załuski library had been taken by the Russians, but in 1811 Stanisław Zamoyski

opened his great library in Warsaw to the public. The Czartoryski Historical Museum at Puławy had grown into a remarkable eclectic collection,
and their library, also opened to the public, was a treasure-house of early
manuscripts. In 1817, the year the Austrians founded a German University
at Lemberg (Lwów), Józef Ossoliński opened a Polish archive and library in
the city, the Ossolineum. In 1829 Edward Raczyński did the same in Poznań,
which was also endowed with a museum by the Mielżyński family. Adam
Tytus Działyński founded the Poznań Society of Friends of Learning, which
began publishing manuscript sources in the 1840s, and his library and
collections also became a public institution. Everything from old coins
to folk-songs was collected and documented, and publications, such as
Samuel Bogumił Linde's *Great Polish Dictionary* (1814), underpinned academic study.

The seeds sown by Stanisław Augustus flourished everywhere. The
literary revival of the late eighteenth century continued to bear fruit with a
new generation of poets. The musical scene he had encouraged produced
composers such as Karol Kurpiński, Marya Szymanowska and Józef
Elsner, and gave birth to the genius of Fryderyk Chopin. The architects
fostered by Stanisław Augustus came to maturity at the beginning of the
century and over the next three decades dotted the countryside with an
elegant style of neo-classical manor-house which became typical.
Kubicki's Belvedere Palace, Marconi's Pac Palace and Aigner's grandiose
Radziwiłł Palace and St Alexander's Church enhanced the Warsaw of
the Congress Kingdom. The last of the Italian architects to come to
Poland, Antonio Corazzi, contributed four monumental landmarks to the
capital: the Bank of Poland, the Staszic Palace, the Treasury, and the
Grand Theatre, which breathed a Romantic element and a sense of scale
into Polish neo-classical architecture. The Warsaw of the 1820s was an
imposing and elegant city, projecting all the self-assurance of a society
which was, to all intents and purposes, in control of its own destiny.

This condition could not last, for two reasons. One was that the Russian
attitude to what was happening in Poland grew increasingly sour. The
other was that the post-Napoleonic generation of Poles was growing up in
an atmosphere of ideological anticlimax and was not temperamentally
prepared to let things trundle along the course of compromise. There was
much heated discussion among students, particularly at the University of
Wilno, where societies of 'Philomaths' and 'Philareths' burgeoned. It was
all fairly harmless, but the Russian secret police has never been known to
consider any discussion harmless and when, in 1821, Major Walerian
Łukasiński founded a Patriotic Society, it began to investigate further.

In 1823 the Russian police went into action. The main blow was directed
at Wilno University, where the Professor of History Joachim Lelewel was
sacked and a number of students arrested. Other arrests followed, includ-

ing that of a young poet, Adam Mickiewicz, a former student, now a teacher in Kowno, and the author of an *Ode to Youth* whose vague stirrings of liberation the censor could not understand but did not like. The University was further chastened by the removal of Adam Czartoryski, the curator, which followed the dismissal of Stanisław Potocki from the post of Minister of Education. These measures were neither drastic nor cruel but they had the effect of irritating the young and those hitherto content with the status quo. Discussion and conspiracy spread to the army and after the failure of the Decembrist coup of 1825 in Russia, which sought to place Constantine on the Imperial throne, investigations led the Russian police back to Warsaw. As the new Tsar Nicholas clamped down on freethinking in Russia, his lieutenants in Poland began ferreting about in ernest.

The police arrested a number of ringleaders of conspiratorial groups and Novosiltsev demanded, at Nicholas's behest, that they be dealt with in accordance with Russian criminal procedure. The Polish government demurred on constitutional grounds and the men were tried by a tribunal delegated by the Seym. Since their actions could not be construed as criminal under Polish law they were dealt with leniently. In his rage Nicholas actually arrested the members of the tribunal before counter-manding their verdict and imposing his own sentences on the prisoners.

A pattern was emerging which has become classic: having imposed a government and a constitution on a satellite Poland, Russia could not countenance its legal functioning. The government in Warsaw found itself in an untenable position, losing authority at home and suffering insults from Russia. This played into the hands of a small revolutionary element which was spoiling for a fight; while the majority of Polish society, which felt that it was better to weather the storm and hang on to what freedom there was, found it increasingly difficult to keep the atmosphere cool as the Warsaw student and the Russian policeman taunted each other.

The police were on the tracks of a group of cadets who had been hatching nebulous plots under the leadership of Ensign Piotr Wysocki, and tension mounted throughout the early months of 1830. News of the July Revolution in France and the subsequent upheaval in Belgium in September brought matters to a head. Nicholas intended to send an expeditionary force made up principally of Polish troops to crush the revolution in Belgium, and mobilisation was decreed on 19 November 1830. The conspirators had no plan and no programme, but they felt that time was running out. On the night of 29 November 1830 one group broke into the Belvedere Palace to assassinate Grand Duke Constantine while another attacked the Russian cavalry barracks in the Łazienki Park. Everything went wrong. The Russians were alerted in time and the Grand Duke escaped the knives of the assassins. An attack on the Arsenal by another group of conspirators was more successful. Groups of conspirators

118 The Belvedere Palace, rebuilt in 1818 by Jakub Kubicki for Grand Duke Constantine. It was here that the conspirators attempted to assassinate the Grand Duke on the night of 29 November 1830, sparking off the Insurrection against Russia.

120 The Seym votes the dethronement of Tsar Nicholas as King of Poland on 25 January 1831.

119 Prince Adam Jerzy Czartoryski; by Aleksander Oleszkiewicz. Himself the natural candidate to the throne, the prince became President of the National Government. He did not believe an all-out war with Russia could be won, and placed his hopes in the diplomatic support of England and France.

ЗО ИМЯ БОГА
ЗА НАШУ И ВАШУ
ВОЛЬНОСТЬ

121 Captured Russian standards carried in triumph as the Polish army marches back into Warsaw across the Vistula after the victories of Wawer, Iganie and Dębe Wielkie, April 1831; painting by Marcin Zalewski.

122 This Polish flag from 1831, bears the Russian inscription: 'In the Name of God. For Our Freedom and Yours.' It was the internationalist flavour of these sentiments that led Karl Marx to place the Polish cause in the vanguard of the struggle for revolution, but they produced little effect, and the Insurrection was defeated by Russian troops. Conservative Europe, sympathetic in principle but anxious lest the Polish Insurrection upset the status quo, breathed a sigh of relief, a feeling encapsulated in the words of General Sebastiani, the Minister of the Interior, spoken to the French Chamber of Deputies, that 'Order has been re-established in Warsaw,' the title of this contemporary French satirical lithograph, (**123**) showing a Russian Cossack standing over a heap of corpses and ruins.

and armed rabble roamed the streets lynching Russians and Polish collaborators, and, by mistake, two of the best Polish generals. Having done their bungling best, the conspirators had got nowhere. The Grand Duke was alive and well, the Russian units were intact and the Polish troops waited in barracks for a sign from a credible leadership.

Few people of any standing in Poland believed in a revolution of this sort and fewer still believed in the possibility of success in an all-out confrontation with Russia. Prince Franciszek Ksawery Drucki-Lubecki, the Minister of Finance, took the initiative of co-opting Czartoryski and other figures of standing to join him in a National Council. In order to keep the army together and restore order General Chłopicki was proclaimed 'Dictator' on 5 December. He too felt that there was no point in confrontation, and tried to deal with the whole matter as an internal Polish problem. He granted Constantine safe-conduct out of Warsaw, along with his court, his stranded units, even his police spies and his political prisoners, and he despatched Lubecki to St Petersburg to negotiate. But the Tsar refused to receive him. Eventually on 7 January 1831 the Tsar delivered a message to Lubecki demanding the unconditional surrender of the Poles as a precondition to any negotiations. This inflamed patriotic fervour throughout the country. Talk of accommodation was branded as defeatist, and, seeing no other way out, Chłopicki resigned. The Seym acknowledged a state of Insurrection and, under pressure from below, on 25 January 1831 burnt all bridges by voting the dethronement of Nicholas as King of Poland. A new government was formed under Czartoryski with Michał Radziwiłł as commander-in-chief. The Kingdom of Poland had seceded from Russia.

In February a force of 115,000 Russian troops under General Diebitsch marched on Warsaw. The Polish army, consisting of some 30,000 men, blocked his advance successfully at Grochów on 25 February. At the end of March General Jan Skrzynecki sallied forth and routed the Russian corps separately in the three battles of Wawer, Dębe Wielkie and Iganie, obliging Diebitsch to withdraw to the Lublin area. The position of the Russian forces was parlous, with Diebitsch isolated and the Guard Corps on its way to reinforce him easy for the Poles to intercept. General Dwernicki had been sent with a small force to Volhynia to co-ordinate the local action, while Generals Chłapowski and Giełgud marched into Lithuania to raise the standard there. The Poles were well set to win the campaign. They called up reserves of 80,000, and with the Lithuanian and other contingents, up to 200,000 passed through the ranks. Including all their available reserves, the Russians only numbered some 250,000. The Polish soldier was more motivated and the officer corps more experienced than the Russian. The Insurrection also attracted valuable volunteers from abroad. Hundreds of Napoleonic officers took part, including General Ramorino, the son of Marshal Lannes (Marshal Grouchy wanted to come, but insisted on too high a rank). The next largest contingent were Germans, who also supplied over a hundred military surgeons, and there were volunteers from Hungary, Italy and Britain.

The Polish high command was not up to the situation. The new commander-in-chief, Skrzynecki, did not believe in the possibility of ultimate victory and felt that the less blood was spilled before negotiations were resumed the better. He therefore dragged his heels and failed to intercept the Guard Corps. When this joined up with Diebitsch's army, he could not avoid its attack. He was caught up with and defeated on 22 May at Ostrołęka. Diebitsch died of cholera and was replaced by General Pashkievich, who tidied up his forces and prepared for a new advance. The Polish position was growing weaker, while Skrzynecki's apathy was beginning to tell on morale.

This reflected the political situation in Warsaw. Czartoryski exhibited a Hamlet-like inability to commit himself. Convinced that if the Poles defeated the Russians, Austria and Prussia would feel it necessary to invade, he felt that the ground had to be prepared diplomatically before any further decisive action was taken. Missions were sent to London, Paris and Vienna in order to secure support and finance, and to offer the throne of Poland to a Habsburg archduke or a member of the British royal family in return for assistance. King Louis-Philippe made sonorous speeches about French military support and there was a moment when it looked as though the diplomatic efforts would yield fruit. The events taking place in Poland aroused strong international sympathy and engaged the poetic fancy. In Germany, this gave rise to a whole genre of *Polenlieder*. In America, Nathan Parker Willis wrote odes to Poland, while in England the young Tennyson 'wrote a beautiful poem on Poland, hundreds of lines long, and the housemaid lit the fire with it.' The French were not to be outdone, and Delavigne, Béranger, Musset, Vigny, Lamartine and Hugo were among those who wrote poems glorifying the Poles' struggle. Public sympathy for the Polish cause was beginning to be translated into action – and not only in Europe. On 23 May 1831 the Aldermen and Council of New York made a strong declaration of support, while Boston offered standards for the Polish regiments. In Paris, James Fennimore Cooper had started a Polish-American Committee to gather funds for the rising.

Given time, some of this feeling could have been brought to bear effectively. But the lack of political determination at the top and the absence of a coherent military strategy meant that the Polish forces were not being used to effect. Meanwhile Pashkievich had started to move again. He marched westwards, bypassing Warsaw to the north, and swept round to attack it from its least defensible western side. Instead of delivering a flank attack on the moving Russian columns, Skrzynecki sent two army corps off in different directions to create diversions. On 6

September 1831 Pashkievich attacked Warsaw. After two days of heroic but costly fighting over every inch of earthwork, the new commander General Krukowiecki capitulated and withdrew with the rest of his forces. The Poles still had some 70,000 troops in the field but these were dispersed in various parts of the country. Continued resistance seemed pointless. On 5 October the main force of the army crossed the border into Prussia to avoid capture by the Russians, while other units sought refuge behind the Austrian cordon, followed by most of the political figures.

The nineteen-year-old poet Zygmunt Krasiński, who had watched developments from Geneva, explained in a letter to his English friend Henry Reeve dated 16 November 1831:

> The executioner's axe, the thongs of the torturer are out of date, even with such Tatars; But there will be sledges leaving for Siberia, spies who will denounce, prisons which will engulf: young men will be made into soldiers for life, geniuses exiled or crushed; hearts will be frozen, broken by persecution, not violent, but clandestine, numbing, everyday persecution, applied morning and evening in the form of affronts of every kind, aggravations at every moment. In the first month a constitution will be granted only so that it can be destroyed in those that follow, with article after article suspended, with the idea cleverly removed to leave only the word; laws will be mutilated, institutions abolished, schools closed down, their teachers replaced by servile ignoramuses; the corruption of virtue will be protected, the Holy Church will be turned into a scarecrow so that noble hearts may turn away from it; baseness will be rewarded with crosses and honours which will be showered on the traitors and the ignoble; the people will be brutalised with vodka, the nobles with epaulettes and position; and those who resist will have prices put on their heads or be dealt with in good time.

It could have been a list of instructions issued by St Petersburg, so accurate was Krasiński's perception of the future. With all the self-righteous indignation of injured virtue, Nicholas took his revenge on those who remained in the Kingdom. He declared the constitution of the Kingdom null and void, and abolished the Seym and all other organs. The Universities of Wilno and Warsaw were closed down, along with the Warsaw Polytechnic, the Krzemieniec High-School, the Society of Friends of Learning and other educational establishments. In exchange, Warsaw was endowed with a Citadel from which Nicholas promised to bombard the city to rubble if there was any disturbance. General Pashkievich was named Prince of Warsaw. Russian generals and officials were given estates confiscated from Polish families. Poland became a Russian satrapy.

Ten people, with Adam Czartoryski at the head of the list, were condemned to death by decapitation, and a further 350 to hanging (most of them had already left the country). While a generous amnesty was trumpeted to the world, 10,000 officers were sent off to hard labour or service as simple soldiers in Russian regiments in the Caucasus. Over 800 'orphans' (children whose fathers had either been killed in the fighting or gone into exile) were taken from their mothers and given to Russian infantry regiments to bring up. In the Kingdom 3,176 families had their estates confiscated and countless families of minor szlachta were degraded. In Lithuania and the Ukraine the punitive measures took on an industrial scale. General Muravyov, nicknamed 'Hangman Muravyov' by the Russians not the Poles, rampaged around the countryside stringing people up and burning whole villages on the whiff of a suspicion of sympathy for the Polish cause. In Podolia, 5,000 families of minor szlachta were dispossessed of everything, degraded to peasant status and transported to the Caucasus. They were the lucky ones. A few years later no less than 40,000 families of szlachta from Lithuania and Volhynia were conveyed to Siberia in the same fashion. The accent was on humiliating the proud, degrading the noble, removing the vertebrae. Prince Roman Sanguszko, who was of Rurik's blood and might have qualified for some respect in Russia, was sentenced to hard labour for life in Siberia and made to walk there chained to a gang of convicts. When his wife, a friend and former lady-in-waiting to the Empress, fell at the feet of Nicholas and begged for mercy, she was told she could go too. She did.

The fate of the exiles was less lurid but no more enviable. Some 8,000 senior officers, political and literary figures found themselves consigned to a life of hopeless waiting. Few of them believed as they crossed the cordons that they would not live to fight another day. Theirs was supposed to be a tactical withdrawal. Many of the soldiers took service in the new Belgian army, and the French tried to pack as many as they could off to regiments in Algeria. Others converged on Paris, which became the focal point of Polish political and cultural life. It was there, amid bitterness and mutual recrimination, that the next campaigns in the battle to recapture Poland were planned and prepared.

The émigrés carried their differences of opinion with them into exile, and two principal groupings emerged in Paris: the Czartoryski Party and the Polish Democratic Society – one can safely ignore the dozens of Carbonarist-inspired factions whose names (Young Poland, The People's Revenge, Union of the Sons of the People, etc.) are more striking than their record. The Czartoryski faction dismissed conspiracy and revolution, pinning their hopes on a diplomatic solution. Prince Adam, referred to even by his political opponents as the 'de facto king' of Poland, lobbied British Members of Parliament and French Deputies, wrote memoranda and petitions, and maintained unofficial diplomatic relations with the Vatican and the Porte, demonstrating the need for a just solution to the Polish question. He ran a vast network with offices in many capitals which sprang into frenetic activity whenever a crisis loomed in Europe.

The Democratic Society was also remarkably well-run, with a nerve-centre, the Centralizacja, based at Versailles. This was fundamentally a revolutionary organisation committed to starting a mass rising in Poland at the earliest possible moment. But in 1837 the Russians uncovered the network the Centralizacja had carefully laid throughout the Kingdom and Lithuania, and cut a swathe through it with shootings, hangings and deportations to Siberia. The Democrats shifted their activities to the less perilous Austrian and Prussian sectors, where they agitated throughout the 1840s, often playing on anti-manor sentiments in order to gain support among the politically docile peasantry. A peasant rising was planned in both Galicia and Posnania for 22 December 1846. Premature action in Galicia alerted the Austrian authorities, which reacted with speed and perfidy. They appealed to the mainly Ruthene peasantry, explaining that the Polish lords were plotting a rising which would enslave them and offering cash for every 'conspirator' brought in dead or alive. The result was a terrible night of butchery in which bands of peasants attacked over 400 country houses, killing about a thousand people, few of them conspirators. Austrian and Russian troops crushed the Socialist Republic which had meanwhile been proclaimed in Kraków and abolished the free status of the city, which was incorporated into the Austrian Empire. In Posnania the Prussian authorities arrested the entire leadership before the planned local rising even had time to break out.

The revolutionary ardour of the Poles was not extinguished by these events and it revived in the 'Springtime of the Nations' of 1848. In February of that year the Paris mob overthrew the regime of Louis-Philippe; three weeks later the barricades went up in Vienna and Berlin; by the summer there was hardly a state in Europe that had not been affected by disturbances. The Poles needed little prompting. Kraków and Lwów rose and proclaimed provisional revolutionary committees designated by the Versailles Centralizacja which presented a list of demands for autonomy and emancipation of the peasants. In the desperate straits in which it found itself the Austrian government had no option but to countenance the fait accompli.

The Berlin mob had released from prison all the Polish conspirators arrested in 1846 and they went to Poznań to take control of the National Committee which had already formed there. The Berlin government was prepared to concede almost anything to weather the storm and therefore sanctioned the Committee, promising 'national reorganisation' of the Grand Duchy of Posen along Polish lines. Attention then switched to

Frankfurt where the first German Parliament assembled in a mood of pan-European liberalism. The fear that Tsar Nicholas would send in his troops to restore order in Central Europe prompted much talk of a common crusade to liberate Russian Poland and roll back the boundaries of Tsarist autocracy. Poles from all over Europe flocked to Posnania. Even Prince Adam Czartoryski arrived from Paris, greeted along the way like a future king. In Posnania the National Committee had by now some 20,000 men under arms, commanded by Ludwik Mierosławski, and proceeded with a programme of local reforms.

In the early summer the mood in Germany and in the Frankfurt Parliament began to veer away from internationalist liberalism, and deputies representing the German population of Posnania, Silesia and Pomerania began to voice anti-Polish sentiments. As the liberal ardour spent itself, the Berlin government began to contain the crisis. It promised to abide by its plan of 'national reorganisation' in Posnania, but demanded the disbanding of the Polish militias. The National Committee tried to negotiate, but when Prussian forces attacked one of the Polish units the Poles fought back. They won two pitched battles against the Prussian army, at Miłosław and Sokołowo, but were eventually bombarded into surrender with heavy artillery. Talk of reorganisation and autonomy was dropped, and in the end the Frankfurt Parliament voted to incorporate the Grand Duchy of Posen into Germany. As Engels wrily summed it up: 'Our enthusiasm for the Poles changed into schrapnel and caustic.'

In November, the Austrian army bombarded Kraków and then Lwów into submission. The 'Springtime of the Nations' had turned into another bleak winter for the Poles; far from benefiting their cause in any way, it had actually had the effect of removing the last shreds of the constitutional status of the Republic of Kraków and the Grand Duchy of Posen. The Poles had been in the forefront everywhere, yet they had gained nothing. They were among the first on the barricades of Vienna and Berlin; they fought in the Dresden rising; a Polish legion formed by the poet Mickiewicz in Lombardy fought at Rome, Genoa, Milan and Florence; Mierosławski commanded the anti-Bourbon forces in Sicily and then the German revolutionaries in Baden; General Chrzanowski commanded the Piedmontese forces at Novara; wherever there were Russians, Prussians, Austrians or their allies to be fought, there were Poles in the ranks. Their greatest contribution was to the Hungarian war. General Bem, who had saved the day for the Poles at Ostrołęka in 1831, commanded the revolutionary forces in Vienna in 1848 and then Kossuth's army in Transylvania. General Dembiński was the commander-in-chief of the Hungarian forces. They and hundreds of Polish officers fought to the bloody end at Temesvar, while the Czartoryski team backed up the Hungarians with all its diplomatic and material resources.

The returns were nil. Civilised Europe was frightened by revolution and the Polish cause was revolutionary. Statesmen were less and less inclined to listen to Czartoryski, however much they might respect him personally. At the same time the Polish cause had gained in respectability on the left. To quote Marx: 'It is no longer a feudal Poland, but a democratic Poland, and from this moment her liberation has become a point of honour for all European democrats.' Honour, however, came as low on the list of priorities for democrats as for the people Marx despised most at the time, Palmerston and Napoleon III. The outbreak of the Crimean War seemed to be a godsend to the Poles, combining as it did both of the nations most sympathetic to their cause against the arch-enemy Russia. Palmerston was a friend of Czartoryski and had often made strong pronouncements on the Polish question. Napoleon III inherited sympathy for the Polish cause with his political pedigree and his Foreign Minister was none other than Count Walewski, the half-Polish natural son of Napoleon Bonaparte. The Poles began to dream of a Franco-British expeditionary force landing in Lithuania, but Palmerston and Napoleon buried the Polish issue in order to buy Austrian and Prussian neutrality in the conflict. They only allowed Polish units to be raised under the Turkish flag to fight the common enemy in the Caucasus and the Crimea.

The Russian defeat in the Crimea and the death of Tsar Nicholas in 1855 had an immediate effect on conditions in Poland itself. The new Tsar Alexander II visited Warsaw and expressed himself open to suggestions for reform, but warned against political illusion: '*Point de rêveries, messieurs, point de rêveries!*' It was an idle taunt. Any attempt at improvement by the Poles was virtually bound to be seen in St Petersburg as '*rêveries*', as the next few years were to demonstrate.

With cautious optimism, Leopold Kronenberg of the Warsaw City Delegation and Andrzej Zamoyski of the Agricultural Society initiated a discussion of possible reforms. It was the area tackled by Zamoyski that absorbed most attention – the question of the peasants. By the late 1850s more than half of all peasant tenancies had been transformed into money-rents, mainly by voluntary commutation on the part of the landlord. But most small estates still operated on the old labour-rent system. In 1858 the Russian government asked the Agricultural Society to prepare a land reform project. Since discussions were going on in Russia on the subject of the emancipation of serfs, the matter was imminent and began to assume starkly political overtones. It was a question of whether the Polish peasant would thank the Tsar or the Polish intelligentsia for his emancipation.

The Agricultural Society was split on the subject. Zamoyski favoured the introduction of the English system of land-rent, while Tomasz Potocki pressed for giving tenants the freehold of the lands they worked. The Society eventually settled on a scheme which commuted all labour-rents to money-rents with permanent tenancy, to be followed by a turning of tenancies into freeholds by negotiation between landlord and tenant. The country followed the course of the discussion and by 1860 the Agricultural Society had come to be regarded as the de facto Seym, its meetings reported even by the London *Times*. It was soon caught in a cross-fire from the admonitions of St Petersburg and the increasingly strident demands of the Warsaw intellectuals. St Petersburg's strong man in this instance was not a Russian but a Pole, Aleksander Wielopolski.

Wielopolski was an intelligent, urbane aristocrat devoid of the romantic tendency to wishful thinking which marked so many of his contemporaries. He was a man of facts and figures. In 1831 he had been sent to London by the insurgent government to negotiate loans and quickly realised that there was no possibility of Western action on behalf of Poland. From then on he abided entirely by the restrictions imposed by Russia and made no bones of his contempt for the 'revolutioneering' nationalists. He was an immensely capable man who inspired trust in the Russians and was therefore placed in charge of the finances of the Kingdom. In 1860 he came up with a plan acceptable to the Tsar which had all the features of a cautious return to the principles of the Congress Kingdom of the 1820s. Russia conceded a measure of administrative reform in the government of the Kingdom and permitted the creation of consultative bodies; the clamp-down on education was to be eased, the peasant question was to be solved by Wielopolski who was given extensive powers, and Alexander's brother Constantine was sent to Poland as viceroy. For his part, Wielopolski undertook to maintain order and keep Polish political ambitions under control.

This was no easy matter. Wielopolski was disliked for his arrogance and tinged with the brush of compromise. His rival Andrzej Zamoyski was a man of lesser intelligence but greater popularity who was beginning to be propelled by pressures from below. When summoned by Grand Duke Constantine he refused to collaborate, preferring to remain in moderate opposition. Both were trying to walk a rope which was growing dangerously slack. The promise of liberalisation had acted like a tonic on the intelligentsia. Meetings were held, discussions raged in word and print on every aspect of reform, emancipation and autonomy, and the conclusion was drawn more often than not that any accommodation within the concessions envisaged by Russia was impossible. The police listened, people were investigated, and the cells of the Citadel began to fill up with hundreds, then thousands. On 25 February 1861, a meeting commemorating the anniversary of the 1831 rising was brutally dispersed by police. Two days later a religious procession was fired on, leaving five dead. On 8 April a similar demonstration resulted in over a hundred deaths. Disturbances recurred in Warsaw and other cities in a mood of mutual provocation.

On 15 October 1861 Russian troops broke into a couple of Warsaw churches in search of suspects. The hierarchy closed all churches and synagogues in the country in protest. Bishops, priests and rabbis were arrested in response, and martial law was proclaimed.

The patriotic fervour was incited by groups of the left known as the 'Reds' who were the heirs of the Democrats of the 1830s and 1840s. This description covered a spectrum of political outlooks, from mere radicals like Apollo Korzeniowski to socialists like Jarosław Dąbrowski and advocates of terrorism like Ignacy Chmieleński. They were emboldened by the military weakness of Russia demonstrated by the Crimean war, and by the recent example of the Unification of Italy. While liberals saw a Polish Cavour in Czartoryski, radicals saw a Polish Garibaldi in Mierosławski, who was a close friend of Prince Napoleon, nephew of the Emperor of the French.

With the imposition of martial law, the demonstrations ceased and conspiratorial activity started in earnest. The 'Red' Warsaw City Committee set up a countrywide provisional government to co-ordinate a mass rising in 1862. The military commander, Jarosław Dąbrowski, made contact with officers, both Russian and Polish, throughout the Russian army in order to cripple the military response at the moment of outbreak. Plans were well advanced when, in the summer of 1862, the Russian police got wind of the preparations and arrested many of the officers, including Dąbrowski.

Meanwhile, Wielopolski was trying to impose his own solution of the peasant question, which was similar to Zamoyski's proposals of 1859. By now, however, Zamoyski and the Agricultural Society had shifted their position. In an attempt to outbid the Reds they pressed for more radical measures. Zamoyski was summoned to St Petersburg where he was given a reprimand by the Tsar and sent into exile. The Agricultural Society was abolished and Kronenberg's Deputation dissolved. It was the turn of the moderates, known as the 'Whites', to go underground and start plotting.

The Poles had learnt a great deal from their experiences and displayed remarkable professionalism in the art of subversive organisation. The City Committee became the Central National Committee under the chairmanship of Stefan Bobrowski. It had five ministries; a diplomatic service which travelled widely and freely on forged documents, gaining admittance to European chancelleries as well as Russian émigrés' garrets; a treasury which collected donations from sympathisers and 'taxes' from the lukewarm, and even floated an international loan; a quartermastership which purchased and smuggled arms and supplies; a department of the interior which elaborated policy on emancipation of the peasants and the Jews; and a department of justice complete with its own 'stiletto police'. The intelligence department had men in every branch of the Russian army and civil service. The armed forces trained and operated clandestinely in Warsaw under the noses of the Russian army encamped not only in the Citadel but in the squares and streets. General Berg who had been instructed to investigate the conspiracy by the Grand Duke Constantine reported back after some weeks that he had discovered 'only one thing, namely that I don't belong to it.' As an afterthought, he added: 'And neither does your Imperial Highness.'

Wielopolski's compromise was unable to prevent an explosion, and his last attempt at defusing it was responsible for detonating it. He brought forward the annual selective conscription into the Russian army and excluded landowners and settled peasants from the lists. By concentrating the draft of more than 30,000 on the young intelligentsia and the cities he knew that the majority of the conspirators would be caught in the net, while those who purposely avoided it would disclose their identity thereby. In the event, the majority slipped away from home as the conscription approached. On 22 January 1863 the National Committee proclaimed the Insurrection, and that night small units attacked garrisons around the country. There was never any realistic hope of military success. The insurgents numbered no more than about 20,000, ill-equipped and dispersed in bands of between 50 and 500. Their numbers grew periodically, and in all some 100,000 people fought over the next eighteen months, but they were no match for the 300,000 Russian regulars concentrated against them. By virtue of good reconnaissance, timing, and an ability to melt away into the countryside, they managed to harass the Russian forces, cut supply-lines, and occasionally defeat a column which had ventured out of the safety of its fortified camp. They could not capture a single town or take on a full division in pitched battle, as this laid them open to bombardment by heavy artillery. Only in the remoter areas of Sandomierz, Podlasie and Kielce was it possible for units of more than 2,000 men to survive in the open. There was no continuity of command. Ludwik Mierosławski, who was to take control, was defeated while moving in from Posnania. The 'White' candidate Marian Langiewicz did assume overall command, but was soon defeated and forced to withdraw to Galicia.

The main hope of the Insurrection lay outside Poland. World opinion was strongly pro-Polish, and while newspapers ranted against Russian injustice, young men flocked to Poland, from Ireland, England, France, Germany and, most of all, Italy. Garibaldi's friend and aide Francesco Nullo was among those killed in 1863. Some never made it, like the two hundred volunteers who chartered a ship in London, the SS *Ward Jackson*, loaded up with supplies and set sail, only to be stopped by the Danes in the Sound. The largest non-Polish contingent were the Russians, which was a triumph for the ideal of revolutionary solidarity.

Foreign governments were less eager to help. Bismarck made it clear

124 Russian troops bivouac on the square in front of the Royal castle as tension mounts in Warsaw; a photograph taken surreptitiously from behind net curtains by Karol Beyer in 1863.

125 Lourse's coffee-room in the Europejski in Warsaw, one of the first purpose-built modern hotels in central Europe. It was here that the bodies of the five people shot by Russian troops during a commemorative procession on 27 January 1861 were brought. These events supported the widely-held view that civilised life was not possible under Russian autocracy, and that there was no room for compromise, only for insurrection.

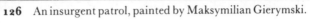

126 An insurgent patrol, painted by Maksymilian Gierymski.

127 An insurgent photographed in Kraków before crossing the cordon to join the 1863 rising in the Kingdom.

128 Jacek Malczewski's 'Halt on the march to Siberia', a typical genre subject for painters at a time when thousands were being packed off into exile in chain-gangs.

that he would help Russia if the need arose. Austria turned a blind eye on the activity going on along its border, which was the only entry-point for supplies. On 17 April 1863 Britain, France and Austria made a joint *démarche* in St Petersburg protesting at the violation of the Vienna settlement of 1815 – ie. against all Russian doings in Poland. Privately, Napoleon III and his ministers had assured the Czartoryski men in Paris that they would send arms and eventually troops, urging the Poles to hold on. It was largely as a result of this that the 'Whites', who were in close touch with their political siblings in Paris, decided in February to join the Insurrection officially and to make a bid for control of the movement. This changed hands more than once over the next months, and in October 1863 came to rest in those of Romuald Traugutt, a Lithuanian landowner from Podlasie. He was a 'White' with 'Red' sympathies, a devout, almost ascetic thirty-five-year-old father of two, a cool, capable man who had reached the rank of colonel in the Russian army and seen service in the Crimean War. He reorganised the National Committee and made it more efficient. He also took control of the military side and, with the help of General Józef Hauke, introduced regular patterns and chains of command. It was largely owing to his leadership that the Insurrection revived in the autumn of 1863 and expanded its area of operations. It had been said that the boundaries of the putative future Poland would draw themselves – with the blood of insurgents. Predictably, they did not stretch very far into the Ukraine, where bands of Polish szlachta were alone to join the Insurrection. In Byelorussia, they included much of the old Commonwealth, with not only the peasants, but also the Jews of towns like Pińsk joining the cause. In Lithuania and even southern Livonia, they corresponded to those of 1772, with mass participation by all classes. It was a slap in the face to the Russian policy carried on in these areas since the first partition: the population had declared for Poland.

In spite of the sympathy generated throughout the world for the Polish cause, it had become clear that no foreign power was prepared to get involved, and without such involvement the continuation of the struggle was of no practical value. As a result, the Insurrection began to peter out in the spring of 1864. On 2 March 1864 the Tsar pulled the carpet from under the feet of the insurrectionary government by sanctioning something which he could not have stopped even if he had wished to: the emancipation of the peasants with full possession of land. In April Traugutt was arrested. Sporadic fighting went on for another six months, but the uprising was over. The Tsar issued an ukase changing the name of the Kingdom of Poland to the 'Vistula Province'. All Polish institutions were abolished, and a period of intense repression began. 'Hangman' Muravyov returned, unmellowed by age. Brutality was meted out on a hitherto unknown scale, the path to Siberia was trodden by chain-gangs numbering tens of thousands of young people who would never return, and the nation went into mourning.

It went into mourning not only for the failure of the Insurrection, but for the whole tradition of insurgency. The 1863 rising was an uncommon achievement – it was no mean feat for a hundred thousand intellectuals, noblemen, workers and peasants to keep Europe's largest military machine tied down for eighteen months. It had also proved that the szlachta were not alone, and the very last engagement was fought by a detachment of peasants. Nevertheless it was the' end of an era in Polish history. Its failure wiped out all hopes of re-establishing Poland by means of insurrection and diplomacy. The defeat of Austria in 1866 and France in 1871 by Prussia seemed to seal the fate of Poland. The last of Poland's fighters took part by the thousand in the Franco-Prussian war as *franc-tireurs*, and the last of its commanders, Jarosław Dąbrowski, died on the barricades in 1871 as commander-in-chief of the Paris Commune. The future belonged to Russia and Prussia, the two policemen of mainland Europe.

17

The Polish Question

The 'Polish Question' haunted nineteenth-century diplomacy like an uneasy conscience, inducing as much discomfort in its friends as its enemies. Britain made many a diplomatic *démarche* on behalf of the Poles; Turkey never let an opportunity pass to show its disapproval of the partitions; the French Chamber of Deputies opened every session after 1830 with a solemn declaration of its intention to restore the freedom of Poland. Yet the governments of these nations were only too keen to bury the issue under a few pious phrases whenever it began to threaten the peace and stability of Europe. The precarious status quo rested on the badly closed grave of Poland. Anyone who valued tranquillity and feared violent upheaval cursed whenever that grave was disturbed.

As the tide of support for the Polish cause ebbed in the chancelleries of Europe it surged in more democratic quarters. It was characteristic that a Polish commemorative meeting held in London in 1841 should have had as its principal speaker a black man from Haiti. As Engels pointed out, every workers' movement of the nineteenth century only ventured beyond its own sphere of interests to make a gesture or a pronouncement on the Polish Question. In 1848 the Paris mob marched on the Hotel de Ville to cries of *'Vive la Pologne!'*, and their sentiment was echoed by the Chartists in England, the Berlin workers who carried Mierosławski shoulder-high out of the Moabit jail, and by every Italian from Mazzini to Garibaldi. It was not gimmickry that put the slogan 'For Your Freedom and Ours'' on the Polish standards in 1831; the Polish nation was the founder-member of the *internationale* of peoples arrayed against the Holy Alliance of monarchs, or, as Marx dubbed it, 'the immortal knight of Europe'.

Marx saw the collapse of the Polish Insurrection of 1831 as one of the most important events of the century. In the resolution he submitted to the Central Council of the First International, he maintained that 'the Poles' struggle for freedom was carried on in the common interest of the nations of Europe and that is why their defeat is a serious blow to the cause of civilisation and human progress.' He saw the Polish Question as seminal, for 'without an independent Poland there can be no truly independent and united Germany' – only a Prussian-dominated empire. In a speech made in January 1867 he was even more explicit: 'There exist only two alternatives for Europe. Either Asiatic barbarism under the leadership of Moscow will fall on Europe like an avalanche – or else Europe will rebuild Poland, cutting itself off thereby from Asia with a wall of twenty million heroes and gaining the respite necessary to achieve its social regeneration.'

It is certainly true that what happened in Poland had an immediate and crucial bearing on the course of events elsewhere. In 1792 the Russian armies expressly mobilised for the purpose could not march against revolutionary France because they were engaged in Poland. The same happened in 1830. As Lafayette explained to the French Chamber: 'The war had been prepared against us . . . Poland was to form the vanguard: the vanguard has turned against the main body of the army.' Had Poland regained her independence it would have been difficult for Austria to maintain its hegemony in northern Italy, for Russia to infiltrate the Balkans, and for Prussia to establish its ascendancy in Germany. Most important, a Poland carved up between the three Powers sealed their cooperation with the enduring bond of complicity and mutual self-interest. An independent Poland would have rendered continued cooperation between them unlikely and sometimes impossible. Poland was the one key that could unlock the chains binding the Holy Alliance of Russia, Prussia and Austria, an alliance which was the greatest impediment to change, revolutionary or otherwise.

What the partitions had done to Polish territory was of less consequence than what they did to the Polish people. They had come at a moment when Polish society was developing a new vigour and a new view of itself. As the state melted away, the nation grew stronger. An unique phenomenon came into existence – the nation without a state. Its sons wandered the globe in search of action or oblivion, usually gravitating towards wars and revolutions. They fought in the French colonial wars and in the Spanish civil wars; they fought in the northern and southern hemispheres, and on both sides of the Atlantic. The Shah of Persia had two Polish regiments in his Imperial Guard. The first officer to die for the Union in 1860 was Captain Blandowski. Another 4,000 Poles fought for the Union, many in the 58th New York Infantry or Colonel Krzyżanowski's United States Rifles, while a further 1,000 fought in the Confederate Army. It was in Ottoman service that such men found a lasting refuge. They were respected by the Turks, with whom they shared Russia as the common enemy, and who valued their services as staff-officers, artillerymen, engineers, cartographers and surgeons. Poles could rise to high positions, provided they embraced Islam, which many did with little apparent reluctance.

Typical is Aleksander Iliński, a wealthy nobleman who fought in the 1830 Insurrection and then went into exile. He took service in the Portuguese army, then fought in the Spanish Civil War (developing a side-line as a successful bull-fighter), and for the French in Algeria, followed by service in Afghanistan and China. In 1848 he was General Bem's aide-de-camp in Hungary, and subsequently joined the Turkish army. He converted to Islam and fought in the Crimean War as General Iskinder Pasha. He later became Turkish governor of Bagdad before dying in Istanbul in 1861.

The Wandering Pole had become a feature of life, but parallels with the Jews start and end there. The Polish 'nation' had never been based on ethnic, territorial, religious or political affinities, but on a coming together of diverse elements. When the state ceased to exist these elements might have been expected to fly off like so many satellites suddenly robbed of the centre of their orbit. Instead of disintegrating into its component parts, however, the Polish 'nation' remained one and continued to live a life of its own. In the mid-nineteenth century 'Poland' existed in the minds of the Poles in a sense that 'Germany' did not for the Germans before 1848. The Poles carried their nation and their country around in their knapsacks wherever fate scattered them: the opening words of Wybicki's Song of the Legions are 'Poland has not perished while still we live'. 'Polishness' became an ethereal moral condition which had nothing to do with the State.

Whether they were Russian, Prussian or Austrian subjects, exiles or prisoners, soldiers or priests, grandees or peasants, the Poles were faced with a dilemma. At its simplest, this was merely the question of how they should react to the situation, both on moral and practical grounds. Should they accept or resist it? This question raised a host of others. Before they could make up their minds on which was the wiser or nobler course to follow they had to consider what it was precisely that they were fighting for, and why. It is one thing to defend one's country, quite another to plan the rebuilding of a state which has ceased to exist. The Polish Question was not just a matter of crowns and frontiers; the Polish cause was not the cause of one tribe against its enemies; 'Poland' was not a geographical area; and Polishness was not an ethnic category. In dealing with the question of what sort of Poland it would be desirable to re-establish, the major considerations were therefore first the definition of the nation and second, since the bonds of Polish nationhood were political rather than ethnic, a decision as to the future political make-up of the country. It was only then that the question of frontiers could be broached.

As early as 1794 many Poles realised that certain sections of the population stood aside, uncertain as to whether the Polish cause was their cause. A Ruthene prince might decide that he was as happy being a subject of Moscow as of Warsaw; a Polish peasant could be forgiven for wondering whether it was worth risking his neck in order to prevent the Polish lord of the manor and king being replaced by Russians or Prussians. On purely tactical grounds therefore, it became necessary to define the Polish cause in such a way as to make it the cause of the majority of the population. This raised another question: were the Ruthene, Lithuanian and Jewish inhabitants of the Commonwealth 'Polish' or not, and should the cause be extended to accommodate them?

Implicit in all this was the need for a new identity, based on a clear interpretation of the past and a precise vision of the future. Polish society was obliged to go back to the beginning and think everything out for itself. The uprisings were in a sense irrelevant to this process, since not one of them was planned by more than an insignificant minority, not one of them had a programme acceptable to more than a small group, and not one of them succeeded in mobilising the whole nation. Yet they were all in some way expressions of the feelings of the nation. That is why the rioting of the November night in 1830 turned into a full-scale war of secession, and why a small group of conspirators could keep a guerilla war going for eighteen months in 1863–64. The risings punctuated a process of thought and self-discovery which might otherwise have turned into meaningless waffle about the nation and its aspirations. They also tested theories and destroyed illusions. The experience of 1794 made it clear that national consciousness had to be fostered among the masses. The military activity of 1797–1815 did involve greater numbers, at least a quarter of a million men, in a way which mixed aristocrats with peasants and initiated a significant number of people from the lower orders to the cult of the national cause. While it revealed that the force was there, it also showed that reliance on foreign support was unwise. The events of 1830 revealed a divergence of interest in different social groups, which 1846 and 1848 were intended to remove by radicalising the issue. In the event, these two risings showed up the pointlessness of amateurs taking on empires with little more than slogans for ammunition. The rising of 1863 was marked by greater professionalism and tactical sense, as well as by large-scale participation of peasants, workers and Jews, but it also revealed, as the American Civil war had revealed, that warfare had taken a giant technological stride towards what it has become in this century.

Each of these struggles highlighted the implications of the Polish predicament, and their increasingly ruthless repression committed more people to passionate participation in activities which they may have originally viewed as futile or even irresponsible. The minor szlachta, traditionally the most reactionary element in the population, were progressively turned into revolutionary extremists. By dispossessing landowners who were involved often very indirectly in resistance, the Powers forced the most docile members of the community into violent opposition. By vindictively penalising members of the aristocracy they forced even this into some measure of resistance. Families which in the 1820s were prepared to see their interest as lying in a realistic allegiance to St Petersburg or Vienna rather than with the hotheads of the Warsaw intelligentsia, were convinced by the image of Prince Sanguszko walking to Siberia in a chain-gang and by the Galician butchery of 1846. While insurrection was undesirable, the reigning order was abominable. There was not a Radziwiłł or Potocki who did not at some stage between the 1790s and the 1860s experience a situation which revealed to him that in time of crisis he belonged not to some superior *internationale* of European aristocracy, but to a hounded nation. The old szlachta solidarity of shared privilege turned into one of shared wrong and suffering, and this embraced anyone who identified with Poland, opening up a whole new channel of inter-class dialogue. The greatest 'collaborator' the aristocracy threw up in the whole century was Aleksander Wielopolski, whose fundamental patriotism cannot be doubted.

Patriotism was not the key issue in the risings, any more than social revolution. They were not, as cliché has it, the romantic gestures of an indomitable people. Most of them were neither planned nor intended, but provoked. In 1794, 1830 and 1863 they were sparked off by impending mobilisation, which was the last straw in a build-up of oppressive and illegal measures by the authorities. The risings were protests not so much against the system itself, but against the lawless behaviour of the author-ities which did not respect the rules they laid down themselves. They were in essence the descendants of the old Confederations, the final sanction designed to prevent the ruler taking advantage of the ruled.

The colonisation of Poland by the Powers did not stop at physical control exerted in relation to need. All three, and most particularly Russia, strove to impose moral conformity and their own values on the conquered natives. To attempt to achieve this through legislation would have been impossible, and the authorities therefore carried on much of their activity in an illegal manner. The Polish mentality is saturated with the notion of legality and reciprocity, and Russian rule in Poland therefore offended not only by its aims, but also by its methods. If someone is tried and convicted to twenty-five years' hard labour under an existing, if barbaric, law, it is one thing. If someone is dragged from his home and sent to Siberia because the police are above the law and do not like his attitude, that is a blow at the basis of civilisation and human dignity. The methods of the new rulers were utterly alien to the moral and cultural metabolism of the Poles, provoking violent gut-reactions whenever they were administered in unnaturally strong doses.

The collapse of the Polish Commonwealth provoked an obvious question: Why? Any failure suggests a post-mortem and the disappearance from the map of one of the largest states in Europe was not an everyday event. After the defeat of 1831 the soul-searching began in earnest. The past was looked into in quest of lessons for the future and both the view that emerged and the lessons drawn from it varied enormously according to the outlook of the various political groupings.

The Czartoryski faction, the political descendant of the Familia and the 'Patriotic' party in the Great Seym, believed that the Constitution of 3 May would have cured the ailing Commonwealth. They were liberals with a penchant for English patterns of political conduct and they believed that Poland's eclipse reflected a breakdown in the proper functioning of diplomacy. Their efforts after 1831 were directed at showing to the other European states the practical desirability of restoring Poland to Europe in the interests of the balance of power. There was no lack of idealism in this political orientation, which had inherited much from its eighteenth-century roots and from the humanist tradition of the old Commonwealth. Stanisław Staszic, a prominent member of this political grouping, held that the only way of bringing justice into international relations was by setting up some kind of Association of Nations, and in 1803 Adam Czartoryski suggested the creation of a Society of States. After the Congress of Vienna he elaborated a system of diplomacy based on morality as well as pragmatic considerations in his *Essai sur la Diplomatie*. Fundamental to the thinking of Czartoryski was the notion of morality in politics, and he considered the self-proclaimed guardians of conservatism such as Nicholas I and Metternich as the robber barons of Europe, bound to bring the system into disrepute and to provoke violent revolution in the end.

The socialist elements of the emigration were influenced by the works of the historian Joachim Lelewel, leader of the Patriotic Society and a member of the Insurrectionary government in 1831. Lelewel had looked into the past and seen something altogether different from the vision of the liberals. He developed a theory that the social and political structure of ancient Slav societies in the pre-Christian era had been based on peasant communities. It was a vision of rural democracy later favoured by Russian historians and it held a strong attraction for many on the left of the political spectrum. According to Lelewel the Constitution of 3 May was a piece of pious Western liberalism alien to the spirit of Polish society.

The manifesto of the Polish Democratic Society, published in 1836, rejected the liberal idea of giving the peasants their land – i.e. turning them into mini-capitalists. 'The question of property is the question of our age,' it proclaimed, in the conviction that 'the land and its fruits are common to all.' It therefore concluded that 'private property must be transformed into common property.' The majority of the Democrats were minor szlachta who had lost everything with their country. Many were condemned to a life of wandering among strangers in dire poverty. Horrified by the prosperity they encountered in London and Paris, revolted by the materialistic values of society in these cities, they developed an unbounded faith in impending revolution and a hunger for the Second Coming. Their programme therefore tended towards upheaval and cataclysm rather than the allotment of freeholds to peasants within the framework of the old system.

An interesting offshoot of this movement was the London Commune, founded in 1834, whose manifesto, written by Stanisław Worcell, a former member of the wealthy szlachta and son of a senator, contained the phrase: 'Property is the root of all evil.' In 1835, a Community of the Polish People was established at Portsmouth, and in the following year another on the island of Jersey. These took the form of agricultural communes, consisting of some two hundred peasants and penitent gentry who sought regeneration through work. They were strongly influenced by two philosophers of peasant origin, Ludwik Królikowski and Father Piotr Sciegenny, who propounded a Socialist Millenarianism which represented the French Revolution as the harbinger of the Second Coming.

There were many splinter-groups among the émigrés, particularly on the left. It was a sad world of threadbare heroes and lost causes, of endless discussions and arguments carried on in damp London basements and freezing Paris garrets, a world of self-sacrifice and pettiness. And there was no lack of extremists at the other end of the political spectrum.

Henryk Rzewuski, a magnate whose family had been associated with the Confederation of Targowica, was himself a patriot but his view of the past was more indulgent than most. A gifted writer, he published in 1839 *The Memoirs of Soplica*, a sort of historical novel which presents all the most dismal features of Sarmatism with nostalgia, showing up as picturesque and heroic even such muddle-headed oafs as Karol ('My Dear') Radziwiłł. This provoked acid criticism from the 'realists' of both liberal and democratic persuasions, but two years later Rzewuski astonished everyone by taking an even more 'realistic' view himself. In 1841 he published a book pointing out the bankruptcy of the Polish cause, the pointlessness of fighting an order which was there to stay, and the desirability of accommodation with Russia.

Rzewuski and others tried, in word and deed, to respond in the most appropriate way, both ethically and rationally, to a state of affairs which they found baffling. It was not just that the country had been rubbed off the map. A whole culture had been wiped out and replaced by a different set of rules and realities, a sort of limbo administered by bureaucrats. To make sense of a predicament is to give oneself hope and it is therefore not surprising that so much time and energy and printers' ink was devoted to this end. With the intelligentsia divided between three empires and scattered in exile, the printed word assumed enormous significance, and the fact that this was an age rich in literary talent ensured that the men setting up communes in Portsmouth and Jersey were not cut off from their fellows who had remained in Poland to farm their estates.

The first traces of the Romantic movement in Polish literature appear in the 1790s. The heart began to rule the mind just as the ravished motherland was being enslaved; the Polish Romantic heart could beat for no other damsel in distress or unattainable object of love. Poets like Karpiński, Kniaźnin and the young Adam Czartoryski wrote of the expiring Commonwealth as lovers. Their immediate successors sang the praises of her vanished accomplishments.

The historical Romanticism of Walter Scott encountered a unique response in a society which could only look back with longing. Byron's fascination with the indomitable spirit of the free struck a chord in the imagination of people to whom the life of a Mazepa was familiar. His splenetic view of the modern world echoed the feelings of thousands of young Poles consigned to a life of aimless redundancy. If Niemcewicz's *Historical Cantos* (1816) placed history before emotion, Antoni Malczewski's poetic tale *Maria* (1825) and Seweryn Goszczyński's *Castle of Kaniów* (1828), a magnificently gory tale of Cossack rebellion, were full-blown Romantic evocations of past freedom. Like the politicans, the poets raked through history in search of a vision. They were no more blind to the inadequacies and corruption of the Commonwealth, but their judgements reflected the spirit of Romanticism. The rational approach of a Stanisław Augustus offended them on aesthetic grounds, as it lacked what they saw as the uncompromising heroism of a Sobieski or, more recently, a Józef Poniatowski safeguarding his honour in the watery grave of the river Elster. This futile tragedy, prints of which hung in every Polish home, was held to be worth more than all the painstaking work of the eighteenth-century reformers. The poets searched the past for its glorious moments in order to give comfort and self-respect to their readers.

Much of the retrospection was concerned not with historical accuracy or melodrama, but with discovering the nature of the culture which flourished in the Commonwealth. By the 1820s its peculiar civilisation seemed as distant as Victorian times to twentieth-century man, and it exerted a powerful fascination on the dispossessed Poles. What they wanted was the essential truth not the factual, folklore not archaeology. In 1818 the historian Zorian Chodakowski had published a work on early Slav culture which he reconstructed from folklore. Lelewel's approach, though sounder, was hardly less mythical. If it made for bad history, it also gave rise to the greatest literature and music.

At an early age Fryderyk Chopin (1810–49) became fascinated by the rhythms and harmonies he heard in the Mazovian countryside. He studied this musical idiom and used it to create, in his Mazurkas, entirely original jewels of a timeless peasant culture. In his Polonaises he distilled the quintessential characteristics of courtly Sarmatism in musical form. His friend Stefan Witwicki published a collection of *Bucolic Songs* (1830) which clearly harked back to Kochanowski and Szymonowicz, while another friend, Józef Bohdan Zaleski, scoured the lore and legend of his native Ukraine for echoes of the vanished world. Rzewuski's *Memoirs of Soplica* were inspired by an attempt to understand and explain the vagaries of the Sarmatian manner. The greatest poet of the age, Adam Mickiewicz (1798–1855), contributed a classic to the quest. His *Pan Tadeusz* (1834) is a novel in verse, a mock-heroic and realistic yet curiously fairy-tale-like evocation of country life in Lithuania. It is also a fascinating document which sums up szlachta attitudes, charts the issues faced by this class in transition, accurately describes country pastimes and customs, gives the best account of bear-hunting in Polish literature, and leaves the reader wistful yet baffled. Written in Paris at a time when Mickiewicz had already condemned the values of the Commonwealth and was leaning heavily towards the left of émigré politics, it could hardly be more telling. As they searched for answers to present problems, such men could not avoid hankering for the past, which assumed a symbolic significance. The old quest for the lost state of innocence, present in Polish literature from the sixteenth century, was becoming inextricably confused with the quest for the lost motherland, or rather, the state of being that had vanished with it. For the émigrés in particular, Arcadia became indistinguishable from Poland.

Not all Polish Romantic literature was obsessed with the motherland, and Mickiewicz had started out writing lyrical works inspired by his favourite poet Trembecki. In 1822 he published *Ballads and Romances*, which earned him critical acclaim, and in the following year *Grażyna* and *Forefathers' Eve*. The first is a tale of self-sacrifice and honour culled from historical folklore, the second a dramatic work based on the pagan Lithuanian custom of invoking the dead on All Souls' Eve, which presents a series of tortured souls recounting their errors and sufferings. In the same year Mickiewicz was imprisoned. He was exiled to St Petersburg, and in 1825 to Odessa, where he wrote *Crimean Sonnets*. In Odessa he shared a mistress with the Chief of Police for Southern Russia and this generous man's favourable reports secured him a transfer back to Moscow. The next two years were important for Mickiewicz. He made friends with a number of Russian writers, particularly Pushkin, and he came to understand, and fear more than ever, the nature of the Russian state. It was in 1828 that he wrote, in *Konrad Wallenrod*, his first overtly political poem.

Juliusz Słowacki (1809–49) was not essentially a political poet either.

Born in Volhynia and educated at Wilno University, he was a sensitive man whose early life was marred by an unhappy exalted love for an older woman, and he began by writing melancholy and self-indulgent verse. He published his first works in Paris in 1832 and in the following year wrote a cycle of poems under the title *In Switzerland*, whose pantheistic theme brings them close to the French Romantic tradition. The same is true of *Kordian* (1834), a play in verse whose hero is a perfect *enfant du siècle*, searching for the meaning of life in the arms of a courtesan and on the slopes of Mont Blanc. Słowacki was a virtuoso of words, images, mood and colour, and there is something both baroque and futuristic about his style. He moved with facility from the melodramatic, almost lurid atmosphere of *Mazepa* (1839) to the sparkling satirical *Fantazy* (1841), a picture of upper-class inanity. In 1836 Słowacki made a journey to Palestine, and the resulting poem, *Voyage to the Holy Land*, is a spiritual meditation. In Lebanon, he wrote the prose poem *Anhelli*, in which he represents Polish exiles in Siberia as blind victims rather than as the noble fallen heroes whose martyrdom was given constructive meaning by the likes of Mickiewicz. An avid reader in many languages, Słowacki shows the influence of Shakespeare and Walter Scott, of Byron and Lamartine, of Calderon, whose works he translated, and of everything that appeared on the Parisian operatic and dramatic stage, of which he was a devotee. Yet he is thoroughly unlike his European contemporaries.

George Sand dubbed Mickiewicz 'the Cousin of Byron and Goethe', but the three had little other than talent in common. The cult of love, the obsession with the self and the yearning for heroic action which were such distinctive hallmarks of European Romanticism were not indulged in by the Poles. The lyrics of Mickiewicz lack vigour and their eroticism is subdued; the soul-searching of Słowacki is spiritual not sentimental; and Polish yearnings for action were politically motivated. After 1831, personal emotion was superseded by spiritual, ethical and even political themes which demanded exploration with an intensity that increasingly cut Polish literature off from other contemporary cultures. The scattered and disoriented nation looked to the poets to make sense of things and the poets grew into the role of the spiritual leaders, the oracular high-priests who strove to provide some answers.

Mickiewicz was the one who took the lead in this direction. In *Konrad Wallenrod*, an historical tale about a Lithuanian child captured by the Teutonic Knights and brought up as one of them, rising to the Grand Mastership of the Order and then leading its armies to defeat at the hands of his own people, Mickiewicz explored the idea of patriotic action through collaboration with the enemy. In the second part of *Forefathers' Eve* (1832), a mixture of Greek tragedy and medieval morality play, he touched on the whole range of moral and ethical problems confronting the Poles in captivity, and on the questions of good and evil in political life. He then addressed himself to the subject of suffering.

The aftermath of 1831 was hardly spectacular and there were no hecatombs of corpses to weep over. Yet the Poles suffered terribly. They suffered not because their bodies had been tortured, but because their hopes had been crucified. They suffered too because they were alone. Europe and the world seemed to care little about the great wrong that had been done to Poland, and as her sons cried out for justice they were answered with silence. The only thing that could save them from total despair was some kind of faith in the very fact of their martyrdom and sacrifice. In 1832 Mickiewicz held out a candle in the darkness of this despair. In *The Books of the Polish Nation* he suggested that Poland had been crucified in the cause of righteousness. The crucifixion would expiate the political sins of the world and lead to resurrection. This messianic image made sense of everything and gave hope where there had been only despair. Christ too had cried out on the Cross and and been answered with silence, but by His death He had conquered death itself. Through their suffering the Poles would conquer persecution.

Few were naïve enough to take this literally, but at some level of the subconscious the messianic vision was a healing balm for every suffering Polish soul. At some level in their consciousness the Poles rejected a reality which excluded their aspirations. It was not a question of escapism, but an attempt at belittling the reality by the discovery of another, deeper truth, and the Poles were not the only people in search of new faith. In the second quarter of the nineteenth century philosophers in every part of Europe sought to replace the faith in reason of the Enlightenment and the faith in action of the Napoleonic period with patterns of thought that could face the challenge of a changing world and the industrial revolution.

Polish philosophy largely grew out of the new German philosophy of Kant and Hegel, but was also strongly influenced by French thought. Bronisław Trentowski (1808–69) and Karol Libelt were pupils of Hegel; others, like J.K. Rzesiński and Gustaw Ehrenberg, probably a natural son of Alexander I and a prominent conspirator, were strongly influenced by him. In applying himself to the concept of the nation, Trentowski rejected Hegel's idea of 'rational states' based not on nationality or culture but on practical considerations, and himself evolved a national philosophy of action. He attempted to produce a practical programme for the complete 'regeneration' of Poland. Very close to him was the remarkable figure of Józef Maria Hoene-Wroński (1776–1853). Bafflingly, he fought for Kościuszko at Maciejowice, then served on Suvorov's staff, and then transferred to Dąbrowski's legions within the space of four years. He settled in France where, in 1804, he had a vision of 'the absolute', and published a vast corpus of work, some of it purely mathematical, but most of it devoted to restructuring the relationship between science and life. He envisaged a cosmic fusion of the arts and sciences into a system which would regenerate mankind. He also tried to elaborate a system of history, in which the fate of Poland played a seminal part. The Polish philosopher who contributed most to European thought was August Cieszkowski (1814–94), also a pupil of Hegel and a classmate of Marx, whose influential writings on the primacy of the will and the relation of Christianity to Socialism were published in French or German.

Mickiewicz stopped writing poetry in 1835 and thereafter expounded his thoughts in the lectures he gave at the Collège de France. In the 1840s he came under the spell of Andrzej Towiański, a charlatan who founded a cabalistic sect in Paris. His messianic vision took on a political tint, and his lectures became openly revolutionary. In 1848 he went to Rome to raise a Polish legion. He pestered the Pope, Pius IX, on one occasion seizing him by the sleeve and shouting: 'Let me tell you that the Holy Spirit resides today under the shirts of the Paris workers.' He did raise his legion, in Lombardy, and took part in a series of revolutionary actions, but by the following year he was back in Paris, editing the international socialist periodical *La Tribune des Peuples*. Many socialists viewed him with suspicion, for his thought and his actions were continually leaping beyond the bounds of their assumptions. Like many Romantics he had come to see Poland's downfall in terms of the people having been betrayed by an inept élite. It only needed a small admixture of Lelewel's historical theory to turn this into a conviction that the people were the nation and the szlachta alien interlopers. At the same time Mickiewicz was intelligent enough to realise that the answer to the Polish problem did not lie in social revolution. His faith in socialism was qualified from the start, and the events of 1846 did not fail to qualify it further. A devout if at times rebellious Christian, Mickiewicz kept trying to arrive at a synthesis of Christian Socialism and to construct a programme of action which fitted the historical moment. It was in this context that his youthful admiration of Napoleon resurfaced. For Mickiewicz, Napoleon was the incarnation of elemental force, intuitive and superior – almost the hand of God. As he cast about in search of some tangible reality on which to pin his hopes, he fixed on the figure of Napoleon III, in which he saw the 'Providential Man' through whose agency great things could be achieved. His socialist colleagues were appalled.

So was Słowacki. He too had been briefly fascinated by Towiański, he too was a socialist, he too entertained messianic visions, but he had a sense of humour and proportion. He rejected the vapourings of Mickiewicz and although he also elaborated a cosmic Christian view of history and the world in the last great poem he wrote, *King-Spirit*, it was a personal vision without political application. A similar attitude was to be taken by the younger post-Romantic Cyprian Norwid (1821–83), an orphan of poor

Mazovian szlachta who hoped to make a career as an artist. He had to take jobs as a draughtsman and even as a manual labourer, and in 1852 he went to America in search of better conditions. He soon returned to Europe, to one of London's poorest quarters and then to Paris, where he ended his days. He is one of the most original, profound and intellectual of all Polish poets, his works full of subdued irony and layered imagery. He recast Polish poetic diction and built his syllabic verse on natural speech rhythms, eventually finding his way to free verse forms in which he was a forerunner of Laforgue and Pound. His most important work was not published in his lifetime and it has been twentieth-century editors and critics who have in course of time perceived his true greatness. Norwid was a lost soul wandering through a materialistic world which offended him aesthetically and prevented him from fulfilling himself. Much of his poetry revolves round the problems of work and creation; he was also interested in history and the condition of Polishness. It was he who pointed out to abstract theoreticians that 'a nation suffers, therefore it is not an idea'. He looked up to men like Mickiewicz but rejected the messianic vision as a dangerous heresy and could see that their programmes were politically inept.

By the late 1840s the thinking of such figures was going round in decreasing circles. As it gathered in lurid imagery underpinned by hallucinatory mysticism, it became almost pathological. This was inherent in the conundrum of their predicament, and partly the result of personal misery. Słowacki dying of tuberculosis in Paris and the poverty-stricken Mickiewicz supporting seven children and a wife who had lost her senses could not be expected to take anything but an embittered view. These men lived only on their own faith, with 'not one real hope, not one drop of living water' to sustain them, as Alexander Herzen observed. 'Like a tree without fresh sap, they withered and faded away; they were becoming alien to their own country without ceasing to be aliens in the lands in which they were living. These were sympathetic towards them to some extent, but their misfortune lasted too long, and there is no good feeling in the soul of man that does not wear out.'

Of the three major Romantic poets only Krasiński managed to avoid this predicament, and as a result his thought is more consistently balanced and lucid than that of the others. Unlike them, he was an aristocrat who never knew physical poverty or hardship, but he suffered with no less intensity, for his birth had placed him in an unenviable position. Krasiński was born in 1812 and christened Napoleon Stanisław Zygmunt by his father, a general in the Grande Armée, but the first of these names was dropped as the general became a prominent reactionary in the Congress Kingdom and a trusted servant of the Tsar. The boy's life at school was made awkward by the unpopularity of his father. He was the butt of

endless taunts and eventually had to be sent to complete his studies in
Geneva. It was there that the outbreak of the 1830 rising found him. He
was painfully torn between the desire to join his fellows in the rising and
obedience to his father in St Petersburg, who forbade him to do any such
thing. By the time he was twenty he felt alienated from his contemporaries
and knew that his inactivity had branded him in the eyes of the intelligentsia.

These feelings gave rise in 1833 to the *Undivine Comedy* a verse play of
extraordinary power and significance. The hero, a young aristocrat, is
elected to lead the noble forces of conservatism resisting revolution. He
finds himself in a dilemma, since he knows his cause to be the right one but
holds all his supporters in contempt. He is fascinated by his opponent, a
proto-bolshevik who coolly controls the masses he leads and is prepared to
sacrifice them in pursuit of power and of a philosophy that can only be
described as dialectical materialism. He is a blueprint for any twentieth-
century national-socialist dictator. As a play the *Undivine Comedy* is prob-
lematic, but as a series of images and discussions it is powerfully incisive.
Krasiński was fully aware of how despicable the forces of conservatism were
with their complacent denial of spiritual values and of compassion for the
less fortunate, yet he was terrified by the brutal cynicism and the lust for
power of the revolutionaries.

While most Poles viewed what was happening in Central Europe as a
question of national oppression, and while socialists brought it all down to
a struggle between revolution and reaction, Krasiński saw the situation in
a different light. The Czartoryski faction had long been at pains to point
out that the Holy Alliance, which arrogated to itself the right and the duty
to defend European civilisation and legitimacy, were bandits not policemen, and that they had no conception of what legitimacy, let alone
civilisation, really were. Russia posed as the guardian of old values, while
Prussia invoked a cultural and civilising right to its Polish territories. They
could count on the Western constitutional monarchies' love of peace and
respect for legitimacy to prevent them from supporting the Polish cause, as
they had, by sleight-of-hand, turned it into a revolutionary one. Hence
Metternich's declaration that the Polish cause 'does not declare war on the
monarchies which possess Polish territory, it declares war on all existing
institutions and proclaims the destruction of all the common foundations
which form the basis of society.' In terms of sheer intellectual dishonesty,
the statement can hardly be bettered.

Krasiński instinctively perceived the essence of the evil which the
Czartoryski faction had identified politically. The Russian system was, as
he put it in a letter to Pope Pius IX, 'a huge merciless machine, working by
night and by day, crushing thousands of hearts and minds every minute';
'the irreconcilable enemy of all spiritual independence'. The bureaucratic

apparatus of the police state was the real enemy of European civilisation, and it was all the more dangerous for masquerading as its champion, as it perversely encouraged and strengthened the forces of revolution, which were equally destructive. He saw the importance of Poland as the only possible counterbalance to both. 'To make Poland a free, constitutional, moderate state would be to save her, and with her the world,' he explained in a letter to François Guizot, Louis-Philippe's minister whose conservatism was to be the immediate provocation for the 1848 revolution. 'It would at one stroke kill all the wild hopes of the Tsars and the destructive hopes of the demagogues, whose very real power is based on the profound and hideous injustice of the present European system.'

It was by those who thought like Czartoryski and Krasiński, and in the first place by his friend Chopin, that the Marquis de Custine was briefed before he left Paris: it is not surprising that his *Lettres de Russie* bear traces of this thought. Interestingly enough, the views of the most aristocratic of all Polish poets were echoed in the reflections of Karl Marx, who saw in the inexorable advance of Russian power the greatest threat to Europe, not least because it sanctioned the ambitions of Prussia. 'The fall of Poland is the cradle of Russia, the advance of Russia is Prussia's right to expansion,' he wrote; 'there is no Prussia without Russia . . . Prussia is Russia's jackal.'

If Krasiński's perception was cooler than that of his peers, he lacked the conviction that sustained Mickiewicz to his bitter end, brought on by cholera in Turkey in 1855, while helping to organise Polish units for the Crimean war. Krasiński could see no promise in any programme. He too went through a phase of messianic exaltation: 'Where there is pain, there is life, there is resurrection,' he wrote to Słowacki, 'only where there is abasement shall there be no resurrection.' At the end of the day the poets and the philosophers had to admit that there was no answer to the Polish Question – no political answer and no spiritual answer. It remained a question of faith and hope. The only thing the Poles could do was to cling to their Polishness. Not their patriotism or their political hopes for the resurrection of Poland, but quite simply the state of mind and the code of Polishness. As Krasiński exclaimed in his last major poem, *The Dawn*: 'You are no longer just my country; a place, a home, a way of life; the death of a state or its birth; but a Faith – a Law!'

18

Captivity

It would be wrong to see the hundred years between the Napoleonic wars and the Great War of 1914 purely in terms of conspiracies and insurrections. Oppressed peoples do revolt, but they also carry on eating, working and breeding, and it is these unspectacular activities which absorb the overwhelming share of the national effort at all but the most critical of times. The Poles were no exception, and their instinct was to get on with life as best they could. It was the inability of the three Powers to provide a congenial framework within which their new subjects could live that kept the Polish problem in an explosive state. Moral considerations aside, they cannot escape the charge of extraordinarily inept colonialism. During a century when states like Britain and France could easily and profitably control vast and populous continents, the three greatest Powers of the European mainland devoted incomparably greater resources in troops, funds and gigantic bureaucracies to policing a small, thinly populated and easily accessible country in their midst, with lamentable results. The only thing that made Poland a difficult country to colonise successfully was that the legacy of the Commonwealth did not include a native civil service or police force which could have been employed by the new masters. The entire apparatus of social control had to be imported, with the result that authority never lost its alien garb.

Prussia gained most in real terms from the partitions and should have had little trouble in digesting its share. This was not large, it was hemmed in on three sides by Prussian lands, and it was infiltrated by people of German origin. The area that had fallen to Prussia in the first partition was integrated into the Prussian kingdom proper. Wielkopolska with the city of Poznań was defined in 1815 as the Duchy of Posen, a semi-autonomous province with its own representative bodies and institutions. The Prussian administration was heavy-handed and contemptuous of the erstwhile Polish élite, but there was no overt persecution. In 1830 the Prussian army kept a close watch lest the province should attempt to emulate the rising in the Kingdom, but the popularity of the Polish cause in Germany prevented any further action. Large units of the Polish army entered Prussian territory in 1831 to avoid capture by the Russians, and they were greeted deliriously by Germans and Poles alike. In some cases the Prussian army ill-treated the disarmed soldiers or handed them back to the Russians, but this was done stealthily.

In 1848, however, the Germans of Posnania felt threatened by Polish aspirations, and their fears, couched in strident calls for the 'defence of Germandom', met with response from the nascent nationalism of their brothers throughout Germany. The Poles were branded as 'a nation of lesser cultural content' by one speaker at the Frankfurt Parliament, and henceforth, Posnania was to be turned into a bastion of the Teutonic world. The failure of the 1863 Insurrection, the unification of Germany and the promotion of the Prussian kings to the status of German emperors in 1871 weakened the position of the Poles further. On being incorporated into the German Empire, Posnania lost its separate status, but this meant that Polish deputies were returned to the Reichstag. What had been a marginal colonial question now became an internal problem. When Bismarck declared his *Kulturkampf* – the war on Catholic and regionalist tendencies in the Empire – Polish deputies found new allies in the Catholics of Bavaria and Westphalia. The equation of Catholicism with 'foreignness' prompted Catholic Germans in Posnania and Pomerania to identify with the Poles. Similarly, Pomeranian peasants who had never asked themselves whether they were Poles or Germans but knew that they were Catholics, declared themselves to be Polish, since this had become synonymous with being Catholic.

The original Prussian analysis had been that once the nobility and clergy had been emasculated, the peasant masses would turn into loyal Germans. In fact, while the parish clergy and the smaller landowners were nationalist, the Church hierarchy and the aristocracy were happy to co-operate. The Archbishop of Poznań and Gniezno, Mieczysław Ledóchowski, was typical in his pro-German attitude, which made him extremely unpopular with the intelligentsia and most parish priests. In 1874, however, Bismarck pushed him into such a tight corner with his attacks on the Church that even he had to protest. He was imprisoned and turned into a national hero overnight. After this, Polish nationalism and the Catholic Church made a common front. It was a formidable alliance which managed to blunt the main thrust of German colonial policy, aimed at the Polish language. From the beginning of Prussian rule, German became the language of instruction in schools. In 1874 the use of Polish textbooks was forbidden by law. In 1876 German became the exclusive administrative language, and no other was countenanced in anything from a law-court to a post-office. In 1887 the study of Polish as a second language was abolished throughout the educational system. Parish priests

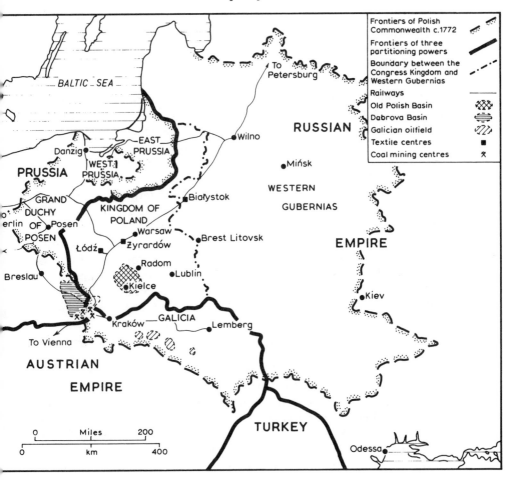

The lands of partitioned Poland, c.1860

played a crucial role in the preservation of the language by holding clandestine classes, and this in turn endowed it with a quality of catechumen sanctity.

The clergy also rallied the peasants to resist the economic onslaught, giving advice and information on everything from agriculture to taxation, and it was they who introduced the co-operative movement into Posnania in 1871. In 1886 Bismarck made an extraordinary speech in which he advocated a campaign to buy out Polish landowners, suggesting that they themselves, being endemically irresponsible, would be far happier spending cash at the roulette tables of Monte Carlo than farming their estates. A Colonisation Commission was set up with a capital of 100 million marks to finance this operation. The Polish landowners fought back by establishing their own Land Bank which could bail out those in difficulty. In Pomerania the Junkers steadily gained ground in the battle for possession of land, but in Posnania the Poles held their own and even reversed the process.

This was no mean achievement since these provinces supported an intensive and competitive agricultural industry. By 1895 over 40 per cent of all farms had some machinery. This competitiveness created redundancy in the rural population (60 per cent of the whole), which led to large-scale emigration, particularly to the United States. This benefited the position of those left behind in more ways than one. The earliest emigrants set off in groups, often led by a priest, with the intention of beginning a new life. This was true of the first Polish settlement, founded in 1854 at Panna Maria in Texas, and of later ones at Czestochowa, Polonia and Kosciuszko in Texas, of New Pozen in Nebraska, and similar communities in Virginia and Wisconsin. The United States was dotted with at least half-a-dozen Pulaskis and some fifteen Warsaws (often spelt Wausau in the South). This form of emigration merely relieved the pressure at home. From the 1870s onwards the emigrants went primarily in search of work, and they found this in the industrial and mining centres of Pennsylvania, New Jersey, Michigan and Illinois. As well as setting aside part of their salary to support Polish priests and build their own churches, they also regularly sent money back to their families at home. At the same time, a landless peasant could return home after twenty years in the Chicago canneries with enough capital in his pocket to buy a smallholding.

The year 1890 marked the end of the Bismarck era and the new Chancellor Leo von Caprivi made concessions to the Poles in return for their votes in the Reichstag. This change of mood was not to last. In 1894 three Junkers founded the Deutscher Ostmark Verein, an organisation vowed to the promotion of German interests in the east. This played on German fears and phobias, invoking racial theories of Slav inferiority and propounding 'scientific' conclusions that, for instance, the Polish language was 'not a cultural medium'. It evoked a powerful response throughout Germany and was backed up in ruling circles. When visiting Marienburg Kaiser Wilhelm II called on the spirit of the dead Teutonic Knights to 'join the fight against Polish impudence and Sarmatian effrontery'.

The whole panoply of cultural, economic and political repression was once more brought to bear against the Poles. Government investment and officials poured into Posnania – the province had more of both than any other in the Reich. Officials and policemen who agreed to retire in Posnania were given higher pensions. The Colonisation Commission bought up tracts of land and gave them to German colonists. In 1898 a series of special laws turned the Poles into second-class citizens. As the pressure mounted, the Poles grew increasingly efficient and inventive.

When it became illegal for them to buy land they set up co-operatives and, in 1897, a Land Purchase Bank, which bought the land and leased it to Polish farmers. When a law of 1904 forbade Poles to build houses on their land the peasant Drzymała started a *cause célèbre* by moving in a carvan, generating much unfavourable publicity in Europe for the German government. It was a tribute to the ingenious response of the Polish peasants to any measure that the government was finally obliged in 1908 to pass a stark expropriation law permitting compulsory purchase of Polish lands by Germans.

What industry there had been in Posnania had all been in German hands, but in the 1870s the Poles began to take over. Hipolit Cegielski started a factory making agricultural machinery, then founded sugar-refineries, and eventually built up a huge industrial complex in Poznań. Others followed suit. The need to help the Polish farmer impelled Poles into the cattle and grain markets, to cut out German and Jewish middlemen. Competition reached such a pitch that in the first decade of the century the Poles began to boycott German-owned businesses and shops, insisting on always 'buying Polish'. Although the draconian legislation continued, the battle for the province was largely won by then. The German-speaking population of Poznań fell between 1860 and 1890 from 41 to 34 per cent and in Danzig (Gdańsk) from 75 to 72 per cent. In rural areas the drop was much sharper. Far from smothering the Polish element, the German tactics had hardened it. Nowhere was this more apparent than in areas where Polish nationalism had been dormant until it was awakened by government intervention. The attempt to underline the 'unpolishness' of the Kashubians (a distinctive people of the Pomeranian seaboard) and the Mazurians (the natives of the southern part of East Prussia) was a fiasco, and in the 1890s both areas sent Polish deputies to the Reichstag. In 1903 Upper Silesia, which had been cut off from the Polish state since the fourteenth century, returned a Pole, Wojciech Korfanty, to the Reichstag.

The Austrians had a better chance of dealing in a satisfactory way with their Polish acquisitions. Austria was the only Catholic Power of the three and culturally it was the least unsympathetic. Yet the partitions coincided with the reforms of Joseph II and these went against the grain of Polish political and social principles. Swarms of officials regulated every aspect of life with a bureaucratic rigidity which offended the local population. Reforms in peasant–landlord relations hardly improved the status of the peasant and managed to bind both parties in a complicated system of fiscal and legal obligations which soured relations between them.

Austria saw Galicia as a pool of manpower for its armies and a source of agricultural produce for the Empire, and discouraged attempts at developing the area economically. The province was heavily taxed. A huge

Habsburg bureaucracy hampered the functioning of the representative Assembly set up in Lwów (now Lemberg) in accordance with the Congress of Vienna's resolutions, and aggravated the antagonism between the Poles and the Ruthenes and Jews, who between them made up about half of the population of 3.5 million.

In the 1830s Leon Sapieha founded a Land Credit Society, a Savings Bank and a Technical Academy, but when at his instigation the Lemberg Assembly asked Vienna for permission to study reform of manor–cottage relations, it met with flat refusal. Metternich was not going to allow any co-operation between the intelligentsia and the peasants. Austrian policy was revealed in all its cunning in 1846, when the Governor of Galicia, Count Stadion, incited the peasants against the landlords. In 1848 he granted personal freedom and the possession of land to the peasants, and at the same time began to foster a Ruthene national movement in eastern Galicia to undermine Polish influence there.

Martial law was imposed in 1848 and remained in force until 1854. The appointment of a Polish governor, Agenor Gołuchowski, was little more than a piece of window-dressing, since he was a loyalist trusted by the emperor. Things began to change in 1859. Austrian defeats in Italy signalled the beginning of a protracted crisis which would transform the structure of the Habsburg state. Taking advantage of the situation, the Poles carried out reforms and by 1864 they had established a *de facto* autonomy, with their own Seym, a Polish viceroy to represent the emperor, and the right to send deputies to the Reichsrat in Vienna. Polish became the official language, and education within the province was left in the hands of the Lemberg Seym.

For the next fifty years the Poles of Galicia were allowed to rule themselves with remarkable freedom. They also supplied more than their fair share of ministers and even prime ministers – Alfred Potocki, Kazimierz Badeni, Agenor Gołuchowski junior, Julian Dunajewski and others – to the Vienna cabinet. The wealthy szlachta of Galicia were supported by an influential conservative intelligentsia which believed in a minimalist approach. They managed to keep more radical elements under control and worked within the bounds imposed, concentrating their patriotism on areas such as education. Materially, Galicia was the most backward of the Polish lands. Great estates continued to operate on traditional lines, while tiny farms barely supported large peasant families. This caused unrest and the foundation of a Peasant Party, which brought about a major strike of farm workers in 1902. It also caused waves of emigration to the United States, which eased conditions in the villages (the money sent back by the emigrants in the early 1900s has been calculated as 50 million dollars per annum). The establishment of industries was hampered by competition from the Empire's well-established industrial province of Bohemia. The only exceptions were coalmining and oil-drilling. Oil was struck at Borysław in 1850 and by 1910 Galicia was the largest single producer in the world, with five per cent of the world market.

Russia's Polish problem was more extensive and more crucial to its own internal affairs than that of either of the other two Powers, and it offered a wider range of solutions. In the event, it was bungled hopelessly. It turned into a major internal ulcer, and soured relations between Russia and the Western Powers. There were two basic options. One was to incorporate all the Polish lands into the Empire outright. The other was to leave them as a semi-autonomous unit which could be kept loyal by the promise that at some stage in the future a war against Prussia or Austria would lead to the reconquest of Posnania and Galicia, culminating in the reunification of Poland.

Russia tried both of these alternately and as a result its policy over the century between 1815 and 1914 was often incoherent. Between 1815 and 1830, and to a lesser extent between 1855 and 1863, Russia delegated the administration of Poland to the Poles themselves. In both cases what it gave with the right hand it took away with the left; it gave legal rights and balked when these were invoked. For the rest of the century, it ruled the area directly, with varying degrees of harshness. The lands of the Commonwealth taken by Russia were originally divided up into two categories: the large strip of Lithuanian, Byelorussian and Ukrainian lands were incorporated into Russia as the Western Gubernias, while the rest, the Kingdom of Poland, was treated as a separate administrative and political entity. There were moments when the Western Gubernias were shunted closer to the Kingdom administratively, suggesting a restoration of the old unity, and others when the Kingdom itself was absorbed more intensively into the Russian Empire. This lack of consistency served Russian long-term interests poorly. Throughout the eighteenth and nineteenth centuries the majority of Poles were prepared to face up to reality and accept some measure of hegemony. Russia's inability to appreciate this and to build constructively on it has been one of her greatest historic failures.

The traditional view of what happened to Polish society during the years of captivity defines four principal categories of reaction: collaboration, passivity, resistance and emigration. These are often used as a guide according to which Polish society can be broken down into groups. The collaborators are the conservative and wealthy who make compromises in order to continue enjoying a reasonable life: the passive are those who are not prepared to sully their hands with collaboration yet do not believe in resistance, the revolutionaries are the heroes who refuse to abide by compromise, and the émigrés are those who have chosen exile or had it forced upon them. This falls short of any serious understanding of the situation and how it affected

society. Only for very few was there ever a choice between abject collaboration on the one hand and unbending resistance on the other. The occupying
powers did not present this kind of dramatic choice unless it was unavoid-
able. They had subtler ways of putting pressure on people.

What preoccupied most Poles was how best to maintain the Polish way of
life and cultural aspirations within the limited means reality had imposed,
in order to ensure their survival until the situation changed for the better. A
penniless, tempestuous and radical young man might believe that the only
way of upholding Polish values was by revolution and struggle, however
hopeless. A landowner who realised that both for him and for the thousands
of peasants who lived on his estates war was the greatest calamity, might
decide that the sensible thing to do was to conciliate the occupying power
and extract as many concessions as possible. Between these extremes there
was a whole scale of intermediate positions. Few held to one or other of these
for long. The inconsistency of Russian policy produced a cyclical trend of
reaction, as did the ultimate hopelessness of either course. Those who
sought accommodation would eventually come up against a brick wall,
whereupon they would either rebel or emigrate. Those who fought or
emigrated often came to see the futility of their actions and returned to
passive coexistence or even collaboration. Some of the most violent
revolutionaries became advocates of loyalism, and vice-versa.

The view of Russians and Poles hating each other is a cliché which ignores
the facts. Contacts between the Commonwealth and Muscovy were beset by
mutual suspicion from the earliest times. Contacts between Poles and
Russians were a different matter. They fought hard and bitterly on many
occasions, but while the Germanic occupant in Galicia or Posnania was
always an alien through and through, there was considerable cordiality
between Poles and Russians whenever hostilities ceased. One of the most
nobly sympathetic characters in Polish nineteenth-century literature is the
Russian major in Słowacki's *Fantazy*. From the Polish officers mixed up with
the Russian Decembrists right down to the common cause made by Polish
and Russian social revolutionaries in the 1880s and 1890s, there was a base
of generous fellow-feeling and kinship. The act of dethronement of Nicholas
by the Seym in 1831 was preceded by a ceremony in honour of the
Decembrists, and accompanied by protestations in the press to the effect
that 'We love the Russian people'.

This love was never allowed to develop. Whenever Russian armies
marched in, the Poles would veer towards the attitude that the Russians
were hopeless primitives incapable of grasping the concept of civilisation
and too brutish to allow others to enjoy it, an attitude in which contempt and
even pity outweighed hatred or fear. The Russians would retreat into their
traditional view of the Poles. Any review of Polish characters in Russian
literature will reveal a gallery of arrogant rogues, idlers, drunkards and

cowards. The Russians never understood the Polish preoccupation with civil liberty and constitutional legality. They tended to view a constitution as a totem to be admired rather than as a mechanism to be used. Throughout the nineteenth century the inhabitants of the Kingdom enjoyed greater personal rights than those of the Empire, yet the Poles always seemed to be whingeing about persecutions which appeared trifling to the average Russian. There was a residual feeling that the Poles were spoilt and cantankerous. To the Russian who knew nothing of Nicholas's refusal to negotiate, the 1830 rising was an act of unwarranted aggressiveness. In 1863 the Anglo-French denunciations of Russian behaviour produced an outbreak of rampant chauvinism and fury against the Poles for having impugned Russia's honour. The fact that Poles had swaggered about Moscow in 1610 and 1812, and that Polish pretensions, which included the 1772 frontiers, struck at the very heart of the Russian state's modern greatness, did little to assuage these insecurities. Any Tsar who offered too many concessions to the Poles could expect to meet with grumbling at home, as Alexander I discovered. While the Polish poets wrote odes to the memory of the Russian Decembrists, Pushkin answered Mickiewicz's *Digressia*, a poem likening Russia to a frozen prison, with *The Bronze Horseman*, and sprang to the defence of his country during the 1830 Insurrection. In 1863 Alexander Herzen lost half his readership overnight when he published a pro-Polish article in his journal *Kolokol*.

The effect of Russian attitudes on life in the Polish lands depended on the political ramifications of a given field of human activity. In the purely economic area there was little interference and no exploitation. If anything, the Kingdom did rather well out of the fact that it was the most industrially advanced component of the Empire.

Economic activity began to flourish when the political situation stabilised in 1815. The next fifteen years saw something of an economic miracle achieved in this hitherto predominantly agricultural country. In 1816 Stanisław Staszic was appointed Director of the Department of Industry, a post which he held for the next eight years. He encouraged the development of mining and reactivated the production of steel in the Old Polish Basin around Kielce. He built the first zinc mills and the first steel rolling mill, and organised a Mining Corps run on semi-military lines with a remarkable system of compensation and pensions. The production of iron, copper and zinc increased. Coalmining, which began to use steam-power for pumping, doubled its output between 1824 and 1836. The 1830s and 1840s saw continued development in spite of political problems and a new smelting centre was developed in the Dąbrowa Basin, whose Huta Bankowa was one of the largest steelworks in the world.

The architect of Poland's economic recovery was Prince Franciszek Ksawery Drucki-Lubecki, one of the founders of the Congress Kingdom, a man who believed firmly in making the best of the situation and gained the confidence of the Tsar. In 1821 he took over the Treasury, which became the leading entrepreneur. He sought to build up Poland's economic power in such a way as to make it industrially self-sufficient. An unpopular figure among the Romantics, Lubecki was clear in his own mind about how the Polish cause could be best served. His efforts were cut short by the 1830 Insurrection, but some of his creations, such as the Bank Polski established in 1838, carried on his programme. He brought new ideas to the Polish economic scene, including direct intervention, credit and protection. In 1825 he set up the Land Credit Society, which enabled private estates to clear debts and fund improvements or new ventures. These included sheep-rearing, distilling and the production of sugar-beet which, with the starting of the first sugar refinary in 1826, opened an important new avenue of agricultural industry.

The most spectacular product of Lubecki's policies was the Polish textile industry. In 1821 the government assisted the establishment of a weaving centre in the village of Łódź. By 1830 Łódź had over 4,000 inhabitants and a number of steam-powered spinning-machines. The production of wool tripled between 1823 and 1829, and the production of cotton quintupled between 1825 and 1830. Łódź exported to Russia and even China, and by 1845, when it was linked by rail to Warsaw, it had become the principal supplier of the Russian market. By then Łódź had 20,000 inhabitants, in spite of new textile centres at Białystok and Żyrardów, started in 1833. While the years following the 1863 Insurrection appear as a period of stagnation, this is not evident from the industrial statistics. Between 1865 and 1879 the number of power-looms in Łódź increased twenty times. The value of production of cotton rose from five million rubles in 1869 to 25 million in 1889. By 1900 Łódź had 300,000 inhabitants and over 1,000 factories.

Poland's industrial revolution was unspectacular by European standards, and in 1900 nearly 70 per cent of the population still lived in the country. Yet the pace was breathtaking. The number of steam engines in use increased twenty-five times between 1853 and 1888. The value of the Kingdom's overall industrial production increased by over six times between 1864 and 1885. Centres like Łódź, Warsaw (which reached over half a million inhabitants in the 1880s) and the Dąbrowa Basin employed a workforce which doubled over the twenty years after 1860 to some 150,000. Fortunes were made and lost in the speculative ventures to which the boom gave rise. Foreign capital, often brought in by entrepreneurs who came to settle, flooded in from France, Germany, England, Belgium and Italy, accounting for up to 40 per cent of the entire industrial capital. A new class of Polish tycoons sprang up, mostly from the Jewish population of the cities. Families like the Kronenbergs, Rotwands, Wawelbergs and

129 A peasant family from southern Mazovia, photographed by Karol Beyer in the 1850s, and **130** two Ruthene peasants from Prince Czartoryski's estate at Sieniawa in Galicia, photographed in 1893. Even taking into account the fact that the Mazovian peasants are in their Sunday attire and the Ruthenes in working clothes, the economic and cultural differences are glaring, particularly remembering the forty years between the pictures.

131 Prince Władysław Czartoryski, photographed in Kraków in 1880, in traditional Sarmatian formal wear.

The physical need to survive and prosper turned out to be just as strong a motor as the urge for freedom when the smoke of the risings was blown away.

132   The weaving-hall of Karl Schleiber's cotton-mill in Łódź, which by the 1880s had become one of the three greatest centres of textile production in the world, along with Manchester and Lille.

133   An early steam-plough, brought in to reinforce the economic struggle against the German settlers in Poznania; photographed in the 1890s

Epsteins amassed wealth, became assimilated into Polish society and married into the aristocracy.

Poland achieved such progress both because of and in spite of Russian policies. Between 1819 and 1822 the Kingdom was part of the same customs area as Russia. In 1831 a tariff barrier was imposed between the two states. These tariffs were imposed and lifted several times, often for political reasons, creating enormous problems for Polish industry. In the 1870s Russia switched to protectionist policies, within which the Kingdom was included, and this created the conditions for the Polish boom of the next decades. Three-quarters of the cotton produced in Łódź in the 1880s was exported to Russia. The metallurgical industry of Warsaw and the Old Polish Basin increased its output by over thirty times in the last quarter of the century, largely as a result of the expansion of railways in the Russian Empire. The Lilpop railcar and rail factory in Warsaw was the largest in the whole Empire and grew fat on the spread of the Russian network. By the 1890s Russia accounted for 90 per cent of Poland's trade, a huge captive market. In the late 1890s Russia began her own industrial revolution, which meant that engineers and technicians trained in Poland found new scope for their skills. Vast numbers of these men invaded the Empire to build bridges, lay tracks and manage mines and factories from the Urals to Manchuria. On the industrial level, the colonial relationship was reversed and favoured the Poles rather than the Russians.

This was not so in agriculture, which was subject to political considerations, as it was the economic base of the potentially rebellious szlachta. It also involved the peasant question, which had a direct bearing on the ability of the Poles to mobilise the masses in support of their cause. The manner in which peasant emancipation was introduced in 1864 was almost entirely shaped by the inherent political undertones. The decree was full of phrases about 'the lords who have oppressed you', which were supposed to give the peasants the impression that their 'little father the Tsar' was liberating them from the Polish nobles. The idea was to drive a wedge between the szlachta and the peasant, and to ruin the minor szlachta, who were the most nationalist element in the country. On the other hand, the wealthier szlachta constituted a conservative element on which the Tsarist authorities hoped to build support.

There were five areas which the decree tackled: the abolition of labour-rents; the commutation of money-rents into freehold possession of land; the distribution of land to landless peasants; the questions of grazing and wood-gathering rights on manorial land; and finally the setting up of peasant councils under Tsarist administration which would put an end to landowners' influence over village affairs. The consequences were not long in making themselves felt. The landless peasants were given too little land to survive on. The compensation to the landlords was paid out not in cash as in Russia, but in negotiable bonds which immediately plummeted in value.

Thousands of small landowners had to sell up and move to the towns. Large estates were hardly affected. Their owners had mostly switched to money-rents long before, they had capital reserves to employ farmhands and bribe local officials, and they could afford to fight in the courts over pastures and grazing rights. The richer peasants bought out the hitherto landless who had been given plots too small to survive on. While land in peasant ownership increased by nearly 10 per cent in the next twenty-five years, the number of landless peasants increased by 400 per cent during the same period. The doubling of the population in the second half of the century only aggravated the land hunger.

The peasants were not grateful to the Tsar for what they had received. The landless ones had hoped for larger holdings. The richer ones felt they had improved their position by their own efforts. They resented the new system of commune administration which brought them into contact with Tsarist bureaucracy. The intended confrontation between village and manor never materialised. The economic ruin of thousands of szlachta families did not fulfil Russian intentions. Those who remained in the country assimilated with the richer yeoman-peasants, strengthening defiance in the villages. Those who drifted to the cities had an even more profound effect. They brought nationalism and Sarmatian culture into the middle-classes into which they married. As a result, no distinctly middle-class culture evolved in Poland, where shopkeepers and bank-clerks continued to affect the manners and outlook of the szlachta of Sobieski's time.

The partitions had pulled the Polish province of the Church to pieces. Six dioceses found themselves in Austrian Poland, under the primacy of the Metropolitan of Lwów. Warmia (Ermeland) and Wrocław (Breslau) were directly affiliated to Rome. The rest of the dioceses incorporated into Prussia were placed under the administration of the Protestant Church of Prussia. The dioceses of the Western Gubernias were subordinated to the Metropolitan of Mogilev, while those of the Kingdom were placed under the newly-created Archbishopric of Warsaw. After 1830 there was not even a nominal Primate. The Papacy was entangled in the European diplomatic web in an effort to preserve its diminishing temporal status and did nothing to support the Polish cause, even condemning the uprisings of 1794 and 1830. All three Powers took measures against the Polish hierarchy. The Josephine reforms in Austria subjected it to the state. Prussia gradually dissolved Church property in the course of the century and took over the appointment of bishops. But even the *Kulturkampf* stopped short of the kind of measures adopted by Russia.

In 1801 the Polish Church was subjected to a secular administrative body in St Petersburg. After 1831 half of the convents and monasteries were closed down. After 1864 all Church property was confiscated and virtually all monastic orders disbanded. The clergy were forbidden to write to Rome on pain of immediate deportation to Siberia. Seminaries and other Church institutions were placed under police inspectorate, and all sermons had to be passed by the censorship. In 1870 the government decreed that the Catholic liturgy was henceforth to be said in Russian. Recalcitrant priests were flogged or deported and peasants were terrorised by the police, but there was such determined resistance that the authorities relented and in 1882 signed a Concordat with Rome, which brought some improvement.

Russian policy towards the Uniates was one of extermination. In 1773, just after Catherine the Great had taken over a large part of the Commonwealth in the name of religious toleration, troops were sent into the villages to 'convert' Uniates to the Orthodox Faith. The persecution abated after the death of Catherine, but Nicholas took up the crusade for Orthodoxy with a vengeance. Between 1826 and 1838 a huge operation was mounted which, as one historian has pointed out, was the spiritual ancestor of the Stalinist purges. Uniate peasants were ordered to abjure their faith and children were mutilated and butchered before their mothers as an inducement. Where even this failed to sway the devout peasants, there were massacres and deportations. A further such campaign was carried out in the 1870s. These crusades failed to stamp out the Uniates, who would hold their services in woods or across the cordon in Galicia. Instead of inspiring loyalty to St Petersburg, it made them look to Poland and to Austria as havens of toleration, and contributed to the rise of Ukrainian nationalism.

The Polish peasants were particularly incensed by attacks on the Catholic faith, with which they associated themselves even more than with the nation. Throughout the nineteenth century the village priest was the peasant's closest adviser and staunchest support in the struggle against oppression and injustice. The peasants resented state interference no less in education, by which they set great store. The educational system in the Western Gubernias had been Russianised after 1831. After 1864 a set of new edicts forbade the use of Polish in any printed form, even on shop-fronts and hoardings, while written Polish was forbidden in any official correspondence. At one stage it even became illegal to give Polish Christian names at baptism. Legislation in the Kingdom was less draconian. Nevertheless, in 1869 the Warsaw Main School which had replaced Warsaw University after 1830 was shut down and in turn replaced by a Russian University. In 1885 Russian was substituted for Polish as the teaching language, even in elementary schools. Children were not allowed to address each other in anything but Russian within the precincts of the school.

Polish culture and the Polish way of life were under continuous threat of extirpation. With the ranks of the intelligentsia thinned by successive risings, repressions and waves of emigration, a nation of which at least four-fifths were peasants seemed in dire peril of losing all but its folk-dances and superstitions. Yet the combined onslaught of Russia and Prussia on Polish nationality had unexpected results. The fifty years between the end of the 1863 Insurrection and the outbreak of the Great War saw a resurgence of intellectual activity all over partitioned Poland.

As the last of the Romantics were passing into legend on the barricades of the Paris Commune in 1871, the mood of Poland swung round. This reaction was led by a group of historians at the Jagiellon University, with their publication in 1869 of *Stańczyk's Portfolio*. The figure of Stańczyk, the supposedly wise and cynical jester of Zygmunt Augustus, was an emblem of their realistic and self-critical view. They suggested that the Common-wealth's downfall was not a martyrdom of the innocent, but the inevitable collapse of a state which had ceased to function because of the blindness of its citizens and the inefficiency of its political institutions. They saw the tradition of insurrection in the same light. They pointed out in historical terms what most of Polish society was coming to realise anyway – that the succession of uprisings had been costly failures which had destroyed the best elements in the nation and provoked greater repression.

The Galician intelligentsia had always favoured realistic accommoda-tion and a minimalist policy of concessions in return for loyalty. But it would be wrong to see the swing in Polish attitudes in terms of the 'collaborators' having triumphed in their argument with the 'insurgents' merely because these had been defeated in 1863. Many of the 'insurgents' had themselves become convinced of the pointlessness of their policy. The brand of minimalism known as 'organic work' which had been practised in Posnania for the last thirty years could be seen to have produced results. This was based on a general effort by all to improve themselves and their work in order to stand up to the 'superior' Germans. Encouraged by the clergy and the intelligentsia, the inhabitants of Posnania had been per-suaded to keep their houses cleaner, tend their gardens better, work harder, bake better bread and to educate themselves and their children. It was a curious application of the Protestant ethic in the fight against the German Protestants, and its consequences were a slow but real economic and social victory over them.

It was not until the latter part of the century that the idea of organic progress through mass self-improvement achieved the status of theory. The works of Auguste Comte, John Stuart Mill and Charles Darwin appeared to hold special relevance to the Polish problem. Material concepts of progress born of the industrial revolution in England and France exerted a profound fascination on Polish intellectuals as they gazed at the primitive peasantry of Galicia operating the three-field system as they had done in the thirteenth century. The Romantic concept of the nation as spirit or divine body had given way to the concept of the nation as an organism. The nebulous dreams of the Romantics' New Jerusalem were superseded by 'scientific' visions of an earthly paradise.

The high priest of this Positivist Movement (as it became known) was Aleksander Świętochowski, fittingly not a poet but a journalist. Throughout the 1880s he edited the Warsaw weekly *Prawda*, one of a range of periodicals catering to every social and professional group, which spawned a horde of essayists and publicists who became a feature of Polish intellectual life. Świętochowski criticised old habits of thought, questioned sacred values, and dwelt on material aspects of everyday life. The ingredients of the new literature were to be, according to the writer Eliza Orzeszkowa, 'a burgher, a banker, a factory-owner, a merchant, tails and top hats, machines, surgeons' instruments, locomotives'. Next to the periodical, the principal pulpit for these views was the stage.

The dramatic works of Mickiewicz, Słowacki and Krasiński were not written for the stage, since there had been no theatre in which they could be performed. As they were taken up with ethical or political argument and relied heavily on symbolism, they took a fantastical, disembodied form unique in European drama, challenging, and sometimes impossible, to stage. The new theatres which did spring up in the 1860s, in Poznań, Lwów, Kraków, and later Warsaw, encouraged a more realistic dramatic tradition. This had been kept going throughout the Romantic period by Aleksander Fredro (1793–1876), an aristocrat who had served as aide-de-camp to Napoleon before settling down to the life of a country gentleman in Galicia. His plays are direct descendants of Polish eighteenth-century theatre, written in elegant and expressive verse. All are comedies set in the world of the country szlachta, but they often touch on serious issues, however lightly. By the 1850s realist drama attracted other authors, including Józef Korzeniowski and his namesake Apollo Korzeniowski, a minor poet noted more for his political activity as one of the 'Red' leaders in 1863, but most of all for having sired a boy who was to became famous as the English novelist Joseph Conrad. The importance of the theatre as a forum for expression, however veiled, grew with increasing cultural persecution in the second half of the century.

If the periodical and the stage were used to propound the Positivist creed, it was the novel and the short story that actually formulated it. The novel form never developed in the eighteenth century and the first Romantic novel in Poland was the dismal, if touching, *Malwina* (1816) by Princess Maria of Württemberg, a sister of Adam Czartoryski. This was followed by a spate of historical novels inspired by Scott. The most interesting is by Michał Czajkowski, who fought in 1831 and subsequently emigrated to Turkey, where he converted to Islam. He commanded a division against the Russians in the Crimean War but later returned and settled in Volhynia (apparently on the best of terms with Alexander II who stood

godfather to his child) before ending his life by shooting himself. His novel
Wernyhora (1838) created a prophetic Cossack bard who has became a stock
figure in Polish thought. A more talented writer, and one who was to
contribute five hundred volumes of prose to Polish literature, was Józef
Ignacy Kraszewski (1812–87). He started writing in the 1840s, covering
subjects as varied as Nero's Rome and pre-Piast Poland, Napoleonic times
and contemporary events. He also wrote several novels on peasant life,
which are among his best.

The first to broach subjects which had a bearing on contemporary
Poland was Józef Korzeniowski, sometimes referred to as the Polish Balzac
because of his acute social observation. *The Speculator* (1848) could be
labelled as the first attempt at a psychological novel in Polish literature.
But it was Eliza Orzeszkowa (1841–1910) who developed the novel as an
instrument of social investigation and ethical polemic. She was a spirited
lady from Lithuania who took an active part in the 1863 Insurrection
before settling down to a life of writing. An ardent feminist, she was also
concerned with breaking down the barriers of social constraint in the
interests of other groups caught in the trap of poverty or prejudice, most
notably the Jews. Her best novel, *On the Niemen* (1888), which is set among
the poorest type of landed szlachta whose extended families lived lives
indistinguishable from those of the wealthier peasantry, is her most
obviously 'Positivist', stressing as it does the ennobling qualities of a life of
hard work close to the land.

Another woman, Gabriela Zapolska (1857–1921), wrote novels and
plays which dwelt more specifically on the exploitation of women by
society. Her most famous play, *The Morality of Mrs Dulska*, is a fierce
indictment of the hypocrisy and double standards surrounding the sexuality and treatment of women. The frequent imprisonment or exile of the
menfolk in a family left women in positions of great responsibility for its
survival, and their participation in conspiratorial and even guerilla activity tended to place them on an equal footing with men. As a result, they
were voicing views and demands on the subject of sexual equality and
freedom that were not heard in England or France until after the First
World War. Not all were as truculent as Zapolska. The most talented
woman writer of the period was Maria Konopnicka (1842–1910), a
life-long friend of Eliza Orzeszkowa, who separated from her husband
after ten years of marriage and moved to Warsaw. She began writing in a
women's journal in the late 1870s, published three collections of poems in
the 1880s and then her first volume of short stories. She was concerned
with eternal conflicts, with suffering and injustice, but in time she grew
more belligerent and her nationalism came to the fore. Typical of this late
period was the long poem *Mr Balcer in Brazil*, which dealt with the fate of
peasant emigrants to the new world.

Another who was concerned with the fate of the emigrants – to the extent of travelling to the United States himself – was Henryk Sienkiewicz (1846–1916). Ostensibly a Positivist dedicated to the diagnosis and cure of social ills, Sienkiewicz wrote stories which explored the predicament of the less fortunate with a lightness of touch and a sense of humour that assured him of great popularity. He also displayed a Romantic nationalism not entirely in keeping with the current ideology. He indulged this by writing a trilogy – *With Fire and Sword*, *The Deluge* and *Pan Wołodyjowski* – an historical adventure covering the Cossack Mutiny, the Swedish Wars, and the Turkish War of the mid-seventeenth century. With its brisk, enthralling narrative, its lack of unnecessary characterisation, and its masterful use of historical atmosphere, this work is redolent of Alexandre Dumas, and it was written to comfort and to boost the morale of the Poles. In this it was eminently, even alarmingly, successful. The imagery of the past it conjures up is so powerful, the values which Sienkiewicz saw in the Commonwealth are made so straightforward, and the sense of Christian mission implicit in the heroism and sufferings of the protagonists are stated with such convincing candour, that the book had a great influence on how the Poles of the next generations looked at themselves and their national destiny. It is an updated version of the *Antemurale* myth, and it has held more Poles spellbound in this century than the original did in the seventeenth. In the late 1890s Sienkiewicz returned to social problems with works such as *The Połaniecki Family*, but he soon looked into the past again. *Quo Vadis*, an international publishing success which won him the Nobel Prize, was followed by *The Knights of the Teutonic Order* (1900). This was written against the background of the anti-Polish onslaught in Posnania, and as a result it is the proto-Bismarckian (even proto-Nazi) aspects of the Order's activities which receive the most profound treatment. Although he was immensely talented, Sienkiewicz had a tendency to subject his creativity to an often naïve set of historical, ethical and political perceptions. Patriotism of this kind does not make good literature. Nor does it make for great music, as an analogy which springs to mind well demonstrates. Stanisław Moniuszko (1819–72) was a fine composer, as anyone who listens to his great E flat major Mass will recognise. Yet the compulsion to write 'national' operas wasted his talent and produced unmemorable music.

The best Polish novelist of the nineteenth century was Aleksander Głowacki (1847–1912), who wrote under the pen-name of Bolesław Prus. He was a member of the minor szlachta, but his penniless father was a functionary and his education was cut short for lack of money. He was wounded during the Insurrection of 1863 and spent some time in prison after it. As a young man he had been fascinated by mathematics and the natural sciences, which he had studied before being obliged to earn his living, as a contributor of humorous pieces to periodicals. His first attempts at serious writing displayed an almost analytical gift of observation of cause and effect. His earlier work is typically Positivist in its faith that progress can cure, but with time a degree of scepticism and even fatalism crept into his writing, greatly enhancing its literary value.

In 1885 Prus published *The Outpost*, a novel about a peasant who refuses through thick and thin to sell his patch of land to the German colonists who are gradually taking over his Posnanian village. The peasant, Slimak, is in fact an utterly unheroic character whose obstinacy is the result of unthinking superstition and pig-headedness; it is therefore his faults rather than any supposed virtues, patriotic or otherwise, that carry him through to victory. This kind of realism raised Prus above the subjective crypto-political programming which cramped and often reduced other writers of the time. The same is true of his next novel, *The Doll* (1890), set in Warsaw. The hero, Wokulski, is a new man, a man of deep experience, a positive capitalist who dreams of using his immense fortune in the service of science and progress, but eventually squanders it on wooing an insipid high-born young lady. Again Prus seems to mock believers in the new dawn of progress. Despite his virtues and intelligence, Wokulski can be lured away by frivolity from the high ideals he has set himself. Both Wokulski and his old friend Rzecki, a typical minor nobleman brought up on the Romantic tradition, though ostensibly opposites, are two sides of the same character, endlessly swinging between one type of hope and another. They represent the story, in microcosm, of the Polish intelligentsia during the nineteenth century. The young of the 1880s would be snapped at by their parents whenever they enquired wistfully about the heroics of 1863, and at the same time they would be taken on a pilgrimage to some forest to weep over a tussock which was the grave of an insurgent.

The themes of Prus's novels are typical of the Positivist movement, but the conclusions he arrived at were not in keeping with its original optimism. He was too wise a man and too honest an artist not to have perceived its shortcomings. Positivism and the programme of organic work which accompanied it had produced impressive results. Everything from hygiene to education had been affected. People who had brains were encouraged to use them to pursue specific goals rather than waste them on planning hopeless risings. It is largely thanks to this that Poland did not disappear from the intellectual map of Europe along with its frontiers. Compared with other European nations, the Poles contributed little to the scientific advances of the nineteenth century. Ignacy Łukasiewicz succeeded in distilling crude oil in Galicia and built the first kerosene lamp in 1853; Zygmunt Wróblewski and Karol Olszewski of the Jagiellon University were the first to achieve liquefaction of oxygen; in 1898 Maria Skłodowska-Curie discovered Polonium and went on to pioneer research into radiation; the organic chemist Jakub Natanson, the biochemist

Marceli Nencki and a number of others added in various ways to the sum of human knowledge. At least the Poles could be seen to be indulging in something other than conspiracy.

The shortcomings of Positivism lay not here but in its failure to provide a panacea. Whatever their political views, people still needed to be given hope and solace. For a brief period the implied promise of organic regeneration had suggested such hope, but the limited scope of the theory soon became apparent, and Poles began to look elsewhere for spiritual sustenance. The problem was not a new one. In the 1840s when the increasingly mystical utterings of the Romantics had begun to leave readers behind there was a surge in the popularity of several poets whose message was less frightening, and relief was found in the bucolic lyricism of Władysław Syrokomla, the aesthetic folklore of Teofil Lenartowicz and the robust patriotism of Wincenty Pol.

Painting also played an important part in this respect. When disaster overtook the Commonwealth, artists began to render not the present but the past, often in idealised form. Horace Vernet's pupil January Suchodolski (1795–1877), Józef Simmler (1823–68) and Juliusz Kossak (1824–99) created a tradition of patriotic genre painting – lancers on picket duty, Husaria on the march, or similar scenes which implied the glories of the past. After the death of the great Romantic poets, this function of painting took on extra significance. It was indulged with greater abandon by artists such as Artur Grottger (1837–67), who covered the entire 1863 Insurrection in a series of symbolic scenes, and Jan Matejko (1838–93), a fine painter best known for monumental canvases of great moments in Polish history. Even more than literature, the painting of this period created a gallery of images which embalmed for all time the myths and heroes of a bygone age. King Bolesław entering Kiev; Bathory taking the surrender of Pskov; Sobieski at Vienna; Kościuszko at Racławice – these are images in the mind of every Polish schoolboy. The depiction of defeated heroes such as Poniatowski and Kościuszko was not avoided. The stress was on the enduring and transcending nobility of their actions at the moment of failure, to suggest that failure itself was not important.

The greatest painter of the first half of the century was Piotr Michałowski (1800–55), a wealthy nobleman who treated paintings as a dilletante pursuit. Having completed scientific studies, he became, under Lubecki, head of the Department of Mines and Foundries in the Congress Kingdom and of arms-production during the 1830 Insurrection. As an émigré in Paris he became a pupil of Charlet. He was profoundly influenced by the works of Géricault and emulated them with his curious mixture of the real and the symbolic, producing pictures which were both study and icon. He made use of historical subjects, particularly from the Napoleonic wars, and into these he injected a sense of power and an impressionism that make them almost emblematic. He also displayed a realist interest in prosaic subjects, and his studies of peasants and of Jews are among his most magnificent works.

The depiction of the lower classes, not as figures in a landscape but as social studies, not for the picturesqueness of their rags but for their implications, was a reflection of Positivist interest in such matters, but the painters did not go the same way as the writers. There were those like the portrait-painter Henryk Rodakowski (1823–94) and the Rome-based academic painter Henryk Siemiradzki (1843–1902), who concentrated on technical mastery rather than national or political programmes. The majority of painters, however, continued to fulfil the function of the eye through which national dreams could be gazed on. This is the more surprising as most of them were brought into the orbit of the Munich School through their studies, and this tended to discourage both the Romantic and the political undertones.

Józef Brandt (1841–1915), the leading Pole of the Munich School, was a fine naturalist painter who returned again and again to historical subjects and military-patriotic genre painting. Józef Chełmoński (1849–1914) dwelt on a nostalgic vision of Polish rural life – a sort of *sielanka* in pictures. Alfred Wierusz-Kowalski (1849–1915) was more marked by the taste of the Munich School, yet his devotion to the countryside of the Ukraine and its lore, in which he seems to search for some kind of essence of old-Polish ways, is a tendency inherited from the Romantic poets. This compulsive return to the eternal theme haunting the Polish subconscious is well illustrated by the finest painters of the period, the Gierymski brothers. Maksymilian Gierymski (1846–74) was an exceptional naturalist painter, and while he frequently tried to get away from what might be called the Polish complex by painting neutral and sometimes sugary genre subjects, he was ineluctably drawn into creating some of the most mysteriously evocative of all Polish patriotic art with his scenes from the 1863 Insurrection. His brother Aleksander Gierymski (1850–1901) was a realist and later the first Polish painter to move towards Impressionism. He spent most of his active life abroad, and much of his subject-matter and its treatment are indistinguishable from the mainstream of contemporary European art. Yet his studies of praying Jews or peasant women are suffused with a nostalgia full of national implications.

Painting seemed to be saying what literature either could or would not. It was like a safety-valve through which the repressed Romantic nationalist aspirations of the Positivist generation could be relieved. Consciously, Polish society had decided to be modern, positive and constructive, to put dreams and hankerings out of its mind. These could not, however, be obliterated, and they survived in the subconscious, surfacing occasionally in the works of writers like Sienkiewicz, and more often in painting. The brutality or at best dreariness of life under Russian, Prussian or Austrian rule denied society any constructive outlet for its energies and aspirations, and they therefore built up into powerful frustrations which always seemed to come full circle and find expression in assertive patriotism.

19

The Making of Modern Poland

A hundred years of suppression had failed to stifle the power of the Polish volcano, and its rumblings grew louder in the last decade of the nineteenth century. By 1900 there were seventeen million Poles in the world, and if the vitality of a society may be gauged by the refusal of its young to be bound by the compromises of their parents, then the generation that came to maturity in the 1890s rates very high. Too young to remember the gallows of 1864, they felt little fear, but they saw little point in heroic acts of defiance. To them it seemed clear that if the mysticism of the Romantics had got Poland nowhere, the Positivist belief in material progress had produced little beyond an aesthetically offensive bourgeois society. Both seemed flawed by their very acceptance of limitations. The new generation rejected the breast-beating attitude to Poland's history taken by the Romantics, it rejected the naïve panacea of the Positivists, and it despised both the docility of the Loyalists and the rashness of the Insurgents. Their own rebelliousness was less blustering and more confident. It was born of the realisation that the vital forces of Polish society had survived a century of partition, and out of a liberation from the complexes and emotional reactions emanating from the psychosis of failure.

The new assertiveness bred forms of political activity which were realistic and modern. But the confusion which inevitably stemmed from trying to break with the past while being emotionally drawn to it littered the political arguments with reworkings of older formulae and reactions to them. The pressures underlying this ideological reshuffle appear most clearly on the cultural scene of the 1890s. The liberation from patterns of thought which had dictated behaviour over the preceding hundred years had an immediate impact on artistic expression, which cast off the restrictive programmes and shifted its attention from promoting the national cause to art for its own sake.

This had the most salutary effect on music, which had not flourished in Poland since the days of Chopin. Even fine composers such as Stanisław Moniuszko (1819–72) and Henryk Wieniawski (1835–80) had been faced with the choice between limiting their creative possibilities by subjecting them to nationalist demands or remaining outside the mainstream of Polish life if they followed their own inspiration. Ignacy Jan Paderewski (1860–1941) continued to court national relevance in his compositions into the early 1900s, with disastrous results such as his grand symphony *Polonia*, but he was by then an exception. In the 1890s Polish music had broken free of such dependence, and a string of composers, including Władysław Żeleński (1837–1921), Mieczysław Karłowicz (1876–1909), Karol Szymanowski (1882–1937) and Ludomir Różycki (1883–1953) opened a new musical tradition which still flourishes today. They did not abandon nationality along with nationalism, nor did they jettison the past in their modernism. The greatest of them, Szymanowski, created a highly personal folkloric idiom in much the same sense as Chopin had done.

Similarly, Polish painters shed the compulsion to produce nationalist iconography, without losing sight of the native land. The Impressionist style was taken up by Władysław Podkowiński (1866–95), Józef Pankiewicz (1886–1940), Jan Stanisławski (1860–1907), Olga Boznańska (1865–1940), and Gauguin's friend Władysław Slewiński (1854–1918). Yet Polish Impressionism did not entirely conform to its French model and retained an element of nostalgic Romanticism. The Viennese Secession and Art Nouveau movements exerted a powerful influence on painters such as Leon Wyczółkowski (1852–1936), Stanisław Wyspiański (1869–1907) and Teodor Axentowicz (1859–1938), but this too was qualified by national traditions. Even the symbolist and surrealist Jacek Malczewski (1854–1929) filled his work with hazy allusions to eternal Polish preoccupations.

The Positivist movement did not make for good poetry any more than it made for good music. The only man who had managed to transcend its bounds was Adam Asnyk, an agronomist and doctor who was a member of the 'Red' government in 1863 before he turned to poetry. In the last decade of the century Polish writers came under the spell of English and French poetry, and passed through a rapid succession of fads, such as aestheticism, symbolism and fascination with poorly understood cultures of the East. But when the froth subsided it revealed a fresh new poetry which took most of its inspiration from native traditions, most notably from the Romantics. The first of the neo-Romantics was Kazimierz Przerwa-Tetmajer (1865–1940), a typical 'decadent', resentful of the materialistic culture which the industrial revolution had spawned. He was distinguished by a fresh appreciation of nature, particularly that of his native Tatra mountains. Another was Jan Kasprowicz (1860–1926), the son of a peasant from Kujavia who managed to complete a higher education at Leipzig before settling in Lwów to write. His early works were concerned with the miseries of peasant life, but in the 1890s he turned to the new aestheticism, passing through symbolist, religious and metaphysical phases before returning to folklore. The best of this generation, and one of the finest Polish poets of the twentieth century, was Bolesław Leśmian (1878–1937). Born into a middle-class Warsaw Jewish family, he went to university in Kiev and lived for a time in Paris before taking up a lawyer's career in his native city. He was a great innovator, coining words and introducing unusual metrical patterns, and his work shows a continuous spiritual progress, a quest for the essence of the world as revealed through anything from nature to sexuality.

The interest in symbol and colour, in folklore, surrealism and mythology, and in the enduring spell of the great Romantics, gave rise to a movement usually referred to as 'Young Poland' which spanned painting and poetry and came together in the theatre. The realistic drama of the Positivists was superseded by experimental theatre which began, for the first time, to stage the disembodied plays of the Romantics, and particularly of Słowacki. It is fitting that the greatest literary figure of this movement, Stanisław Wyspiański (1860–1907), should have been a painter. A remarkable artist whose work is both impressionistic and symbolist, Wyspiański was deeply affected by a visit to Bayreuth. On his return to Kraków he devoted himself to translating poetry into action and combining the aural with the visual, by collaborating on theatrical productions, and eventually writing plays himself.

His literary career is crammed into the last seven years of his life, yet he managed to write dozens of plays, some of them amongst the best in the Polish language. Some were modelled on Greek tragedy, but most were impressionistic dramas in the tradition of Mickiewicz and Słowacki. This is true of his first, and one of his best, *The Wedding*, a study of Polish attitudes and visions of the past and future given form by the characters assembled at a village wedding. While he adhered to no programme, Wyspiański dwelt at length on the moral implications of the Polish predicament and reactions to it, analysing the significance and worth of patriotic action in its various forms. His attitude as well as his artistic expression was vigorous and rebellious, reflecting the political and cultural mood of his generation.

The novelist Stefan Żeromski (1864–1925), often referred to as 'the conscience of Polish literature', carried on the same political debate. His first major novel, *The Labours of Sisyphus* (1897), has an underlying Positivist theme in its depiction of the struggle for honesty in education. In *Ashes*, written seven years later, Żeromski constructed an historical saga which is a glorification of the insurrectionary tradition. From these opposite viewpoints, he constructed a new kind of robust socialist patriotism. He was not exclusively or even predominantly a political writer, and he is at his best on the theme that fascinated him most, the problem of evil in human affairs, which he analysed in such novels as *Story of Sin*.

The other foremost novelist of the period was Władysław Reymont

(1867–1925), the son of a village organist who was in turn a tailor's apprentice, a monk, a clerk, and several other things before he became a writer and won the Nobel prize. His *Promised Land* (1899), a Zolaesque novel set in the rapidly expanding industrial centre of Łódź, provides the final verdict of his generation on the Positivist faith in regeneration through material progress: 'Villages were abandoned, forests were felled, the earth was deprived of its treasures, rivers dried up, people were born – all for that 'Promised Land', for that polyp which sucked them in, crushed and chewed up people and things, the sky and the earth, giving in exchange useless millions to a few and hunger and hard work to the masses.' There is an epic quality to Reymont's writing, and this comes out strongly in his greatest work, *The Peasants* (1902–09).

This literature dwelt on social issues not with the sadness of the powerless spectator. Polish society did not accept that what was happening in Łódź was the responsibility of the Russian government. It continued to think as a society in control of its own destiny, and reality did not deter it. When, in the 1880s, an association backed by the Church began to wage an effective campaign against alcoholism amongst the lower orders, the Tsarist authorities banned it as a subversive organisation. Yet the Poles continued to consider themselves as being wholly responsible for the fate of their society. This was ultimately why the nation continued to function as an entity, and why the Polish problem would never go away.

As the Tsarist government clamped down and Russianised education, clandestine classes began to be held for the teaching of Polish language, history and religious instruction. By the late 1880s this began to take on the proportions of a national movement, with a 'flying university' consisting of eminent teachers giving unofficial instruction to several hundred students. According to Russian sources, clandestine education at some level involved one-third of the entire population of the Kingdom by 1901. Conspiracy, illegal presses, and the smuggling of books once again became a natural adjunct to Polish social life, and political conspiracy was not far behind. Most of the political activity was still legal and semi-official. By the late 1870s, peasant co-operatives and self-help groups in Galicia had turned into a Peasant Party, and the workers of the cities had begun to organise unions. A Polish socialist movement gathered momentum, and in 1879 the first Zionist Congress met and the Jewish Socialist Union, the Bund, was founded in Wilno.

The mirage of achieving something through loyalism was finally dispelled in the 1890s. The death of Alexander III in 1894 augured change, and when the young Nicholas II visited Warsaw in 1897 various loyalists courted him. Nothing came of it. If the permission to erect a statue of Mickiewicz in Warsaw in 1894 looked like a gesture in the right direction, the decision by the Tsar in 1897 to build a vast Orthodox church dedicated to St Alexander in the middle of the city's largest square was an obvious affront. In the following year the Polish Socialist Party managed to purloin and publish a secret memorandum from the Governor of Warsaw to the Tsar in which he described the loyalists with scorn and derision. Only in Galicia were the fruits of loyalism evident and henceforth this would act as the Piedmont for the subversion of the Kingdom and Posnania.

The main currents of Polish political action defined themselves at about the same time. The socialist movement had suffered a setback in 1884 when the Russian police arrested the leadership of Ludwik Waryński's Proletariat party. Waryński was sentenced to sixteen years' hard labour, four were hanged, and dozens of others were imprisoned or exiled. The remnants were brought together with other splinter-movements by Stanisław Mendelson and transformed in 1893 into the Polish Socialist Party (PPS). In the following year another group of socialists led by Rosa Luxemburg and Julian Marchlewski founded the Social Democratic Party of the Kingdom of Poland (SDKP) which rejected nationalism. This movement soon began to disintegrate, but was revived in 1900 by Feliks Dzierżyński, who added Lithuania to the name (SDKPL). Although it grew to an impressive size, this party played a greater part on the Russian than the Polish political scene ('Bloody Feliks' became the first head of the Cheka and its successors, OGPU and GPU). The PPS on the other hand quickly gained in influence in all three partitions. In 1894 it started publishing a clandestine organ, *The Worker*. The editor, Józef Piłsudski, was a gifted conspirator whose early life reads like a novel. He had spent five years in Siberia for helping to supply Alexander Ulyanov (Lenin's brother) with explosives for a bomb which was thrown at the Tsar in 1887. He was twice sprung from Russian jails by his colleagues. After escaping from prison in St Petersburg in 1900, he dodged from Tallin to Riga, thence to Kiev (where he managed to compile and publish an edition of *The Worker*) and Lwów, then to London, from where he entered Russia again on forged papers. If he was deft at moving the presses of *The Worker* from hiding-place to hiding-place, he also made it interesting reading, with the result that by 1899 the illegal paper had a circulation of 100,000. Piłsudski used it as a platform for his own views, and this helped him to win the leadership of the PPS.

The PPS was the spiritual descendant of the Democrats of the 1840s, and adopted a viewpoint which was not new. The national issue deformed Polish socialism from the start and made it unlike any similar movement in other countries. The foreign oppressor often appeared to be a greater threat to the working class than the capitalist. The national issue was a thorny one for adherents of socialism, but, as Engels pointed out in a letter to Kautsky, 'Polish socialists who do not put the liberation of their country in the first place of their programme would be like German socialists who didn't demand in the first instance the abolition of laws against the socialists, the institution of a free press and the right of assembly and association.' The first published programme of the PPS specified that Poland should exist within the 1772 frontiers, as a federation of nations: a multi-ethnic state based on the premises of self-sufficiency, cultural hegemony and the need to offset the might of Russia. It ignored the budding nationalism of the Ukrainians and Lithuanians, which was to create problems for the party in the future. It also failed to appeal to the Jews. As a result of mass expulsions from the Western Gubernias in the 1890s, vast numbers of Jews settled in the Kingdom, of whose entire population they now made up 14.6 per cent. The *Litwaki*, as they were known, did not even speak Polish. They were strong in the Bund, which in 1898 allied itself with the Russian Social Democratic Party, turning its back on the PPS and the cause of Polish independence.

The other party to evolve at this time was, unlike the PPS, something of a new departure. It was the Polish League, founded in 1887, renamed the National League ten years later, and eventually fixed as the National Democratic Party. Neither conservative nor revolutionary, it rejected loyalism and castigated the Positivists, but believed in resistance through realistic and businesslike means. Its membership included the bourgeoisie, the déclassé szlachta and large sections of the peasantry. It was less aristocratic than the PPS and less Romantic in its outlook. It was dominated by Roman Dmowski (1864–1939) whose political philosophy was practical, logical and implacable. In 1903 he published *Thoughts of a Modern Pole*, in which he departed from the traditional ideas of the nation as spirit, as organism, as cultural entity: he saw it as a physical unit whose definition needed yet to be forged. He criticised traditional Polish values, arguing against such concepts as toleration. For him, minorities, whether based on caste, religion or ethnic differences, were alien bodies within the nation. He liked the notion of 'healthy national egoism' and despised the principle of Christianity in politics. This violated the most sacred values of the Commonwealth. In terms of political culture, it was the exact opposite of the philosophy that had brought the Commonwealth bloodlessly through the Reformation. According to Dmowski, the existing conditions were not conducive to building a state that could survive in the modern world. As he gazed on the ruins of the Commonwealth, with its disparate elements each developing its own ideal of the future, the notion of starting again where it had left off seemed as romantically impractical as the idea of putting the Habsburg Empire back together would now.

In the National League Dmowski intended to create an all-Polish pressure group, an underground political apparatus which could unite like-minded people into a disciplined and ideologically homogeneous force. In 1899 the League founded a Society for National Education, and gradually extended its influence over cultural associations. It proceeded to extend its control over other political groupings, including peasant parties and factory workers' unions.

Józef Piłsudski was very much the product of his szlachta origins and his landed milieu in Lithuania. He was proud, rebellious and deeply rooted by sentiment and ideology in the values of the Commonwealth. He took to active subversion at an early age, and in 1904 he set up terrorist commandos known as *Bojówki* to carry out acts of sabotage and diversion. The outbreak of the Russo-Japanese war in the same year was a bugle-call to him. The humiliating defeats suffered by Russia delighted the Poles, but also made them anxious, as thousands of young Polish conscripts were being killed in the East. Piłsudski went to Tokyo with a series of proposals. He suggested the creation of a Polish Legion out of Russian prisoners of Polish origin and offered the Japanese a guerilla war in Poland to tie down Russian troops. In return, he wanted the Japanese to demand the establishment of an independent Poland at the peace negotiations. The Japanese were wary of getting involved. This wariness increased when Dmowski also arrived in Tokyo to torpedo Pilsudski's plans.

On 13 October 1904 the PPS organised a massive demonstration in Warsaw. When the police shot at the crowd, Piłsudski's armed squads returned the fire. The fighting squads of the PPS then launched a campaign of attacks on Tsarist officials. While hostilities escalated in the Kingdom, Russia itself heaved with unrest. In the new year, in the wake of the bloody clashes on the streets of St. Petersburg, the PPS proclaimed a general strike which lasted for two months and involved some 400,000 workers all over the Kingdom, in spite of severe reprisals by Tsarist troops. In May 1905 the Russian fleet was disastrously defeated at Tsushima. Unrest spread through the forces, and the crew of the battleship *Potyomkin* mutinied on the Black Sea. In June barricades went up in Łódź and the workers resisted the troops and police for three days. In October the Tsar issued a manifesto promising the Kingdom a constitution, but during the demonstration held to celebrate this troops opened fire on the crowds, and on 11 November a state of siege was declared. In December revolution broke out in Moscow and on 22 December the PPS called for a rising of all the workers in the Kingdom.

Events in Poland were dominated by a struggle for control between the Socialists and the National Democrats. During the June 1905 unrest in Łódź, when the PPS had called for action and the National Democrat controlled Workers' Union had opposed it, there were clashes between the two and even bloodshed. When the Imperial Manifesto turned the Russian Empire into a constitutional monarchy and announced elections to the Russian parliament, the Duma, the National Democrats were keen to take advantage, while the PPS boycotted the elections on the grounds that they endorsed Russian government in Poland.

134 A Warsaw street-scene photographed in 1905 but quite familiar in essence to Poles from any generation of this century. The increasingly repressive Tsarist administration only fuelled the conspiracies it was trying to stamp out, and certainly helped Józef Piłsudski (**135**) to launch his campaign of terrorism. This portrait was painted by a colleague while Piłsudski was a German prisoner in the fortress of Magdeburg in 1917.

136 A lancer of the First Brigade of Piłsudski's Polish Legions, which fought not so much *with* the Austrians as *against* the Russians from 1914 until disbanded in 1917.

Dmowski opted for a form of loyalist bargaining, demanding greater participation in the government of the Empire. At the first elections to the Duma the National Democrats gained 34 seats. With others elected in the Western Gubernias, there were 55 Polish members. He assumed that this would carry some weight, but he was mistaken. In the first twelve months of the new Constitution, 2,010 people were killed by the army and police, and over a period of three years the Governor of Warsaw signed over 1,000 'political' death-sentences. Dmowski's attempts at bargaining with the government came to nothing, while opponents in Poland denounced him for selling out. Nevertheless, he continued building up the Polish lobby in Russia's government, and as European diplomacy lurched from crisis to crisis, this policy began to make sense. In *Germany, Russia and the Polish Question* (1908) he argued that Germany was the greater threat to Poland and that Poland must side with Russia in any conflict between the two. He pointed out that Poland was the key to dominion in East Central Europe, and that there would be room for bargaining when the Powers went to war.

The PPS found itself in trouble when the dust had settled after the events of 1905. It had failed to bring about armed insurrection and was left protesting out in the cold. It was split with dissension and in 1907 actually separated into two different camps. Piłsudski managed to keep control of the larger, and his thinking prevailed. This too was becoming dominated by the approaching war, and his scheme was diametrically opposed to Dmowski's. As Piłsudski asserted in a lecture delivered in Paris in 1914, 'only the sword now carries any weight in the balance for the destiny of a nation.' He had established a para-military training-school in Kraków, and by the summer of 1906, 750 people in five-man squads were operating all over the Kingdom. During the twelve months of that year they killed and wounded nearly 1,000 Tsarist officials and officers, and carried out raids on prisons, tax-offices and mail-trains. The most spectacular was the hold-up at Bezdany in September 1908 of the heavily guarded train carrying the Kingdom's taxes to Russia. In 1908 the *Bojówki* were replaced by the Union for Active Struggle, an apolitical Polish 'army' founded by three members of the PPS: Kazimierz Sosnkowski, Marian Kukiel and Władysław Sikorski. With the unofficial approval of the Austrian authorities, 'sporting' clubs sprouted all over Galicia, followed by a Riflemen's Union. In 1912 Piłsudski reorganised these on military patterns, and by June 1914 he had nearly 12,000 men ready to take the field. When Europe went to war, he took up arms in the Polish cause. He saw Russia as the greatest enemy, and the Central Powers as the cloak under which to begin his operations.

On 2 August 1914 Piłsudski's first cavalry patrol crossed the border from Galicia into the Kingdom, followed four days later by a battalion of

Riflemen. They occupied Kielce briefly in the name of Poland before being forced to withdraw by Russian troops. Their point had been made. They were not going to watch passively as the Powers fought each other over Polish territory. On 27 August Austria agreed to the formation of two Polish Legions with their own uniforms and colours under the command of Austrian army officers of Polish nationality. These quickly grew to a strength of 20,000 men and over the next two years created something of a legend. Although they had no more of a country than they could carry in their heads, morale was high and these young men fought like lions in the conviction that some day they would march into a free Poland. As in Dąbrowski's Legions, officers were addressed as 'citizen', and the almost mystically revered and loved Piłsudski was simply 'the Commander'. Piłsudski was careful to underline that they were neither Austrian troops, nor, effectively, allies of the Central Powers.

All three Powers were keen to engage the sympathy of the Poles in general, and desperate to ensure the loyalty of their own Polish subjects in particular (between 1914 and 1918 some 450,000 Poles died and 900,000 were wounded fighting in the Russian, Prussian and Austrian armies). At the same time, they were careful not to make firm undertakings. The Proclamation of Grand Duke Nikolay on 15 August 1914 promised autonomy for the Kingdom to which captured parts of Galicia and Posnania were to be joined, but the details were left vague. Dmowski pressed for greater commitment on Russia's part and suggested the formation of a Polish army in Russia, but the government was reticent.

By August 1915 the whole area of the Kingdom had fallen to the Germans, but they too were slow to reach a decision on its future. Endless schemes were passed back and forth between Berlin and Vienna on the subject, culminating in the Proclamation of the two Emperors of 5 November 1916, in which they promised to set up a semi-autonomous Kingdom of Poland made up only of areas conquered from Russia. The project was doomed to failure. The Germans needed cannonfodder, and the kingdom was created so that a *Polnische Wehrmacht* could be raised. They originally hoped to organise this on their own but soon realised that they could not do without Piłsudski. Piłsudski had already achieved much of what he had set out to do, by demonstrating that Poland represented a military as well as a moral force. But he had no intention of being used to further German plans. He agreed to join the Council of State of the new Kingdom as head of the military department, but insisted on explicit guarantees that its forces would not be German 'colonial troops' as he put it, and would never be used against the British or French. The Germans were not prepared to grant such terms, so Piłsudski resigned. In July 1917 he was arrested. The Polish units already raised refused to take the oath of allegiance and were disbanded. The men swelled the ranks of the Polish

Military Organisation (POW), an underground network set up across the entire area of the Commonwealth by Piłsudski in the previous two years, a silent army which awaited his signal.

Dmowski had gone to the West in 1915. His predictions had come true: the real enemy was Germany, and Poland had become the crucial factor in any solution of the conflict in the East. By 1916 the war was as much about Poland as it was about Alsace-Lorraine, something which was coming to be recognised by statesmen who in 1914 hardly knew where Poland was. As President Woodrow Wilson put it in his address to the US Senate on 22 January 1917: 'Statesmen everywhere are agreed that there should be a united, independent, and autonomous Poland.' Dmowski devoted his energies to informing and directing the opinions of these statesmen. A number of his colleagues had been engaged in this activity from the beginning, most notably Henryk Sienkiewicz until his death in 1916, and Ignacy Paderewski. In June 1917 France sanctioned the formation of a Polish army on French soil. In September France recognised Dmowski's National Committee in Paris as a provisional government of the future Poland. Britain, Italy and America followed suit. Thus by the autumn of 1917 there was a Polish government and a Polish army recognised as co-belligerents, if not formal allies, of the Entente.

The Entente could only do this because their ally Russia had, under Kerensky's government, agreed to the principle of an independent Poland. But October brought the Bolsheviks to power. The entire Eastern front collapsed, and the German army occupied the whole area of the Commonwealth. In March 1918 the Bolsheviks signed the Treaty of Brest-Litovsk, leaving it to the Germans. As a protest against this new peace, General Haller led the Second Brigade of the Legions, the last Polish unit fighting for Austria, across the front to join up with Polish units which had similarly left the disintegrating Russian army. Over the next two years units such as these bobbed about on the swell of the Russian Revolution and Civil War in a desperate effort to keep together and maintain their fighting potential for the day it could be used in the Polish cause. They were often defeated or disbanded, and sometimes forced to serve 'White' Russian generals at the behest of the Entente, but they mostly survived to fight for Poland. General Haller managed to make his way to Paris and take command of the Polish army being formed there, known as the Blue Army on account of its French uniforms.

The German Kingdom of Poland still had no king, and was ruled by a Regency Council made up of Poles. But even as revolution toppled first the Habsburg and then the Hohenzollern thrones, the Germans and the Austrians did not desist from their imperial machinations on Polish lands. The Germans had for some time been fostering the formation of a small ethnic Lithuanian state which could be a German satellite. Austria was contemplating a Habsburg Kingdom of the Ukraine. On 1 November 1918 Ukrainian flags were hoisted on the public buildings of Lwów and the Ruthene regiments of the Austrian Army took over the city. Piłsudski's POW units and the mainly Polish inhabitants fought back and regained control, but they were besieged within a small area. The newly-established Lithuania claimed Wilno and areas of the Grand Duchy inhabited by a majority of Poles. Before it had even come into existence Poland was at war with two of its components.

On 7 November 1918 the socialist Ignacy Daszyński proclaimed a Polish Peoples' Government in Lublin. On 10 November, the day before the Armistice in the West, Piłsudski was freed from his German jail and arrived in Warsaw. He was met at the station by Zdzisław Lubomirski and Archbishop Kakowski, who handed over to him the powers of the Regency Council. All over the country his POW and ex-Legionaries disarmed German troops and took control. Piłsudski then sent a telegram to the governments of the Entente announcing that 'the Polish state has arisen from the will of the whole nation.'

What no Pole could have fancied in his wildest dreams had happened: the three Empires had been shaken by revolution and reduced to impotence within the space of a year. Poland was free. But the collapse of the three Empires had created new problems. New antagonists had sprung up to dispute Poland's claims and a number of minority groups within its heartlands were hostile to it. Lithuania, which had nothing to do with the old Grand Duchy except its name, claimed large areas of what no Pole could consider as anything but an integral part of his country. The new Czecho-Slovak state invaded the area around Cieszyn, inhabited by a Polish-speaking population. The Ukrainians were fighting over Lwów and areas of Galicia. There was even a Byelorussian nationalist movement which disputed Polish claims to parts of what had been the Grand Duchy. The Germans who had settled over the last century were inimical, and the millions of Jews were fearful of and in large measure hostile to the new Polish state.

All these problems were further complicated by the peace negotiations in Paris. The Polish negotiators, Dmowski and Paderewski, found that Poland had few friends when the bargaining started, and that hardly anyone had any knowledge or understanding of Poland's past. Some of the most influential 'experts', particularly J.M. Keynes and E.H. Carr of the British delegation, held views of the most extraordinary racial arrogance on all the nations of Eastern Europe. Lloyd George was fond of voicing German-inspired views that 'the Poles have always been a troublesome people . . . a people who have never succeeded in governing themselves.' As they quarrelled amongst themselves over the African spoils of Germany, the ministers of the Entente were quick to accuse Poland of 'imperialism' when the latter occupied Lwów, a city which had been part of the Polish realm for over six centuries, and waxed indignant over Polish 'annexations' in areas which did not have a clear majority of ethnically-Polish inhabitants. What they did not realise was that Polish claims in the East were the legacy of all radical thought over the last century. It was the Democrats of the 1830s and later the socialists who upheld the idea of Poland not as just another smug nation-state, but as a multifarious organism held together by its own specific dynamics. Even Marx had consistently maintained that the appropriate frontiers for Poland were at least those of 1772. To the Western statesmen the issue seemed to be one of possessions and area. To the Poles the issue was not one of expanse, but of ideology. The Western statesmen failed to grasp this, and they felt the Poles ought to be more grateful. Clemenceau felt it necessary on more than one occasion to remind Paderewski 'that it is to the endeavours and sacrifices of the [Western] Powers that the Polish nation owes the recovery of its independence.' The Poles could be forgiven for thinking otherwise.

Poland's frontier with Germany depended entirely on the decisions reached by Wilson, Clemenceau and Lloyd George, and these were subject to every consideration except that of Polish reason of state. It was only in Silesia, where an uprising against the Germans by the population proved effective, that the Poles were able to break this rule. All of Prussia and Pomerania was awarded to Germany, and Gdańsk was left as a Free City under League of Nations administration, linked to Poland by a thin corridor through German territory. Poland's frontiers with Russia, on the other hand, depended not on words uttered at Paris, but on actions in the field.

Piłsudski had strong opinions on the subject. He was no 'modern Pole' like Dmowski, and 'national egoism' came second to a number of traditional considerations. The old slogan of 'for your freedom and ours' was still ringing in his ears, and he felt a responsibility towards the Ruthenes and Lithuanians. At the same time, Piłsudski realised that merely rebuilding a small Poland next to a vast Russia would offer slim chances for the future. This led him back to the notion of the Commonwealth of Three Nations. He felt the only sensible and just solution to be a federation of Poland, Lithuania and the Ukraine. Poland could tolerate giving up Wilno to a Lithuania which was bound up with Poland, but not to a foreign state. The same applied to Lwów and other areas.

Unfortunately for Piłsudski the dialogue with the Lithuanians and the Ukrainians began only after shots had been exchanged. It proved impossible to reach any agreement with the Lithuanians, who were deeply suspicious of Poland and knew their own claims to be extremely weak. There was more common ground with the Ukrainians, and negotiations started soon after the fighting over Lwów had ceased. But no solution to

the problems of the Ukraine, Byelorussia and Lithuania could be adopted
without reference to what was happening in Russia. In August 1918 the
Bolsheviks had declared all the treaties of partition null and void – which
did not mean that they were willing to see Poland make itself at home
within its 1772 frontiers. Throughout 1918 and 1919 they were too busy
fending off White offensives to bother much about the Polish frontier.
Piłsudski too was worried by the successes of the Whites. Their leader,
General Denikin, made it quite clear that he envisaged only one Russia –
great and indivisible. Piłsudski certainly did not wish to see him established in Moscow with Allied backing, for then not only Poland's eastern
frontier, but her whole sovereign status would be dependent on deals made
between Moscow and Paris. Piłsudski therefore refrained from any military activity against the Bolsheviks which might help the Whites, and even
made a secret peace with Lenin, in spite of urgent appeals from London
and Paris that he should support Denikin.

When the Whites had been decisively defeated, in the winter of 1919, the
Bolsheviks began to prepare plans for exporting the revolution through
Poland to Germany. While the Bolshevik government launched a formidable 'peace offensive', protesting their willingness to grant Poland the most
extensive frontiers, they built up their forces facing Poland from four
divisions in January 1920 to twenty by the end of April. Piłsudski had his
own plans. The Bolsheviks had already flooded into the Ukraine, ousting
the Ukrainian nationalist forces of Ataman Semyon Petlura from Kiev.
Petlura was forced to fall back westwards, and to seek Polish protection.
Piłsudski seized the opportunity to sign an alliance with him, and in the
last days of April he launched an offensive into the Ukraine. On 7 May
1920 the Polish army marched into Kiev.

Piłsudski hoped that Petlura would raise a sizable Ukrainian army. This
would permit Polish troops to be transferred north, to face an alarming
Russian concentration there. Progress was slow and Petlura's forces
did not grow to more than 30,000 before the Russian attack came in the
north. Polish forces in the area managed to contain it along the Berezina,
but on 5 June the Cavalry Army of Budyonny broke through to the south of
Kiev, precipitating a chaotic Polish-Ukrainian withdrawal. On 4 July the
five Russian army groups in the north launched a second offensive, and
over the next six weeks the two Russian prongs, under Tukhachevsky and
Yegorov, advanced inexorably into Poland.

The Bolsheviks announced the overthrow of the bourgeois order and
successfully agitated among workers all over Europe to block supplies
being shipped to Poland. Western governments were unhelpful. Lloyd
George's attitude was that 'the Poles have quarrelled with all their
neighbours and they are a menace to the peace of Europe.' On 12 August
the Red Army reached the defences of Warsaw and newspapers all over

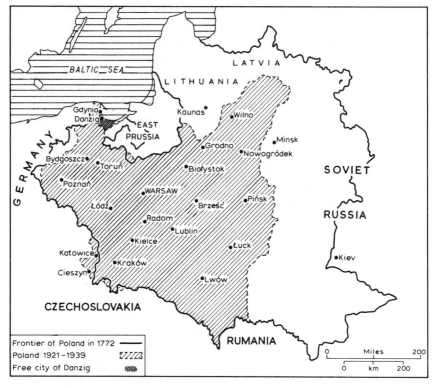

The Polish Republic

Europe announced the city's fall. But on 15 August Piłsudski launched a
daring flank attack which virtually annihilated the entire Red Army in
Poland. After another Polish victory on the Niemen, the Russian front
collapsed. Polish troops reoccupied large areas of Byelorussia, Podolia and
Volhynia before an armistice was signed on 16 October.

At the negotiations which followed in Riga a combination of pressure
from the Entente and of the fact that the Ukrainian national movement
had proved too weak, forced Piłsudski to abandon his federalist scheme.
The negotiations were conducted by the peasant leader Jan Dąbski and
Stanisław Grabski, a National Democrat, who saw no reason to demand
the retention of areas with high proportions of non-Polish inhabitants. The
result was a compromise which satisfied few. Both Wilno and Lwów
remained with Poland, but other historic areas of the Commonwealth were
left out. Over two million Poles were left outside the boundaries of the new
state, which included large Ruthene, German and Jewish minorities.
Nevertheless, there was once more an independent Poland, with an area of

388,600 square kilometres, the sixth largest state in Europe by population. As Piłsudski had said, when opening the first sovereign session of the Polish Seym on 10 February 1919: 'A century and a half of battles, sometimes bloody and sacrificial, has found its victory in this day. A century and a half of dreams of a free Poland have come true at this moment.'

20

The Republic

The Promised Land is always something of a disappointment to those who have viewed it from afar. The Poles had dreamed of it so long that it was inevitable they would find their new condition wanting. They had associated every problem and evil with the unnatural state of captivity. The sudden removal of this only revealed that the problems and blemishes were within themselves. And all the pent-up aspirations released from this captivity rapidly came into collision with one another. The Poles had dreamed of their Arcadia individually, and had to live in it collectively. This gave rise to an entirely new problem: authority had to be respected, bureaucracy co-operated with, the police desired, the army admired. All manifestations of state power, which had been distrusted since the fourteenth century and loathed since the end of the eighteenth, now had to be accommodated among the most sacred elements of a Poles' life, and it did not come naturally. For too long all virtue had lain in opposition. This marked the attitude of the peasant to the policeman as much as it did that of the general to his government. It deeply marked the only deputies to the Seym who had any experience of parliamentary practice: when they had sat in the Duma or the Reichstag they only blocked and opposed. This augured ill for the political life of the resurrected state.

The constitution adopted in March 1921 was based on that of the French Third Republic: it consisted of a Seym of 444 deputies elected by proportional representation, a Senate of 111 seats, and a president elected by both houses. Neither president nor Senate had extensive-powers, most of which were in the hands of the Seym. Proportional representation has a tendency to spawn small parties, particularly in a country with numerous ethnic minorities, and no less than 31 were represented in the Polish Seym. The concentration of power in the hands of an assembly with no overall majority led, as it must, to a rapid turnover of cabinets. This was made all the more inevitable by a desperate and insoluble economic crisis, and by two problems specific to Poland. One was that a hundred years of living within one or other of three entirely different cultures had marked the mentality and behaviour of every Pole. Those Brought up in a Prussian mould found it extremely difficult to work with those of more urbane Habsburg habits, let alone with those schooled in the Byzantine inefficiency of the Tsarist bureaucracy. The other problem specific to the Polish scene was the nature of the political parties. The principal currents of Polish politics had originally been differentiated by views of how independence was to be achieved and what form it should take, and not so much by who should rule the country. When independence came, it was not ideology, but factions, such as the peasants, the middle classes, the workers, the Jews or the Ruthenes, which gave rise to the political parties. This ruled out the possibility of durable coalitions, since conservative-minded peasants hungry for land could not coexist with conservative-minded landowners, and left-wing industrial workers who wanted low food-prices could not maintain an alliance with left-wing peasants who wanted the reverse.

The strongest single party were the National Democrats, but their views alienated most of the others, and they could therefore not sustain a coalition which would give them an overall majority for any length of time. Neither left nor right could form a government without the centre, while the 20 per cent of seats in the Seym held by the various Jewish, German and Ruthene parties could have a dramatic influence at times of crisis. Between November 1918 and May 1926 no less than fourteen different governments took office and dissolved amid fractious bargaining. The sense of instability was only enhanced when the first president of the Republic, Gabriel Narutowicz, was assassinated by a lunatic two days after his inauguration in December 1922.

The atmosphere of tawdriness and dissension which attached itself to parliamentary politics provoked a chorus of public opinion calling for 'strong government'. Only one man in Poland enjoyed the sort of public esteem and personal authority needed to provide this: Józef Piłsudski. In the early 1920s Piłsudski withdrew into sullen retirement on his little estate of Sulejówek, whence he exerted a muted but pervasive influence through his writings, his Sibylline pronouncements on various matters, and his very absence from public life. He had a strong following in the armed forces and was respected by people on the right and the left of the political spectrum, by the most chauvinist Poles and by the Jewish minority.

On 10 May 1926 the leader of the Piast Peasant Party, Wincenty Witos, formed the latest in a succession of cabinets too weak to rule effectively. Two days later Piłsudski marched on Warsaw at the head of a few battalions of troops, and demanded the resignation of the governmnent. Witos was ready to resign, but President Wojciechowski ordered him to stand firm and called out the army. Some units dragged their feet, others backed Piłsudski, and the railwaymen refused to move regiments loyal to the government. After three days' street-fighting Wojciechowski and Witos resigned.

The Seym offered the presidency to Piłsudski, but he declined and put forward the name of an eminent scientist and one-time member of the PPS, Ignacy Mościcki, who was then elected. Piłsudski himself briefly served as prime minister, and then handed over to Kazimierz Bartel, a respected politician of the People's Party. Piłsudski had no policy beyond 'cleaning up the mess' of parliamentary bickering, and took little interest in the day-to-day affairs of government. He was far more interested in the army, which he saw as the key to Poland's survival and a repository of its chivalric values, and the only formal title he accepted was that of Marshal. He hovered on the sidelines, part-dictator, part-monarch, his role ill-defined, his influence paramount. By these means he managed to conserve his popularity: he was at once accessible and aloof, and while he was the lynchpin on which the whole regime was hung, he was not too firmly locked into any programme or policy to forfeit his essentially non-party appeal. If his manner, which grew increasingly surly, and his methods, which became more peremptory, were denounced by many, his purpose could be faulted by few. He was a national hero embalmed in the legend of his life of struggle for the freedom of Poland, embodying rebellion as well as authority. He was what every monarch might aspire to be – a man of his times who evokes all the finest traditions of the past.

The only formal change that took place after the coup of May 1926 was a slight amendment of the constitution, strengthening the powers of the president. But if the machinery of government remained largely intact, it ceased to function properly. The opposition in the Seym was ignored and treated with mounting scorn by Piłsudski and his followers. After the elections of 1928, in which his non-party ruling bloc (BBWR) failed to get the majority he had hoped for, what little respect he had for parliamentary procedures finally evaporated. Few people had been dismissed from their posts or penalised after the coup, but those who persisted in truculent opposition were hounded and eventually silenced by petty means. One or two even died in more or less mysterious circumstances.

Long years of conspiratorial activity had taught Piłsudski to use trusted men to carry out his plans and to obviate institutional channels. He gathered round him a bevy of trusties from the PPS, the *Bojówki*, the Legions or the POW. They were men like Walery Sławek, honourable, naïve, devoted, a man with no political ideas of his own and few talents; or Edward Śmigły-Rydz, a soldier and patriot with the soul of a second-in-command and a political programme to match. To Piłsudski they were his 'boys', to the man in the street they were 'the colonels'. They were the levers through which the Marshal exerted power. By 1930 they had taken over in the government and in the administration, and they backed up their increasingly authoritarian rule with a barrack-room ideology of 'cleaning up' political life which earned the regime the name of *Sanacja* (literally 'sanitation'). Opposition leaders such as Witos were arrested in 1930, later to be put on trial on charges of conspiracy, the freedom of the press was gradually restricted and elections were rigged. With the death, on 12 May 1935, of Józef Piłsudski, this ruling clique tightened its grip, and the country continued as a dictatorship without a dictator. A new constitution was adopted in April 1935, reducing the Seym to a more manageable 208 deputies elected from 104 constituencies. This cut out small parties which had thrived on proportional representation. The powers of the Seym were curtailed and those of the president extended, but it was not President Mościcki who ruled. The camarilla of 'colonels' continued in control, dominated by the éminence grise of Marshal Smigły-Rydz, head of the armed forces.

The political opposition posed no threat to the government. The National Democrats were in disarray, with significant segments of their membership splitting off to form other parties. The peasant parties and the PPS were powerless. In 1936 a group of concerned constitutionalists, including Wincenty Witos, General Józef Haller, General and ex-Prime Minister Władysław Sikorski and Ignacy Jan Paderewski, met at the latter's home near Morges in Switzerland and founded the Morges Front, in an attempt at rebuilding a respectable centre-right opposition. There was little they could do, as the means for parliamentary action were limited. A number of parties had boycotted the elections of September 1935, but the government had founded the Camp of National Unity (OZN), which sucked in frustrated National Democrats as well as malcontents from smaller parties. The only weapons left to the opposition were strikes and demonstrations, but these were put down with force, and even brutality.

European politics of the 1920s and 1930s are unedifying, and few countries can look back on the period without some measure of embarrassment. Unemployment, confrontation, constitutional crises and military coups were the small change of contemporary politics. Poland was no exception. The twenty years of the Republic saw the breakdown of parliamentary procedures, the use of intimidation, and the rise of shoddy national-socialist philosophies. Yet in a number of respects the case of Poland was very different. The *Sanacja* regime failed to turn it into a one-party state, and inter-war Poland never drifted towards the sort of bullying, disciplinarian, national-socialist world of youth-movements and marches which enveloped so much of Central Europe. The one factor that militated against Piłsudski's universal popularity was his propensity to act tough, a characteristic that tended to earn a leader unbounded admiration in most neighbouring countries. This was partly due to the survival of the old values of the Commonwealth: liberalism, Sarmatian individualism and dislike of authority. But it was also inherent in the human shape of the Polish Republic. The peacemakers of 1918 had attempted to create nation-states in Central Europe, but the communities embraced by the Commonwealth had been so interwoven that merely contracting its frontiers did not produce a homogeneously Polish state. The Republic was about half the size of the Commonwealth in 1772. In 1920 it had a population of 27 million, but only 69 per cent of this were Poles: 17 per cent were Ruthenes, nearly 10 per cent were Jews, and 2.5 per cent were Germans. This created enormous problems. The Polish 'nation' of the Commonwealth had been open to all nationalities, but when Poland was resurrected as a nation-state in 1918, the new 'nation' could only be based on the linguistic, cultural and religious tradition of the dominant group. The German, Jewish, Ruthene and other minorities were automatically excluded unless they assimilated and adopted more than just the passport of their country. And in the case of the three largest minorities, assimilation was the last thing they wanted.

The Ruthenes who inhabited the east and south-east of the country were treated as second-class citizens by local administrators and police, and with suspicion by the central authorities. This was to some extent justified. These were the poorest areas of Poland, and discontent was fuelled by Soviet Russia in the east and by Germany via Slovakia in the south-east. In 1930 a Ukrainian nationalist organisation funded from Germany began a campaign of terrorism and sabotage. The authorities responded with a ten-week 'pacification'. Troops combed the area, burning down restive villages and incarcerating terrorists and activists in the internment camp set up at Bereza Kartuska in 1932. In 1934 the Ukrainians managed to assassinate the Minister of the Interior, Colonel Bronisław Pieracki, but the extremists were undermined by the reaching of an agreement in the same year between the government and the principal Ukrainian party (UNDO). Calm returned to the countryside until 1939, when the extremists re-emerged as a German fifth-column.

Relations with the German minority were more decorous but no more cordial. The *Volksdeutsche* resented having been marooned in a foreign country and felt no loyalty to Poland. With the rise of Nazism in Germany, they became increasingly strident in their denunciation of the Versailles settlement, demanding the return to the Reich of large areas of Posnania and of the Free City of Danzig. But even this hostility did not pose the same problems as the Jewish minority.

In 1772 the Commonwealth sheltered some four-fifths of the world's Jews. They fitted comfortably into its political, economic and cultural framework, and there was no 'Jewish problem'. After the partitions they became the citizens of three different states into which they did not fit at all.

Prussia treated them as unwelcome vermin, Austria as a social anomaly which ought to be regimented into society, and Russia as untouchables who were to be tolerated only beyond the Pale of Settlement – i.e. the old borders of the Commonwealth. Their specific function and place within the society of the Commonwealth was destroyed, and the age-old Polish-Jewish symbiosis decomposed. Far from fulfilling a useful commercial and political function as they had done in ages past, the Jews were now in direct economic competition with the déclassé szlachta, the urban proletariat, the budding Polish middle class and even the peasants. In the second half of the nineteenth century Russia pushed the Pale of Settlement further west, with catastrophic results. Some 800,000 Jews from Lithuania and Byelorussia were forced to migrate to the Kingdom, where they generated overcrowding and resentment among their Polish brethren. Speaking Russian not Polish, these *Litwaki* were unwelcome to the Poles trying to create a new national consciousness, and came to be viewed as Russian interlopers. A minority continued to assimilate into Polish society and play a worthy role in it, but the Jewish community as a whole did not identify with Polish aspirations. While many were active in the PPS and fought in Piłsudski's Legions, many more supported the Bund which was hostile to the Polish cause. There was little Jewish enthusiasm for Dmowski's National Democratic movement, which openly proclaimed its belief that all those who were not prepared to assimilate completely should be encouraged to find new pastures, and whose members often gave vent to violently anti-Semitic feelings.

The collapse of law and order in November 1918 produced a rash of anti-Jewish outrages in country areas and in towns such as Lwów and Pińsk. Further violence and some shootings took place in the wake of military operations between the Poles and the Bolsheviks, since some leaders of the Bund had called on all Jews to further international revolution by supporting the Red Army. Hostility towards the Jews was inadvertently heighted by American and British Jewish pressure groups at the Paris peace talks of 1918. It was at their insistence that states such as Poland were made to sign 'Minority Treaties', which subjected their treatment of their Jewish citizens to international scrutiny. As well as encroaching on their sovereignty, it was an insult to the Poles with their long tradition of toleration. The life-blood of anti-Semitism is the fact that a Jew can be identified in almost any camp or faction and then the whole race accused of guiding it. In the first two years of Polish independence, powerful groups of American and British Jewry were seen to be advocating the curtailment of Polish sovereignty apparently in unison with German interests, while Jews were in the forefront of the Bolshevik invasion of 1920. The average Pole felt the Jews were not on the same side as him.

The census of 1931 revealed that there were 3,113,900 Jews in Poland, representing 9.8 per cent of the entire population. They made up over 30 per cent of the population of Warsaw, a fairly standard figure for most of the larger cities, with exceptions such as Białystok's 43 per cent. In smaller county towns the proportion was much higher, reaching 60 per cent, 70 per cent and in a handful of cases over 90 per cent of the entire population. Since the majority wore long black gaberdines, side-locks, beards, and spoke mainly or exclusively Yiddish rather than Polish, these 'minorities' were extraordinarily conspicuous. They were equally conspicuous in their economic relationship to the rest of the population.

The occupational breakdown of the 1931 census reveals that only 0.6 per cent of those engaged in agriculture were Jews. They made up 62 per cent of all the people making a living from trade in Poland, and the figure for the town of Pińsk was 95 per cent. Their fortunes fluctuated dramatically during the economically unstable twenties and thirties. Every time a new peasant co-operative was founded or a village combined to sell its produce direct to the buyer, the livelihood of several Jewish families vanished. By 1936 at least 1,000,000 Jews in Poland were losing their source of subsistence, and by 1939 just over that number were totally dependent for their survival on relief from Jewish agencies in the United States.

Polish representatives to the League of Nations urgently stressed the need for mass emigration. The desire to be rid of the Jews went hand in hand with concern for their plight, but should not be overestimated: the same representatives also appealed to the League to facilitate large-scale emigration of poor Polish peasants from the overpopulated countryside. Relations between the Poles and the Jewish minority varied enormously; they were far more complex than and rarely as bad as is usually made out. Abraham Stern, the son of a dentist from Suwałki and a great admirer of Piłsudski's *Bojówki* visited Poland a number of times after settling in Palestine in order to recruit for the Irgun. The Polish authorities allowed him to buy arms and train men, and facilitated the illegal immigration of Polish Jews into the British Mandate.

While the majority of Jews in Poland were caught in a poverty trap, they never managed to dispel the envy surrounding the community as a whole. In 1931 46 per cent of all lawyers and nearly 50 per cent of all doctors were Jews. These professions were what every peasant's son coveted as the first step to social advancement, and to him there seemed to be a great Israelite barrier to fulfilling his aspirations. The Jews were far more successful at getting into universities than dim-witted locals who believed higher education to be their birthright. Even the struggling village shopkeeper appeared to the peasants as an exploiter who should have no place in their new Poland.

There were moments when these feelings came to a head, and occasional rioting led to looting of Jewish shops, but these occurrences were insignificant in the context of other popular disturbances resulting from economic factors. Law and order were precarious, and the police force was about half the size of that in Britain and France in relation to the respective populations. An anti-Semitic campaign began in the mid-1930s at the University of Lwów, where the preponderance of Jews offended the career prospects of the other students, and spread to other universities and technical colleges, resulting in some cases in the introduction of admission quotas based on percentages of the population.

The National Democrats, denied power for so long, had by now largely lost their sense of identity as well as much of their membership. In an attempt at gaining the hearts of the younger generation and of the disgruntled masses as a whole, they began to veer towards classic anti-Semitism. They made much of the Jewish and 'Masonic' entourage of President Mościcki, but this did not stop their fringes being eaten away by several small openly fascist parties, the most notorious of which, the Falanga, carried out petty assaults on Jewish shops and synagogues. The decay of parliamentary politics was reflected in the rise of a shabby anti-Semitism, and students at some universities even demanded the institution of Jew-benches. Yet at no point in this process did the sort of biological anti-Semitism of the Nazi or anti-Dreyfusard variety catch on in Poland. The points at issue were political, cultural and to some extent religious, but most of all they were economic, and these affected the Jewish community hardly more than the rest of the population.

Economically, the country created in 1918 made no sense at all. Along with four legal systems, the Republic inherited six different currencies, three railway networks, and three administrative and fiscal systems. There were huge discrepancies between the agriculturally advanced Posnania, the primitive rural economy of Mazovia and the industrially developed Silesia. Galicia, the grain-basket of the Habsburg Empire, and the Kingdom, which had been the industrial centre of the Russian Empire, were cut off from their respective markets. The area had been ravaged by six years of war. Eleven million acres of agricultural land had been devastated, six million acres of forest felled, and over four million head of livestock removed by the Germans alone. According to Vernon Kellogg of the American Food Mission, one-third of the population were on the point of starvation in 1919.

As 64 per cent of the entire population lived off the land, there was, quite simply, far too little to go round. The political solution to this problem was Land Reform, which, from 1925, annually distributed 200,000 hectares to the landless peasants at the cost of large estates. But this only aggravated the problem, by multiplying the number of tiny, inefficient farms. In 1939 there was still only one tractor for every 8,400 hectares of arable land, and yields were up to 50 per cent lower than in neighbouring Germany.

The only lasting solution was massive inudstrialisation, but this was made no easier by the fact that in 1918 the retreating German army had carried out a gigantic operation quaintly termed 'the de-industrialisation of Poland', which left no factory, railway-station or bridge standing and no piece of machinery in place. The state came into being with vast debts to the Allies (for equipping and arming the Blue Army and supplying armaments between 1918 and 1920), and the unbelievable obligation of making war-reparations to Austria and Germany. Poland was not the only country rebuilding its economic life and therefore had to compete for credits. Foreign capital saw the new country as a rather uncertain investment.

The result was a bumpy economic start. In December 1918 the US dollar bought 9.8 Polish marks; in December 1923 it bought five million. At that point Premier Władysław Grabski managed to balance the budget and to stabilise the situation with the introduction of the Złoty. Nevertheless, foreign capital eluded Poland, while Germany waged a tariff war against it. It was not until 1929 that production had at last reached the pre-1914 levels, only to sink to an all-time low in 1932.

In spite of extremely unfavourable conditions, a host of teething-troubles and outside factors over which the Poles had no control, the Republic's achievements in the economic field are impressive. It was created out of three derelict rumps of different Empires and lasted only twenty years. Yet by the end of those twenty years it was the eighth largest producer of steel in the world, and the ninth of pig iron. It exported 12 million tons of coal, 1½ million tons of crude oil, 95,300 tons of textile fabrics, and 138,000 tons of yarn, and was beginning to develop a chemical industry. Its most spectacular achievement was directed to the sea. Gdańsk was dominated by its predominantly German population, which yearned for incorporation into Germany. Poland therefore decided to build its own port. The dredging of the new harbour was started in 1924, in the fishing village of Gdynia. By 1938 Gdynia was the busiest port in the Baltic, with 12,900 ships calling yearly. A Polish merchant marine of over 80 ships was built up, as well as a navy.

The management of the economy was made all the more difficult by the hopeful assumptions of every social group in the euphoria attendant on the recovery of independence. In 1918, even before the fighting was over, the first Polish government passed decrees on social insurance and an eight-hour working day. In 1920 the government launched a health insurance scheme, and in 1924 an unemployment insurance act. The 1930s saw the building of remarkable state housing schemes for the low-paid, and by then Poland had the highest levels of social security in the world. In a situation where minimal benefits and strict austerity would have been useful, the authorities had to accede to overblown demands and expectations. Such was the case with education, a subject which was treated very

The Republic created by the Paris Peace Conference of 1919 was a compromise in every sense, and none of the political or ethnic minorities was happy with it. For the first time in Polish history, the intelligentsia and the creative artists were alienated by the ideology of the political establishment. The new seat of the provincial government of Silesia at Katowice (**137**) epitomises the vigour, capability and ambition of the resurrected state, as well as its blind optimism. It contrasts vividly with the work of artists such as Stanisław Ignacy Witkiewicz, whose *Temptation of St Anthony* (**138**) painted in 1922, is characteristically pervaded by a sense of impending catastrophe.

seriously. Over the twenty years of independence illiteracy was virtually halved. By 1939 the six universities of Kraków, Warsaw, Lwów, Wilno, Poznań and Lublin contained 48,000 students, almost a third of them women, while a further 27 technical colleges provided higher education for greater numbers. The standards achieved in the Polish educational system during the 1930s compared very favourably with those of other countries, particularly in the humanities and pure science.

Retrospectively, it appears that the overriding problem faced by Polish society in its new role as a sovereign nation was one of identity. There was a Sapieha foreign minister, a Zamoyski presidential candidate, a Potocki ambassador and members of szlachta families in every officers' mess, but it was not their values that triumphed in the new Poland. Nor did those of the nineteenth-century intelligentsia. Piłsudski and Dmowski had already been superseded by the movements they had created. The higher echelons of government and of the administration were largely filled by new men of disparate origins who had been tempered in the furnace of conspiracy, jail, and struggle for independence. They were united by their common experiences and service in the army, which played a major role in forging a new national consciousness. They were the pinnacle of a mushrooming bureaucracy, the newly created administrative class of a country which had done without one for a thousand years. These men believed themselves to be the rightful élite of the new Poland, and they quickly assumed a mongrel Sarmatism. While they too identified strongly with the new state, many members of the landed classes, the old intelligentsia, and particularly the artists, became alienated.

The liberation of the country in 1918 freed writers and artists from the duty of serving the national cause, and their first reaction was one of relief. As the poet Jan Lechoń (Leszek Serafinowicz 1899–1956) put it: 'And in the Spring, let me see only Spring, not Poland.' During the 1920s he and his colleagues, a group of lyrical poets publishing in the monthly *Skamander*, were able to indulge themselves and explore themes which had in the past been overridden by the need to write something positive from the national point of view. Julian Tuwim (1894–1953), a product of the Jewish middle class of Łódź, produced humorous, exotic works, giving vent to his taste for the bizarre and the demonic. Kazimierz Wierzyński (1894–1969), a veteran of the Legions, wrote exuberant lyrical poetry for its own sake, like his companion-in-arms Antoni Słonimski (1895–1976). It was the first time that subjects such as sexuality could be explored, and the first time that homosexuality appeared as an element in literature and society. In this respect, Jarosław Iwaszkiewicz (1894–1981) was a literary landmark. A native of the Ukraine, he was fascinated by the East and by the associations between music, verse, colour and the senses. He helped the young composer Karol Szymanowski, another native of the Ukraine, a suppressed homosexual who could find no place for his thoughts and feelings within the Polish cultural context, to find meaning and fulfilment in a Dionysiac view of the world. It was Iwaszkiewicz who wrote the libretto to Szymanowski's opera *King Roger* (1920–24), which explores the theme of the transcendental nature of sensual love.

The most interesting figure on the Polish literary and artistic scene was Stanisław Ignacy Witkiewicz (1885–1939). He embodied and stated – in the most extreme ways – most of the problems faced by Polish artists of the first half of the century. He was brought up at Zakopane in the Tatra mountains and studied painting in Kraków before embarking on travels which took him all over Europe, India, Ceylon, Australia and New Guinea, no doubt encouraged by his close friend the anthropologist Bronisław Malinowski. In 1914 he went to war as an officer in the Russian army. He was decorated for bravery, but did not confine himself to soldiering, devoting all his spare time to the study of philosophy and the exploration of hallucinatory drugs (on which he published a book in 1932). Instead of shooting him in 1917, his soldiers elected him as their commissar, and he eventually managed to return safely to Zakopane, where he settled and rapidly became the centre of a whole range of intellectual and artistic activity.

While he was primarily a painter, Witkiewicz could never put down the pen for long. He wrote some thirty plays, but few were staged in his lifetime, so outrageous were they to contemporary audiences. They are curious mixtures of philosophical polemic and unashamed provocation, with titles such as *The Madman and the Nun: or There is Nothing so Bad that it Cannot Get Worse*. His aim was not 'progammatic nonsense': he was trying to 'enlarge the possibilities of composition by abandoning lifelike logic in art, by introducing a fantastic psychology and fantastic action in order to win complete freedom from formal elements', as he explained in his book *The Theatre*. His two great novels, *Farewell to Autumn* (1927) and *Insatiability* (1930), are no less fantastic, although they have conventional if somewhat picaresque plots, using comedy and melodrama to suggest endless philosophical views of every situation.

Witkiewicz's was an extreme but not atypical example of the disorientation felt by his contemporaries. Their sudden liberation from the duties of the national cause, their experiences during the Great War and the Russian Revolution, and the general sense of transience felt throughout Central Europe in the 1920s and 1930s left them all somewhat disoriented. This was particularly true of prose writers. Some tried the social novel, others built on their wartime experiences, others looked for some new form. One of the most interesting is Bruno Schulz (1893–1942), whose obsessively fetishistic erotic drawings are no less remarkable than his magical, Kafkaesque stories. A Jewish native of Drohobycz, he was gunned down on the street by the Gestapo. The most gifted prose writer was the enfant terrible of respectable landed szlachta, Witold Gombrowicz (1904–69), whose surrealist novel *Ferdydurke* caused a sensation when it was published in 1938.

For poets, musicians and painters, the equating of Arcadia with the lost motherland, and of violated innocence with occupied Poland, was an obvious and fruitful source of creation. It was made all the easier by exile, as the cases of Mickiewicz and Chopin demonstrated, since it was easier to refine feelings at a distance from reality. Bringing the idyll face to face with reality in 1918 created problems, and not only for those who had dwelt on the lost state of innocence. The denial of statehood sometimes has the effect of creating nations where there were none, and certainly in the case of Poland, and more recently of Israel, it created a myth which those called upon to do so found it hard to live up to. For conservatives who found the new Poland disappointingly populist or for socialists who found it depressingly reactionary the problem was one of discontent. For artists the problem was more crucial. When Szymanowski gave his first concert in a free Poland, the hall was half-empty. Literature and art were becoming luxuries, rather than the life-giving manna they had been. Redundancy is a cruel prospect for the creative artist, and it was particularly cruel for the descendants of such national bards as Mickiewicz to find themselves strumming irrelevancies on the sidelines.

The Polish intelligentsia of the nineteenth century had devoted its energies to thought largely because there was no other field open to them. In 1918, this intelligentsia was turned into an administrative middle class and bolstered by a new intake of the men of action who had helped create the Republic. It began to display all the philistinism of any other middle class confronted by avant-garde expression, seeing it increasingly as a manifestation of 'degeneracy', a blot on the otherwise 'healthy' aspect of the nation. Writers were speaking to a shrinking public, a small 'radical intelligentsia'. They keenly felt the paradox that in their own free country they were more alienated from the people than those writers of the previous century who could not be read openly. Their alienation turned to bitterness and even anger. In the grotesque poem *Herrings in Tomato Sauce*, written in 1936, Konstanty Ildefons Gałczyński (1905–53) brings Władysław the Short, the king who had struggled to reunite the fragmented country, back to life: 'Well, you wanted your Poland, now you've got it!' he is told.

Some managed to keep writing lyrical poetry ignoring the political situation, others grew more sombre in their work. Lechoń stopped joking in the 1930s. Gałczyński turned to right-wing politics, while others drifted in the opposite direction. Słonimski went to Soviet Russia in 1932 looking for answers. Bruno Jasieński, a futurist who turned to poetry of social protest, went to live in Paris, where he wrote a novel in French for which he was expelled, and then to Moscow where he wrote a Socialist Realist novel before being liquidated by Stalin. Władysław Broniewski, a former Legionary and a veteran of the 1920 war, became a communist and wrote verse denouncing the system in Poland.

There was an important group of Polish artists in Paris, dominated by the remarkable painter Tadeusz Makowski (1882–1932). But Poland remained the scene of vibrant avant-garde activity. In painting, the idiosyncratic naturalism of Eugeniusz Zak (1884–1926) was succeeded by the expressionist surrealism of Witkiewicz, who was superseded by a school of 'formists'. In literature, too, a 'formist' avant-garde challenged the poets of the *Skamander* group, only to be succeeded by waves of 'catastrophists' in the mid-1930s, reflecting a growing pessimism. Julian Tuwim revealed his fears in the long poem *Ball at the Opera* (1936), an apocalyptic allegory of society's sins dancing their way to the end of the world. A year later, Słonimski published his novel *Two Ends of the Earth*, in which Warsaw is bombed by a dictator called Retlich and the two survivors are placed in a concentration camp. Witkiewicz had taken a pessimistic view of the world long before. Now many of his contemporaries were arriving at one. A younger group, based in Wilno, including Czesław Miłosz (b.1911) and Jerzy Putrament, were just starting out on their literary careers, and they made impending catastrophe an article of faith. It is not difficult to see why. Ultimately, it would not be up to the Poles to define their future or their national identity.

Ever since 1918 the precious gain of Polish independence had been at risk, in the face of inevitable German revanchism and the fundamental reluctance of Russia, Tsarist or Bolshevik, to be rolled back eastwards. Under Stalin and Hitler they were fast building up to a position from which they could reject what was to Germany a humiliating frontier settlement, and to Russia a tactical, time-gaining peace. It was clear that war would come, and all but the most sanguine and ill-informed realised that Poland did not stand a chance on her own.

With all the wisdom of hindsight it is impossible to suggest a foreign policy that might have saved Poland. Between 1932 and 1939 Polish foreign policy was conducted by Colonel Józef Beck, who saw clearly that in the diplomatic game Poland had nothing to offer: no dependable allies, reserves of power or crucial facilities – except as a theatre of war. Since the Western Powers demonstrated at the Locarno Conference of 1925 that they would bend over backwards to avoid another war, Central European states had to fend for themselves. In 1932 Poland signed a non-aggression pact with the Soviet Union. This brought Polish-German tensions to a head, with demands that Danzig be returned to Germany. Piłsudski even considered the possibility of following through with a Franco-Polish attack on Germany after Hitler came to power. But Hitler stepped in with conciliatory offers and in January 1934 Poland and Germany signed a ten-year non-aggression pact. Hitler was keen to meet Piłsudski and discuss plans for a German drive into the Baltic countries in conjunction with a Polish drive to the Black Sea. The Poles were not, however, going to be talked into giving Danzig to Germany in return for tracts of an ungovernable Ukraine.

After the *Anschluss* with Austria in the spring of 1938 it became obvious that the West would be of no practical use to Poland in time of trouble. Beck could not turn to the Soviet Union for a full military alliance, since no Pole who knew his history could consider allowing 'friendly' Russian troops on to Polish soil. The only hope was to placate Germany in the hope of staving off aggression and of eliciting a convincing promise of military support from Britain and France, who were naturally anxious to wean Poland away from Germany's influence. In October 1938, after the German seizure of the Sudetenland, the Poles reoccupied the Zaolzie (the part of Cieszyn which the Czechs had annexed in 1918). It was intended partly as a show of force and partly as a strategic measure to strengthen Poland's southern flank against German attack – a consideration which also prompted a Polish ultimatum to Lithuania to open diplomatic relations and declare her neutral intentions. These moves had little practical effect beyond giving liberals abroad the unfortunate impression that Poland was a strutting bully little better than Germany or Italy.

On 22 March 1939 the German government delivered an ultimatum to Poland demanding that Danzig should become part of the Third Reich, along with the strip of Polish territory dividing East Prussia from the rest of Germany, the so-called 'Polish Corridor'. Poland could go no further down the road of co-operation with Germany, and the ultimatum was duly rejected. On 31 March Great Britain offered an unconditional guarantee of Polish territorial integrity, and in the following month a full military alliance was signed by Britain, France and Poland.

There followed three months of uneasy calm. Optimists saw this as a sign that the situation had been contained and peace assured. In fact Germany was using the time to make her final preparations. Hitler put pressure on Rumania, forcing her to secretly rescind her defensive military alliance with Poland, and started negotiating with Stalin. In August, the foreign ministers of the two states, Ribbentrop and Molotov, signed a secret protocol concerning the future of Poland.

On the evening of 31 August 1939 a dozen German convicts were dressed in Polish uniforms and told to attack a German radio station in Gleiwitz in Upper Silesia. Early next morning, as the world awoke to the remarkable news that Poland had attacked the Third Reich, the Wehr-macht invaded Poland in defence of the threatened Fatherland. Two days later, on 3 September, Great Britain and France declared war on Ger-many. Two weeks after that, on 17 September, when it became quite clear that they would do nothing further to help their ally, the Soviet Union invaded Poland from the east. A new partition of Poland had been accomplished.

21

Ordeal by Fire

The Polish Republic of 1918–39 had its faults, but it was not a political failure. The next six years would reveal what it had achieved and fully vindicate the reputation of a regime which it is all too easy to criticise. At the beginning of 1939 Poland was hardly prepared to fight a war, let alone face the combined onslaught of Nazi Germany and Stalinist Russia. Economically weak and militarily deficient, the country was rent by its foreign minorities and its political factions. It might have been expected to fall apart not only as a military power, but as a state. Yet the Poles who fought on every front between 1939 and 1945 were the soldiers of the Polish Republic, loyal to its legitimate government and to the political edifice of prewar Poland. Their discipline and unity of purpose must be put down to its credit. Indeed, it could be said that the vicissitudes of the Polish effort during the war, its glories and its inadequacies, its victories and its defeats, reflect the achievements and failures of the Republic.

The September campaign was a case in point. Hitler gambled everything on the probability that the Allies would not respond immediately, and therefore threw everything he had at Poland in the hope of overunning it first. On 1 September some 1.8 million German troops invaded from three sides: East Prussia in the north, Germany in the west, and Slovakia in the South. They were supported by 2,600 tanks, of which the Polish army boasted barely 180, and over 2,000 aircraft, which quickly wrested control of the skies from the 420 planes of the Polish Air Force. The Polish Army had neither the equipment nor the training to stand up to this hurricane of armour. Its 1,500-mile defensive screen was pierced by eight German spearheads, while the Luftwaffe carried out massive bombing raids on Polish cities. By 6 September the Polish command had lost control; by 10 September the Germans had overrun most of northern and western Poland; on 14 September Warsaw was encircled.

Once the first shock had worn off, Polish commanders reacted with determination. The Pomeranian and Poznanian army groups under General Tadeusz Kutrzeba held off the Germans in a two-day battle at

Kutno. They then fell back on the Vistula and Bzura rivers, whence, reinforced by other units, they launched a counter-attack which threw the Germans back and won a breathing-space for other retreating Polish units. In order to avoid encirclement, the Polish command had ordered a withdrawal to the region of Lwów, where a new line of defence was being organised, pivoting on the frontiers with neutral Russia and friendly Rumania. But on 17 September Russian armies invaded from the east, and it was revealed that Rumania had, under German pressure, renounced its military alliance with Poland. The continued defence of this last corner of Poland was impossible, and the campaign was over. Warsaw, besieged since 14 September, capitulated two weeks later; the garrison on the Hel peninsula off Gdańsk held out till 2 October; General Kleeberg's Polesie Defence Group surrendered at Kock on 5 October after a week of fighting on two fronts against Germans and Russians. Smaller units continued to fight in various parts of the country until the spring of 1940, when their remnants went underground.

The September campaign is usually portrayed as a courageous fiasco and characterised by the image of lancers charging tanks. It is difficult to understand why. In September 1939 no European army could hope to defeat the Wehrmacht, and the Poles did not intend to try. It had been agreed with the British and French staffs that in the event of aggression, Poland was to hold down the German forces for a period of two weeks, which would allow the French time to throw 90 divisions, 2,500 tanks and 1,400 planes across the virtually undefended Rhine. The Poles held on for twice that time, but not a single French footsoldier moved forward, while the RAF confined itself to dropping leaflets on German cities. As Marshal Śmigły-Rydz explained: 'I was the commander of a sector which had to be sacrificed in order to give the others the time and opportunity to organise and prepare.' In this context the campaign was remarkably successful. The Poles tied down the German forces for over three weeks, and would certainly have managed to keep going longer had the Russians not invaded (which they certainly would not have done had the French attacked Germany, as Stalin was reluctant to engage his forces and strictly adhered to the hyena policy). For all its inadequacy, the Polish army acquitted itself valiantly, taking a greater toll of German men and equipment than the Franco-British effort of 1940. The Germans lost over 50,000 men, 697 planes and 993 tanks and armoured cars. But their dogged resistance cost the Poles nearly 200,000 in dead and wounded.

In October the country was divided between its captors. The larger Soviet zone was incorporated into the Soviet Union and over the next few months about 1,700,000 of its inhabitants were transported to labour camps in Siberia or the far north of Russia. The Germans incorporated Pomerania, Silesia and Posnania into the Reich, while the remainder of

The Nazi-Soviet partition of Poland, 1939

their conquests was designated as the General-Gouvernement. This was a colony ruled from the Royal Castle on Wawel hill by Hitler's lawyer-friend Hans Frank. He declared that the concept of Poland would be erased from the human mind, and that those Poles who were not exterminated would survive only as slaves within the new German Empire. The process began at once. Priests, landowners, teachers, mayors, lawyers and persons of influence were summarily shot or sent to a concentration camp which was started at Oświęcim (Auschwitz). The humbler elements of the population were shunted about in a vast programme of rearrangement whose logic is difficult to follow. Over the next five years about 750,000 Germans were imported into the areas that had been attached to the Reich; 860,000 Poles from the same areas were resettled in the General-Gouvernement, while a further 330,000 were shot. In all, some 2,000,000 Poles were moved out of the Reich into the General-Gouvernement, while 1,300,000 Poles were taken from the General-Gouvernement and shipped to the Reich as slave labour. In May 1940 the Jewish ghetto of Łódż was sealed, and the same was done in Warsaw and other cities. Over the next four years 2,700,000 Polish citizens of Jewish origins were taken from these ghettos and murdered. Like Frederick and Catherine before them, Hitler and Stalin, having decreed that Poland had ceased to exist, were determined to bring this about in the most ruthless manner. The inhabitants of the area were to endure a long nightmare which defies concise description. Yet not for a moment did there cease to be a Polish Government and a Polish Army.

There was a relatively smooth transition from the divided political scene of peace-time to a government which combined democratic respectability with authority. In the last days of September 1939 President Mościcki, who was interned after he crossed the Rumanian frontier with what was left of his government, appointed Władysław Raczkiewicz, former President of the Senate, as his successor. On 30 September Raczkiewicz formed a Government in Paris under the premiership of General Władysław Sikorski, who also became commander-in-chief of the Polish armed forces. A National Council consisting of senior representatives of all the major parties was convened under the symbolic presidency of Ignacy Paderewski and the chairmanship of Stanisław Mikołajczyk, leader of the People's Party. The Government was recognised by the Allies and proceeded to re-form the Polish armed forces with escapees filtering through from Eastern Europe and émigré Polish volunteers from France and the United States. By June 1940 these numbered 84,500 men in four infantry divisions, two brigades and an armoured brigade, an air force consisting of 9,000 men, and a navy of 1,400. Polish units took part in the ill-fated battle for Narvik, and then in the French campaign of June 1940. Three-quarters of the land forces were lost in the fall of France, but the remnants followed the government to Britain, where they began to organise once again. By 1945 there were 220,000 men in the Polish Army under British command. The Polish Air Force, which accounted for 12 per cent of all German aircraft destroyed in the Battle of Britain in the summer of 1940, grew to a strength of ten fighter and four bomber squadrons. It flew a total of 86,527 sorties, lost 1,669 men, and shot down 500 German planes and 190 V-1 rockets. The Polish naval ensign flew on some 60 vessels, including two cruisers, nine destroyers and five submarines, which were involved in 665 actions at sea.

The struggle went on in Poland with similar continuity. The day before the fall of Warsaw on 28 September, a group of senior officers established a resistance command which assumed authority over units operating throughout the country and built up its own. Out of this grew the Home Army, Armia Krajowa (AK), directly subordinated to the commander-in-chief in London. By 1944 the AK numbered nearly 400,000 men and women, which made it the largest resistance movement in occupied Europe. The operations began in what might have been a spectacular way. On 5 October 1939 Hitler took the salute at the German victory parade in Warsaw standing on a podium filled with enough explosives to blow him and his entourage into the sky, but a last-minute change in German plans meant that the man responsible for detonating the charge was moved from the vicinity. Open resistance and assassinations of German personnel provoked such massive reprisals on the civilian population that they had to be abandoned in favour of less glamorous activities, such as intelligence-gathering for the Allies. An efficient system of couriers and radio-links provided rapid communication with London, and the extension of the AK into concentration camps and factories worked by Polish slave labour all over Germany meant that the net was cast wide. As well as derailing trains, blowing bridges and cutting communications, the AK operations embraced the wholesale sabotage of German military material – engines, view-finding and navigation equipment for tanks, guns and planes – at source in the factories which produced them.

The extraordinary courage and ingenuity of the resistance were reflected in underground life as a whole. The government continued to hold sway through the Delegatura, an executive based in Warsaw with its own consultative committee drawn from all parties. The Delegatura was the political master of the AK and controlled everything in Poland from underground law-courts to the flying universities and clandestine schools, much as the City Committee had done in 1863. The life of the nation was lived in hiding. For a period of six years, education at every level was carried on secretly in indescribable conditions. Bombs were manufactured, plays were staged and books were published under the nose of the Germans, and hardly a national holiday passed without the Polish national anthem and *God Save the King* being broadcast all over the city through the official German megaphone system. The whole spectrum of activities was carried out with an efficiency and a wit that tend to obscure the difficulties and dangers involved. Torture, concentration camp and death awaited anyone on whom German suspicion fell, and many thousands paid the price.

The only organisations which the Delegatura and the AK did not control were the Jewish resistance movement and the small fighting organisations affiliated to the extreme right and left. The Nazis quickly set about sealing off the Jewish community from the rest. While this was a simple operation in the ghettos and *shtetls* full of Orthodox or Hasidic Jews who stood out by their dress, it was more complex in the case of Jews who had assimilated into the Polish middle classes or intelligentsia. Faced with the death penalty for assisting or sheltering a Jew, most Poles were reluctant to interfere, while some elements of the extreme right even regarded the whole operation as a rather favourable development. At the same time countless Poles did risk their lives to hide Jews and provide them with false papers, and in 1942 the AK set up a special commission of assistance which was responsible for saving the lives of 10,000 Jews. It also supplied the Jewish resistance with a quantity of arms before and during the fighting in the Warsaw ghetto. Followers of the extreme right in politics had formed the National Armed Forces (NSZ), which remained independent of the AK. This was of little significance at this stage, although it did sow a certain amount of confusion. On the other hand, the People's Army, affiliated to the Polish Workers' Party and Moscow, was to cause considerable problems for the Delagatura.

The Polish Communist Party had never been a significant force on the political scene. In the mid-1930s its leadership was imprisoned, and the bulk of the activists sought refuge in Russia, where in 1938 Stalin liquidated the higher echelons and dispatched the rest to concentration camps. The only senior Polish communists to avoid this fate were those, like Władysław Gomułka and Marceli Nowotko, who were safe inside Polish jails. In December 1941 Nowotko was instructed by Moscow to found the Polish Workers' Party, but he was assassinated less than a year later on orders from Stalin. Gomułka, who had been organising underground units in south-eastern Poland, became leader of the party, and it was under his leadership that the People's Army was founded as an equivalent to the Delegatura's AK. Moscow was building its own structures as an alternative to those of the Polish government, without as yet defining the role they were to play.

This uneasy situation reflected the anomalous position of Poland in the Allied camp. In 1940 the Allies were at war with Nazi Germany, but Poland was also technically at war with Soviet Russia, which had invaded as an ally of Germany. General Sikorski made several attempts to clarify the position through talks with Stalin, without success. But on 22 June 1941 Hitler launched operation *Barbarossa*, and as the Soviet Armies disintegrated under the impact, Stalin became more amenable. On 30 July an agreement was signed whereby Poland and the Soviet Union became allies. All Polish citizens imprisoned in Russia were to be released and formed up into a Polish Army which would fight alongside the Red Army.

The official cordiality was undermined by severe tensions. Although Russia repudiated the Ribbentrop-Molotov pact of 1939, it did not recognise Poland's prewar frontier. Polish prisoners were released grudgingly and some were rearrested. The army forming in southern Russia under the command of General Władysław Anders was exposed to provocations and attempted infiltration by communists. As time passed, Anders grew puzzled and then uneasy about the fate of some of his colleagues. He had drawn up lists of those officers he knew had been captured by the Soviets in 1939 and would prove useful to him now. As the last prisoners trickled in from camps in the far north, it became clear that some 15,000 officers, including several generals and an admiral, were unaccountably missing. The Polish ambassador in Moscow was given no satisfactory explanation. Sikorski personally took the matter up with Stalin, and was fobbed off with a promise to investigate and a profession of friendship to the Poles. Meanwhile, General Anders' army was being harassed and even had its food rations withheld. Two years in the notorious Lubianka prison had taught him to fear the worst, and he finally decided to take his army and its horde of Polish waifs and strays out of the Soviet Union to Iran, where the British needed it.

On 11 April 1943 German radio announced that mass graves had been discovered in the forest of Katyn near Smolensk containing the bodies of 4,231 Polish officers, each with his hands tied behind his back and a bullet in his head. The first sample of names given (they all had their documents and uniforms) tallied with those on the list made out by Anders in 1941. The Russians accused the Germans of the massacre. The Polish Government demanded an investigation by the International Red Cross, whereupon, on 26 April, Russia accused the Government of bad faith and collaboration with the Germans, and broke off diplomatic relations. There is no reasonable doubt that the executions had been carried out by the Russian NKVD in the spring of 1940.

The inhabitants of Warsaw heard of the Katyn massacre one week before SS Brigadeführer Jurgen Stroop launched the operation to slaughter the remaining inhabitants of the Warsaw ghetto. The whole area was reduced to rubble over the next three weeks as the Jewish resistance defied the German onslaught. The ruins were still smouldering when, in June 1943, the commander of the AK, General Stefan Rowecki, was arrested in Warsaw by the Gestapo. On 5 July, the plane in which General Sikorski was travelling back to London crashed on take-off from Gibraltar, killing all its passengers. With sabotage as the most likely cause, suspicions of Russian involvement and British connivance were immediately aroused, never to be satisfactorily proved or dispelled. Everything seemed to be conspiring to crush the spirit of the Poles and further to weaken their hopes of independence.

After the Russian victory at Stalingrad in November 1942, Stalin's position in the Allied camp became unassailable. He now began to denounce the Polish Government as a phoney clique with no real following in the country, and he started recruiting his own Polish army in Russia, out of those Poles he had failed to release two years previously. As Stalin's position grew stronger, that of the Polish Government grew weaker. The death of Sikorski removed from the scene the one man Churchill and

Roosevelt felt they could not ignore. He was succeeded as prime minister by Stanisław Mikołajczyk, and as commander-in-chief by General Kazimierz Sosnkowski.

Stalin insisted that the Polish frontier of 1939 was unsatisfactory, arguing that it should be moved westward to correspond more accurately to the areas in which Poles constituted an overall majority, and he adroitly seized on the 'Curzon Line', a cease-fire line pulled out of a hat by British diplomats in 1918. Fearful lest Stalin turn round and make peace with Hitler if crossed, Roosevelt and Churchill tried to persuade the Polish Government to accede to the Russian demands. The Poles could not sign away large areas of the country without losing authority in Poland. Nor did they believe that such a concession would guarantee Russian friendship: it would only demonstrate their own weakness.

Mikołajczyk wanted to negotiate directly, but Stalin became increasingly evasive. The Teheran Conference of November 1943 had revealed to him the extent of his power over Churchill and Roosevelt. There was no good reason for him to tie his hands on an issue on which he now perceived he would have both entirely free. Time was on his side, not on that of the Poles. In January 1944 the Red Army crossed the 1939 Polish-Russian frontier in pursuit of the retreating Wehrmacht. Soon he would have his divisions in Poland, while those of the Polish Government were in Britain and Italy. He even had the 80,000 men of the First Polish Army commanded by General Berling, an ex-Legionary who had been imprisoned in 1939 and persuaded to remain in Russia. Ironically, the Polish Government's one remaining asset in Poland, the huge AK, turned out to be a political liability. Its long-awaited show of force was reduced to a peripheral episode of pointless heroism which profited only Stalin.

The AK command had been preparing a full-scale rising to coincide with Allied plans. After the British and American advance through Italy into Austria, the Polish Second Army Corps of General Anders was to race ahead into Poland from the south, while a special independent parachute brigade waited in England to be dropped in to support the rising. But the Soviet armies advanced faster than those of the Allies. In the event, Poland would be liberated by the Red Army, while Anders battled from Monte Cassino to Ancona and Bologna, and the parachute brigade was destined to meet its effective end in the battle for Arnhem. The AK therefore had to face the fact that it would be liberated by allies who did not recognise it or its government. As they prepared to conduct military operations against the Germans, the Poles realised that they would simultaneously have to make a political stand against the Soviets. Their plan, code-named *Tempest*, was to conduct operations in the German rear in support of the advancing Soviet troops. AK units were to make contact with Red Army commanders and combine further operations. It was an attempt to bridge on the battlefield the chasm which had opened in the political world.

In April 1944 the 6,000-strong 27th Division helped the Red Army capture Lwów. In July the 5,000-strong local AK units similarly assisted in the battle for Wilno. In both cases, the Red Army and AK units co-operated with cordiality, but two days after the celebratory bear-hugs and handshakes, all the AK officers were arrested or shot, and their men pressed into Berling's First Polish Army. Discouraging as this was, the AK command still clung to the hope that the Soviets might behave differently once they crossed the 'Curzon Line' into territory which they formally recognised as Polish. These hopes came to nothing, and after the joint liberation of Lublin at the end of July, the AK units taking part met with a similar fate.

In June Stalin had told Churchill that he would only consider negotiating with the Polish Government if certain changes were made within it. Roosevelt suggested that he agree any such changes directly with Mikołajczyk, and after strong Allied pressure, Stalin agreed. Mikołajczyk flew to Moscow on 26 July, but by this time his position was parlous. Stalin had collected a number of his client Poles into a 'Union of Polish Patriots', and in Lublin on 22 July a group of these, under the leadership of an erstwhile member of the PPS, Edward Osóbka-Morawski, constituted themselves as the 'Polish Liberation Committee'.

The AK command had to think fast. The Red Army crossed the Bug on 20 July, and on the following day news broke of the bomb plot against Hitler. On 23 July the German administration began to evacuate its offices in Warsaw, while endless columns of *Volksdeutsch* settlers, stray German soldiers and camp-followers clogged all roads leading west. On 27 July Soviet units crossed the Vistula at Magnuszew, and Russian guns could be heard in Warsaw. On 29 July Moscow Radio broadcast a message from Molotov addressed to the inhabitants of Warsaw, calling for an uprising against the Germans. 'There is not a moment to lose,' it urged. The AK command were only too aware of this, and they were caught on the horns of a harrowing dilemma.

An uprising in Warsaw was a terrifying prospect. The AK would almost certainly be wiped out and the civilian population was bound to suffer. If they did not rise, the Soviets would brand them as Nazi sympathisers, while the Germans would blow up most of the city, which they had extensively mined. The AK command also knew that it would be hard to restrain their own units, which had waited five years for the moment they could openly fight the Germans. Units of the People's Army were preparing to go into action, and this would provoke a general free-for-all which nobody would be able to control. The Delegatura consulted their superiors in London, who advised against a rising and stressed that the Allies would be unable to support it in any way, but left the final decision up to the men on the spot. The Delegatura left it to the military. There was no room for manoeuvre, and not much choice. After a meeting of senior officers, the commander of the AK, General Tadeusz Bór-Komorowski, made his decision. With the advance units of the Red Army in Radzymin, only 12 kilometres from Warsaw, and the thud of their guns rattling the windows, he gave the order to start the uprising on the following day.

At 5 p.m. on 1 August 1944 units of the AK went into action all over Warsaw. Their initial aim was to clear the enemy from the city and seize enough arms to equip their reserves. This plan might have been feasible in the volatile atmosphere of the last days of July, but by 1 August the Wehrmacht had reinforced pickets and garrisons throughout the city and was moving fresh Panzer divisions across the Vistula. The AK units failed to take a number of their primary objectives. They did not manage to expel the Germans from a crucial east-west axis running between the older part of the city to the north and the large area of suburbs to the south. Over the next couple of days they extended the area under their control, but failed to take the airport, the main station, or any of the Vistula bridges. By 6 August they had fought to a standstill and from then on could only defend themselves. This they did for a total of 63 days.

The Germans quickly mobilised a special force under the command of General von dem Bach. It included the SS Viking Panzer Division; an assortment of military police battalions; the notorious brigade of SS Sturmbannführer Dr Oskar Dirlewanger, composed entirely of German convicts spared the noose in return for their promise of proving their enthusiasm for the Fatherland; a battalion of riff-raff from the Near East, the SS Azerbaidjan; and several units of Russian prisoners-of-war drafted into the 'Russian National Liberation Army'. Following their capture of the Wola suburb, they indulged in a butchery of the civilian population which shocked even the German command. Over the next weeks the Korpsgruppe von dem Bach advanced from all sides, gradually pushing the AK back, house by house, and slaughtering the civilian inhabitants as they went. The Luftwaffe relentlessly divebombed the areas defended by the Poles, while long-range artillery poured in shells. Conditions were indescribable. Short of ammunition, medical supplies, food and even water, the soldiers of the AK fought on with courage and ingenuity (the German casualty figures of 17,000 dead and only 9,000 wounded testify to the care taken with every bullet). They managed to capture several tanks and a great many other weapons, but they desperately needed air-drops of arms, ammunition and medical supplies from the west and a Soviet advance against the Germans from the east if they were going to regain the initiative. Although they held on for eight weeks, neither materialised in any real form.

The first Allied arms drops took place on the night of 4 August, but the price paid was enormous. The planes flew a round trip of 2,500 kilometres from northern Italy, and of the 320 British, Polish, South African and American crews which took part in the sorties, nearly half never made it back to base. Churchill suggested a shuttle operation and requested landing facilities on Soviet airfields for the RAF, but Stalin refused.

A couple of days after the outbreak of the rising, Moscow radio denounced it as a conspiracy against the Soviet Union. Stalin personally told Mikołajczyk, who was still in Moscow, that 'the Soviet command dissociates itself from the Warsaw adventure and cannot take any responsibility for it.' On 20 August Churchill and Roosevelt sent a joint appeal couched in the strongest terms, to which Stalin replied that since the Poles had started the business they must bear the consequences, and described the AK as 'a handful of power-seeking criminals.' He justified his refusal to help by explaining that giving more weapons to the AK would only prolong the sufferings of the civilian population, and that the most effective way of helping them was by an early Soviet capture of Warsaw.

Nobody doubted this. The AK had only decided to rise believing it to be imminent. On 2 August, however, the sound of Soviet guns, which had been such music to the people of Warsaw, began to recede and finally died away. Stalin invoked a number of technical reasons why his armies stood idle for the next six weeks, but while there were certainly military difficulties involved, the real reasons lay elsewhere. The AK and Delegatura represented the element of leadership which believed that Poland should control its own future as a sovereign state. This was not among Stalin's intentions, and sooner or later this leadership would have to be eliminated. But this would not be easy with a fully mobilised AK standing behind it, and the operation would have strained the capacities of even the gigantic forces of repression at Stalin's disposal. It was therefore something of a godsend to him that the Germans were doing the dirty work for him, and to him it would have been madness to interfere. He could claim complete innocence while reaping the fruits of a crime which he would otherwise have had to commit.

Neither his thinking nor the essence of his actions changed even when, after increasingly forceful demands from Churchill and Roosevelt, Stalin agreed to a shuttle operation. On 13 September his own air force appeared over Warsaw to drop supplies. Soviet forces at last occupied Praga, the east-bank suburb of Warsaw, and on 16 September Berling's Polish troops attempted to cross the Vistula. On 18 September 100 Liberators of the USAF carried out the first shuttle-drop, but by then the Polish-held areas of the city had shrunk so far that most of the supplies fell into German hands.

The AK held three main areas – the Old Town to the north, the city centre, and the large residential suburb of Mokotów to the south – as well as several smaller districts. Communication between these was poor, and

139 Winter 1944. King Zygmunt III stands amid the ruins of Warsaw defiantly brandishing the Cross he wanted to plant in Moscow, while the Red Army were implanting their own creed on the ruins of Poland.

the large and well-armed units which had congregated in the countryside outside the city could not break through the ring of Germans surrounding their comrades within. The Germans began by liquidating resistance in the western suburbs of Wola and Ochota before concentrating on reducing the stronghold of the Old Town. It was here that some of the fiercest fighting took place, at very close quarters. Bombed into what looked more like some mountainous eyrie than the centre of Europe's eighth largest city, it was fought over inch by inch. After four weeks of dogged resistance, the command of the group defending the Old Town decided to evacuate. On the night of 1 September the remnants of this force, over 4,000 men, climbed down manholes into the city sewers, carrying as many of their wounded as they could. The long trek waist-deep in filth was not made any easier by the Germans pouring poison gas down every manhole they could find, but eventually most of the men emerged in the city centre. This continued to hold out, but towards the end of September the other pockets of resistance were reduced one by one. There seemed to be little point in prolonging the agony and on 2 October General Bór-Komorowski signed the capitulation. Churchill and Roosevelt had stressed that the soldiers of the AK were regular Allied troops, and the Germans treated them accordingly. The civilian population were herded into cattle trucks and sent to concentration camps or forced labour in Germany. They left behind 250,000 dead, buried in the ruins. As soon as they had gone, Hitler's personal instructions went into effect: squads of SS demolition experts, Vernichtungskommando, moved in and proceeded with Teutonic thoroughness to dynamite any building left standing. By the time the Red Army 'liberated' Warsaw in January 1945, there was nobody and nothing to liberate, except for stray dogs and rats. A huge desert of rubble remained as a monument to the city which can rightly claim to have suffered more than any other in the whole war.

In the last hours before the capitulation tens of thousands of people had slipped out, making for the safety of the countryside. Among them were several thousand soldiers of the AK, its new commander, General Okulicki, and the whole Delegatura. The fall of Warsaw was not to be the end of the struggle for the AK, which still had units throughout the country. Yet its role was effectively at an end. Five years of meticulous planning, ingenuity and quiet heroism had yielded impressive results in the field of intelligence-gathering, and accounted for some 150,000 German military personnel. But the opportunity for which these men and women had prepared never materialised. Neither the *Tempest* operations nor the Warsaw uprising gave the organisation a chance to show its full potential. The Polish Government and the AK were outmanoeuvred politically by the Soviets, and the events of 1944 were only the first in a long process, in the course of which the entire Polish leadership was gradually elbowed aside and replaced with men picked by Stalin.

Mikołajczyk's trip to Moscow was politically disastrous. Far from strengthening his bargaining position, the Warsaw Uprising had turned him into a client begging for help. During talks which took place in Moscow in October, under British and American patronage, Stalin demanded that Mikołajczyk accept the 'Curzon Line' as a frontier in the east, in return for which Poland would be compensated with former German territory up to the river Oder. He also wanted Mikołajczyk to dissolve the Polish Government and come to Poland to head a provisional government made up mostly of the Lublin committee.

The Polish prime minister was less concerned with the territorial adjustments than with the open violations of constitutional principles, and he was aware that the majority of his colleagues in London and most Poles throughout the world would reject the idea of such a surrender. Pressed by the British and American governments, he felt obliged, against his better judgement, to demonstrate his goodwill by accepting the compromise. His misgivings were to be fully justified within a couple of years.

On 17 January 1945 the Red Army marched into the ruins of Warsaw and within a couple of months the whole of Poland was in Soviet hands. Stalin was master of the situation and proceeded to state his case with force at the Yalta Conference in February and at Potsdam in July. There was hard bargaining over who should form the interim government in Poland, with Stalin putting forward his men, and Churchill and Roosevelt urging the inclusion of political leaders from London and figures like Wincenty Witos and Archbishop Adam Sapieha. The resulting compromise was an interim government consisting of twenty-one ministers of whom sixteen were Stalin's men, with Edward Osóbka-Morawski as premier and Mikołajczyk as deputy premier. The Allies formally recognised this and withdrew recognition from the Polish Government. The majority of its ministers refused to bow to this fate, and the government exists to this day in London in defiance of the high-handed arrangements of the Great Powers.

The bargaining over the composition of the interim government was, in fact, academic. Behind the Red Army came Stalin's secret police, the NKVD, and with it the new Polish security services, the Urząd Bezpieczeństwa (UB). They were not concerned with the discussions going on at Yalta on the nature of elections to be held in Poland, merely with rooting out of Polish society every element which could be deemed unsympathetic to the Soviet Union. Although General Okulicki had formally dissolved the AK in January of that year, many of its members remained on their guard, while units of the right-wing NSZ engaged in active self-defence. As the NKVD and UB intensified their search for 'reactionaries' (i.e. former AK soldiers), this self-defence grew into a minor guerilla war which cost the lives of some 30,000 Poles and 1,000 Soviet soldiers over the next two years. In May, sixteen men, including General Okulicki and the entire Delegatura, were invited to Moscow for 'talks' and then put on trial for 'collaborating with the Nazis', receiving sentences of up to ten years. Tens of thousands of AK members, former officers, political workers and landowners were dragged in, interrogated, tortured, and often quietly murdered. Up to 16,000 people are thought to have died in this way. Nor were the liquidations confined to the politically aware. Remote areas were the scene of massacres and executions whose motives remain obscure. Surviving Jews too were the victims of murder and at least one pogrom, in Kielce.

The confusion all over the country was intense. About 3,500,000 Germans either fled or were removed, mostly from parts of Germany now taken over by Poland. Their place was being taken by Poles flooding in from every quarter, 2,200,000 returning from slave labour and concentration camps in Germany, 1,500,000 ousted from the Polish lands taken over by the Soviet Union. The Soviet order was imposed ruthlessly at ground level, where the decisions of the political men were as arbitrary as those of their colleagues of the police. Anything could be 'nationalised' in the pandemonium – estates, factories, smallholdings, livestock, pictures and other valuables – and it was unwise to argue the legal points. All the political window-dressing was being concentrated for the benefit of the Allies, and regardless of the lawlessness reigning in the country, this was carried out with zeal in the run-up to the 1947 elections to the new Seym, which were to prove a show-piece of Soviet management.

Mikołajczyk's Polish People's Party (PSL) was the largest contestant, with more members (600,000) than all the other parties put together. The second largest party was the new PPS. Its old leadership having remained in exile or in hiding, it was led by a prewar activist and survivor of Auschwitz, Józef Cyrankiewicz. The party favoured by Stalin, the Polish Workers' Party (PPR), led by Władysław Gomułka, had only 65,000 members in December 1945, just over one-tenth of the membership of the PSL. In the event, however, the PSL received only 10.3 per cent of the vote. One million people were disqualified from voting by bureaucratic sleight-of-hand, thousands more were arrested on the day or beaten up on the way to the polling-stations, which were heavily staffed with members of the security services; 128 activists of the PSL were murdered, 149 of its candidates were arrested, 174 were 'disqualified' and only 28 were elected, of whom 14 were subsequently 'disqualified'. Cyrankiewicz was prime minister. Fearing for his life, Stanisław Mikołajczyk escaped to the West. The Lublin men were in control.

The subjection of Polish political life to Russian norms did not end there. Władysław Gomułka, secretary of the PPR and deputy premier, the principal advocate of 'a Polish road to Socialism', was accused of 'national-ist deviation' and sacked from his post, which was filled by Bolesław Bierut, a staunch Stalinist. This was followed by a purge of 'nationalists' throughout the PPR and a witch-hunt in the army. Those who had served in Polish forces abroad and returned to offer their services to the new state were mostly shot. The Russian Marshal Rokossovsky was put in charge of the army, which was staffed throughout by Russian officers. As the cold war intensified, the purge was carried through to trade unions, local organisations and the street. Typical Stalinist verbiage about 'foreign agents' and 'enemy espionage' invaded everything from a quarrel between two party bosses to a police report on a wayside robbery. A brief affair with a former member of the AK was pretext enough for a girl to be interro-gated, tortured and imprisoned for years. The prisons were bursting, and new concentration camps at Mielęcin and Jaworzno filled up with some 30,000 workers who had dared to strike or even grumble about conditions. Peasants who had been given land in 1945 were forced to give it up and join Soviet-style collective farms.

In December 1948 the remaining deputies of the PPS were forced to merge with the PPR in the new PZPR (Polish United Workers' Party), which henceforth became *the* Party. The remains of the PSL were amalga-mated into the ZSL (United Peoples' Party), which was only nominally independent of the PZPR. In 1951 Gomułka and others who had fallen from grace were imprisoned. Finally, in 1952, a Soviet-style constitution was imposed on the country, which was officially renamed the People's Republic of Poland.

The Poles are the nation who really lost the Second World War. They fought continuously from the first day to the bitter end and beyond. They put more effort into the struggle than any other society; they lost over half a million fighting men and women, and six million civilians; they were left with one million war-orphans and over half a million invalids. According to the Bureau of War Reparations, the country had lost 38 per cent of its national assets, compared to the 1.5 per cent and 0.8 per cent lost by France and Britain respectively. They lost vast tracts of their country and their two great cultural centres of Wilno and Lwów. They also saw the greater part of their heritage destroyed. Although they were faithful mem-bers of the victorious alliance, they were treated as a vanquished enemy: they were robbed of much of their territory and of their freedom.

Even worse than the physical wrongs done to them were the humilia-tions to which they were subjected. Men and women who had risked their lives for six years plotting and fighting against the German order in unspeakable conditions were dragged into jail by their Soviet masters, tortured and accused of collaborating with the Nazis. In the West, their

The People's Republic of Poland

efforts and sacrifices were belittled and ignored. Their continuing martyrdom aroused no sympathy, and their appeals only irritation. They had not
only been consigned to Hell; they were supposed to enjoy it.

The war was a turning-point in Poland's history, and its consequences
are indelible. It was the last stage in the transformation of the multi-ethnic
Commonwealth into a homogeneous nation-state. Like a purification by
fire, it painfully removed all the anomalies which had made the Republic
such a mongrel state. Poland's frontiers were wrenched back to an
idealised original; the minorities which had not been extirpated were
removed; Poles from all over Eastern Europe were concentrated. The loss
of Wilno and Lwów, and the disappearance of the Jewish, Ruthene and
German elements have impoverished the cultural variety of the Polish
world. The compensating factors are political rather than cultural. Szczecin and Wrocław have brought the country physically closer to the heart of
Europe, and Poland is now full of Poles. They are divided neither by race
nor religion, and the experiences of war put the whole society through a
levelling experience. What the war did not achieve in terms of convincing
workers, peasants and intelligentsia that their interests are one, the
socialist regime has successfully done since.

22

Plans and People

After six years of German occupation the Poles were prepared to put up with almost anything. The workers wanted a system which recognised their needs, the peasants wanted land, the young intelligentsia wanted a fresh start, and everyone wanted peace and bread. The new regime needed to deliver only a modicum of these in order to ensure broad-based support. Its signal failure to deliver anything but incompetence, venality and repression over the next forty years is puzzling to anyone not acquainted with the workings of Soviet-style socialism.

While they had few illusions about the Soviet Union and its methods, people were eager to rebuild the devastated country, and ready to shed their prejudices and private interests. Even members of families such as the Radziwiłł and Potocki offered their services and briefly occupied important posts. At the same time, many never reconciled themselves in any way to what had happened. The majority of those stranded in the West at the end of the war chose not to return, and the wisdom of their choice soon became apparent.

The security services, the UB, had originally shown an interest in members of the prewar establishment and officers of the AK. Such qualifications were soon jettisoned. By 1948 there was nobody so humble or so insignificant that he or she did not qualify for the attentions of the UB, attentions which were both meticulous and brutal. It thrust its tentacles into every corner and crevice, gradually spreading fear throughout society as it became clear that there was no such thing as an innocent person. Even members of the Party and the government were not exempt from these attentions – the discreetly named Tenth Department, which received its orders direct from Moscow, was there to keep an eye on them. The Party could not maintain its rule without the security services, and with every crisis it became more subservient to them, permitting them to adopt laws and procedures of their own.

The Party had originally attracted idealists and opportunists alike, and in the former category peasants and workers were well represented. In the wake of Gomułka's dismissal in September 1948, a massive purge of its ranks was carried out, ostensibly to weed out 'nationalists' and 'deviationists' – i.e. those who believed in some kind of democratic socialism. The white-collar element were adept at keeping their heads down, while factory-floor idealists could be tripped up only too easily. As a result, the purge removed an enormous number of its blue-collar members. By the early 1950s the Party was mostly made up of bureaucrats of one sort or another, and being a Party member became virtually synonymous with being a functionary. A vast privileged class sprang up, a *nomenklatura* on the Russian model, and those who contrived to enter this charmed world were soon living a life very different from that of their ordinary compatriots. The higher the benefits and sins of this ruling elite piled up, the less it could afford to admit any other groups to share in the former or witness the latter. Hence dialogue with and accountability to any other segment of society quickly became impossible.

Yet in spite of the fact that this self-perpetuating oligarchy had a huge army and even larger police at its disposal, it could not do entirely as it pleased, for it was dealing with a nation whose most learned intellectuals and simplest peasants alike worshipped democracy and legality. They also worshipped God. This was an anomaly in a marxist state, and it baffled and irritated the theoreticians. If at first the rulers of Poland believed that a mixture of materialism, social engineering, indoctrination and persecution would eventually alter it, they soon had to concede that it would not. The deep and enduring faith of the people was backed up by a Church led by redoubtable Cardinals such as Prince Adam Stefan Sapieha, Archbishop of Kraków, Augustyn Hlond, Archbishop of Gniezno, and Stefan Wyszyński, who succeeded him as Archbishop of Gniezno and Primate of Poland. Stalin's joke about the Pope's divisions ('How many divisions has the Pope?' was the remark with which he dismissed any idea that the Pope might have any influence on the post-war political scene) has been made to look foolish by the formidable skill with which the Polish Church has marshalled, protected and manoeuvred tens of millions of its faithful.

The Church came through the war morally enhanced by its uncompromising stand against the Germans. Thousand of priests had been sent to concentration camps or shot, and no trace of collaboration tainted the hierarchy's reputation. This made it all the more difficult for the new regime to persecute it. In 1949 the Church's lands were nationalised and its charitable institutions taken over by the state. Religious instruction was forbidden in schools and chaplains were banned from prisons and hospitals. In 1952 three bishops and a number of priests were put on trial charged with spying for the United States, receiving sentences of death or imprisonment, and in September 1953 Primate Stefan Wyszyński himself was imprisoned. The government nevertheless moved cautiously, fearful of evoking a mass reaction.

The Church's most solid support came from the peasants, who still made up over half of the population. Marxist planners have never been fond of peasants, and usually try to turn as many of them as possible into 'workers'. In 1945 the peasants' support was wooed by the confiscation and redistribution of large estates. But within a couple of years the same peasants were forced into collective farms on the Russian model. By 1954 there were 10,000 of these, mostly on the territories transferred from Germany to Poland in 1945. The remaining private peasant farms were squeezed by the imposition of compulsory quotas which they had to deliver at fixed prices usually below the cost of production. Force was regularly used to collect the quotas and a newly imposed land tax from the unwilling peasants, and tens of thousands of them were imprisoned. The Party's contempt was nevertheless tempered with wariness, for the peasants exerted an influence on the urban proletariat.

The sort of industrialisation that was implemented in the postwar years in Poland usually has the effect of drawing people from the countryside into the towns, where they soon turn into a rootless and traditionless proletariat. In Poland the process was so rapid and on such a large scale that it backfired. By 1970 no less than 63 per cent of the entire blue-collar workforce had come from the villages. In 1968, 22.3 per cent of industrial workers, 28 per cent of construction workers and 31.7 per cent of transport workers lived in the country and commuted to work, while 10 per cent of industrial and building workers and 15 per cent of transport workers were also part-time farmers. Instead of creating a rootless urban proletariat, the rapid industrialisation had the effect of ruralising the workers of the cities. As a result, they had to be watched. Trade unions were set up to monitor their activities and the personnel manager in any factory was an officer of the UB.

The key to keeping both peasants and workers out of politics was an economic policy that could satisfy their needs – their aspirations could be countered by the alleged need for self-sacrifice in the struggle for socialism. The advancing Germans had done great damage in 1939, and the retreating Germans dynamited everything they could think of. In the wake of the advancing Soviet armies came special units whose job it was to dismantle and remove anything that could be useful back in the Soviet Union, including entire telephone exchanges and tramway installations. The new regime had to start literally from scratch, and this circumstance favoured the usual socialist penchant for central planning and 'thinking big'. A three-year plan was followed by a six-year plan announced in 1950. The State Economic Planning Commission issued rigid directives which often turned out to be unworkable in local conditions of which the planners were entirely ignorant. The commission did not encourage initiative or even questioning by factory managers, so there was little these could do except muddle along by cooking figures and bribing inspectors. Since it was known that factory managers concealed their real resources so as not to be caught out underfulfilling the quotas they might be set, the planners found themselves ignoring reports and estimating the possibilities themselves. The whole process of economic planning, from investment to costs and prices was therefore carried out at a largely theoretical level and was as often as not based on guess-work. Since each factory hinged on the performance of a dozen others, and since a further dozen hinged on its own performance, and since each of these had preordained supplies, capacity and output all calculated from figures which bore scant relation to reality, the results tended to be ludicrous.

Much of the planning defied common sense. New factories were built hundreds of miles away from existing industrial centres, coalfields or manpower pools. The planners had a weakness for vast projects, great steelworks that would be seen and smelt for miles around, like so many monuments to the socialist achievement. This went hand in hand with ideological dictates; the terrifying Stalinist city and steelworks of Nowa Huta were purposely located as a counterbalance to Catholic, traditional and academic Kraków. Few of the products of the intensive post-war industrialisation actually penetrated into the everyday life of normal people. Since all private traders and artisans were squeezed mercilessly for being petty capitalists, it soon became virtually impossible to obtain anything remotely useful otherwise than on the black market.

The pattern of Poland's industrialisation was also dictated by the Soviet Union, which wanted the economies of its satellites to complement its own and which told Poland to refuse Marshall aid in 1947. It was Soviet demands too that burdened it with the obligation to maintain a huge army and police apparatus, and to pay the keep of the Russian armies stationed in Poland. Finally, Poland was bound by trade treaties which crippled the economy. At a conservative estimate some 5,000 million dollars' worth of Polish coal was given away free to the Soviet Union between 1946 and 1955, at a time when coal was virtually Poland's only means of acquiring much-needed foreign currency.

The Russian presence in Polish economic and political life grew steadily. It was not enough that Polish society should accept its fate – it must be re-educated to like it. The process began in the schoolroom. Textbooks, particularly on history, were rewritten and a plethora of new subjects, mostly dealing with Marxism or the history of Russian communism, found its way on to the curriculum. An Institute of Social Sciences under the ideologue Adam Schaff set about creating a new cadre of teachers and experts in every field who would have the right view of things. The Union of Polish Youth brought people up as standard-bearers of socialism. Adults had to endure lectures and courses so that they too might understand the class struggle and marxist economic theory, and everyone was expected to belong to at least one progressive organisation, such as the Polish Women's League or the Polish-Soviet Friendship Society.

In 1948 the Party called for a new Literature and Art of Socialist Realism. The members of the Writers' Union were dragged off on factory visits while their weekly organ *New Culture* lectured them on Marxist theory. Most did not understand what exactly was expected of them by the 'terroreticians' of the Party, and many ceased writing altogether. Painters and sculptors had to turn out representations of workers wielding hammers, soldiers marching forward with their jaws resolutely stuck out towards the new socialist dawn, or steelworkers holding a discussion on the Korean War during their lunch-break. The case of the musicians was perhaps most harrowing of all, since it was not possible to conform to the new regulations without abandoning not only artistic integrity, but all point as well. Andrzej Panufnik, prize-winning composer and conductor of the Warsaw Philharmonic Orchestra, was twice nominated as State Laureate and even awarded the Order of the Banner of Labour for his works. But in 1952 his new *Heroic Overture* was labelled 'formalistic', 'decadent' and 'alien to the great socialist era'. Party activists demanded that the scores be burnt and his music was banned from performance for the next thirty years.

The degree to which Stalinism had been implanted in Poland can be gauged from the events after his death, on 3 March 1953. Katowice was promptly renamed Stalinogród as a mark of respect and subvervience while the Party waited nervously to see which way the wind would blow. After a few months, the signals from Moscow were that a general 'thaw' could take place. People relaxed as the paranoia of the last few years receded, though few deluded themselves that they were now free. Writers who had not published for years now appeared in print, questioning, still in veiled form, some of the tenets of Socialist Realism, journalists actually discussed some of the orthodoxies which had hitherto been taken as gospel, and economists even raised doubts as to whether marxist-leninist theories were foolproof in every circumstance.

Political life was suddenly blown open in 1954 when Colonel Józef Swiatło, deputy chief of the Tenth Department, defected and began a series of broadcasts on Radio Free Europe which regaled the inhabitants of Poland with the inside story of the UB. Even senior Party members were astonished to hear to what extent every aspect of life had been dictated by Moscow. A terrible storm broke. Gomułka and others were quietly released from prison, the head of the UB was dismissed, and the security services adroitly lowered their profile. Party Secretary Bierut admitted

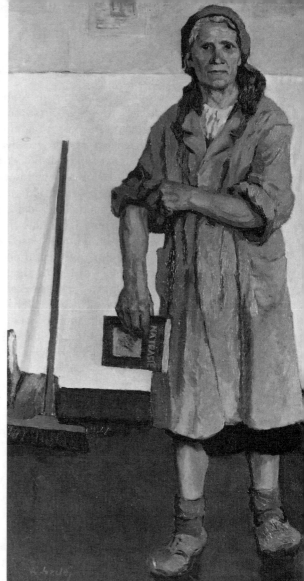

140 The art of Socialist Realism: *Portrait of Bronisława Urbanowicz*, exemplary cleaning-worker at the Gdańsk Politechnic, painted in 1950 by Aleksander Kobzdej. As she rolls up her sleeves to work, she clutches *On the Road*, a book of Socialist guidelines. Just how illusory such 'realism' proved to be can be seen from a 1953 poster, (**141**) on which happy peasants drive a tractor 'towards Prosperity, towards Socialism', and a photograph (**142**) taken thirty years later.

that 'mistakes' had been made, and that there had been a 'tendency to widen the field of activity of the security services', but he wavered. He was in the unenviable position of having to gauge which way Moscow would move next and he therefore zig-zagged between thaw and repression, personally favouring the latter. There were many traditional Stalinists like him in the Party. Their reaction to the Swiatło revelations was not that the system had to be cleaned up, but that security ought to be tightened in such a manner as to prevent a repetition of the scandal.

In February 1956 Nikita Khrushchev made his famous speech to the Twentieth Congress of the Communist Party of the Soviet Union denouncing Stalin's rule. Bierut, who was in attendance, died of a heart attack. The Party was in disarray, as it usually is when anything untoward happens. Khrushchev came to Warsaw to attend the plenary session of the Party's Central Committee, which was to elect a new First Secretary, and he suggested Edward Ochab, who was duly elected. Ochab proceeded to announce a programme of liberalisation, a partial amnesty, which resulted in the release of some 70,000 political prisoners, and the arrest of the Chief Procurator, the Minister of Public Security, and several high-ranking persons in the UB. But this did not herald radical change, as the summer months were to show.

Back in December 1955 the 15,000 workers of the former Cegielski and now Stalin works in Poznań had discovered that bureaucratic venality had cheated them of a percentage of their salary. They remonstrated with their management, took the matter up at district Party level, and finally sent delegates to Warsaw to petition the highest authorities, which ignored them. On 28 June 1956, at the height of the International Trade Fair in Poznań, they staged a demonstration. They demanded that Prime Minister Cyrankiewicz come to talk to them, but he declined. They attacked a police station in which they seized arms, and went on to demolish a radio-jamming station and the Poznań headquarters of the UB. The authorities responded by sending in tanks, and the riots came to a bloody end two days later.

'Foreign agents' were blamed, and reactionaries within the Party argued that such outbreaks were the inevitable consequence of relaxing discipline. While the Party continued its programme of decentralising the economy and democratising itself, a faction of Stalinist die-hards, the so-called Natolin group, called on their allies in Moscow. As the Eighth Plenary Session of the Party opened on 19 October 1956, a delegation headed by Khrushchev flew in unannounced and Russian troops stationed in Poland began to march on Warsaw. The government called out the army, and even distributed arms to the car-workers of Żerań.

The man who averted bloodshed was Władysław Gomułka. He managed to convince Khrushchev that he could contain the situation, and the Soviet units returned to base. Speaking to a huge rally in Warsaw on 24

October, Gomułka declared that 'the Party, united in the working class and the nation, will lead Poland on a new road to Socialism'. It was to be socialism with a human face and a Polish costume. Cardinal Wyszyński was released and the Church was allowed to resume its normal activities in return for a pledge of allegiance to the regime. Marshal Rokossovsky and hundreds of Russian officers were dismissed from the Polish army and sent home. A quarter of a million Poles stranded in the Soviet Union were allowed to emigrate to Poland. Commercial treaties were renegotiated on more favourable terms, and the Soviet Union was to pay for the upkeep of its own troops stationed in Poland.

The changes were largely cosmetic. On 30 October the Soviet government made a general declaration to the world pledging itself to 'respect for territorial integrity, state independence and sovereignty, and non-interference in one another's internal affairs'. On the same day Imre Nagy announced a return to democracy in Hungary, and five days later the Soviet army invaded his country.

Gomułka himself presided uneasily over the revolution which had brought him to power. A purge of Stalinists was being carried out in the ranks of the Party, factory workers in Silesia were sacking their bosses, and 80 per cent of all collective farms were dissolved spontaneously by the peasants. Associations and periodicals suppressed in 1948 sprouted like weeds after the rain, and every group seemed to be formulating demands or demanding justice. The open collecting of funds, medical supplies and blood on behalf of the Hungarian freedom-fighters was a major embarrassment to the Polish government, which found itself obliged (for the first and last time) to take a different line from the Soviet Union in a United Nations vote on the issue. On 10 December the Soviet consulate in Szczecin was stormed by angry workers.

Even the genuine reformers in the Party had to admit that the time had come to close ranks and safeguard its interests. A few months earlier Gomułka had praised the workers of Poznań for having taught the Party 'a painful lesson', but by the middle of 1957 the striking tram-drivers of Łódź were branded with the more traditional epithet of 'hooligans', and 1,500 miners in the Katowice area were fired in the interests of 'discipline'. During the elections of 1957 Gomułka warned against voting for independent candidates, stressing that: 'the crossing out of the Party's candidates is equivalent to crossing out the independence of our country, and crossing Poland off the map of Europe'. The Poles took his point that either the country was ruled by him and the Party or it would be taken over directly by the Soviet Union. In fact, it is impossible to know whom they did vote for, and the rigidity of all subsequent election results defies credulity. The Seym thus elected was a dead body, with debate reduced to a minimum, followed by unanimous voting.

Behind this stodgy democratic façade the Party leadership set about repairing the damage suffered by the *apparat* since Stalin's death. In 1959 the insalubrious figure of General Mieczysław Moczar was placed in command of the security services, and a new campaign of petty persecution was launched against the Church. The government had already tried repression, which had merely turned priests into martyrs. It had tried subversion, by encouraging a movement of 'patriotic priests' who were to reconcile the teachings of Marx with those of Christ, which had turned into a fiasco. Thereafter it followed the course of pettyfogging obstructionism and judicial harassment, while seducing the young into rival activities. Despite this the Church's position in national life went from strength to strength. Faced with the injustice, falsehood and drabness of socialist reality, people of all classes sought solace, truth and beauty in the Catholic Faith. The parish priest was the one man to whom peasants and workers could always turn. The Catholic University of Lublin was the one free seat of learning. For a long time the Catholic periodical *Znak* and the weekly *Tygodnik Powszechny*, both published in Kraków, were the only papers to maintain any editorial freedom. They brought together priests and laymen, who formed the Club of the Catholic Intelligentsia, a discussion-group which grew into a youth organisation offering an alternative to the Party-sponsored associations.

After the 'thaw' of 1956 the universities once more became centres of learning and discussion. Contact with the outside world – through trade, travel, cultural exchanges and the broadcasts of such services as Radio Free Europe – meant that those brought up under Stalin were now able to see that there were options. As the intense fear of the Stalinist era died away, people began to think aloud once more. But the writers were not the ones to lead the discussion. The war had scythed through the established writers of the 1930s, and those who were not killed were scattered – to London, Paris, New York, Buenos Aires or Tel Aviv. Some like Władysław Broniewski, who wrote an ode to Stalin, Konstanty Gałczynski and Jarosław Iwaszkiewicz, who became president of the Writers' Union, managed to conform to the postwar regime. Those who had only just started writing were hit exceptionally hard by wartime experiences. Czesław Miłosz found himself wondering whether it was morally justifiable to write poetry when one could hear the screams of the tortured. He, and colleagues like the novelists Jerzy Andrzejewski, Kazimierz Brandys and Stanisław Dygat began their literary lives anew in 1945, and they strained to put a positive interpretation on the situation. They were not as deeply committed to the new regime as Tadeusz Konwicki who actually produced Socialist Realist novels, but they nevertheless endorsed the system to some extent. As the 'thaw' revealed more and more irrefutably the evils which they had countenanced and in some cases abetted, the more honest felt their moral credibility to be impaired. In a sense, all those who had not openly protested – and there were few like the novelist Stefan Kisielewski, who had derided marxism from the start – were in some sense committed to the socialist road for Poland and the rule of the Party.

The problem of living with such a political past is revealed in works such as *A Contemporary Dream Book* (1963), whose author, Tadeusz Konwicki, was in turn a partisan in the extreme right formations and an obeisant Stalinist. Some, like Kazimierz Brandys or the philosopher Leszek Kołakowski, kept trying throughout the 1960s to accommodate the existing order to some notion of honesty, before finally admitting that, in Kołakowski's words, 'democratic socialism = fried snowballs'. These writers could not speak with the same moral authority as a Mickiewicz or a Krasiński to young people who had not lived through the war. Brought up under socialism and already disillusioned with it, this generation would determine its own political viewpoint, and its political education began in the late 1960s.

While Gomułka grew more reactionary and old-fashioned in his methods, a faction within the Party viewed him as soft and incompetent. General Moczar had rallied the remnants of the Natolin group, breathed new life into the security services, and was only waiting for an opportunity to act. When in 1966 the Polish bishops sent an open letter to the German bishops calling for mutual forgiveness and reconciliation, Moczar's faction denounced the Church for encouraging 'German revanchism'. But it was the Six-Day War between Israel and the Arab states in 1967 that provided the fuse Moczar had been looking for. The Soviet Union and her satellites were on the Arab side, and the Israeli victory was greeted with delight in Poland, partly because it was a slap in the face to Russian policy, partly because Polish society could identify with the Jews, many of whom were of Polish origin. People in the street could hardly conceal their glee that 'our Jews had given the Soviet Arabs a drubbing.' Konstanty Łubieński cast one of the only two votes ever registered against the government in the Seym on its condemnation of Israel. 'Zionist influences' now joined 'German revanchism' as a mortal enemy of Moczar's brave socialist Poland.

In January 1968 Mickiewicz's *Forefathers' Eve* was playing in Warsaw to houses filled with students who cheered the anti-Russian references in the play. The government took the absurd step of banning it. The demonstrations which ensued at the University were dispersed with unwarranted brutality by the police, supported by the Volunteer Reserve of the Citizens' Militia (ORMO), made up of some of the worst thugs (officially 'sociopolitical activists') the Party could muster. Over a thousand students were arrested and thousands more dismissed from the University. A small demonstration on their behalf elicited similar over-reaction, with hundreds of 'sociopolitical activists' doing their utmost to turn it into a pitched battle. The press gave lurid accounts of massive disturbances barely contained by the forces of order, and on 11 March blamed them on 'Zionist agents' taking their orders from Germany. According to Moczar's partisans, a huge conspiracy was being hatched by 'German revanchists' and 'Zionist agents'. Gomułka made a timely but inept speech stating that not all Jews were 'Zionists', but fingers were already being pointed at the Jewish origins of supposed ringleaders among the students, and indeed at those of some high-ranking Party officials. On 13 March a number of senior officials were dismissed for alleged 'Zionism'.

Moczar's partisans played heavily on the fact that during the first years after the war some of the best Party jobs had gone to people of Jewish origin (Stalin had some difficulty in finding enough reliable Polish communists). The envy of the lower ranks did the rest, and a purge began as Party members sniffed at each others' pedigrees. Among the most vociferous of the anit-Zionists were men like Edward Gierek, Secretary of the Silesian Committee of the Party, new men hungry for power. Gomułka was no longer in control, but hung on with grim determination, only too aware that the witch-hunt was deflecting much of the discontent with his own leadership. He decided to grant exit visas to those 'Zionists' who wished to emigrate, and over the next few months up to 20,000 Polish Jews availed themselves of these. Gomułka's own Jewish wife was not among them, nor were some highly-placed Jews who had managed to side-step the attack. Gomułka's position was nonetheless tenuous. He had to reach out for Soviet support, buying it with an enthusiastic participation in the invasion of Czechoslovakia in August of that year, but this did nothing to enhance his popularity within the Party and in the country at large, which was suffering the effects of his economic policy. He had tried to decentralise the economy, but it had proved impossible to shrug off the old habits of central planning. As wages slumped and working conditions declined, absentee-ism and careless work crippled production. The private sector in agricul-ture was starved of investment; socialist principle demanded that it should be eventually phased out, although it was responsible for 80 per cent of all production. Terrified of becoming a debtor, Gomułka resisted imports, including those of grain and animal feed. The result was a fall in the quantity of livestock and, following two bad harvests in 1969 and 1970, a severe shortage of meat.

The cost of living had risen throughout the 1960s, while wages lagged far behind. The sudden increase by an average of 30 per cent in the price of basic food announced on 13 December 1970 therefore produced an instant reac-tion. Workers at the Lenin Shipyard in Gdańsk went on strike and marched in protest to the local Party headquarters. The police guarding the building opened fire on them, so they burnt it down. Similar confrontations took place in nearby Gdynia and in Szczecin, and on the following day the tanks moved in. The fighting spread to Elbląg and other cities on the coast, and on 17 December the whole area was sealed off by the army, while the numbers of dead reached into hundreds.

On 19 December an emergency session of the Politburo assembled without Gomułka, who had suffered a stroke, and voted to replace him by Edward Gierek. Gierek managed to impress the workers with his apparent goodwill, but it was not until he rescinded all the price-rises that the strikes abated. He admitted that the episode was 'a painful reminder that the Party must never lose touch with the working class and the nation', and many, like the Gdańsk workers who shouted 'We will help you!', believed in his sincerity. But the next ten years of his rule were to transform this lack of contact into an unbridgeable chasm. The traditional, unimaginative, committed communists of Gomułka's generation were replaced by a new breed of apparatchiks, true creatures of the Soviet system, devoted to its well-being rather than to its ideology. They felt none of the puritan communists' revulsion for new ideas and experiments, and they fancied themselves as realists with a firm grasp of modern economics.

Gierek entertained ambitious plans for an 'economic leap forward', to be achieved by massive borrowing from the West which was to be repaid through the improved extraction of raw materials and the export of goods produced in new factories built with foreign capital. The spirit of *détente* favoured his scheme, and money poured in from Western banks only too happy to lend. The initial results were dramatic: production rose sharply, and the Polish economy began to grow at a faster rate than any other bar Japan's. The standard of living went up, and its cost went down. Private cars, dishwashers and trips abroad came within the reach of the average citizen. Gierek was out to buy popularity, so the peasants were relieved of the compulsory delivery quotas, and national insurance was extended to cover them. The price of food was frozen at the 1965 level in order to win the hearts of the workers.

It was not long before cracks began to appear in Gierek's economic structure. The new factories were finished behind schedule, while their products proved to be of inferior quality and difficult to sell in the West. The foreign debt spiralled. The only answer was to increase export of coal and other raw materials, and to divert consumer goods originally intended for the home market to exports. The consequences were felt immediately, as shortages of staple items grew more and more frequent. As Gierek juggled with figures, he forgot the lessons of history. In 1975 he raised the prices of 'luxury' consumer goods, which hit the poor and bred resentment, and on 24 June 1976, he raised the price of food by an average of 60 per cent. On the following day strikes broke out all over the country and soon turned to rioting. The price-rises were immediately withdrawn, but the motorised detachments of the Citizens' Militia (ZOMO) went into action, arresting hundreds of workers and methodically beating them up. People were dismissed from their jobs by the hundred, and sentences of up to ten years were handed out.

The crisis brought to the surface a basketful of problems which had been obscured by Gierek's economic fireworks. His panacea of economic progress was based on an assumption of technical competence on the part of the Party cadres, but while membership had risen to a record three million, quality had not. The new men lacked the commitment to socialist ideals of those they replaced and brought neither a sense of realism nor managerial ability in its stead. The principle of negative selection that attracted society's dross into the Party was avenging itself. Rather than curing the ills endemic to socialist economies, they added to them, for, as often happens, corruption came in on the tail of incompetence. It was corruption on a vast scale, spreading through every branch and twig of the system in the most flagrant manner, giving birth to a vast kleptocracy that bred massive resentment throughout society.

Gierek had leapt at every opportunity of credit and co-operation offered by the spirit of *détente*, and compensated for this by increasingly servile behaviour towards the Soviet Union. Polish capital and personnel were committed to Soviet development projects; Polish goods produced from dollar investments were sold on for useless rubles; and the level of 'fraternal aid' to 'liberation movements' in Angola and elsewhere in the third world rose sharply. While he flew off on official visits to France, Germany and the United States and hosted their presidents in Warsaw, he also had to go to Moscow and, in 1975, play host to a none too happy Alexey Kosygin. The Soviets wanted tangible tribute, in the form of a series of amendments to the Polish Constitution. Poland was to be constitutionally committed to Socialism, to the 'leading role' of the Party and, most important, to a 'fraternal alliance' with the Soviet Union. In addition to being larded with references to the Great October Revolution (1917), the constitution was also to contain an insidious clause which made civil rights dependent on 'the fulfilment of civic duty', but this was dropped as a result of howls of public protest and the vehement intervention of the Church.

The breadth of the public response and the fact that Gierek felt obliged to give in were twin symptoms of a radically altered relationship between government and people. It was not that the authorities had grown soft or neglected their defences – the budget of the Ministry of Internal Affairs remained larger than those of the Ministries of Culture, Health and Education put together. It was simply that society had grown more assertive and politically more mature. It had emerged from the nightmare of Stalinism with its élite either dead, exiled, or discredited. When Gomułka came to power, it seemed as though the Party might grow into a leading role, but this illusion was quickly dispelled, and people were held together only by their instincts and the need to survive. Methodical disinformation by the authorities kept them confused and isolated. The country was cut off from Europe not merely by the Iron Curtain, but also by the West's lack of interest in, and indeed intellectual flight from, the realities reigning behind it. Intellectual fashions current in the West dictated attitudes which were favourable to the Soviet Union and little short of contemptuous of the 'reactionary' arguments of Poles who tried to draw attention to reality. This bred a sense of alienation in the Polish intelligentsia. It also bred a grim determination in the new articulate generations which sprang from the working class and the peasantry, who, for obvious reasons, were less sensitive to what intellectuals in Western Europe might think of them.

The 1968 invasion of Czechoslovakia shook the image of Soviet benevolence entertained in the West. In the 1970s increased travel in both directions engendered human contacts, while Polish culture and thought began to percolate into Western consciousness. Early contacts with the outside world were purely artistic, and since Poland had no great painters, it was music that led the way. The impressive flowering of Polish music since the War produced such composers as Grażyna Bacewicz, Kazimierz Serocki, Tadeusz Baird, Krzysztof Penderecki, and the dominant figure of Witold Lutosławski. The Polish presence made itself felt in areas such as poster art and above all the performing arts. Jerzy Grotowski's Theatre Laboratory of Wrocław has had a lasting effect on attitudes to acting and staging throughout the world, while Tadeusz Kantor's revolution in the art of mime has had a similar impact.

If these figures did little more than remind the world that Poland still contained a vibrant society, it was through the medium of film that something more of a message was transmitted. The Polish Film School of Łódź produced a string of directors who placed Polish cinema in a class of its own – Walerian Borowczyk, Krzysztof Zanussi, Roman Polański and primarily Andrzej Wajda. Each evolved a specific style of mixing philosophical themes with a visual dimension, which in Wajda's case is almost impressionistic. By their ability to create ambience and a setting which hinted at deeper realities, they were able to bring home to audiences both in Poland and outside a whole range of truth which would never have got past the censor in literary form.

Literature has been the most crippled form of expression since the war, and most writers have fallen casualty to their own attempts at analysing a state of affairs which is essentially nonsensical. Having to accommodate the horrors of war and Stalinism without giving up hope in the world, and having subsequently to live in a system which by its moral corruption and its intellectual absurdity created a way of life in which nothing is what it is said to be, the thinking man was more often than not reduced to a state of mild paranoia. His thought and writings were dogged by doubt, anxiety and a desperate search for absolutes or at least shreds of truth to which he might cling. This was not easy in a state in which, as the Czech writer Vaclav Havel pointed out: 'Power is a prisoner of its own lies; therefore it must falsify. A man need not believe in all these mystifications. He must, however, act as if he believed in them, or he must at least silently tolerate them, or at the very least get along well with those who operate according to them. In other words, he must "live the lie".' The only writers who avoided drowning in this mire and left work of lasting value are those who managed to transpose their emotions and their intellectual reactions on to a plane which distanced them from everyday life.

The most extreme example of this is the work of Stanisław Lem, who used science fiction as a vehicle for philosophical debate about Man's moral relation to the Universe. Another is Sławomir Mrożek, whose plays, half fable, half reality, permitted him to explore themes relevant to Polish conditions without tying them down to reality. His play *Police* (1958), in which the sudden conversion of the last political prisoner in a totalitarian state leaves the secret police in peril of redundancy and therefore obliged to recruit volunteers from its own ranks to become subversives, is one of the greatest expositions of the unique relationship between logic and absurdity which characterises Soviet socialism. Witold Gombrowicz, who had been stranded in the West by the war and subsequently settled in France, also wrote on themes which were apparently disembodied but in reality closely linked to the problems confronting the individual in a totalitarian state.

The poet Tadeusz Różewicz, an active soldier of the AK, was so affected by the experience of war that he came to view everything, including conventional literature, in a bitter light. He was almost an existentialist, an angry man venting his spleen through works which are nevertheless poetic, and which include a number of plays belonging to the realms of the absurd. His contemporary and companion-in-arms, Zbigniew Herbert, is another whose view of life is overshadowed by the trauma of the war. But his reaction is not one of anger. It is an attempt at piecing together from the shattered remnants of physical things the furniture of a new life, and the process of creating his crystalline verse is a reaffirmation of faith in art and beauty. Herbert, who is sometimes reminiscent of Norwid in his contemplative awareness of objects and their form, is culturally the most European of his colleagues, hence his international popularity. Yet his work, and that of Czesław Miłosz, is, like the experience of most Poles, so intimately connected with the historical reality of horror, suffering, hatred and love, that it skirts the emotion and flees the sentiment which are so central to the poetry of other contemporary cultures. The greatest of Poland's post-war poets, Miłosz shares many characteristics with Herbert, most notably a classicist emotional spareness and elegance, but he is also a more political person. After the war he embraced the new regime with an enthusiasm which he has had some difficulty in living down since he settled in the United States in 1960. While few are left cold by the power and beauty of his works, many in Poland remain dubious of the moral integrity of his statements.

Since the war Polish culture has evolved in a great semaphoric concert of individuals scattered throughout the world, transmitted through émigré journals and publishing houses of which the Paris monthly *Kultura* and imprint Instytut Literacki are the most distinguished. There is therefore nothing provincial or geographically hermetic about the way in which Polish thought has developed. Yet in spite of, and perhaps partly because of, this richness, it has been slow to penetrate the consciousness of the rest of the world. Nevertheless, by the mid-1970s, the barriers that had cut the Poles off psychologically from Europe seemed to be crumbling. The droves of young Poles visiting the United States, England and other European countries provided access to information of every sort. They also fostered relationships with people of other countries and with the old emigration. The opportunity to see other systems in operation gave people brought up under a totalitarian regime a valuable scale of comparison in terms of the civil and political rights they might feel due to them. Their growing self-confidence was underpinned by the work of historians, who were providing an eager and largely ignorant or indoctrinated public with sound and truthful documentation on the country's past which was devoured in search of meaning and precedent. The need for information was compounded by an emotional urge to arrive at a deeper understanding of the old Polish world. Historians such as Paweł Jasienica fed this hunger with their broad, human treatment of subjects such as Jagiellon Poland and the Commonwealth. As in the nineteenth century, the orphaned nation wanted to be told about its unknown parents in sympathetic terms rather than in the cold damning language of socialist historiography. The same desire produced a deeply un-socialist fascination with anything from old pictures to the down-at-heel descendants of magnatial families.

It was therefore a very different society that was confronting Gierek in 1976 from that which had confronted Gomułka in the late sixties. It was not conditioned to endure and resist silently. It was well-informed and no longer believed a word of government propaganda, it knew that a different sort of life was possible, and it knew that the rest of Europe was once more aware of its plight. These feelings were not confined to the intelligentsia. A nationwide discussion was carried on, both at personal level and in *samizdat* or émigré publications smuggled into Poland, and by the middle of the decade political programmes were beginning to take shape. A new sense of strategy was emerging, the most obvious sign which was the formation of the Workers' Defence Committee (KOR) in September 1976 by a group of writers and dissidents. This provided workers with legal advice, sent observers to their trials, and informed the public on their treatment through its *Information Bulletin*. It also collected money to help pay fines and to assist their families. The Committee gradually extended its activities to cover all cases of human rights violations, and mercilessly heckled the authorities on points of law.

It was joined in March 1977 by the Movement for the Defence of Human and Civil Rights (ROPCO), and in May by a Students' Solidarity Committee in Kraków. Periodicals of every sort and an extraordinarily active underground press began pouring forth a torrent of literature. In the same year a Flying University began operating in Warsaw, and discussion clubs burgeoned. The police arrested individuals, raided premises and confiscated materials, but the dissidents were well organised and screened by a wall of sympathy and co-operation on the part of the public. They were also given tacit support and facilities by the Church, which played an active part in defending human rights and helping sacked workers. Gierek could ill-afford to crack down. He had official talks with the Primate, Cardinal Wyszyński, in 1976; in 1977 he visited France, Italy and India, and he hosted Jimmy Carter, Willy Brandt, King Baudouin, Helmut Schmidt and the Shah of Iran in Warsaw. He needed to appear statesman-like in order to stave off economic nemesis. The world recession was hurting the overstretched and incompetently managed Polish economy. The terminal condition of Polish industry spelt chaos, the desperate condition of Polish agriculture threatened crisis. The election, on 16 October 1978, of the Cardinal Archbishop of Kraków to the Holy See meant that the crisis could, when it came, no longer be controlled locally.

To the Poles the election of Pope John Paul II was not only a solace in their misery, as well as a great national honour, it was also the final breach in the wall behind which they had been kept since 1945. The Pope's visit to Poland in June 1979 was an extraordinary event, and it had a profound effect in reaffirming the Poles in their spiritual and cultural values. It acted as a catalyst on a number of processes which were changing the position of Polish society and its view of itself. It brought to a head the growing sense of the power of that society in the face of coercion, a sense that had been evolving over a dozen years at least. It brought millions together at rallies and open-air Masses: people came forward and counted each other. The Papal visit had opened new channels of communication, and it is no exaggeration to say that Polish society was transformed by it. It was the crowning element in a build-up of the Polish presence in the world. The Polish Question once more hovered over the international stage.

While people throughout Poland learned to view their future in terms of free will and community, the hapless Gierek was foundering in the morass of his economic miracle. His sums did not add up, and in July 1980 he again made the mistake of balancing the books by drastic rises in the price of food. A rash of strikes broke out in response, but this time their tenor and their strategy were entirely new.

At dawn on 14 August 1980 a previously dismissed electrical fitter climbed into the Lenin Shipyard in Gdańsk to lead a strike over the illegal dismissal of a fellow-worker, Anna Walentynowicz. His name was Lech Wałęsa. A participant of the 1970 strikes, he knew that workers out in the open were no match for tanks, and in years of discussion with KOR and underground workers' cells, he had forged a strategy and defined goals. He occupied the shipyard and demanded that representatives of the government come to listen to a whole list of demands. Enterprises all over the country staged similar sit-ins, and an Interfactory Strike Committee was formed to co-ordinate the movement, with advisers from KOR on hand.

The government quickly gauged the strength and determination of the movement and on 31 August signed an agreement with the workers. This was no mere settlement of wage-claims or disputes over working conditions. It was a whole package involving the establishment of free trade unions, the freedom of information, access to the media and civil rights. Historically, it was a seminal event. It was the first authentic workers' revolution in European history, and ironically, it was directed against the 'dictatorship of the proletariat'. Communism presupposes that the working masses can be manipulated and exploited by policies of bread and circuses, and that only a marxist-leninist party can save them from this. Yet in this instance it was the Party that juggled obsessively with economics, and it was the uneducated masses that had raised the questions of principle and of workers' rights. As the Italian communist leader Enrico Berlinguer pointed out, it was the final demolition of the myth that something tangible had been achieved for the proletariat by the October Revolution in 1917.

It was appropriate that the new trade union should take the name of 'Solidarity', since it was this very feeling between all segments of the nation that gave it such strength. Soon the various unions affiliated to Solidarity had over ten million members, which, in a population of just over 35 million, represented virtually everyone of working age. Over the next fifteen months Polish society took a warm bath in its own values as the rigidity of imposed styles of action and thought fell away and the sense of human dignity re-entered people's dealings with each other. Every facet of life was affected by the novel sense of freedom and renewal. Knowledge and information on every subject from politics to ecology was made available and disseminated in huge quantities. Writers pulled out of their bottom drawers things they had never conceived of publishing; film-makers set about making films they had only dreamt of making; people stopped looking over their shoulders. With the negative influence of the Party removed, workers quickly devised better ways of doing their work. A mood of quiet optimism and deep exhilaration reigned despite the fact that the political situation was ominous and the economic conditions catastrophic.

The harvest of Gierek's economic policy was a bitter one. The foreign debt reached giddy heights while the machinery bought with borrowed currency either fell to pieces or ground to a halt for lack of spare parts. What trimming Gierek had attempted in the late 1970s had resulted in skimping at the last moment, so that many projects suffered in the finishing stages, while a scale of pollution unknown elsewhere in Europe added to the misery of the population. A freeze on foreign spending applied without sensitivity ruined what little chance there was of muddling through, and hit the health service in the most tragic manner. By the summer of 1981 there were widespread shortages of drugs, and no syringes to administer them with. Malnutrition and diseases connected with dirt and deprivation reached epidemic proportions, and while foreign charities went into action on a gigantic scale, the government ignored the issue entirely.

The Party had not only lost control, it had fallen apart. Hundreds of thousands handed in their cards and one milion of its members joined Solidarity, but the senior echelons hung on, hoping for the best. The Polish *apparat* no less than its masters in the Kremlin were taken aback by the depth of feeling that came out into the open and the sheer breadth of the movement. No modern government had ever faced such a total revolt. None has faced an opposition so full of the courage of its convictions and so serenely sure of itself. It is clear that at no time did the ruling élite seriously consider honouring the promises made to Solidarity in the Gdańsk agreement of August 1980, and its apparent compromise was dictated solely by its own disarray. A succession of reshuffles of leadership yielded no new sense of direction, and while the official press laboured the subject of the Party's 'leading role', there was less and less evidence of any activity on its part. It was inevitable that the vacuum created by its tortoise-like behaviour should suck Solidarity further and further in. It was also inevitable that differences of opinion should emerge within the ranks of the movement. Lech Wałęsa stuck to his original strategy, in the view that Solidarity was a trade union and not a political movement. Others believed that since the Party had discredited itself entirely and seemed to be shirking its responsibilities, the one movement that did represent the nation should insist on some degree of power-sharing. Solidarity was not a mindless revolution, but an articulate political opposition, one with a coherent vision combining socialism with democracy and state management with private and co-operative ownership. Its thinking, not bedevilled like that of the West by left/right stereotypes, was pragmatic and fresh. Many saw in it the germ of a compromise between Polish society's democratic aspirations and Poland's inescapable position within the Warsaw Pact. It also held the key to any real economic recovery.

The situation began to resemble that of 1863 in many respects. Wałęsa had made a deal with the authorities which satisfied him and the majority of his countrymen. The authorities failed to honour their agreement and kept making gestures designed to provoke. Wałęsa found it harder and harder to control his supporters, some of whom were begining to assume a defiant and openly rebellious attitude towards the entire system, and by extension, towards the Soviet Union. Matters came to a head at Solidarity's First National Congress which convened near Gdańsk in September 1981. The Congress constituted the first democratically elected national assembly since the prewar Seym, a fact that lent its deliberations enormous gravity. While Wałęsa and the moderates attempted to pin the discussion down to matters concerning Solidarity and the Gdańsk agreement, many of the delegates, frustrated and incensed by the government's bad faith, kept raising issues of principle that went far beyond these confines. On 8 September the Congress even passed a motion to issue a statement of sympathy and support to all the downtrodden peoples of the Soviet bloc and to 'all the nations of the Soviet Union'. It was a proclamation that the Poles were, as in 1831, and 1863, fighting 'For Your Freedom and Ours'.

The Soviet Union had tolerated what was happening only because it could not do otherwise. It was diplomatically isolated as a result of its invasion of Afghanistan, and economically dependent on the West, which, for once, seemed prepared to make more than pious noises. In effect, the almost universal sympathy felt by ordinary people throughout the world for the Polish people and their revolution was gradually undermined by political reactions to the movement. British Thatcherites waxed lyrical about trade unionism in Poland, French communists denounced the Polish working class, while Western bankers whined about the billions they had lent to Gierek. It soon became apparent that Western politicians would make use of Solidarity but not support it. The scale of the movement and its charismatic leader's immense popularity throughout the world nevertheless dictated caution in the Kremlin.

One thing the Soviet Union could under no circumstances countenance, however, was any idea of the dismantling of its *apparat* in Poland. The Party might fumble and stumble, but while the Party was there, the Soviet leash was on the Polish dog. However much it had been loosened by the Gdańsk agreements, it could always be tightened in due course. It was when the *apparat*'s monopoly of power came into question that the Soviet Union felt compelled to act. It will be a long time before it is known exactly what was planned when, by whom and for what date, but it is clear that the choice of

143 A Gdańsk shipyard worker making his confession during the sit-in strike of August 1980. Such images irritated the Polish Communist authorities less than the communist parties and socialist fellow-travellers of the West, who found Solidarity a difficult movement to accommodate in their political canons.

General Wojciech Jaruzelski, a man blindly faithful to Moscow and the head of the only section of the *apparat* which still functioned, as prime minister in February 1981 was one of a number of steps taken to make a clamp-down possible. This came on the night of 13 December 1981.

In a complex operation carried out with surprising efficiency, virtually the entire leadership of Solidarity were arrested. Thousands of people were dragged from their beds and ferried through the freezing night to prisons and concentration camps, while tanks patrolled the snow-covered streets and impressive quantities of ZOMO stormtroopers were deployed in potential trouble-spots. Communications were cut and a 'State of War' was declared. The workers were unprepared, and there was little resistance. The Wujek mine in Silesia was the scene of a spectacular underground occupation, which ended in tragedy as the enraged ZOMO opened fire on the surrendering miners. Their colleagues in the Piast mine held out longer, but the last 900 came to the surface on 28 December. Although a few Solidarity leaders remained in hiding and mounted a campaign of underground opposition, the movement was ostensibly crushed. In all, some 10,000 of its members were detained, while another 150,000 were hauled in for 'preventive and caution- ary talks'. Jaruzelski was soon in a position to start releasing the detainees. In December 1982, a year after its imposition, the 'State of War' was suspended, and six months later, lifted. By then a number of special powers had been brought in that made it unnecessary.

Jaruzelski had certainly managed to bring Poland back to Moscow's heel with a minimum of bloodshed and unpleasantness. But he was less successful in his attempts at 'normalising' the situation. He claimed that he had acted only to prevent worse bloodshed, hinting darkly that the Soviet Union had been about to invade. He set up a Patriotic Movement for National Regeneration, which people were pressured to join, often on pain of losing their jobs. He tried to promote an image of fairness, by arresting Gierek and a number of the worst fraudsters of his entourage.

Few people were impressed, either in Poland or abroad. The United States protested in the strongest terms and imposed stringent trade sanctions. Other Western countries followed suit. This hit the already chaotic economy and Jaruzelski's attempts at reviving it very hard. He had imagined that crushing Solidarity and outlawing strikes would do the trick. Plans and reform programmes were announced, but nothing came of them, and the economy stagnated. The zloty was devalued twice, in 1983 and 1985. Inflation rose to around 70 per cent. Although trade sanctions against Poland were eased, non-cooperation by Solidarity and the parlous condition of the Soviet and other Comecon economies militated against any improvement in the situation.

The underground leadership of Solidarity insisted that economic progress could only be achieved in partnership with itself, and regularly appealed to the authorities to open negotiations. But the General claimed that the only representative of the workers was the docile official union established in October 1982. At the same time, he kept making what he hoped would be seen as concessions. Most of those detained, including Wałęsa, were released by the beginning of 1983, and in July of that year a general amnesty was announced. Those, like Jacek Kuroń and Adam Michnik, who were being held on charges of attempting to overthrow the state, were not brought to trial.

But such moves did not reflect any change of attitude. Soon after being released, Wałęsa was accused of fraud and tax evasion, and he was frequently harassed by the police. Lesser mortals were simply bullied, beaten up or murdered. In November 1985 up to 100 senior academics were dismissed in a thorough purge of the educational system. A steady stream of political refugees rushed to the West, in stolen planes, in boats and a multitude of ingenious ways. Although the Pope was allowed to visit the country in the summer of 1983, a vicious campaign against the Church was launched at about the same time. A number of priests were beaten up, and several murdered. Only in one case was the murder pinned on the security services, and on 27 December 1984 three policemen were tried for killing Father Jerzy Popiełuszko.

This trial was something of a turning point, showing as it did that the security services and the party were no longer masters in their own house. Public opinion both at home and abroad had to be placated. Gorbachov's proposed reforms and pandering to Western opinion robbed them of the certainty that they could count on Soviet force. Jaruzelski, now Head of State, controlled not only the army, but also, through his interior minister General Kiszczak, the security apparatus, and he was clearly distancing himself from the Party. The Party's tenth congress in July 1986 revealed its waning influence. The number of workers in its ranks had fallen to an all-time low, and many of its members were uttering unorthodox sentiments. A few months later,. Jaruzelski formed a 'Consultative Council' including a number of independent figures, though hardly representative of the nation.

In 1985 a new government had been formed with the economist Zbigniew Messner, a man with a low party profile, but his efforts at curing the country's economic ills got nowhere. The economy was running itself into the ground, and by 1987 the foreign debt had gone up to $37.6 billion. A mood of despondency descended on the country, and a vast economic migration of over half a million joined the political refugees. Those left in Poland took to black-marketeering and petty trading on a gigantic scale for survival. The new diaspora helped to revive the consciousness of the old emigration, and this supported the country, both morally and materially, through the dark and hungry days.

Although still outlawed, Solidarity was reasserting its influence and now operated almost openly. When price rises were announced in 1986, it threatened a nation-wide stike, and the proposals were withdrawn. The government's claim that the movement had been crushed was beginning to look very empty. Every foreign statesman visiting Poland trod the path to Wałęsa's home, and consulted him on whether to ease sanctions or not. But repeated calls by Wałęsa, by the Primate, and by foreign governments, that the authorities should talk to Solidarity were ignored. Indeed, many of the Party die-hards were keen on a fresh clampdown. But if he was not on Solidarity's side, Jaruzelski was not on theirs either, and he stood in their way. Consciously or not, he was to be the Trojan Horse through which the Party's hegemony would be breached.

The Pope's third visit to his native land, in June 1987, was almost as important as his first, and it was by far the most political. He talked to Wałęsa and had several discussions with a more attentive Jaruzelski. But the General still baulked at the idea of talking to Wałęsa, and made no new move, allowing the country to drift towards what anyone could foresee was a major crisis.

The volume of public protest was rising steadily, with groups as disparate as the refounded PPS and ecological movements joining the fray. Austerity measures introduced in the spring of 1988 caused widespread strikes. In the summer, ZOMO units stormed mines in Silesia. Solidarity called for a general strike to take place on 1 September. On 26 August General Kiszczak announced that he had been authorised to hold consultative talks with opposition groups. A meeting with Wałęsa and Bishop Dąbrowski took place immediately, and it was agreed that 'round table' talks would be held in October. Wałęsa called off the strikes, and a new government under Rakowski was formed, with a few independent figures.

But while the round table was ready by the prescribed date, the talks did not start. There was disagreement about exactly who should take part, and about the scope of the talks. Wałęsa and the Church representatives wanted them to cover not only economic issues, but constitutional ones as well. As fresh dates were set and then cancelled, it began to look as though the Party was up to its old gerrymandering tricks. To everyone's surprise, the talks did finally begin, on 6 February 1989.

It soon became clear that what the talks were really about was the elimination of the Party's influence from every domain of public and private life. Abandoned by the General and cut off from its traditional sources of power, there was little it could do, but its two million members included the security services and most of the army, and there were plenty who would be prepared to fight for their positions. For all his liberal talk, nobody could be sure how Gorbachov would react to fundamental change in Poland, the cornerstone of his military system. The opposition negotiators therefore trod warily, allowing generous terms for the capitulation of the nomenklatura. At the same time, the great kleptocracy, seeing the imminent end of its rule, began asset-stripping the state in grotesquely ingenious ways.

The talks ended on 5 April, in a spirit of harmonious agreement that seemed hard to believe. Solidarity and the Church recovered their legal status, the right of free association and freedom of speech were guaranteed, as was the independence of the judiciary. Most important of all, democratic elections to a new bi-cameral parliament were to be held in June. The Party reserved 65 per cent of the seats in the lower house for its own members, allowing opposition candidates to contest the remaining 35 per cent. The elections to the new Senate were to be entirely open. The next elections, to be held in 1993, were to be completely free. The constitution had been rewritten. General Kiszczak declared that the agreement 'closed a chapter in our history and opened a new one'. But the chapter he thought was opening was to close very soon indeed.

The elections were held in two rounds. The first, held on 4 June, was a fiasco for the Party. Solidarity-approved candidates won outright in all but one of the open seats, while thirty-three of the Party's nominees standing for seats reserved for the Party, including General Kiszczak and Prime Minister Rakowski, failed to get the minimum number of votes required. An embarrassed Jaruzelski had to ask Wałęsa whether he would agree to change the rules so that some of these could be re-run at the second round. Wałęsa obliged magnanimously. Solidarity's victory was as complete as it could be. It had won 99 out of the 100 seats in the Senate, with the remaining one going to a non-party businessman. In July, the new parliament met to elect a President. It was symptomatic that a couple of days before, Jacek Kuroń went on television to explain that it was essential to allow this post to go to Jaruzelski, in order to reassure Russia on Poland's position within the Warsaw Pact. The General was duly elected, by one vote.

Jaruzelski invited Solidarity to join the Party in a coalition government, but they refused. He then tried to form a government with Kiszczak as Prime Minister, but failed to secure backing for this in the Seym. After some more horse-trading, in which Wałęsa played a decisive role, Tadeusz Mazowiecki, a Catholic intellectual and editor of Solidarity's weekly paper, was put forward. On 12 September, he formed a government dominated by Solidarity nominees.

In 1944 Stalin himself had declared that trying to establish communism in Poland was like fitting a saddle to a cow. It was a nonsense from the start, and it was bound to fail. The cow could not throw off the saddle, but it worked its shoulders and arched its back in such a way that it slid off. The Poles achieved their ends without upsetting any entrenched interests or provoking dangerous reactions, and the way they acted throughout was a tribute to the political maturity of the population as a whole. There was nothing dramatic about the events, and no heady celebrations. Indeed, the elections were only partly free, the reviled Jaruzelski was still Head of State, and many of the old *apparat* remained in place. But there was no gainsaying the fact that Poland was free once more. Quietly, without fuss, the crown was replaced on the national eagle and the People were dropped out of the country's name. In November, Wałęsa, the symbolic head of state, was invited to address the American Congress as the leader of a free nation, an honour only granted to Lafayette and Churchill before him.

Shortly after the Polish elections, the Hungarians dissolved their communist party and began a series of reforms that led to a declaration of independence from the Soviet bloc. A couple of months later, the Czechs brought down the rule of the party in their country, and soon after that, the people of Eastern Germany threw out their communist leaders and tore down the Berlin Wall. Six months after the elections which seemed such an unbelievable victory, the Yalta system had disintegrated and Central Europe was unrecognizable. The Poles could derive deep satisfaction from the knowledge that they had contributed more than anyone to bringing down the Soviet system. But how the future unfolds depends once again not so much on the Poles as on what happens in Russia and Germany. For there is no getting away from the fundamental problems heaped up in this area by History.

Further Reading

Polish history is unevenly and poorly covered in English, and existing books are not always reliable. In compiling the list below I have omitted those which are out of date or unreliable, and I have included a number of books in French which are superior to those available in English on a given subject, or which cover an important subject on which there is nothing in English. Those who are interested in following up particular subjects will find that a great deal of very useful work has been published in journals of one sort or another over the past twenty years. Comprehensive guides to this, and to all literature on Polish subjects, can be found in *Poland Past and Present: A Select Bibliography of Works in English* by Norman Davies (Oriental Research Partners, Newtonville, Mass., 1977), and *Bibliography of Books in Polish or Relating to Poland published outside Poland since September 1, 1939*, ed. Zdzisław Jagodziński, London, 1985.

1. General histories which provide greater detail on some areas of political history:

Reddaway, W.J. (ed.) *The Cambridge History of Poland*, 2 vols, Cambridge, 1951
Fedorowicz, J.K. (ed.) *A Republic of Nobles, Studies in Polish History to 1864*, Cambridge, 1982
Leslie, R.F. (ed.) *The History of Poland since 1863*, Cambridge, 1983
Davies, N. *God's Playground, A History of Poland*, 2 vols, Oxford, 1981

2. Constitutional and legal histories:

Wagner, W.J. *Polish Law through the Ages*, Stanford, 1970
Jędruch, J. *Constitutions, Elections and Legislatures of Poland 1493–1977*, Washington, 1982
Czapliński, W. (ed.) *The Polish Parliament at the Height of its Development*, Wrocław, 1985
Konopczyński, L. *Le Liberum Veto*, Paris, 1930

3. Cultural histories:

Miłosz, C. *The History of Polish Literature*, Berkeley, 1983 (contains useful list of Polish literature available in English translation)
Krzyżanowski, J. *A History of Polish Literature*, Warsaw, 1978
Brown, M.H. and Wiley, R.J. (eds) *Slavonic and Western Music*, Oxford, 1985
Knox, B. *The Architecture of Poland*, London, 1971
Morawińska, A. *Polish Painting, 15th–20th Centuries*, Warsaw, 1984

4. Books on specific periods and subjects, listed in chronological order of subject:

Vana, Z. *The World of the Ancient Slavs*, London, 1985
Jażdżewski, K. *Poland*, London, 1965
Knoll, P. *The Rise of the Polish Monarchy: Piast Poland in East Central Europe, 1320–1370*, Chicago, 1970
Kłoczowski, J. (ed.) *The Christian Community of Medieval Poland*, Wrocław, 1981
Manteuffel, T. *The Formation of the Polish State, 963–1194*, Wayne University Press, 1985
Barraclough, G. (ed.) *Eastern and Western Europe in the Middle Ages*, London, 1970
Jasienica, P. *Jagiellonian Poland*, Miami, 1978
Gąsiorowski, A. (ed.) *The Polish Nobility in the Middle Ages*, Wrocław, 1984
Mączek, A. (ed.) *East Central Europe in Transition, from the Fourteenth to the Seventeenth Centuries*, Cambridge, 1985
Kozakiewicz, H. *The Renaissance in Poland*, Warsaw, 1976
Fiszman, S. (ed.) *The Polish Renaissance in its European Context*, Indiana, 1988
Armitage, A. *The World of Copernicus*, East Ardsley, 1971
Segel, H.B. *Renaissance Culture in Poland: The Rise of Humanism 1470–1543*, Cornell, 1989
Zins, H. *England and the Baltic in the Elizabethan Era*, Warsaw, 1972
Tazbir, J. *A State Without Stakes: Polish Religious Toleration in the 16th and 17th Centuries*, Warsaw, 1973
Jobert, A. *De Luther à Mohila: La Pologne dans la Crise de la Chrétienté*, Paris, 1974
Kot, S. *Socinianism in Poland*, Boston, 1957
Reczlerski, W. *The Protestant Churches in Poland*, London, 1944
Goldberg, I. *Jewish Privileges in the Polish Commonwealth*, Jerusalem, 1985
Pollard, A.F. *The Jesuits in Poland*, Oxford, 1892
Dembkowski, H. *The Union of Lublin*, Boulder, 1982

Przeździecki, R. *Diplomatic Ventures and Adventures: Some Experiences of British Envoys at the Court of Poland*, London, 1953
—— *Diplomatie et Protocole à la Cour de Pologne*, Paris, 1934.
Targosz, K. *La Cour Savante de Louise-Marie de Gonzague*, Wrocław, 1982
Gasztowtt, T. *La Pologne et l'Islam*, Paris, 1907
Francastel, P. (ed.) *Utopie et Institutions au XVIII Siècle*, Paris, 1963.
Jobert, A. *La Commission d'Education Nationale en Pologne*, Paris, 1941
—— *Magnats Polonais et Physiocrates Français*, Paris, 1941.
Stone, D. *Polish Politics and National Reform 1775–1788*, Boulder, 1976
Lord, R.H. *The Second Partition of Poland: A study in diplomatic history*, Cambridge, Mass., 1915
Walicki, A. *The Age of Enlightenment and the Birth of Modern Nationhood: Polish Political Thought from Noble Republicanism to the Age of Kosciuszko*, Oxford, 1989
Wolff, L. *The Vatican and Poland in the Age of the Partitions*, Boulder, 1988
Leśnodorski, B. *Les Jacobins Polonais*, Paris, 1965
Leslie, R.F. *Polish Politics and the Revolution of November 1830*, London, 1956
Wandycz, P. *The Lands of Partitioned Poland*, Seattle, 1975
Namier, L.B. *The Revolution of the Intellectuals, 1848*, London, 1946
Leslie, R.F. *Reform and Insurrection in Russian Poland 1856–1865*, London, 1963
Walicki, A. *Philosophy and Romantic Nationalism: The Case of Poland*, Oxford, 1982
Komarnicki, T. *The Rebirth of the Polish Republic*, London, 1957
Gerson, L. *Woodrow Wilson and the Rebirth of Poland, 1914–1920*, New Haven, 1953
Senn, A.E. *The Emergence of Modern Lithuania*, Princeton, 1959
Dziewanowski, M.K. *Joseph Piłsudski: A European Federalist, 1918–1922*, Stanford, 1969
Davies, N. *White Eagle, Red Star: the Polish-Soviet War of 1919–20*, London, 1972
Zamoyski, A. *The Battle for the Marchlands*, Boulder, 1981
Polonsky, A. *Politics in Independent Poland 1921–39*, Oxford, 1972
Rothschild, J. *East Central Europe between the Two World Wars*, Seattle, 1975
Carpenter, B. *The Poetic Avant-Garde in Poland 1918–1939*, Seattle, 1983 ·
Mendelssohn, E. *The Jews of East-Central Europe between the World Wars*, Bloomington, Indiana, 1985
Gutman, Y. *The Jews of Warsaw 1939–1943*, Brighton, 1982
Garliński, J. *Poland in the Second World War*, London, 1985
Bethell, N. *The War Hitler Won*, London, 1972
Zawodny, J.K. *Death in the Forest; The Story of the Katyn Forest Massacre*, London, 1971
Garliński, J. *Fighting Auschwitz*, London, 1976

Anders, W. *An Army in Exile: The Story of the Second Polish Corps*, London, 1949.

Nowak, J. *Courier from Warsaw*, London, 1983

Ciechanowski, J.M. *The Warsaw Rising*, London, 1974

Hanson, J.K.M. *The Civilian Population and the Warsaw Uprsising of 1944*, Cambridge, 1982

Polonsky, A. *The Great Powers and the Polish Question*, London, 1976

Dziewanowski, M.K. *The Communist Party of Poland*, Boston, 1976

Mikołajczyk, S. *The Pattern of Soviet Domination*, New York, 1948

Chęciński, M. *Poland: Communism, Nationalism, Anti-Semitism*, New York, 1982

Abramsky, C., Jachimczyk, M., and Polonsky, A. (eds) *The Jews in Poland*, Oxford, 1986

Abramsky, C., Jachimczyk, M. and Polonsky, A. (eds.) *Polin; a journal of Polish-Jewish studies*, vols 1–3, Oxford, 1986–9

Karpiński, J. *Countdown: the Polish Upheavals of 1956, 1968, 1970, 1976, 1980 . . .*, New York, *1982*

Garton Ash, T. *The Polish Revolution*, London, 1983

5. *Useful biographies, listed in chronological order of subject:*

Champion, P. *Henri III Roi de Pologne*, Paris, 1943

Morton, V.B. *Sobieski, King of Poland*, London, 1932

Laskowski, O. *Sobieski, King of Poland*, Glasgow, 1944

Fabre, J. *Stanislas Auguste Poniatowski et l'Europe des Lumières*, Paris, 1952

Cazin, P. *Le Prince-Evèque de Varmie Ignace Krasicki*, Paris, 1940

Backvis, C. *Stanislas Trembecki*, Paris, 1937

Gardner, M. *Kościuszko*, London, 1920

Krakowski, E. *Le Comte Jean Potocki*, Paris, 1963

Kukiel, M. *Czartoryski and European Unity, 1770–1861*, Princeton, 1955

Welsh, D. *Adam Mickiewicz*, New York, 1966

Zamoyski, A. *Chopin*, London, 1979

Gardner, M. *The Anonymous Poet of Poland: Zygmunt Krasiński*, Cambridge, 1919

Gömöri, G. *Cyprian Norwid*, New York, 1974

Zamoyski, A. *Paderewski*, London, 1982

Terlecki, T. *Stanisław Wyspiański*, Boston, 1983

Stone, R.H. *Bolesław Leśmian: the Poet and his Poetry*, Berkeley, 1976

Reddaway, W.F. *Marshal Piłsudski*, London, 1938

Jędrzejewicz, W. *Piłsudski: A life for Poland*, New York, 1982

Bethell, N. *Gomułka*, London, 1969

Micewski, A. *Cardinal Wyszyński: A Biography*, San Diego, 1984

Index

Compiled by Richard M. Wright.
(Italic page numbers refer to illustrations)